Palgrave Studies in Economic History

Series Editor
Kent Deng, London School of Economics, London, UK

Palgrave Studies in Economic History is designed to illuminate and enrich our understanding of economies and economic phenomena of the past. The series covers a vast range of topics including financial history, labour history, development economics, commercialisation, urbanisation, industrialisation, modernisation, globalisation, and changes in world economic orders.

More information about this series at
https://link.springer.com/bookseries/14632

Spyros Sakellaropoulos

The Evolution of the Political, Social and Economic Life of Cyprus, 1191–1950

palgrave
macmillan

Spyros Sakellaropoulos
Department of Social Policy
Panteion University
Athens, Greece

ISSN 2662-6497 ISSN 2662-6500 (electronic)
Palgrave Studies in Economic History
ISBN 978-3-030-91838-5 ISBN 978-3-030-91839-2 (eBook)
https://doi.org/10.1007/978-3-030-91839-2

The title is an extended and updated version of the first three chapters of the original Greek title *The Cypriot Social Formation (1191–2004)* published by Topos Books, Athens 2017.

Cover credit: Keystone Press/Alamy Stock Photo

This Palgrave Macmillan imprint is published by the registered company Springer Nature Switzerland AG
The registered company address is: Gewerbestrasse 11, 6330 Cham, Switzerland

In memory of my grandfather,

Spiros Sakellaropoulos

Contents

List of Maps

Chapter 2

Chapter 3

Chapter 4

CHAPTER 1

Introduction

This book examines the evolution of the politics of society and economy in Cyprus from the conquest of the island by Richard the Lionheart up to the 1950 referendum. To put it somewhat differently, an attempt will be made to examine the organization of Cypriot society from the time that it emerged from Byzantine control until the beginnings of the internationalization of the Cyprus question. Undoubtedly a period which extends through a duration of approximately nine centuries includes many kinds of change and it is no easy task to detect a red thread connecting all this historical development. But there is something that imparts character to it and makes possible an interpretation of all this interest in controlling the island: its particularly advantageous geographical position. Situated between Europe, Africa and Asia, Cyprus has always been an important centre of military and economic activity in the wider region. This is why the Franks occupied it during the Crusades.

The problem the Franks had to face was neither the—non-existent—enmity of the locals nor the failed attempts of the Byzantines to reoccupy it. The basic problem beyond a certain point in time, primarily in the fifteenth century and subsequently, was the Ottoman threat, which boiled down to inability to reproduce the feudal mode of production. The fact that feudalism had reached its economic and military limits propelled the West into discovery of the New World, to the deployment of science for

S. Sakellaropoulos, *The Evolution of the Political, Social and Economic Life of Cyprus, 1191–1950*, Palgrave Studies in Economic History,
https://doi.org/10.1007/978-3-030-91839-2_1

the organization of production, and by extension to gradual transition to a new social system, capitalism. Which is why the economically more advanced Venetians took over the task of ruling Cyprus at the end of the fifteenth century. But all that this development achieved was to delay what was evidently ever more likely: Ottoman conquest.

The Ottomans enjoyed military supremacy in the region and the West were no longer interested in domination simply through conquering territory. What had become the priority for them was the extraction of precious stones and raw materials from their colonies, along with the growth of trade on a capitalist foundation. Cyprus no longer had the importance that it had possessed in previous centuries given that the potential for developing trade relations with the Ottoman Empire but also with Asia as a whole were limited at that time. Thus, the Ottomans, after first dominating the Mamelukes, who until them competed with them in the S. E. Mediterranean, will be able to conclude Cyprus in their own territory.

That said, the Ottomans installed a system of social power corresponding to the Asiatic mode of production. Land was owned by the state; cultivators had rights of occupancy, and tax collection was assigned to officials of the state.

Nevertheless, towards the end of the sixteenth century the Ottoman Empire found itself confronted by a long-protracted crisis which was to last until its collapse on the eve of the First World War. The crisis was linked to the inability adequately to administer all the vast expanses it had conquered, but also to the penetration of early forms of capitalist organization which exposed the weaknesses of the less productive Asiatic mode of production.

The advent of crisis within the Ottoman Empire would have corresponding consequences in Cyprus, with numerous revolts, in which usually there was joint participation by the two largest communities (Muslims and Orthodox), breaking out against the economic oppression to which they were subjected for the sake of ensuring payment of taxes so that the excessive public deficits might be reduced. To solve this problem the Sublime Porte decided to grant the Orthodox hierarchy unprecedented powers of tax collection so as to introduce some order into the fiscal operations of the state, but also to curtail the power of private tax farmers who, having expelled the public officials, were escaping almost all control. This change would significantly upgrade the Cypriot Church, in a way which could not be compared with anything prevailing elsewhere in the hierarchy in other Ottoman regions. The hierarchy would be exercising *both* a political role as representative of the Orthodox *and* an economic role as an important landowner, *but also* an administrative role as a tax collector. This would trigger a series of new insurrections, in which a significant role was played by Muslim peasants, who turned against the Orthodox hierarchy *too,* perceiving it as a co-participant in the overall power structure.

Something should be underlined at this point which is a basic thesis of the present book. Undoubtedly the lives of the Muslim and Christian rural population were characterized by numerous common points throughout the era of Ottoman rule, which is why one many times sees joint uprisings against unjust rulers and excessive increases in taxation. But this does not invalidate *another* aspect of the reality, namely that apart from the points in common there were also important differences between the two communities. The Orthodox paid more tax, and enjoyed fewer political rights, than Muslims. The latter, unlike the Christians and despite the different mode of operation of the Orthodox Church by comparison with the situation in other parts of the Ottoman Empire, felt that Ottoman power was "something theirs". The education of the two communities was also entirely different in content, underlining the differences exposed by religion. In terms of social life, Cyprus was far from being what could be called a multicultural community. It is arguable that while social relations were not hostile or non-existent, the two communities to a large extent lived parallel lives. This situation was to be intensified in the aftermath of two developments: The first being the economic progress of the Greek Cypriots as merchants in the wider region, in contrast to the Turkish Cypriots who preferred to continue to occupy themselves with farming or public administration. The second has to do with the gradual emergence of the Hellenic identity among the Greek-speaking Orthodox, which metamorphosed into the demand for the creation of an independent Greek state. This tendency made its appearance in Cyprus also, and the Cypriot Orthodox, after the massacre of the notables in 1821 but also with the participation of many of them in the Greek Revolution for independence, would acquire Greek national identity. Given the formation of the Greek state in 1830, this development may have contributed even further to the diffusion of Greek identity but for the time being the Greeks of Cyprus did not advance the demand for *Enosis* of Cyprus with Greece. This was because on the one hand there was the sense that nothing like that was feasible in the present phase because of the strength of the Ottoman Empire—let alone that the fledgling Greek state was not demanding it—and on the other because an important fraction of the Orthodox elite, and specifically the Church hierarchy, continued to see itself as officialdom and part of the upper strata of the Ottoman administration and society. This is the point in time when I consider it proper for the Orthodox Christians of Cyprus to begin to be called Greeks of Cyprus or Greek Cypriots, as reflected in the terminology used in this book.

The continuing crisis of the Ottoman Empire and the perennial Russian threat obliged the Porte, after its defeat in the Russo-Turkish War of 1878, to seek an alliance with the British, with the cession of Cyprus in exchange. Almost immediately after that, without being able to avoid vacillations and internal conflicts, the Greek Cypriots began to submit to their new masters the demand for *Enosis*. As a result, apart from the British the Muslims of Cyprus *also* began to raise vehement objections to such a prospect, arguing that if the cession of Cyprus to the British should ever end, the island must be returned to the Sublime Porte. The British took advantage of this disagreement, establishing institutions (Legislature, Education) which not only emphasized the existing differences between the two communities but, utilizing the Muslims as de facto allies, assigned them an upgraded role in relation to the Greek Cypriot majority.

One interesting development has to do with the role of the hierarchy through the nineteenth century. In the first phase the institutional innovations adopted by the Ottoman Empire may not, indeed, have entailed a downgrading of the Church but rather enabled the emergence in political positions *some* sections of the rising bourgeois class. This fact, subsequently, would play a catalytic role in shaping the strategy of *Enosis* as it later emerged under British rule. Two tendencies were constructed inside the hierarchy: the so-called traditional, which aspired to maintain the position of the Church as a mechanism of State in the period of Ottoman administration and the likewise so-called modernizing, which in collaboration with the fledgling bourgeoisie sought to establish a Cyprus moving towards capitalism as part of the modern Greek nation state. Unlike the traditional faction which espoused agricultural development and variants of simple commodity production within a pre-capitalist state formation, the modernizers perceived the great potential offered to the Cypriot economy by the introduction of the capitalist mode of production. The conflict ended with the ascendancy of the modernizers and a change in the Church to a leadership whose strategy corresponded better to the current reality. The new Church hierarchy that emerged at the turn of the twentieth century undertook political representation of the demand for *Enosis*. On the other hand, the Muslims began to construct their own Turkish national identity, frequently clashing with Greek Cypriots over the *Enosis* demand. We thus reach the point in time when it is appropriate for them to be called the Turks of Cyprus, or Turkish Cypriots, terms which I choose to utilize from a certain point and onwards in the narrative presented in this book.

So, within this context of antagonism towards the two communities, the British administration would start to be bombarded with Greek Cypriot memoranda seeking *Enosis*, generating continual clashes with the Muslims. The British, for their part, proposed cession of Cyprus to Greece, for the first time in 1912 in return for the conferral of bases in Ionia and for the second time in 1915 in return for the participation of Greece in the First World War. In neither case was there a positive outcome, for different reasons. But what was important was that the Greek Cypriots concluded that the question of *Enosis* could be an object for negotiation with the British, the more so because there was the precedent of the British ceding the Ionian Islands to Greece in 1864. But in the aftermath of World War I, with France and Italy occupying a stronger position in the wider region, and on the other hand with the increased use of the aircraft as a weapon of war, the position of Cyprus was upgraded, and this would preclude its cession to Greece. Moreover, for the Greek state raising the question of Cyprus was not a priority.

So, the Greek Cypriots would find themselves isolated as they continued to demand *Enosis* and made the relevant overtures to the British government. When it all proved futile at that time, in the early 1920s, they would opt for the practice of abstaining from the elections to the Legislative Council, with a view to pressuring the British and bringing the subject back to the forefront. But apart from the steadfastly dismissive stance of the British the Greek Cypriots had to deal with the reactions of the Muslims, for whom the process of shaping a Turkish national identity was now completed. The transformation had been assisted by the mobilization of the Muslims on the one hand though the perennial endorsement of the demand for *Enosis* by Greek Cypriots and on the other through consolidation of the sentiment that from the political majority they had been under the Ottoman Empire, following the transfer of political power to the British they had been transformed into a political, demographic, and economic minority. If to all this is added the fact of nation states having been created in regions which had hitherto been part of the Ottoman Empire along with the objective reality of the use of the Turkish language and the Muslim religion, all the factors emerge which led to the acquisition of Turkish national identity. Of course, this process did not come about automatically given the existence of a section of the Muslim elite which felt more closely connected with the Ottoman identity but also with the British administration.

Essentially what had happened was that the overall context within which the Cyprus question had been framed had been greatly modified. For a start, the Greek defeat in Asia Minor (1922) and the establishment of the Kemalist state had profoundly altered the realities and the power balance. Greece had suffered a broad-scale military defeat and it had become clear that it would not be easy to claim territory in which Turkey was also interested. Moreover, Turkey had been organized as a robust secular state able for the first time to function as a much more stable pole of attraction for Turkish Cypriots than the shaky Ottoman Empire. At the same time, it was evident that the British, irrespective of which party was in government, were increasingly persuaded that they should not give up Cyprus.

It was within his phase of development that the 1931 revolt took place. It was considered by the popular strata at this time that questions like the very heavy taxation and unfavourable social conditions within which they were required to live could only be resolved by liberating themselves from British domination, which was why they proposed to pursue the strategy of the Greek Cypriot bourgeoisie which sought *Enosis* so that it too could conduct its activities more satisfactorily with lighter taxation.

The crushing of the revolt would lead to the tension of repression and destruction of such political liberties as had been attained. It is interesting that in the new conditions stringent limitations were also imposed on the supporters of Kemalism, who shortly before had managed to secure the majority of Turkish Cypriot votes. Beyond its authoritarianism Britain now aspired to a "Britishization" of the two communities. Naturally in such a circumstance there could not be any question of *Enosis,* the more so given that Greece itself was not prioritizing it, not wishing to damage its good relations with Britain.

The outbreak of World War II, the difficult position in which Britain initially found itself, the occupation of Greece by the Axis forces, the participation of the USSR on the side of the Allies, all this would change the until then authoritarian political scene as well as bringing the question of *Enosis* back to the fore. At the same time, the establishment of AKEL would imbue the Communist movement with legalized status and modify the power balance within Greek Cypriot society, greatly increasing the influence of the Left. A role in this was played by the fact that AKEL, unlike its predecessor the Communist Party of Cyprus, was to adopt the demand for *Enosis*.

Following the end of World War II, the demand for *Enosis* was placed on a new basis, given that the crisis of colonialism that then emerged had led to many countries acquiring their independence and created a very favourable environment for the presentation of such demands. The Greek Cypriots submitted it with the utmost urgency. In response, apart from the reactions of the British, who notwithstanding their internal disagreements did not wish to embark on such a discussion, the stance of the Turkish Cypriots included the creation of political parties and purely Turkish Cypriot workers' federations and the organization of rallies against *Enosis*. And the relations between Left and Right were throughout this period exceptionally hostile. The Greek civil war affected the Greek Cypriot political forces, albeit by refraction, and an existential anxiety was generated in the Greek Cypriot bourgeoisie, which persisted in the demand for *Enosis* but saw AKEL, and not the British, as enemy number one. Seeing that the British continued to regard the occupation of Cyprus as of indispensable value and that all they were disposed to accept was the institution of a Self-governing Constitution, AKEL agreed to participate in the relevant discussion to be conducted under the auspices of the Consultative Assembly. The Greek Cypriot Right then condemned AKEL as a traitor to the nation. The narrow limits of the political freedoms that the British side was willing to grant led the Consultative Assembly to failure and to AKEL changing its line, once again assigning priority to the goal of *Enosis*. But this vacillation, in conjunction with the defeat of the Greek Left in the civil war, would have as one of its consequences a diminution in the influence of AKEL and consolidation of the political hegemony of the Right and the ecclesiastical hierarchy.

But apart from the conflicts within the Greek Cypriot community, something which must certainly be noted is that the official Greek state throughout this period was ambivalent over *Enosis*. Undoubtedly, they wanted *Enosis* to go ahead so as to expand once again the borders of Greek territory. But they had to confront the reaction of the British, who were the key ally of the Greek ruling class in the Greek civil war. It was for this reason that they were so wary, vis a vis the Greek Cypriot efforts, to broach this subject and to pressure the British side.

Given this situation where nowhere was there to be seen any favourable prospect for the achievement of *Enosis,* an initiative was taken by the Greek Cypriots for the holding of a referendum, a development which met with active opposition both from the British and from the Turkish Cypriots. The overwhelming endorsement of *Enosis* from the participants in the referendum would be a watershed in the history of the Cyprus question. Seeing the almost unanimous vote for *Enosis,* the Greek Cypriots would decide to internationalize the Cyprus question, publicizing it at the international level, persuaded that in this way they would secure the sympathy of other states and would accordingly be able to exert greater pressure on the British. This would mark the beginning of a new decade in which the Cyprus question would be included in the agenda of international issues, culminating in the proclamation of the independent state of Cyprus in 1960.

Before closing this introduction, I feel it appropriate to mention all the people to whom I am obliged for the assistance of every kind that was made available to me during the writing of this book. To begin with I must thank the Palgrave publishing house which for a second time does me the honour of accepting my work for publication. I should also mention that the work in question is to a significant extent a revised version of the first section of my book "The Cypriot social formation 1191–2004: From creation to partition", which was published in Greek in 2017 by Topos editions, and for publication of which I am deeply indebted to Vangelis Georgakakis and Giannis Karachalios.

That said, I am evidently called upon to thank Loukas Axelos and Charalambos Tsardanidis who were so kind as to read a previous version of the text and make very useful observations. I also owe a debt of gratitude to Fay Retsa for her unfailing presence and support. At the institutional level I wish to thank my department, the Social Policy Department of Panteion University, which once again showed the importance it attributes to fraternal solidarity and assistance. Finally, I would like to convey my gratitude to the staff of the Panteion University Library, always willing to respond to my every bibliographical need, and in particular to Dimitra Legga, who hastened with persistence and zeal to meet my scholarly requirements.

Last but by no means least the present work could not have been enriched and upgraded from the Greek edition if had not been for the fruitful dialogue with several colleagues with extensive knowledge of the Cyprus question but also for their assistance in gaining access to difficult-to-find material. They are Alexis Alekou, Nikos Christofis, Daphnos Economou, Giannos Katsourides, Christos Kyriakidis, Michalis Michail, Nikos Moudouros, Petros Papapolyviou, Stavros Tombazos, Nikos Trimikliniotis, It is obvious that any deficiencies in the present edition weigh exclusively on the writer, as does the economic cost entailed in conducting research for which no funding was available from a relevant grant.

Spyros Sakellaropoulos
Athens,
June 2021

Interplays between external and internal forces over time

1. The Period of Frankish Rule (1192–1478)

    a. At the level of internal contradictions there is the ruling feudal class with class-support from the urban bourgeoisie. On the other side are the dominated classes of paricii, *perpiarii* and lefteroi (free tenants)
    b. At the level of internal contradictions in 1373 the Genoans succeed in occupying Famagusta, remaining there until 1474
    c. In 1426 the Egyptian Mamelukes occupy Cyprus and henceforth the island is obliged to pay tribute each year to the Egyptian Sultan.
    d. The above development in combination with the economic hardship but also the gradual promotion of Venetians to key positions of political power will contribute to the beginning of the period of Venetian supremacy from 1474.

2. The Period of Venetian Rule (1474–1571)

    a. Within Cypriot society the ruling class is comprised of nobles and feudal lords and the dominated classes of *francomati* and parici (serfs).
    b. The internal conflicts within the ruling class induce a section of the Cypriot aristocracy to seek the intervention of foreign powers to overturn Venetian rule (1520–1550)

c. In the 1550–1565 period there are popular uprisings and demands are put forward by some villagers that power should be assumed by the Ottomans.
d. The growing geopolitical significance of Cyprus for the Ottoman Empire leads the latter to declare war on the Venetians in 1570 and ultimately to occupy the island the following year.

3. The Ottoman Period of Occupation of Cyprus (1571–1878)

a. 1580–1620: insurrections of the Christian population aim at re-establishing Christian rule on the island
b. 1650–1790: joint revolts of Muslims and Christians on issues of taxation
c. 1790–1830: conflicts between Muslims and Christians around economic and political issues. A significant contribution to this is made by upgrading the role of the Orthodox Church within the system of Ottoman power in Cyprus but also by Orthodox Christian connections with the newly established trade networks
d. 1830–1840: resumption of joint revolts of Muslims and Christians on issues of taxation
e. 1853–1878: military clashes between the Ottoman Empire and Russia lead the former to cede Cyprus to Britain in return for British protection from the Russians. The overall weakening of the Ottoman Empire is also attributable to the fact of economic decline, which has been underway since the seventeenth century.

4. The Period of British Rule (1878–1950)

a. 1878–1910: Conflicts between Greek Cypriots over the expedience of raising the demand for *Enosis* with Greece.
b. Gradual adoption of Turkish national identity by the Muslims of Cyprus and confrontation with Greeks over the question of *Enosis*.
c. The question of *Enosis* acquires additional pertinence and urgency in the course of the First World War when Britain and the Ottoman Empire are in opposite camps. The more so when to induce Greece to participate on the side of the Entente Britain proposes that Cyprus be ceded to it, irrespective of whether that is possible given the desire of the Greek leadership at that time to maintain a stance of neutrality.

d. But the new geopolitical situation brought about by the ending of the First World War contributes to Britain's deciding to keep the island in defiance of the urgent claims of the Greek Cypriots
e. The rise of the Kemalist movement and the establishment of the Turkish state exerts a significant influence on the consciousness of the Turkish Cypriots, who divide into Kemalists, who prioritize articulation of claims against British rule, and traditionalists, who seek continuation of unimpeded collaboration with the British
f. The development of capitalism, as elaborated in the first decades of the twentieth century, intensifies the socio-economic contradictions on two planes: in the agricultural sector where the poor farmers are forced into continual borrowing from wealthy creditors, leading them into gradual loss of their property, and in the urban sector where workers in industry and trade live in conditions of harsh exploitation by their employers
g. The abovementioned developments contribute to the emergence of the Communist current in Cyprus
h. The incursion into Cyprus of the global economic crisis contributes in two ways to deterioration in workers' living conditions: on the one hand with the rise in unemployment and cuts in wages and on the other through increases in taxation.
i. 1931 sees the revolt of the Greek Cypriots against the British as a result of two factors: firstly the discontent triggered by annulment of the prospect of *Enosis* and secondly the unrest produced by the reduction in income
j. Violent suppression of the revolt takes the island into a period of authoritarian colonial rule. But the outbreak of World War II and the need to bring Cypriots into the ranks of the British Army, in conjunction with Greece's participation in the war on the side of the Allies, obliges the British to proceed with a political liberalization.
k. This democratization leads to the emergence of a three-sided confrontation that is to set its stamp on all of the 1940s: (i) the establishment of AKEL (Communist Party of Cyprus) as a mass organization, in conjunction with the effects of the civil war in Greece, contributes to the emergence of intensifies enmity between the Greek Cypriot Right and the Greek Cypriot Left, (ii) the return of the demand for *Enosis* but also the founding of Greek Cypriot political agents is countered by the creation

of unified Turkish Cypriot political and syndicalist organizations, (iii) The decision by the British that after the war Cyprus will remain under British domination produces great unrest both in the Greek Cypriot Right and in the Greek Cypriot Left, a situation culminating in the 1950 referendum.

CHAPTER 2

From Richard the Lionheart to the Occupation of Cyprus by the Ottomans

1 The Occupation of Cyprus by Richard the Lionheart

In the course of the third Crusade Richard the Lionheart occupied Cyprus (1191), which was under disintegrating Byzantine administration, as was all of the once-powerful Byzantine Empire. Richard was faced with a twofold problem: on the one hand, there was the military control of the island, in a situation where significant forces could not be devoted to it; on the other, there were the demands of the French king Philippe Auguste for a sharing of the booty. Finally, given that money was needed for him to pay his soldiers, who were besieging Acre, as well as for recompensing the French, though as regards the latter case it is not known what happened finally, the decision was taken to sell the island to the Templars for 100,000 besants (Sakellarios 1890: 413). To be able to pay this sum the Templars sought to extract it from the Cypriots, establishing a toll that amounted to 1/48 of the price of food. This demand triggered an insurrection on 5th July 1192. The revolt was successfully repressed but it had been made clear that the occupation of Cyprus was generating numerous burdens for the Temple. A decision was therefore taken to ask Richard to cancel the sale. There then appeared on the scene a certain Guy de Lusignan, scion of a powerful family of Poitou, who had been crowned King of Jerusalem in 1186, but for a number of reasons his

S. Sakellaropoulos, *The Evolution of the Political, Social and Economic Life of Cyprus, 1191–1950*, Palgrave Studies in Economic History,
https://doi.org/10.1007/978-3-030-91839-2_2

authority had been challenged by the Barons, the Crusaders and indeed by Richard himself. The purchase of Cyprus offered a new opportunity for the exercise of power. De Lusignan therefore proposed to the King of England that he, Guy de Lusignan, should pay the 100,000 besants. The agreement was signed and in May 1192 Guy was installed as master of Cyprus (Richard 1995b: 2–3) (Map 1).

The reasons that the Crusaders wanted occupation of Cyprus was not unrelated to the intense pressure they were encountering from Muslims in their possessions in Syria and Palestine. Cyprus was a secure base because, while its position between Europe and the East made it strategically significant, an attack against it required a powerful fleet and favourable weather conditions. Finally, one important factor was the island's commercial potential. It was for this reason, indeed, that many Venetians and other merchants had already taken up residence there (Pavlidis 1992: 14).

2 The Period of Domination of the Lusignans

The transference of power from the Byzantines to the West did not lead, at least for the first 100 years, at the level of regional organizations, to any particular alterations from the arrangements of the Byzantines. There was the village (*casal*), which was either an independent administrative unit or part of a broader administrative entity, the *baliaggio*. Most villages had the character of feudal property. They were initially divided into *despotates (despotia)* that is to say estates that were cultivated directly by the landowner, and into plots that were rented by villagers. But there is evidence that around the end of the fourteenth century there was an important change in the mode of administration and the island was divided into 12 regions, each of which was under the direction of a Crown official (*chevetaine*). These officials were engaged basically in harvesting taxes and other royal revenues. This development must be linked to changes in the regime of exploitation on royal estates from a franchising or rental-based policy to their direct management by the Crown (Edbury 1991: 194).

A second administrative-institutional change that should be mentioned is the downgrading of the role of the Orthodox Church. In accordance with the relevant decisions of 1220 and 1223, the number of Orthodox bishops was reduced from fourteen to four and were placed under the supervision of the Latin bishops of Paphos, Famagusta and Limassol and the Latin archbishop of Nicosia. At the same time, both the election of

Map 1 In 1191 in the course of the Third Crusade Richard the Lionheart seizes Cyprus from the Byzantines. He sells it initially to the Templars and subsequently to the Lusignan Franks (*Source* https://en.wikipedia.org/wiki/History_of_Cyprus#/media/File:Atlas_Van_der_Hagen-KW1049B13_007-CYPRVS_INSVLA.jpeg)

a bishop and the ordainment of a priest required permission from the local feudal lord. Initially the Orthodox clergy did not agree to this, but in 1260, the Orthodox bishops were to recognize the authority both of the Pope and of the Latin bishops, who were able to impose ecclesiastical penalties as they could with their own flock (Kalogirou 1994: 57), an arrangement which was to prevail up to the Ottoman occupation. What is interesting is that this acceptance from a purely formalistic viewpoint means that erstwhile Orthodox priests had been transformed into Roman Catholics who merely retained Orthodox ritual.[1] But this formal change did not lead to assimilation by the Catholics, because they remained as before different both in terms of the content of their faith and in their external attributes and ceremonial. At the beginning of the fifteenth century, there are reports of a failed attempt to effect a secret reunification of the Church of Cyprus with the Orthodox Patriarchate of Constantinople (Koureas 2001: 270–272).

At the level of social morphology, the society of Cyprus was structured as follows: there was the ruling class, comprised of big landowners and including the King, the Catholic Church and senior state officials. Feudal property was an intrinsic element in their cohesion. A feudal estate could be comprised of land or of an annual cash income (Richard 1995a: 357–358).

Guy de Lusignan assigned 200 fiefs to armed nobility and 300 to knights with an income of 400 besants. The land he distributed came either from imperial estates, from the Orthodox Church or from the property of private citizens who had left Cyprus. A distribution of this kind is indicative of Lusignan's desire to limit the size of fiefs so that they could not become competitive with royal authority (Collenberg 1995: 793).

The Assembly of adult peers, feudal lords and knights comprised the High Court, which was presided over by the King himself. The King was not able to punish any of the nobility without the consent of the High Court. At the same time, it functioned as the government, determining policies of state, interpreting the laws and instituting new laws. It was

[1] In the event of the episcopal throne being vacated, the clerics of the episcopate elected the new bishop, whose election was ratified by the Latin bishop. The new bishop was subsequently sworn in, declaring that: "I the bishop of (city) ... henceforth pledge my allegiance to the throne of the Church of Rome. I recognize the sainthood of the Pope and accept as my lord .... Archibishop of Nicosia and his duly elected successors. I shall assist, support and defend the Papal power of the church of Rome" (quoted in Kalogirou 1994: 56).

in the High Court that issues of royal succession and vice-regal matters were resolved and all questions pertaining to fiefs and owners of fiefs were placed under its jurisdiction. It was the terrain on which feudal lords gave their consent to the sale of royal lands and the signing of diplomatic treaties (Edbury 1991: 186). As a court of law the High Court involved itself exclusively with the affairs of the nobility. For matters concerning others and for issues between the nobility and ordinary people, the *cour des bourgeois* was the responsible authority. This was a jury court whose members were appointed by the King and were drawn from the local urban Latin population (Pavlidis 1992: 23–24). Its terms of reference covered all aspects of civil and criminal law (Edbury1991: 193).

Class—support of the feudal aristocracy was the urban bourgeoisie. The bourgeois lived within the walls of the city, with corresponding responsibility for its defence. They had secured “urban concessions” in recompense for this obligation. But in reality the military obligation imposed a minimal burden on the Cypriot bourgeoisie, who were primarily merchants and artisans by occupation. The urban concession, which could also devolve upon a member of the nobility but was governed by its own law and could not be identified with a fief, was transferred in accordance with the rules of civil law and took the form of an annual remittance (Richard 1995a: 359).

Another intermediate class was that of the so-called *turcopoles*, who were a corps of mounted soldiers to whom a fief had been assigned of lesser significance than those accorded to the nobility. A *turcopole* received on average half of the amount made available to a noble (Papadopoulos 1995: 765).

Above and beyond that were the people, divided into the following categories:

a. there were the *parici,* who were the most subordinate class and paid to the feudal lord a poll tax of 50 besants annually, as well as at least a third of their production, who were obliged to work as forced labour on the estates of the feudal lord for an average of two days a week and who wore the garment of the serf that is familiar from the West also. Along with all their family they could be sold or exchanged by their lords, who were empowered to punish them with any penalty other than death or mutilation. They were not allowed to leave the estate and the lords regarded them as part of their portable property. Even marriages between *parici* from different estates were forbidden. Apart from that other kinds of deductions from their income were imposed, such as marriage levies, widows' tax, inheritance tax, the *tithe* on animals, payment for use of the mill, of the threshing floor, for the services of the shepherd and the field warden (Hadjidemetriou 2002: 192; Richard 1995a: 365; Arbel 1995: 512; Pavlidis 1992: 33)

b. A little higher on the social scale were the *perpiarii*, who had under the preceding regime purchased their own freedom and the freedom of their family and were obliged to pay 15 golden besants a year (their name is thought to derive from these coins because the name of the coin was *hyperper*). They also continued to pay taxes corresponding to those of the *parici* for the land they utilized and for the seeds. The *perpiarii* enjoyed the right of free mobility and choice of their place of domicile. They were not subject to forced labour requirements or obliged to surrender one-third of their production. The sources refer to them as a remnant from the Byzantine regime when the privilege of freedom for them and their descendants was granted by some dukes or *Katepano* (provincial administrators) and continued to be recognized by the Franks also.

c. Finally there were the *lefteroi* (free tenants) who were former parici who had been liberated either through payment or at the initiative of their masters (Christodoulou 1959: 71). Another term for the *lefteroi* was *francomati*, derived from the French word *franchise* (liberation). Irrespective of whether they lived in the cities or the countryside, they were entitled to manage their own land. If their land was within the boundaries of the fief they were required to surrender only a small proportion of their production, from one-fifth to one-tenth, to the feudal lord. Above and beyond that the feudal lords possessed no other power over them and in any case such obligations as they had were derived from contracts they had entered into and not from the regime of serfdom, as in the case of the *parici*. They accordingly came under the jurisdiction not of the feudal lord but of the courts, and they paid taxes to the King for certain privileges they enjoyed, for example, with salt (Hadjidemetriou 2002: 193). The real reason for their appearance on the scene is to be sought on the one hand in the financial needs of the monarchy and on the other hand in an increase in the general economic prosperity of the *parici*.

Entrenchment of the power of the Lusignans did not seem to add more than in the past to the burdens weighing on the majority of Cypriots. It was the inhabitants of the cities who were in the worst position, given that the Franks imposed personal taxation on them. While the *parici,* by contrast, saw a perpetuation of all the institutional obligations that had burdened them in the Byzantine period,[2] this nevertheless pertained only to the institutional dimension and moved on a somewhat apparent level. What really happened registered more accurately at the level of society. The need to divide the land among such a large number of nobles induced the Lusignans to reduce the area of land the *parici* were allowed to occupy, with the result that their income plummeted dramatically. The situation was to deteriorate even further when the institutional context underwent radical change with the passage of the years and the coming of difficult times, with the forced labour obligation increasing from 12 to 104 days per year (by other accounts to 156) (Pardos 2001: 114). In consequence, relatively soon the farming population's tax obligations were exceptionally high compared with those of other agricultural communities in Europe in the same period. But besides that, the creation of the fiefs was conducive to an organizational model historically characterized by stagnation in human social development, unlike what had prevailed in the Byzantine Empire, where there had been greater flexibility.

One form of improvement for a section of the *parici* was to emerge at the end of the first decades of Frankish rule. It was then, precisely because of the discomfort that had been caused to farmers by the aforementioned state of affairs, that the phenomenon of the *francomati* or *lefteroi* began to make its presence felt. The *francomati* owed their existence to the fact that the Byzantine institution of *Canon Law* remained in force, necessitating the liberation of any *parici* ordained as priests. Needless to say, an attempt was made to impose limits on this ruling, through the related decrees of 1220 and 1222, both through the obligation for there to be

[2] We point out very briefly that during the Byzantine period there were the *parici* who were leaseholders of land belonging to a wider farming community. The community land either belonged to the state or were part of great tracts of land that were property of the Orthodox Church. The community was taxed as a single unit and each leaseholder was obliged to remit to the community his share of the tax. In parallel with this there were different types of slavery. In such cases growers lived in slave villages labouring for the benefit of their master, who paid the taxes, with the farm workers bound to the land (Christodoulou 1959: 70–71).

the consent of the feudal lord and through limitation of the number of monks. Nevertheless, the phenomenon of mass emancipation later made a comeback because in the mid-fourteenth century in his attempt to organize missions against the Ottoman raids in Asia Minor, King Peter (1359–1369) proceeded to free *parici* in return for cash remuneration. The practice was reiterated a few years later when Peter II (1369–1382) permitted the freeing of serfs so as to be enabled to pay the war reparations exacted by the Genoans for the Famagusta War of 1373–1374 (see below) (Antonopoulou 2013: 54–55). These developments may be seen in conjunction with the relative improvement in the economic situation of the farming population which enabled them, once the institutional possibility already existed, to purchase their freedom from the authorities. To all this there should be added, from time to time, the provision of Cyprus with slaves, with consequent increase in the numbers of individuals freed and/or improvement in the life of the serfs. Characteristic from this viewpoint is reduction in the days of forced labour from three to two per week (Richard 1977: 351–352).

3 The Crisis of Frankish Rule

From a certain point onwards the Frankish regime began to stumble. A significant role in this was played by the epidemic of plague which hit Cyprus in 1348. As a result the population figure fell by a third, with a consequent fall in agricultural production and the corresponding revenue, while at the same time, taxation of the nobility increased (Koureas 2001: 277), prompting a sale of Frankish property to Venetians, who founded great estates and thus facilitated their own monopoly of commerce in products such as sugar, cotton and wine (Collenberg 1982: 80). At the same time, the presence of the first Venetian banks lending money at high-interest rates both to the Kingdom and to the nobility contributed to exacerbating the financial straits of Frankish power.

At the most direct level, the crisis of Frankish power started to become perceptible from 1373 onwards, when the Genoans invaded and occupied Famagusta. The Genoan intervention was triggered by the events of 10th October 1372. On that day Peter II, who in Nicosia the previous January, had already been crowned king of Cyprus, was also in Famagusta crowned king of Jerusalem. Bloody incidents then broke out between the Frankish and Genoan communities, with involvement of the Cypriots on the side of the Franks, and the Genoans accordingly sustained great damage (Edbury

1991: 199–200). After that the Genoans sought compensation from the King but he was not able to satisfy their demands and the response of the Genoese was to launch a military intervention. The time had now come for Genoa to realize one of its old dreams, namely occupation of Famagusta. Finally, this city was to be occupied and ceded as collateral for the purpose of paying off the debt to the Genoese (Sakellarios 1890: 502). In reality, the latter were interested in securing exclusive rights to utilization of its port. Finally, after the death of Peter II, King James, who succeeded him on the throne, agreed to definitive cession of Famagusta (Gasparis 2001: 70–71; Sakellarios 1890: 507).

What should be noted is that the fact of even the Pope apparently giving some kind of consent to the mission of the Genoese is symptomatic of the uneasiness that had begun to be felt over the stability of Frankish rule in this particularly vulnerable island. The anxiety, which was not unconnected with the rising power of the Muslims, proved justified when in 1426 the Mamelukes launched an invasion of Cyprus. On the pretext of opposing the Franks' toleration of piracy, the Sultan of Egypt attempted to bring Cyprus under his own control. The defeat suffered by the royal army, with King Janus being taken hostage by the Mamelukes (Sakellarios 1890: 516), who after four days of pillaging and destruction then departed, reduced the island to a state of chaos, foreshadowing what was to follow. The island was divided into four parts: Famagusta remained under Genovese control, Kyrenia was administered by the Franks, the situation in Paphos was anarchic because of the autonomist activity of a mercenary called Sforza, aided by Spanish soldiers. An insurrection of the farming population had broken out in the other areas under the leadership of Re (King) Alexis, from Pentadaktylos, one of the *parici*. The fact that order returned rapidly to the island, except in Famagusta, can in no way conceal the dimensions of the existing problem. For example, the Egyptian Sultan demanded and secured 200,000 ducats in payment in exchange for releasing Janus, along with an annual tribute amounting to 5,000 ducats. In this way, Cyprus was partly losing its independence and there is nothing accidental about the way that henceforth the sultans in Cairo would begin to demand a voice in the affairs of Cyprus.

Events were to accelerate following the death of John II (1458), with a dynastic crisis breaking out between Queen Charlotte and James, John's illegitimate brother James turned to the Mamelukes for assistance and Charlotte sought the help of the West. The Genoese judged that they should support the Queen because their interests in Famagusta were under threat. Venice, by contrast, refused support on account of their specific commercial interests in the South-Eastern Mediterranean, and particularly in Egypt. In 1460, James occupied Nicosia and Western Cyprus and the following year he was to occupy all of Cyprus apart from Kyrenia and Famagusta. Finally, in 1464, he completed his conquest of the whole island (Gasparis 2001: 77).

The emergence of the Ottoman threat but also a range of other factors such as disasters and an epidemic of plague, all making their appearance in the 1470s, served to weaken Cyprus economically and lead to James forging an alliance with Venice through his marriage with Catherine Cornaro. The death of James in 1473 and the coming to the throne of Catherine led to refilling of all the important positions in the Kingdom with Venetian officials, neutralizing what had been regarded as opposed to Venetian interests. The growth in influence of the Ottomans in the surrounding region (given that the Ottoman Sultan Bayezid II [1481–1512] had repeatedly threatened Cyprus during the wars against the Mamelukes commencing in 1484) was used as an argument for the Venetian side to persuade the Sultan of Egypt to accept the divestiture of Cyprus to Venice on the condition that the Egyptians would continue to be paid their tribute. So it was that in 1489 the flag of the Republic of Saint Mark was raised in Cyprus (Sakellarios 1890: 537).

4 The Period of Venetian Rule (1474–1571)

Annexing Cyprus, the Venetians aimed at securing unimpeded functioning of maritime communications, resupply of Venetian ships conducting trade in the Eastern Mediterranean and optimum economic exploitation of the island's resources (chiefly sugar and salt) for the benefit of Venetian commerce. Moreover, using the island as a staging post would facilitate penetration of Asia, along the spice roads (Tsiknakis 2001: 84) (Map 2).

To secure these objectives, the Venetian Republic took pains to ensure the best possible military defences for Cyprus and the installation of a strong local government.

The Venetians retained the social system of feudalism: the administrative organization of the island was divided, as before, into 12 regions: (Nicosia, Famagusta, Carpasia, Limassol, Mesaoria, Larnaca (Alykes), Paphos, Kyrenia, Avdimou, Chrysochou, Pentagyia and Mazotos). Head of the administration was the Doge, a Venetian citizen, elected through

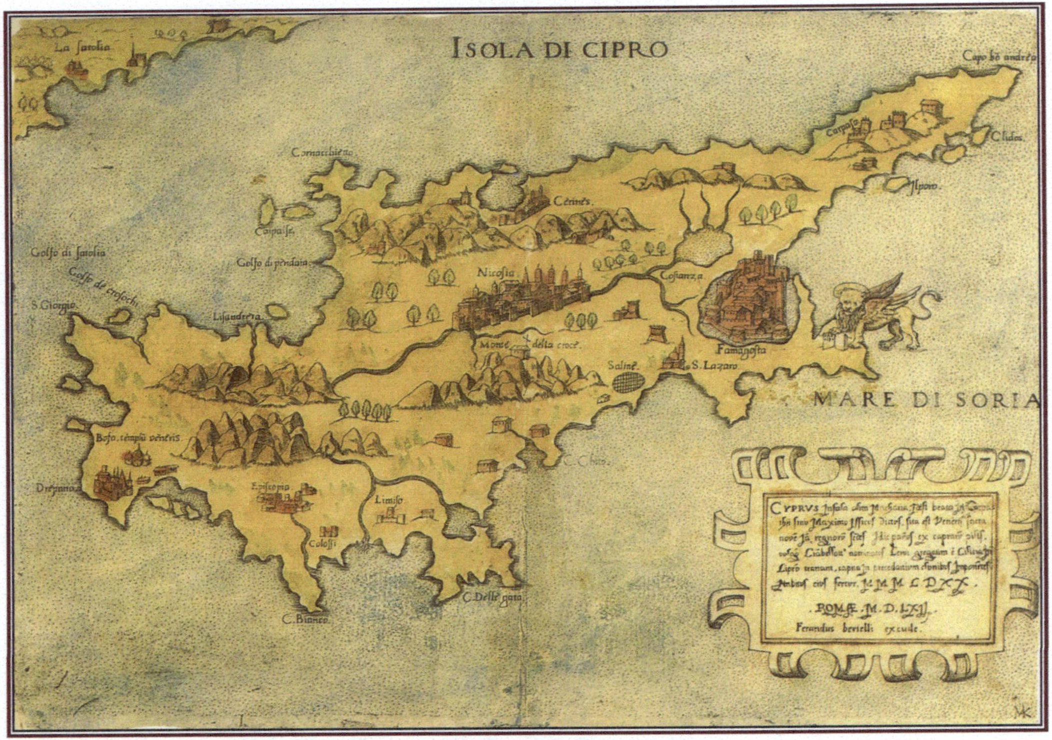

Map 2 In 1474 the Venetians succeed the Franks as masters of Cyprus (*Source* https://italiancyprus.com/2021/05/venezia-and-cyprus-connections/)

secret ballot by the Great Council of the patrician class for a two-year term of office. The Doge governed with the assistance of two counsellors, known as Administrators, also serving a two-year term and similarly elected by the Great Council. This three-member authority represented the Republic of Venice (Aristeidou 1990, I: 37–30; Sakellarios 1890: 539). The legislative powers were exercised exclusively by the competent bodies of the Republic of Venice. The High Court was abolished and the councils of Nicosia and Famagusta established which after, in some way, represented the corresponding districts to the Venetian authorities. We say "in some way" because the abolition of the High Court removed all rights for exercising power from the Frankish nobility. On the other hand, the council of Nicosia conveyed the demands of the aristocracy of that city, whereas, given the very limited presence of nobility in Famagusta, the council of the latter primarily reflected the interests of the bourgeois strata (Arbel 1986: 207–210).

The social structure was not significantly different from that of the period of Frankish rule and comprised the following categories: (a) at the top of the pyramid were the nobles and the feudal rulers; they were followed by (b) the bourgeoisie, that is to say, those inhabitants of the cities who did not have an aristocratic title but were economically well off, such as merchants, manufacturers, medical doctors, lawyers, notaries, mariners, soldiers, civil servants, etc. (c) the ordinary people, namely country people and city dwellers not belonging to one of the aforementioned social groups. The population fell into two subcategories. There were the *francomati* and the *parici* (serfs). The *francomati* retained free status, surrendering to the feudal lord between a sixth and a quarter of their production, with the land they cultivated belonging to them. They needed the permission of the authorities to marry and in cases of intermarriage with *parici* were relegated to the category of *parici*. But it should be noted that this freedom was a freedom within the agrarian context, that is to say, the *francomati* were excluded from the freedoms and opportunities enjoyed exclusively by members of the urban community (Arbel 1995: 517; Aristeidou 1998: 374–375) and with the passage of time, as the period of Venetian rule wore on, they saw their lives deterioriating (see below). The *parici*, on the other hand, was in an inferior condition to that of the *francomati* because they were absolutely subordinated to the control of the feudal lords without any rights at all. They were regarded as an inseparable part of the fief, and the feudal lords continued to have the right to lease them out, to lend them, to sell them or transfer them, together with their property, like other movable objects and tools (Aristeidou 1990: 91–93; Kyrris 1985: 246).

Available data indicate that the life of the Cypriot population was much worse than it had been in the times of the Lusignans. Venetian rule was much more oppressive than Frankish rule had been, with the farming population living in harsher conditions and the machinery of state riddled with corruption (Aristeidou 1990: 96). The taxation that had been imposed was the heaviest of all the territories ruled by Venice. Characteristic examples were the increase in the days of forced labour from two to three a week, the existence of a separate tax on cereals sold in the Nicosia area or the tax on buying and selling of small quantities of food by private citizens or indeed the imposition of tax even on ownership of domestic pets (Aristeidou 1998: 378). *At the same time the following were* introduced: *obligatory deliveries of wheat,* upgrading in maintenance of municipal records to ascertain the numbers of *parici*, who they were, where they were, *the requirement that the francomati participate in forced labour, and from a certain point onwards* a limitation on freeing of *parici* (Richard 1977: 352).

Many scholars of the subject maintain that this stance of the Venetians reflected a conscious policy aimed at enabling feudal lords to extract as much income as possible so that they would not turn against the Venetian Republic, while at the same time, avoiding the creation of a political alliance between the aristocracy and the dominated classes (Hadjidemetriou 2002: 251). *This is how it was decided that the parici would be retained on a mass scale.* Given this situation, the Venetian government undertook a series of measures. In 1484, a decision was announced that the freeing of a subject belonging to the state-run lands would be possible only by permission of the Council of Ten. Above and beyond that an attempt was made to institute stricter controls to stop *parici* escaping from villages on Crown estates. Systematic population censuses were conducted and it was determined that only *parici* who were small traders or craftsmen could purchase their freedom, whereas stiff penalties were introduced for ship's captains who transported serfs illegally out of Cyprus. Limits were placed on the appointment of *parici* as clerics or village jurymen and there was a weakening of the right of the cathedral of Nicosia to free exposed infants, that is to say the children of serfs, who were left at its entrance. Provisions were introduced for prosecution of those who abandoned their babies at this church in the hope of having them freed. Finally, strict controls were imposed on the resort to monastic life which led to evasion of the duties of serfdom (Arbel 1995: 519; Antonopoulou 2013: 162).

Of course, these policies, which imposed drastic burdens on the life of the Cypriot rural population, were bound to spark revolts and reaction. The Venetian administration therefore endeavoured to introduce a number of measures that might offer some relief from the weight of their remaining obligations. Venice wanted, in other words, to retain the framework of serfdom while lightening the burden for those operating within it. The landowners' jurisdiction over *parici* was thus abolished and the *Regimento* established in Nicosia as court of first instance for all matters involving the serfs. There was a reduction in serf indebtedness; serfs reaching the age of 60 were exempted from all obligations to the fief apart from a symbolic contribution. The widow's tax was abolished on state-owned properties. Inheritance tax was no longer imposed; the marriage tax was not collected on Crown lands and there was recognition of the right of secondary beneficiary *parici* to hereditary entitlement. Together with this economic relief, a range of "social policy" measures were adopted. A doctor was appointed to provide medical care for serfs on Crown estates, with authority to exempt *parici* from duties they were not in a position to perform owing to the state of their health. A special allowance for the appointment of wet-nurses was established for serfs who were mothers and unable to breast-feed and the poorest serfs received cereals for purposes of subsistence. The Republic also built huts for *parici* and distributed money for blankets to newly married *parici* women and to orphans. Finally, in 1561–1562, the Council of Ten decided that feudal lords were not permitted to sell or lend *parici* (Arbel 1995: 514–515; Antonopoulou 2013: 197).

On the other hand, the strategy in question—improvement of the living conditions for the serfs—resulted *inter alia* in a gradual deterioration of living conditions for the *francomati* who, owing to their numerical increase,[3] had evolved into a broad social category, and that entailed a contraction of the elements that distinguished them from the

[3] According to data cited by Kyrris, at the end of the fifteenth century and the beginning of the sixteenth, it was estimated that there were 47,185 *paroikoi* or landless tenants and 77,066 free cultivators. In the decade from 1530 to 1540, there were 70,050 landless tenants and 95,000 free cultivators. Finally, in 1562, the number of landless tenants had risen to 83,653 and the number of free cultivators fallen to 47,053 (Kyrris 1985: 246).

serfs. Specifically, from as early as the beginning of the period of Venetian rule, all *francomati* between the ages of 15 and 60 were obliged to work ten days a year on the fortifications of Famagusta or Kyrenia or else pay five besants, and later this time was reduced to six days or three besants. Moreover, a number of rules were introduced which generated a framework within which it was conspicuously difficult for *francomati* to survive. Like the *parici*, the *francomati* were enroled in the lists of the land register, paid the tithe and the salt tax, surrendered a part of their income to the landowners, were obliged to perform coastguard duties and were conscripted into assisting with public works. They were able to conclude agreements on land usage with the proprietor of the land but this was for a limited time period. In other words, the division of the farming population into two separate social categories seems gradually to have undergone contraction, because through these institutional changes what the Venetians were seeking was the creation of a numerically large social category of subordinate strata with insignificant differences between them. This was a development which on the one hand institutionalized the social downgrading of the *francomati* but on the other contributed to the creation of a broader social layer for whom there were many reasons to be discontented with the existing situation, a reality which essentially could not be changed by the limited improvements accorded to the *parici*.

It is within this context that one may comprehend the various attempts at overthrowing the regime that took place in the final years of Venetian rule, which were qualitatively different from what had been seen before. Up until 1550, all attempts at changing the power structures had involved movements of Cypriot aristocrats urging foreign notables (the Sultan, the Duke of Savoy, the Sultan of Egypt and the German emperor Maximilian) to assist in overthrowing Venetian rule.[4] Henceforth what one had were initiatives by Cypriot villagers (1551[5] and 1565) who wanted the Grand Vizier to have the Ottoman Empire intervene on the island to secure

[4] Also see the relevant data cited by Aristeidou (Aristeidou 2001: 592–594).

[5] In the related documents from 1551 the 47 signatories, Cypriot villagers from 13 settlements, charged that the Venetians exercised unjust and oppressive power on the island, petitioned that the Sultan should free them from this "hostile", as they called it, administration and make them his subjects. They assured the Sultan that he could be indemnified to the sum of 8,000 ducats a year, which was the sum paid annually by the villages (Apostolopoulos 2001: 671).

their liberation.[6] To this, there should be added to popular insurrection of 1562 and 1565. The revolt of 1562, headed by Iakovos Kritikos seems to have been quickly crushed by the Venetians (Aristeidou 1980: 6). But there was also the revolt of 1565 by the people of Nicosia, which was triggered that year by a severe drought. There was hardly any germination of grain and the plan was that the very little production that was concentrated by the authorities in state warehouses should be sold at high prices. Then the insurrectionary crowd blockaded the houses of the administrators, forcing them to open the warehouses and distribute the grain (Aristeidou 2001: 595).

The overall conclusion is that with the strategy they adopted the Venetians underestimated the climate of social discontent that had been generated. Only as the end of their rule approached (1569–1570), seeing the threat that was looming and fearing the possibility of an alliance being concluded between Cypriots and the Ottomans, did the Venetians consent to the authorities liberating the serfs and offering additional freedoms to the *francomati,* cutting back on forced labour. But it was already too late because shortly thereafter the war would start that would end with the occupation of Cyprus by the Ottomans (Arbel 1995: 520).

5 On the Fall of the Venetians

The rise of Ottoman power and the conquest of Constantinople in 1453 sharpened the conflict between Ottomans and Mamelukes. Finally in 1517, the Ottoman Sultan Selim I (1512–1520) occupied Egypt and put an end to the supremacy of the Mamelukes. Given that the Ottomans had in the meantime conquered Syria-Palestine, the result was that Cyprus found itself encircled by regions dominated by the Ottomans. Selim's next move was to send envoys both to Cyprus and Venice to announce that he was the new master of Egypt. The Venetians feared that the Ottomans might occupy the island and accepted the new situation, along with an obligation to pay tribute to the Ottomans, in 1521 signing a relevant treaty with them (Pavlidis 1992: 337–338). This move by the Venetians was regarded as an important diplomatic success considering that in

[6] As Apostolopoulos observes "The Venetians themselves in their memoranda emphasized the danger of the lower strata of the population collaborating with the Ottomans, in a potential clash on the island between Venice and Turkey" (Apostolopoulos 2001: 669–670).

December 1522 the Ottomans also invaded Rhodes, so that the Hospitaller knights were forced to surrender and take refuge in the West. As Hill aptly observes (Hill 1951, Vol III: 834), it is impressive that Cyprus succeeded in remaining in the hands of the Venetians for half a century.

Of course the above outcome is attributable to a number of skilful diplomatic moves by the Venetians. The tribute was paid regularly and they did not hesitate to flatter the Sultan by congratulating him officially for the conquest of Rhodes! Above and beyond that, since the Ottomans had conquered almost all the Eastern Mediterranean apart from Crete, Cyprus was not of any strategic significance for them besides the fact that it would entail involvement in war with the Venetians. Besides that, there were objections within the court of the Sultan, given that Venice's commercial activities were to the advantage of Ottoman possessions. Last but not least, during all this time, the Sultan was conducting military operations in other areas (from Hungary to Libya) and had his attention focussed on them (Pavlidis 1992: 343).

But the big change in the Ottoman mood occurred with the coming to the throne of Selim II (1566–1574), who wished to commence his reign with a conquest, and Cyprus presented him with an easy solution. Apart from that, a role was played by the need for securing Cyprus's ports for the sake of safer pursuit of trade with Syria and Egypt and elimination of the phenomenon of piracy. With Cyprus as their base pirates were attacking ships travelling from Egypt to Constantinople. But the most significant factor was related to the fact that after their expansion over an area extending from Asia Minor to Syria, Palestine and Egypt, the Ottomans could not tolerate the presence of a Christian Cyprus as a shard in the body of the Ottoman Empire. They were anxious that it could become a staging point for European fleets in the Eastern Mediterranean, at a time when Pope Pius V was busy assembling an alliance of all the Christian states (Pavlidis 1992: 364).

Another important factor was the collapse of Venetian commerce in the East, a by-product of geographical discoveries.[7] The decline of trade in the Mediterranean and the opening up of new sea routes in which

[7] As Braudel put it most pertinently: "The time has surely come to turn on its head that hoary and misleading explanation, still sometimes encountered, that it was the Turkish conquest which stimulated the great discoveries, whereas the reverse in fact occurred, for the great discoveries robbed the Levant of much of its appeal, enabling the Turks to extend their influence and settle there without too much difficulty" (Braudel 1996: 667).

other countries became commercially active (Tsiknakis 2001: 85) was to lead to a financial crisis in Venice and would contribute to the military weakening of Cyprus (Zachariadou 1997: 7). There was even further deterioration in the situation when at the end of 1569 the Venetian shipyards were destroyed by fire. The conjuncture now seemed favourable for the Ottomans launching an attack on Cyprus. Military preparations got under way and a little later, in February 1570, the message that Selim was to send to the Venetians was only too clear: "From you we are demanding Cyprus, which either you will give to us of your own accord or we shall take it by force. Do not awaken the anger of our fearsome blade. Otherwise we shall wage the harshest of wars of against you, everywhere. And do not rely on your wealth, for all at once we shall make it flow away from you, as the raging torrent flows. See to it that you do not anger us" (quoted in Pavlidis 1992: 366). The ultimatum, written in threatening language, was rejected by the Venetian Senate by 220 votes to 199 (Aristeidou 1980: 35) revealing how strong was the minority who believed it was not worthwhile staging a confrontation with the Ottomans.

There would be no point to a detailed exposition of the events of the occupation of Cyprus.[8] Nevertheless, it is worth mentioning one point concerning the attitude of Orthodox Cypriots to the invasion. On the basis of what has been asserted before, what emerges is that the accumulated discontent that characterized the behaviour of the Cypriot rural population towards the Venetians induced them not to regard the Ottomans as foreign conquerors. That fact played a part in the way the villagers did not side militantly with the Venetian army. The only people who willy-nilly fought against the Ottomans were the Cypriots of Nicosia and Famagusta, precisely because there was no other option for them.[9] Our view is that the choice of non-involvement was furthered by what happened at Lefkara. There the village surrendered without a fight and its inhabitants were not harmed by the Ottomans, who believed that in this way they would set an example for other towns so that they would not resist. To forestall that eventuality the Venetians attacked at night and massacred the inhabitants of Lefkara. The result was that instead

[8] For a fairly extensive description see the third chapter of the second volume of the *History of Cyprus*, Nicosia: Odysseia, pp. 69–86.

[9] For Nicosia, in particular, there is a reference in a Venetian document cited by Aristeidou: "[...] the inhabitants, 22,000 of whom were combat-worthy, did not want to defend the city [...]" (Aristeidou 1980: 128).

of becoming afraid, the people of Cyprus welcomed the coming of the Ottomans.

With the local population not inclined to fight and the West oriented to its new possessions, the future of Cyprus was pre-ordained. The savage battles which broke out on 13th July 1570 and were to finish on 17th August 1571 would end with the incorporation of Cyprus into the Ottoman Empire.

6 Conclusion

The conquest of Cyprus by the West emerges as a product of the continuing crisis of Byzantium, a crisis which was to culminate in the occupation of Constantinople. The annexation of the island appears at first to have been something fortuitous but it subsequently appears comprehensible as having comprised a strategic point in the process of acquiring control of the Mediterranean, which was not to be relinquished. Frankish rule was to lead to a transition to the feudal mode or production, which was characterized by social stagnation and the attachment of the peasant to the land. With the passage of time, it would become clear that the new system was more authoritarian and more exploitative for the popular strata of Cyprus.

The problems for the Franks were to start from the fact of their fixation on a “traditional” feudal mode of production with an orientation on extra-economic activities. This social system fell into crisis with the strengthening of the positions of two powerful military antagonists: the Egyptian Mamelukes and the Ottomans. The Franks’ obligation to pay a tribute to the Sultan of Egypt ushered in a generalized crisis of the power system, contributing initially to the Venetians’ becoming entrenched in key positions and in a second phase ceding Cyprus to Venice. The fact that it was the Venetians who in these difficult conditions undertook the responsibility of governing should come as no surprise. Engaged for centuries in commercial activities, Venice found it easier to handle a more elevated status in the feudal world, overcoming aspects of the crisis of the feudal system, which was a system based primarily on extra-economic coercion. Of course this strategy too had its limits, which were to surface following the discoveries in the New World and the emergence of the first forms of capitalist organization of trade and production. To put it somewhat differently, the question of the sovereignty of Cyprus exemplifies the difficulty of reproducing the feudal system in different forms, particularly when it comes into conflict with the more centralized—and for that reason more efficient—Asiatic mode of production (adopted by the Ottomans), but also with the emergence of a different social system, the capitalist mode of production. The Westerners are integrated into the dynamic of the capitalist mode of production and in consequence lose a certain amount of territory. But it is the potentialities opened up by incorporation into the new productive system that lead to the Venetians *marginally* not accepting the Ottoman ultimatum for peaceful surrender of Cyprus. Essentially, the Venetians' having adopted a different *overall* strategy the Cyprus question puts them in a difficult position. In that context, their diplomatic virtuosity will not be able to conceal, on the one hand, the fact that in any case the island was in a state of seigniory, initially to the Mamelukes and then to the Ottomans, and on the other, the Ottomans' geopolitical need to liquidate all Christian power in the Eastern Mediterranean. Of course in the long-term historical perspective these territorial losses would be counterbalanced by the effects of the dynamic of capitalism, which would confer a multiplicity of benefits on those social formations that adopted the system. In contrast, persistence in maintaining the Asiatic mode of production would gradually lead to the Ottoman Empire being sidelined and transformed into the "Sick Man of Europe".

In any case, there is one point that should be emphasized vis à vis the internal limits of feudal sovereignty: the organization of social power in Cyprus within a "classical" feudal framework did not permit the forging of social alliances. The "sterilized" vertical social organization did not generate the prereqisites for broader social coalitions. In reality, there were two different social worlds: the feudal lords and the rural population (similarly divided between *parici* and *francomati*). In a first phase, transference of sovereignty to the Venetians lowered the living standards of the farming population. The reason for this was that the Venetians' attempt, beyond a certain point in time, to improve the lives of their subjects, would clash with the policy of lowering the living standards of the *francomati*. This social reality could not generate stable social alliances conducive to reversing the military balance and the growing Ottoman threat. Indicative from this viewpoint is the existence of Cypriot initiatives for the Ottomans to take power in Cyprus. Within that context, there is nothing surprising about the relative ease with which the Ottomans conquered the island.

References

Antonopoulou, M.-E. 2013. *The Social Position of Farmers (Parici and Frangomata) in Venetian-Occupied Cyprus (15th and 16th Centuries)*. Athens: Poreia (in Greek).

Apostolopoulos, C. 2001. An Attempted Approach to the Ottoman Empire by the *parici* of Venetian-Occupied Cyprus (1551). In *Proceedings of the Third Cyprological Congress*, vol. II Medieval Section Nicosia, 669–689 (in Greek).

Arbel, B. 1986. Urban Assemblies and Town Councils in Frankish and Venetian Cyprus. In *Proceedings of the Second International Cypriological Congress*, ed. T. Papadopoulos and V. Egglezakis, vol. II, 203–213. Nicosia: Association of Cypriot Studies.

Arbel, B. 1995. Cyprus Under Venetian Rule. In *History of Cyprus*, ed. T. Papadopoulos, vol. IV, Medieval Kingdom Venetian occupation, Part I, 455–536. Nicosia: Makarios III Institute (in Greek).

Aristeidou, A. 1980. *Unpublished Documents on Cypriot History from the Archives of Ragusa (16th century)*. Nicosia: Cyprus Centre of Scientific Research (in Greek).

Aristeidou, A. 1990. *Unpublished Documents on Cypriot History from the Archives of Venice. Vol. I (1474–1508)*. Nicosia: Centre of Scientific Research (in Greek).

Aristeidou, A. 1998. Rich and Poor in Venetian-Occupied Cyprus. In *Rich and Poor in the Community of the Greco-Latin Orient*, ed. C. Maltezou, 373–385. Venice: Hellenic Institute of Venice (in Greek).

Aristeidou, A. 2001. Unknown Attempts to Organize Revolts or Insurrections During Venetian Rule. In *Proceedings of the Third Cyprological Congress*, vol. II, Medieval Section, 570–598. Nicosia (in Greek).

Braudel, F. 1996. *The Mediterranean and the Mediterranean World in the Age of Philip II*, vol. II. Oakland: University California Press.

Christodoulou, D. 1959. *The Evolution of the Rural Land Use Pattern in Cyprus*. London: A. P. Tayler & Co.

Collenberg de Rudt, W.H. 1982. Le declin de la societe franque de Chypre entre 1350 et 1450. *Kypriakai Spoudai* 46: 71–83.

Collenberg de Rudt, W.H. 1995. Structure and Origin of the Class of the Nobility. In *History of Cyprus*, ed. T. Papadopoulos, vol. IV, Medieval Kingdom Venetian rule, Part I, 785–841. Nicosia: Makarios III Institute (in Greek).

Edbury, P. 1991. *The Kingdom of Cyprus and the Crusades, 1191–1374*. Cambridge: Cambridge University Press.

Gasparis, C. 2001. Race for Predominance: Venice and Genoa in the Medieval Kingdom of Cyprus. In *Cyprus Crossroads of the Mediterranean*, 61–82. Athens: National Research Foundation (in Greek).

Hadjidemetriou, K. 2002. *A History of Cyprus*. Nicosia.

Hill, G. Sir. 1951. *A History of Cyprus, vol. 3, The Frankish Period 1432-1571.* Cambridge: Cambridge University Press.

Kalogirou, A. 1994. The Clash Between the Latin and Orthodox Church in Cyprus. In the collective volume, *Some Crucial Hours in Cypriot History*, 19–61. Nicosia: Municipality of Nicosia (in Greek).

Koureas, N. 2001. Social Aspects of Latin Rule in Cyprus, A Politics of Separation. *Yearbook of Cypriot Society for Historical Studies* V: 254–284 (in Greek).

Kyrris, K. 1985. *History of Cyprus*. Nicosia: Nicocles Publishing House.

Papadopoulos, T. 1995. Structure and Functioning of the Feudal Polity. In *History of Cyprus*, ed. T. Papadopoulos, vol. IV Medieval Kingdom Venetian Rule, Part I, 759–784. Nicosia: Makarios III Institute (in Greek).

Pardos, A. 2001. The Ideological and Cultural Platform of Cypriot Resistance (12th-16th Century). In National Research Institute, *Cyprus Crossroads of the Mediterranean*, 109–152. Athens (in Greek).

Pavlidis, A. 1992. *History of the Island of Cyprus*, third volume: From 1192 to 1571. Nicosia: Filokypros (in Greek).

Richard J. 1977. Une Economie Coloniale? Chypre et ses Ressources agricoles au Moyen-Age. In *Byzantinische Forschungen. Internationale Zeitschrift fur Byzantinistik, herausgegeben*, ed. von Adolf M. Hakkert and Peter Wirth, Band V, 331–352. Amsterdam: Verlag Adolf M. Hakkert.

Richard, J. 1995a. The Political and Social Institutions of the Medieval Kingdom. In *History of Cyprus*, ed. T. Papadopoulos, vol. IV, Mediterranean Kingdom Venetian Rule, Part I, 333–374. Nicosia, Makarios III Institute (in Greek).

Richard, J. 1995b. The Formation and the Foundations of the Medieval Kingdom (1192-1205). In *History of Cyprus*, ed. T. Papadopoulos, vol. IV Mediterranean Kingdom Venetian Rule, Part I, 1–20. Nicosia: Makarios III Institute (in Greek).

Sakellarios, A.A. 1890. *The Cypriot Question, i.e. Geography, History and Language of the Island of Cyprus from Antiquity Until Today*, vol. 1. Athens (in Greek).

Tsiknakis, K. 2001. Cyprus in the Maelstrom of Competition Between the European Powers (15th-16th Century). In *Cyprus Crossroads of the Mediterranean*, 83–108. Athens: National Research Foundation (in Greek).

Zachariadou, E. 1997. *Cyprus in the First Century of Ottoman Occupation (1570-1670).* Nicosia: Leventis Foundation (in Greek).

CHAPTER 3

The Ottoman Period (1571–1878)

1 The Organization of Production in Cyprus and the Economic Condition of the *Rayah*[1]

The period of Ottoman occupation is characterized by the predominance of the Asiatic mode of production, a mode of production quite different from the corresponding feudal mode of production that had enjoyed supremacy during the periods of Venetian and Frankish rule, but consonant with what had been imposed throughout the Ottoman Empire[2] (Map 1).

The basic features of the Asiatic mode of production can be summarized as follows: (a) No private ownership of land (b) the community of peasant farmers is characterized by the existence of powerful binding ties and collective organization of production (c) land belongs to the state and for that reason the greater part of the social surplus product, which takes the form of tribute tax, is directed towards the centre of power (d) peasant farmers possess freehold rights only on the condition

[1] The term *rayah* was employed initially to designate subjects or peasant farmers irrespective of religion. But it gradually came to denote the non-Muslim subjects who paid taxes. It is also used in this sense in Ottoman texts on the subject of Cyprus, and Muslim taxpayers are called *ahali* (Hadjikyriakou 2019: 76).

[2] For the functioning of the Asiatic mode of production in the Ottoman Empire see Islamoglou and Keyder (1977).

S. Sakellaropoulos, *The Evolution of the Political, Social and Economic Life of Cyprus, 1191–1950*, Palgrave Studies in Economic History,
https://doi.org/10.1007/978-3-030-91839-2_3

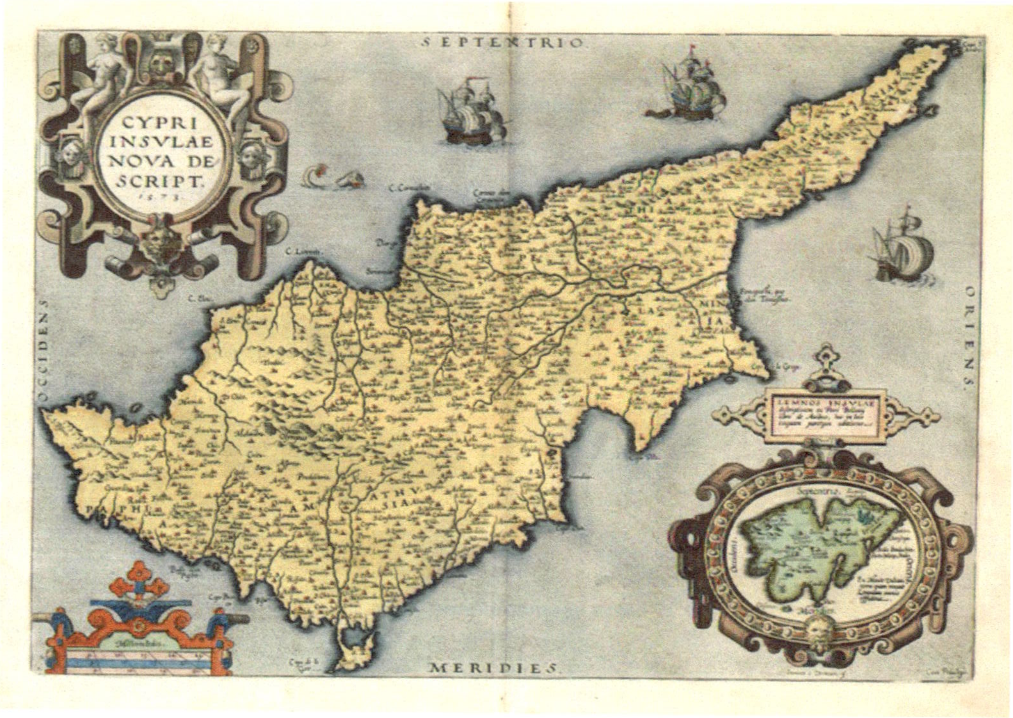

Map 1 Coming from Constantinople, the Ottomans displace the Venetians and occupy Cyprus (1571) (*Source* https://sanderusmaps.com/our-catalogue/antique-maps/mediterranean-sea/old-antique-map-of-cyprus-by-abraham-ortelius-8079)

of belonging to a community (e) management of surplus product brings into existence a ruling class linked to management of state functions and sustained by the surplus product (f) organization of the power centre is consolidated in the form of the despotic state (g) from the moment that they fulfill their financial obligations towards the central authorities, the communities possess a measure of autonomy, administered by a stratum of local leaders and religious officials who collaborate with the regional, and in some cases with the central, authorities (h) the state officials have no hereditary rights over their position but are appointed by the power centre and function as executive instruments for implementing its decisions (i) the economy is not adequately monetarized and commerce exists for satisfaction of the aristocrats and hegemons (Milios 1996; Mandel 1996).

Now more specifically, from the fourteenth century onwards activation of the Asiatic mode of production within the Ottoman community meant acceptance of a regime of state ownership of land,[3] with the sovereign entitlement belonging to the Sultan, who had the right to receive the land rent and the surplus product of the lands under cultivation. At the administrative level the land rent and the surplus product were divided between the military leadership, comprised of timariots—*Sipahis*, and the religious leadership. The timariots—*Sipahis* received the tax revenue and conscripted in the name of the Sultan, and the core of the *timar* was the so-called *kilic* (sword),[4] which was the income that was regarded as sufficient for supporting the timariot-*Sipahi*. These were essentially state officials, recallable by the Sultan, whose activities, i.e. the collection of income from taxation, were regulated by law, while at the same time they were required to keep a military force in a state of combat readiness to serve as reinforcements, if needed, for their province's armed forces (Sarris 1990: 55).

This practice had been introduced precisely so that the state could secure its income. The *Sipahi* had specific powers. He implemented the

[3] As N. Sarris observes, this does not mean that there was no private property anywhere. What was important for the rulers was on the one hand to increase state revenues and on the other to ensure that landowners did not become so powerful as to place in jeopardy the power centre. The regime of land ownership accordingly varied from region to region (depending on the local conditions, the utility of the land and the conditions under which production was conducted). It is therefore more correct to say that private property was limited but not eliminated (Sarris 1990, Vol. 2: 54).

[4] Conquest through the sword.

land laws. He had the right to lease uncultivated expanses on the basis of a contract to interested farmers. The lessor/tenant paid a sum in advance to rent the land and undertook the responsibility of cultivating it uninterruptedly and paying the prescribed taxes without having the right to alter land use.

At the end of the sixteenth century the abovementioned took the form of leasing taxation revenue following an auction (*muzayede*). This was the practice of *mukataa*[5] that is to say cession of *iltizam* (tenure) of state lands (*mukataalu*) whereby the lessor of the taxes paid a sum determined by the central administration and in return had the right to recover the taxation revenue from specific regions or specific economic activities (Cvetkova 1979: 93).

In this way the lessor secured a significant profit because he was given the opportunity to appropriate quite large sums from taxpayers, only a part of which went to the central administration. This was because through such an arrangement the Ottoman state took delivery of the tax revenues sooner and without its own involvement. All the dangers entailed by tax collection were avoided and the amounts delivered were much greater than the state would "normally" have obtained, not only because it itself initiated the collection process but because the sums acquired included all the money that competitors would have given surreptitiously to win preference for their own tenders (Cvetkova 1979: 93).

The lessor had the right to divide the region into smaller segments and sublet it to smaller-scale tenants answerable to him. Initially the lease was for a specific brief period (*tahvil*) of no more than one year to three years, but subsequently a system was instituted of granting lifelong contracts (*malikane*). This happened because practices of super-exploitation of peasant farmers had been noted, with lessors impatient for quick and large profits.

Nevertheless, the result of this development was that the Ottoman state would lose some of its control of Ottoman territory, to the advantage of private interests. The conclusion of contracts of lifelong duration meant

[5] In the Ottoman Empire this characterization was given to taxation units or regions, to sectors of state property, sources of revenue, which the state ceded to private individuals. Usually the *mukataa* involved state taxation, customs offices, salt marshes, harbours, mines, mints, land included among the estates (*haas*) of the Sultan, etc. (Cvetkova 1979: 93).

that lessors could start behaving like governors of the areas they had under their jurisdiction, the more so because the Ottoman state demanded of the administrators and military that they should help the lessors with tax collection. The next stage was the significant accumulation of capital which the tax farmers employed for the expansion of usurious activities. The situation worsened every time that the State, encountering urgent economic difficulties, was forced to accept the demands of the lessors, who many times themselves imposed the terms of the lease contracts.[6] Finally at the end of the eighteenth century the new system brought total debasement to the role of the *Sipahis* who, lacking the capital to tender for a taxation lease, were ultimately marginalized (Michael 2005: 53–54).

In this context the farming population finally saw their position deteriorating since, in their attempt to extract more profits, the lessors increased taxation taking advantage of the fact that they were not accountable to the power centre for the revenue they collected. The upshot was that a new social group called the *Ayan*[7] by the mid-eighteenth century had removed significant regions from the control of the central government, with local regulations overshadowing the official laws and decrees (Michael 2005: 55). According to Cvetkova "The new terms enabled the feudalist military leaders, and particularly the wealthiest of them, who owned numerous manorial estates generating huge incomes and were correspondingly powerful, to aspire [...] to removing these feudal concessions from the control of central government. The political conjuncture of that time offered extensive opportunity for progressive transformation of those dependent temporary fiefs into hereditary property and accordingly the creation of a right to private ownership" (Cvetkova 1979: 102).

But what should be noted is that although the making available of state-owned lands, through enactment of certain political, administrative and economic functions, was the most customary means for securing their emancipation from central government control, it was not the only one. The process was often triggered by the reaction of the peasant cultivators to the abuse by state officials, whereupon the rural population sided with the local notable, whom they saw as their protector.[8] Faced with

[6] For presentation of a series of such cases see (Cvetkova 1979: 93–94).

[7] For the role of the Ayan also see paragraph 13 of the present chapter.

[8] As we shall see subsequently, this became particularly obvious in the case of certain insurrections, in Cyprus also.

the prospect of recession, the timariots additionally took into account the dependence that characterized these villagers' relations with their masters by virtue of the loans which had been extended to them (Sarris 1990: 131).

The most important tax to be collected by a *timar* owner was the tithe, whose basis was all the produce generated by the cultivator. It was always paid in kind, and the amount extracted by the *timariot* varied from one region to another. The second most important tax was in money. Its basis was land rent and was determined in accordance with the area of land. For Christians this type of tax was called *ispendj* and for Muslims *ciftresmi*. Apart from these basic taxes the *timar* owner also collected other taxes associated with product manufacture and with stockbreeding (Michael 2003: 10).

So cultivators of land were not proprietors but occupants. They had been granted the right of inheritance of their plot but they were not able to buy or sell that land. But if they failed to pay their land rent the *timar* owner could withdraw their right to cultivate the land and award it to another community (Gazioglou 1990: 121). They differed in a number of ways from the serfs of the feudal mode of production given that a proportion of their product, which was either entirely free from any association with forced labour or else was associated only to a very limited extent, was surrendered to the State; they were not obliged to hand over anything to *timar* owners and, most importantly, through a series of procedures they were able to secure independence from any requirement imposed by the *timar* (Divtcioglou 1979: 117–119; Asdrahas 2003: 251). The most common tax was the *tithe* which, like poll taxes was imposed only on non-Muslim populations (Milios 2000: 238).

As for the role and the organization of the communities, it should be mentioned that they were structural elements of the Ottoman system both on the economic plane (collective organization of production, disposal of the surplus product remaining for the benefit of the community following deduction of tax) and on the political by virtue of the internal hierarchy created generated out of the existence of the *proestoi* (notables), who had the task of mediation with the *timariot* (Milios 2000: 242).

In the case of Cyprus the cultivators were state-employed peasant farmers, given that the state regulated the legal status and the owners of the land did not have rights over production but simply tax revenue collection rights. All in all, the Orthodox *rayah* was obliged to pay a sum total of taxation that was channelled to four different recipients: to the

State treasury, which was where the poll tax revenue was dispatched (see below); to the *Sipahis,* who received the land tax; to the church hierarchy, who levied various ecclesiastical donations; and to the parish priests, who received an annual contribution from their parishioners (Michael 2005: 143).

One important question that must be answered is whether the lives of Cypriots improved after the Ottoman conquest. The sources indicate that there was certainly a limitation placed on the institution of forced labour. According to a 1572 *ferman* of the Sultan, from at least two days, forced labour was limited to one day, and that was to be either at the State sugar mills or at clearing in the fields and other related work. Inalcik in fact says that there are no testimonies to indicate that even this is true (Inalcik 1973b: 133) and that in any case the volume of forced labour in the sugar mills was reduced significantly from the end of the sixteenth century onwards when the sugar refineries in Cyprus went into a decline and the cultivation of sugar cane was replaced by that of cotton, which was exported to Europe for the textile mills. Aristeidou puts forward a more moderate assessment, arguing that the *rayia* had either to perform forced labour duties on works of public benefit or work two days a week on the estates of the beys and the *Sipahis* (Aristeidou 1980: 41). That said, as far as taxation is concerned, the Ottomans abolished the burdensome tax on salt and taxes on newborn animals. On the other hand they introduced a slight increase in the tax on wine, they imposed the *inspenje* tax to be paid by all Christians, which was set at 30 akchas (aspers) and they maintained at the same levels the tax on sheep, the poll tax, which now took the form of *jizye* and was linked to the exemption of all non-Muslims from military service, and the *tithe,* which fluctuated around the level of 1/5 of production at most (whereas under the Venetians it had been between 1/3 and 1/6 of production) (Inalcik 1973b: 126).

So, it seems that in the first period there was a lightening of the Cypriots' economic obligations. This is also shown by the fact that in the first years of Ottoman administration revenue from the island was just 200,000 ducats (1585) whereas under Venetian rule it reached the sum of 361,000 ducats (Zanettos 1910, Vol. I: 1034). But with the passage of time this was to change, and taxation would increase. Characteristic is the example of the *tithe*, which in the eighteenth century rose to 1/3 of production. To this must be added the proliferation of usury, to which the farming population necessarily resorted so as to be able to pay in cash a whole range of taxes. It should be noted that if the cultivator was not able to pay the amount of tax he was deemed to owe, the tax collector confiscated his plough and his donkey and sold them at a very low price (Karouzis 1977: 32). Above and beyond that, as time passed other taxes were introduced, such as the taxes to pay accommodation and other expenses of the tax collector, the right of *Pasha* (*saillanet*), the Pasha's furnishing, the travelling expenses of the Pasha, the product taxation and in some areas the taxation on water (Ioannou 1996: 25; Grivaud 1983: 179).

To conclude, if we compare all this in the Ottoman period as a whole with what happened in the pre-Ottoman period we see that the differences are not very significant (Kyrris 1985: 253–254) because while there may have been a reduction in forced labour, a considerable number of new taxes were also introduced. In this connection it has been calculated that a skilled Muslim worker needed 22–26 days' wages to pay his annual taxes whereas a Christian needed 33–37. It is important to note that this discrimination did not involve taxes that were related to some kind of return to the taxpayer. They amounted simply to a penalty for being of a different religion (Sarris 1990: 186).

The situation was deteriorating and worsened further when, at the beginning of the eighteenth century, taxation was ceded to the Grand Vizier who, apart from the civilian and military administration, also transferred collection of revenue from Cyprus to the Muhassil (Cypriot governor), for a price (see below). From the moment of his installation in Cyprus the latter's only goal was to extract the greatest possible profit from the "investment" he was making. To quote the words of Lord Sandwich, who visited Cyprus in 1738, the Cypriots "are the poorest and most oppressed of the Sultan's subjects because they are taxed at the whim of the Muhassil who, having purchased his post at great expense, recoups the sum by imposing heavy financial burdens on his unfortunate subjects".[9]

Note that this way of allocating taxation produced a conflict of interests between the Muhassils and the *Sipahis*: the excessively centralized taxation of the markets and payment of taxes in cash reduced the Siphahis' income and left the countryside derelict. The basic difference between the Muhassils and the *Sipahis* was that the former lived on the island for a brief period during which they had to amass very large sums whereas the latter had long-term interests. This contrast was arguably the key factor

[9] Quoted in the *History of Cyprus*, Vol II p. 139.

behind the insurrections that broke out on the island, as will be made evident later in this chapter.

2 Administration

In the Ottoman administrative context Cyprus was to be situated within a broader administrative unit—eyalet or Pashalik (one of the 35 of the Ottoman Empire, specifically the 7th) which included eight military provinces (sanjaks) divided into Kadiluks.[10] The smallest administrative division was the nahiye (Sakellarios 1890: 558). It should be noted that the timariot system applied in the Sanjaks and mostly covered the hinterland. Kyrenia, Paphos and Famagusta were not part of the timariot system. They were integrated into the saliyane system, which was under the direct administration of the *Kapudan Pasha,* Ottoman Admiral of the Fleet, to whom taxation revenues were channelled. We would have to wait until the beginning of the seventeenth century for that to change and for the districts of Paphos, Famagusta and Kyrenia to become Sanjaks (Zachariadou 1997: 15; History of Cyprus 2010 Vol. II: 88).

The governor of Cyprus was the beylerbey,[11] and later (see below) would take the title of muhassil. His headquarters were in Nicosia, which would remain capital of the island. Second in the hierarchy was the chief, or Aga, of the Janissaries (*yeniceriagasi*), who stood in for the governor in the event of his absence. The beylerbey was under the authority of the Grand Vizier, represented the Sultan and had overall administrative, military and taxation responsibility for the island. The head of the *Sipahi*, the *alaybeyi* of Nicosia, also exercised considerable power and his equivalents in Paphos and Famagusta[12] were under his orders. Together with the beylerbey there were four Agas in Nicosia. The first had responsibility

[10] These were administrative districts in which judicial authority was exercised by a Kadi (Michael 2005: 56).

[11] In general terms the title Beylerbey inside the Ottoman Empire symbolized possession of the title of Pasha and membership in the class of Viziers, that is to say military administrators. The Beylerbey was flanked by economic officials, secretaries and personal adjutants, whose task was to appoint and promote the holders of timars, deal with legal cases involving officials, and dispatch tax receipts to the capital (Itzkowitz 2008: 120).

[12] Note that after the abolition of the Pasha's role as administrator of Famagusta, around 1640, and the simultaneous abolition of the position of Pasha of Paphos, the Alay Beyi gained almost complete independence from the central government in Nicosia (Ioannou 1996: 14–15; Hadjikyriakou 2011: 136).

for the Treasury and the other three were in charge of collection and distribution of taxation revenues. The state officials, together with the senior military officers, comprised the divan, a kind of Council of State (Hadjidimetriou 2002: 276). The governors bore the title of Beylerbey until 1670, that is to say during the period when Cyprus remained under the administrative jurisdiction of the Grand Vizier.

From 1670 to 1703 Cyprus was under the authority of the Kapudan Pasha,[13] that is to say the Admiral of the Ottoman Fleet. In the period between 1703 and 1785 Cypus was a *hass*,[14] that is to say a personal *timar* of the Grand Vizier, who appointed the Governor of Cyprus as his representative on the island.[15] The latter bore the title of Muhassil and was responsible for collection of taxes, holding the lease on all the island's revenues following an auction (*mukataa*)[16] and exercising complete administrative and military control over the island (Ioannou 1996: 18).[17]

From 1785 to 1839 authority was passed to the Imperial Divan, with the Kapudan Pasha granted the right to appoint the muhassil on behalf of

[13] According to Hadjianastasis this happened on the one hand because of the problems that had been caused by the power of the governor Ibrahim Pasha, who was recalled and executed, and on the other by the conquest of Herakleion in 1669, leading to a downgrading of Cyprus, something which administratively amounted to transformation of the centre of an eyalet into a province of the Archipelago (Hadjianastasis 2004: 203).

[14] For Hadjikyriakou this starts from 1687 and does not follow a uniform course up to 1785. In 1709 for a brief period it was assigned to second Vizier and it was subsequently transformed into an imperial *hass*, only to revert back to being a *hass* of the Grand Vizier (Hadjikyriakou 2011: 131, 136).

[15] Hadjianastasis maintains that this change was a consequence of the revolt of the Janissaries, who deposed Sultan Mustafa II and installed Ahmed III in his place (Hadjinanastasis 2004: 203).

[16] Essentially it was in this way that the role of the *Sipahis* as leaseholders of land was downgraded. It is explicable on the one hand as a by-product of the increased need of the Ottoman economy for financial liquidity and on the other as a reflection of changes in its military priorities. The emphasis shifted from cavalry units of *sipahis* to the forces of salaried infantry, so that there was no longer any reason for continuation of the privileged position of the *sipahis* (Hadjikyriakou 2011: 133).

[17] According to Hadjikyriakou this was in 1718, when Cyprus ceased to be an eyalet, that is to be governed by an appointed Pasha coming from the military-cum-administrative establishment, and was transformed into a *muhassilik* i.e. administered by a muhassil, a private citizen who had bid in an auction for the right to collect tax revenue (Hadjikyriakou 2011: 131, 136).

the shareholders.[18] The Muhassil acted as representative of the Kapudan Pasha and had limited administrative powers. He could not hire or fire officials; he was known as the Muteselim. The prescribed annual revenues were remitted to the Kapudan Pasha. What money remained after the military and administrative expenses of every province had been met, would go to the empire's central treasury.

From 1839 to 1861 Cyprus—as Sajak—belonged to the eyalet of the islands of the White Sea (Cezair- I Bahr-I Sefideyaleti)[19] with a leaseholder Mutasarrif as administrator. From 1861 to 1868 it was an independent province (mutassariflik) directly subordinated to the Imperial Council and for the two years from 1868 to 1870 it was part of the vilayet of the Dardanelles (Michael 2015a: 114). From 1870 to 1878, due to the activity of Archbishop Sofronios, it was an independent prefecture (mouteriflik) in the orbit of Constantinople (Pavlidis 1993: 9–10; Hidiroglou 1975: 102–103; Michael 2006: 227). For purposes of internal administration, it was divided into six wards (kaza) and six sub-wards (nahiye).[20]

Another important administrative change was upgrading of the function of the Orthodox Church, which found itself again playing a dominant role on the island given that in accordance with a *ferman* published in October 1571 the presence of Latins in Cyprus was banned[21] and

[18] The reasons for all these changes are described in paragraphs 6 and 7. It should be mentioned here, albeit very briefly, that above and beyond its administrative dimension, this specific change had an administrative and tax-related dimension to it. Cyprus, like Smyrna, acquired an *esham* taxation regime. In other words instead of tax collection being assigned for life to one private citizen, it was subdivided into shares with many shareholders (Hadjikyriakou 2011: 135).

[19] This eyalet was comprised of the islands of Rhodes, Cyprus, Chios, Kos, Mytilene, Lemnos, Tenedos, Imvros and Thassos. In one account Samos too was included, despite the fact that from 1832 onwards it enjoyed autonomous status. The reason for the creation of the eyalet including islands separated by a great geographical distance must have to do with the Ottoman power structure's fears of the possibility of new insurrections, after the Greek Revolution of 1821, by the Greek-speaking populations there (Aymes 2004).

[20] The exact arrangement was the kaza of Paphos with nahiyes Paphos, Chrysochous, Kouklion, the kaza of Limassol with nahites Limassol, Koilani, Avdimou, Episkopi, the kaza of Famagusta with nahiyes Famagusta, Mesaria, Karpasia, the kaza of Kyrenia, with nahiye Kyrenia, the kaza of Larnaca with nahiye Larnaca and the kaza of Değirmenlik (Milos) with nahiye Değirmenlik, Dag, Oreini, Morphou and Lefkas (Zannetos 1911: 50).

[21] This happened for purely geopolitical reasons of confrontation with Catholic Europe and in contradiction to the Koran, which teaches protection of the people of the Book

the only religions that were permitted were the Orthodox Christian and the Muslim (Kyrris 1984: 67). The institution of the Archbishopric was thus restored and the functioning of the four Metropolitans returned. A basic role in these developments was played by the existence of the system of the *millet* within the Ottoman Empire,[22] upon which Ottoman rule in Cyprus was to a significant extent supported, both at the administrative level and at that of collecting taxes. It was in this context that in 1572 the Kykkos monk Timotheos mounted the archiepiscopal throne, which had been vacant since the Frankish decree of 1260. Christians were accorded the right to resort to the ecclesiastical courts to resolve their differences. The Church also reacquired a great part of the property that had been taken away from it. This development was due to the fact that the Ottomans thought that a powerful Orthodox Church would not only serve as a counterbalance to the influence of the Latin church, but would also operate as a mechanism for integrating the Orthodox majority into the Ottoman administration. Note, of course, that these political concessions proceeded in parallel with the Orthodox hierarchy's depositing a significant sum in the state treasury. With the passage of time this one-off obligation assumed the form of an annual contribution (Michael 2003: 6–7).

From the seventeenth century onwards Cyprus was divided between three dioceses (Kyrenia, Kition and Paphos) and the archiepiscopate with its seat in Nicosia. This arrangement was chosen by the Church to correspond with the administrative structure, given that—as indicated—from the beginning of the same century the island was similarly divided

(on the condition that they observe their obligations to the Muslim authorities) i.e. Jews and Christians of every doctrine. Finally, after a number of attempts by the Catholics, the Roman Catholic Bishopric in Paphos was re-established in 1629 (Coureas 2009: 96). What is interesting is that, according to sources, the Catholic bishop Vespa was given such a warm reception by the Orthodox Archbishop Christodoulos, with the result that Christodoulos saw the Pope as the primary spiritual leader of the Christians (Hadjianastasis 2015: 155–156). This stance on the part of Christodoulos must be explicable as reflecting the tendency at that time for the Orthodox hierarchy to seek alliance with the Catholic world with a view to overturning Ottoman rule.

[22] This was a system for institutional separation between the religious communities, and not the nationalities, within the Ottoman Empire, so that finally it was religion that determined nationality and not the opposite. The system of *millet* made it possible within the communities for there to be self-management of their educational, cultural, and religious questions.

between three Sanjaks (Kyrenia, Famagusta, Paphos) with the administrative centre in Nicosia, which in turn possessed its own periphery. The Church was enabled in this way to meet whatever administrative needs it was presented with by the Ottoman rule.

Finally, it should not be overlooked how important for the system of administration was the institution of the Dragoman, which was introduced from the first years of the Ottoman occupation. The Dragoman was of the Orthodox faith and generally belonged to the class of political notables comprising the link between the Archiepiscopate and the island's Administrator. His salary was paid by the Ottoman state. Until the mid-eighteenth century he was chosen by the Porte, following a relevant report by the Church, which most times was accepted (Kyrris 1973: 176). Initially his duties did not extend beyond the role of interpreting between the Greek population and the Ottoman administration. But with the passage of time his responsibilities expanded, and he was gradually transformed into a politician (he was assigned diplomatic tasks) and finally into a governmental dignitary with extensive budgetary responsibilities (Michael 2006: 218). In that connection he was put in charge of the population census, the inventory of residents' property,[23] allocation of responsibilities for remission of tax, preparation of the payment of the Janissaries (Kyrris 1973: 177). On the subject of the budget, in the event of disagreement with the Turkish administration, given that he functioned as an intermediary between the Governor and the ecclesiastical hierarchy (Indianos 1938: 16), he had the right to impose a veto and appeal directly to the Sultan. There were cases when the conflict with the pashas led to the latter denouncing the specific Dragouman to the Porte, with the result of his being cashiered at the instigation of the Governor and with the acquiescence of the Porte.[24] But there were also cases, such as that of Markoulis in the seventeenth century, who encountered resistance from the Christians because of the harshness with which he performed his duties (Hadjidemetriou 2002: 278; Hadjinastasis 2011: 164; Kyrris 1964: 10–11).

Essentially the Dragoman operated as yet another agency of power apart from the Administrator and the Hierarchy of the Orthodox clergy.

[23] According to Theocharidis the taxation jurisdictions of the Dragomans had to be linked to adoption of the practice of *mukataa* (Theocharidis 1987: 70).

[24] Hadjibakis' successful expulsion of the Dragoman Chadzijosif, during the 1770's, is a typical case (Indianos 1938: 146).

The more his powers increased the more the role of the Administrator diminished in questions of responsibility for security and supervision of the island, the more so because he was the only non-clerical Orthodox official not implicated through duties of imperial administration in allocation of tax obligations and collection of taxes (Michael 2006: 219). The Dragoman was therefore an organic element in the power system, not only because he exercised a clearly political function but because most times in order to reach this position one had to pay significant sums, which one then had to recoup through taxation (Konstantinidis 1995: 25).

3 Population Movement

Immediately after the conquest of Cyprus, to consolidate the Ottoman presence on the island, the Sultan decided to proceed with implementation of mandatory movement of populations from Asia Minor, while at the same time transferring young women for marriage with the Ottoman soldiers stationed there. In the relevant ferman issued on 21st September 1572 it reads: "Because according to the report of the Turkish governor of Cyprus much fertile land remained fallow in the course of the campaign (we note characteristically that during the invasion around 50 to 60 thousand Cypriots were killed and 10–20 thousand taken prisoner and dispatched abroad—S.S.) it appeared necessary also to colonize the cities to restore the island's previous prosperity". The ferman dealt with mandatory migration of people who lived in Asia Minor[25] on barren, rocky and steeply sloping ground and/or possessed just a small area of land under cultivation. The ferman also stated that the people transferred should be the ones who were notorious for their bad character and their involvement in illegal activities, the unemployed, peasant cultivators who had abandoned farming and moved to the cities, artisans, and individuals who had lodged claims for agricultural property and whose claims applications were still pending. Tax exemption for two years was instituted as an incentive for those who migrated (Hadjidemetriou 2002: 270; Pavlidis 1993: 25–26; Hadjioannoun 1976: 10). The ratio of migrants to the population as a whole in the specific areas concerned must have been one to ten. If

[25] To be precise, the firman was sent to the Kadis of the districts of Alaiye, Manavgat, Karaman, Icel, Bozok and Teke (Pampalos and Theoharidis 2008: 151).

someone tried to escape to a foreign country he had to be arrested and executed (Pampalos and Theocharidis 2008: 153).

The Muslim presence on Cyprus was initiated by the approximately 3,800 soldiers living on the island (Orhonlu 1973: 258) mostly not as a garrison but as settlers, by certain Greeks and Franks who had converted to Islam and by around 3,000–4,000[26] Ottoman subjects who came from Asia Minor. It is worth noting that among the families who finally went to the island, seventy families engaged in a variety of different occupations (carders, blacksmiths, tanners, tailors, shoemakers, etc.) and the overwhelming majority were peasant farmers. In 1581 another 8,000 families arrived in Cyprus (Orhonlu 1973: 260). The population transfer continued in the seventeenth and eighteenth centuries. In these two centuries chiefly criminal elements were introduced, whose presence on the island provoked numerous reactions from existing residents (Kizilyerek 2009: 19–20).

4 The First Insurrections (1578–1668)

During the period of Ottoman occupation numerous insurrections were staged against the regime. In the first years they had more the character of return to Western domination, and accordingly an important role was played by former nobility who were attempting to secure the assistance of the European states.

It is characteristic that just seven years after the advent of the Ottomans on the island there is a report of a joint insurrection of Christians and Muslims, or to be precise Cypriots, Janissaries and Muslim slaves. The revolt resulted in the death of the Beylerbey and of his replacement. The rebels raised the flags of Vienna, Spain and the Pope, in other words the key enemies of the Sultan. At first the revolution was crowned with success and all resistance to it on the island was crushed. The Ottoman Empire was forced to send Kapudan Pasha Uluz Ali at the head of a fleet of 50 ships with Famagusta as their destination. But this move was also thwarted by the rebels (*Historical Encyclopedia of Cyprus* 1979–1980, Vol. 1: 93). After this the insurgents sought allies abroad. But neither

[26] This figure derives from the fact that according to the archives of the Grand Vizier 1,689 families had been chosen (Pavlidis 1993: 27) to migrate to Cyprus. Given that it is not certain that all in fact migrated, it seems that in certain cases people were replaced by substitutes (Orhonlu 1973: 260); what emerges is this conservative calculation.

Spain, which saw a military intervention as being extremely risky in an island very far away from itself and very close to Asia Minor, nor Venice which was pursuing a policy of appeasing the Sultan, nor the Pope, who had no military power, were able to act alone. The only solution could be collaboration between these three forces, as proposed by the Spanish ambassador to Rome, Don Juan de Zuniga. Finally the King of Spain Philip II decided not to intervene, fearing that confronting the Ottoman fleet would necessitate sending very large forces and running a great risk (*Historical Encyclopedia of Cyprus* 1979–1980, Vol. I: 94).

There are also references to another two uprisings before the end of the sixteenth century, in 1587[27] and 1589, but no detailed accounts of them.

In 1606 a particularly important uprising took place led by Petros Aventanios against the Ottomans' attempt to institute abduction of children. In the first phase, despite being inadequately armed, the approximately 12,000 insurgents scored some successes, killing around 3,500 Ottomans, but they were subsequently defeated, with the result that around four thousand Cypriot revolutionaries took refuge in the mountains. That was then the decision taken to send Petros Aventanios to Spain to ask help from King Philip III. What is interesting is that Aventanios placed Spanish conquest of the island in a more strategic context. He thought that such a development would contribute not only to liberation of the Holy Sepulchure but also to the reacquisition of Constantinople and Egypt given the exhaustion of the Porte on account of the war with the Persians (Stylianou 1976: 11). But the Spanish side was not to be tempted by Aventanios' proposals, both because the Ottoman Empire was still flourishing and because the problems that Spain was encountering in the region of Flanders were regarded as much more significant than the question of Cyprus (Stylianou 1975: 337–338).[28] There would

[27] How anomalous the situation was in 1587 is evident from the related message sent on 24th October 1587 by Archbishop Timotheos to the King of Spain Philip II (Papageorgiou 1990: 40–43). Finally the Spanish Council of State convened in May 1588 to deliberate the issue and concluded that for the moment such a mission would be unfeasible but it could probably be conducted at some point in the future (Hadjianastasis 2015: 149).

[28] Above and beyond the mooted involvement of Spain it should be noted that Tuscany at that time indicated interest in Cyprus and accordingly dispatched troops at different points in time. There were even certain military incidents, without this developing into

be renewed overtures in 1611 and 1613, but without meeting with acceptance from the Spanish. The Duke of Savoy[29] was also turned to in parallel but without any result (Hadjianastasis 2015: 152).

It has been calculated that in all 28[30] uprisings took place in Cyprus between 1572 and 1668[31] and all ended badly (Sakellarios 1890: 567–569). Their basic weakness was that they were framed in a context of *potential* broader planning of the West. It was not made clear that Western plans for occupation of the East had gradually receded given the strength of the Ottomans in the South-Eastern Mediterranean—particularly after the occupation of all of Crete in 1669, the importance that the colonies in the New World had for the West, but also the gradual emergence of the capitalist mode of production, which induced Westerners to focus more than in the past on economic activities.

5 The Crisis of the Asiatic Mode of Production in the Ottoman Empire

From a certain point onwards, in both in its general (in the Ottoman Empire) and in its particular (in Cyprus) form, the Asiatic mode of production would begin to show signs of decline which over time would lead to its effacement with corresponding emergence, and subsequent ascendancy, of the capitalist mode of production.

a full-scale siege of Cyprus. The Ottomans' sturdy shielding of Cyprus, together with Tuscany's loss of allies, put an end to these aspirations (Jennings 1993: 364–366).

[29] The House of Savoy considered that because Queen Charlotte of Cyprus (1448–1464) was from this family, the Savoys continued to have rights to the throne even more than a century later. This was the reason for the commencement of relevant discussions with the Cypriot Orthodox hierarchy, without them leading anywhere (Jennings 1993: 361–362).

[30] Particularly after the first fifty years of Ottoman rule there was an observable increase in the disaffection of the local population. The reasons for it are not unrelated to the higher taxation which, as already indicated, the Ottoman power structures begun to impose, one element in wider economic discontent triggered by drought and attacks by locusts (Aristeidou 1980: 45).

[31] 1668 is considered the last time the Cypriot clergy made representations to the Catholic powers—in which above and beyond the offer for them to take possession of Cyprus there was recognition of the primacy of the Pope (Michael 2010: 153–154). The later absence of such practices must be linked to upgrading of the Orthodox hierarchy within the Ottoman administration (see below) (Hajianastasis 2015: 152).

The slowing of the Ottomans expansive capacity that became visible from the end of the sixteenth century, in conjunction with the loss of territory and granting of autonomy status to certain areas, together meant diminution of state revenues and consequent limits to the dominance of the Sultan and contraction in the reach of state power. A significant role in the general crisis was played by the Empire's wars against Persia (1624–1639) and Venice (1645–1669). Establishment of the sea route to the Indies by way of Southern Africa had serious parallel consequences, sidelining as it did the Ottoman ports of the East. There were other external factors such as epidemics, bad harvests, climate change, earthquakes. Moreover the Ottoman currency, the akce, began to undergo frequent devaluations.[32] The cause is to be sought in the influx of gold and silver from America, the impossibility of building trade and the money economy, the growing use of the Spanish "real" in consequence of the expansion of commerce through smuggling[33] but also the huge state expenditures that characterized the period in question (military expenses for unprofitable wars of conquest but also for corresponding defensive wars, the extravagant lifestyle of office holders). The result was that the 1564 budget deficit of 6.6 million akces in 1564 had skyrocketed to 154.3 million by 1650.

The devaluation of the akce and subsequent influx of cheap silver from Europe had further consequences also: from the moment that there could be no increase in the taxes the *Sipahis* could officially impose on their timars, although the face value of the latter remained the same, their real value rapidly plummeted, given that most taxes were paid in cash. The *Sipahis* and the other timariots therefore tried to recoup their income losses by introducing new taxes or arbitrarily increasing the existing ones. The revolts of the Janissaries of that time were similarly motivated by

[32] According to figures cited by Barkann there was a great increase in inflation in 1605/6 when compared to 1489/90 prices in akces increased by 530.66%. Although there was a subsequent fall in inflationary tendencies, prices in 1655/6 were 361.86% higher than the corresponding prices in 1489/90 (Barkan 1975: 11). The situation deteriorated even further at the end of the seventeenth century given the effects of repeated military defeats (see below). Thus, although in 1475 a ducat had been equivalent to 44 akces, in 1680 it was exchanged for 300 akces.

[33] The growth of smuggling is attributable to population increase in the Ottoman Empire obliging the state to proceed to mandatory suspension of exports, with the result that the burgeoning demand for agricultural products in Western countries was covered by smuggling (Islamoglou and Keyder 1977: 49).

reduction in their real income (Inalcik 1997: 25), as was the participation of timariots in rural insurrections (Cvetkova 1978: 83).

To deal with all these economic problems, given the inability for policies to be programmed that might lead to economically productive growth, the Ottoman state was induced to adopt a number of specific options:

a. a tax hike whereby special taxes took the form of regular annual tax payments and increased from 40 akces per taxpayer in 1582 to 535 in 1681, with the poll tax soaring from 40 akces in 1574 to 280 in 1691. This was a transparent move by the central state to unload its losses onto the rayah while simultaneously increasing pressures on the centrifugal tendencies of the timariots.
b. acceptance of lifelong surrender of revenues to officials.
c. adoption of implementation of the *Capitulations* system, that is to say concession of trade privileges to citizens of foreign states (tariff reduction, citizen tax exemption) (Giannopoulos 1975: 99–101). The latter in particular was to make a decisive contribution to the penetration of incipient mechanisms of capitalist intervention into the Ottoman Empire, particularly from the moment that the three Anatolian companies (French, English and Dutch) were becoming active on Ottoman territory (seventeenth century) with the Austrian Anatolian company following in the eighteenth century (Vergopoulos 1975: 71).

From an overall perspective the Ottoman power system existing up until that time was visibly and irreversibly faltering. The conditions that had created it were in the process of disappearing. The *Sipahi* timariots who comprised the backbone of the economy were being displaced, as already mentioned, by an army of mercenary footsoldiers with firearms[34]

[34] As Inalcik testifies: "During the wars against Austria from 1593 to 1606, the need to send into battle infantry troops equipped with firearms resulted in a significant increase in the number of Janissaries (7,886 in 1527 and 37,627 in 1610) [...] During interludes of peace when their services were not required, these mercenaries, lacking salaries and employment, roamed the countryside exacting tribute from the Anatolian population" (Inalcik 1997: 24). To avoid such complications it was necessary for the salary of the Janissaries to be paid immediately along with a number of special gifts they had become accustomed to receiving (Islamoglou and Keyder 1977: 50). When this didn't happen they either took to looting or began to revolt, even against the Sultan.

and an economy that accorded pride of place to monetized economic relations.

As regards Cyprus in particular, the economic crisis had greatly intensified from as early as 1621. As characteristically mentioned that year by the traveller Deshayes de Courmesnin: "There isn't even one Christian resident who has the means to eat bread all year round. Almost everyone survives by eating carob, which the island produces in large quantities. There is no other part of the Ottoman Empire where the inhabitants are so heavily burdened by taxes and so tyrannized. Because apart from the haradji (poll tax) they pay to the Sultan [...] they give to the Beylerbey and the *Sipahi* one fifth of their production. And if after all this taxation they still have something left, it is taken from them by force".[35] A reinforcement role in deepening the crisis was also played by factors such as drought and plagues of locusts, whose effect was to reduce harvests and bring famine. Most peasant cultivators were no longer able to satisfy the Ottoman state's taxation demands and some were forced to leave the island while others embraced Islam to avoid the poll tax.

All the above led to a crisis in the Asiatic mode of production, with the consequence of the Church emerging as the administrative centre of Ottoman power in Cyprus, and the occurrence of a series of uprisings linked to the consequences of this crisis, namely the increase in taxation by virtue of its assignment by the *Sipahis* to "professional" tax farmers and the gradual emergence of early forms of capitalist commerce.

6 The Role of the Church from the Mid-Seventeenth Century Onwards

Essentially from the middle of the seventeenth century and subsequently it has been a "nationalization" of the Church, which emerges as an intrinsic element of the Ottoman power coalition. This means that on the one hand the senior Orthodox clergy are regarded as officials of the Sultan, so that *Berats* are issued for them also[36] corresponding with those issued for other Ottoman officials and on the other that Orthodox religious law is transformed into state law. Christians, in other

[35] Cited in the *History of Cyprus* Vol. II: 116.

[36] It should be clarified that these concessions on each occasion were made to prelates as physical persons and not to the Church as a legal entity.

words are obliged to obey it because it is the law of the State. In the context of dismantlement of its strength, accelerating economic crisis and phenomena of autonomization of timariots in various provinces, the central government needs to acquire an ally to function as its de facto representative in Cyprus. From that viewpoint it is characteristic that in 1660 the Porte withdrew powers of distribution and collection of tax from Ottoman officials in Cyprus and gave them to Orthodox head priests. Above and beyond the political significance of this development, it also had a "technical" dimension to it: the centralized mechanism of the Orthodox Church with the human resources it had at its command enabled it to record the demographic movements within the Orthodox community. The Church's tax collecting structures were in the form of a pyramid starting from the rank and file and ending with the Archiepiscopate. This is something which the administrative functioning of the Ottoman state, in which the first signs of decline were becoming evident, was apparently unable to secure (Michael 2003: 10–11).

The above move was supplemented by abolition of the positions of two provincial pashas (of Famagusta and of Paphos) and the retention only of the Pasha of Nicosia, but with reduced powers. The senior clergy acquired the right to have direct access to the Sublime Porte and to submit reports on public finance. What is interesting is not only that in this way the ecclesiastical hierarchy of Cyprus bypassed the island's Ottoman officials but also that in their visits to Constantinople they were not obliged to notify the Synod of the Great Church, or even the Patriarch himself. This fact signified not only essential recognition of the self-governing character of the Cypriot church but also recognition of its purely political-administrative function. In parallel, as regards the relationship between the church hierarchy and the local Ottoman officials, this was reframed. The Ottoman administrator was obliged to consult the Archbishop in determining the total amount of tax and at the same time seek the strengthening of the ecclesiastical mechanisms for the collection of tax revenue.

7 The Boyacioglou Insurrection and the Administrative Reforms Resulting from it

Towards the end of the eighteenth century what prevailed in Cyprus was a peculiar dual power situation whereby on the one hand there was a legally appointed Ottoman administration and on the other the power of the leader of the Janissaries Boyacioglou. This paradoxical reality has to do with more general developments in the Ottoman Empire but also with the more specific conditions that prevailed at that time in Cyprus.

Specifically, in 1683 the Ottoman Empire failed for a second time to occupy Vienna, and this failure was followed by failed wars against the alliance of Venice, Austria, Poland and Russia, with resultant contraction in Ottoman territories. And this in turn meant a fall in agricultural production because of the needs of military recruitment, devaluation of the currency through an increase in the proportion of copper in its composition, together with higher taxation in the provinces (Mantran 1989: 247–248). The bad situation was made worse by the drought and famine of 1687. It was in the midst of all this that the revolt of the Janissaries broke out in 1687. The Sultan Mehmed IV was deposed and replaced by his brother Suleiman II (Stavridis 2003: 138).[37]

For Cyprus in particular, despite the pertinent content of the important aforementioned administrative changes, they were somewhat timid given the enormity of the problems facing Ottoman rule on the island and in the final analysis they led to a contradictory outcome. This was because the assignment of tax collection to local proxies, compounded by administrative subordination to the Kapudan Pasha, signified a weakening of the Ottoman presence there.

A conjunction of developments in the centre and at the local level may be considered the generative factor behind the revolt of Boyacioglou at the end of the seventeenth century. More specifically, Boyacioglou's movement was launched about 1683 and wound up in 1690 (Sakellarios 1890: 569–570). 1680 and thereabouts was a time of very great poverty, with the result that extensive taxation of cultivators was not feasible. To take out a taxation lease had become an unprofitable prospect and no interested parties turned up at the relevant auctions. In this climate of paralysis, Mehmed Boyacioglou, the head of the janissaries, succeeded in imposing his presence after years of struggling with the Agas. He proceeded to declare himself leader of Cyprus, breaking off relations with the Sublime Porte. Nevertheless, to avert a dispatch of troops by the Sultan, he continued every year to pay the required *jizue* to the tax collectors and until 1686 kept the Muhassil in his position, as indeed he did other Ottoman officials who had been appointed by the Sublime

[37] A revolt of Janissaries also took place in Crete during the same period (Hadjianastasis 2011: 173).

Porte, but real power was in the hands of Boyacioglou (Stavridis 2003: 122–123). In any case for a time the Porte maintained a stance of toleration with him, which however changed when it become known that Boyacioglou was trying to become independent and there were vehement protests from the French community in Larnaca about the debts of Boyacioglou and his followers which were never paid. The upshot of the last-mentioned was a string of complaints by the French ambassador to the Sublime Porte and the issuance of a ferman by the Sultan in 1688 (Stavridis 2003: 127–130). Finally, when Boyacioglou refused to comply a military force was dispatched in 1690, initially headed by Colak Mehmed Pasha and when he was defeated by Boyacioglou the Porte was then obliged to send other troops led by Cifutoglou Ahmed Pasha. Cifutoglou besieged Nicosia, Boyacioglou was forced to withdraw and was finally arrested and executed, along with many of his followers (Pavlidis 1993: 95–97; Hadjianastasis 2011: 167).

At the governmental level the Boyacioglou revolt forced the Porte to proceed with new changes. Sultan Ahmed III, who in 1703 mounted the throne to succeed his deposed brother Mustapha II, took the following decisions whose trend was towards greater centralization of power: Cyprus was withdrawn from the administrative jurisdiction of the Kapudan Pasha and placed under the authority of the Grand Vizier. Beyond that all political and military power was concentrated in the hands of the Muhassil: there ceased to be a special official (the haradji—collector of the haracci) collecting the poll tax because this responsibility too was assigned to the Muhassil, while the four Agas who until recently had been directly appointed by Constantinople were henceforth appointed by the Muhassil, who was head of the armed forces (Zanettos 1910: 1102–1103).

8 The Reforms of 1754

There were no important changes in the first half of the eighteenth century but the intense pressures the Ottoman Empire continued to be exposed to from a number of directions would lead the Sultan to increase even further the power of the Orthodox Church. Thus in 1754 at the request of the Church hierarchy the Palace agreed to reduction and stabilization of the amount of tax paid by Cyprus, irrespective of the total population size. What happened specifically was the various categories of tax were integrated in a sum, 216,419 kurus,[38] for the island as a whole. The hierarchy's achievement was that any subsequent alteration to that sum would have to be split between Orthodox and Muslim.

At the same time in a separate ferman the Cypriot senior clergy were recognized as *Kocabasi* of the island with the responsibility for preparing reports to the Sublime Porte and enjoying immediate access to the Palace so as be able "immediately to present [...] the issues and the proposals of the *rayah* at any time fearlessly" (Archimandrite Kyprianos, Chronological History of the island of Cyprus, pp. 315–316, quoted in Hadjikyriakou 2019: 82). One consequence of the promotion of Church hierarchs to the position of *Kocabasi* was the sidelining of a number of secular personages who aspired to the acquisition of political influence.

This is something rather different from what one saw in other places in the Ottoman Empire where Orthodox people lived. There significant social changes were taking place and the economic development that had already occurred enabled secular figures to seek political office. On the contrary in Cyprus the Church hierarchy was a well entrenched presence in such posts (Michael 2005: 83). The title *kocabasi* was applied to the notables in a society, who were elected and represented it in its dealings with the State authorities. Their duties included distribution of tax revenues, tax collection, the functioning of schools, the administration of justice in agronomic questions (Michael 2005: 85). In this way Church hierarchs emerged as ex officio political representatives of the Cypriots. This peculiarity must be attributable to the developed economic functions exercised by the Cypriot Church,[39] for the pursuit of which a significant role was played by the maintenance of demographic records (births, marriages, deaths) but also to the status of respect accorded to the Church by the faithful (Katsouridis 2009: 128) such that it was impossible during this specific phase for the rising bourgeois strata to be able to compete with it, even at the level of politics.

To all this must be added the fact that the legitimation of the religious hierarchy vis à vis the Ottoman administrator was reinforced in particular

[38] One kuru was the equivalent of 120 akces.

[39] As already mentioned, the conquest of Cyprus by the Ottomans led to a ban on the doctrine of the Latin Church. One of the results of this was that the reconstituted Cypriot Church would take over the property of the Latin monasteries that were eliminated, while gradually succeeding in buying out a number of monasteries that had been occupied by the Ottomans (Katsouridis 2009: 129).

by the differing conditions under which they acted out their roles. The religious hierarchy was elected and so enjoyed popular legitimacy, while the administrator, being appointed, did not. The religious leaders had a lifelong term of office whereas there was a perpetual turnover of administrators, reflecting the changing power balances within the Sublime Porte. It is indicative that in the period from 1754 to 1878 103 Ottoman administrators of Cyprus are recorded, meaning that their average term of office was no more than 1.2 years! By contrast in the same period of time there were only 11 archbishops, with an average term of office of 11.2 years (Michael 2005: 212).

Purely on the plane of economics these changes amount virtually to leasing to the machinery of the Church the revenue that the Ottoman state was able to collect from taxation. The ecclesiastical hierarchy undertook the obligation to guarantee this sum to the Ottoman administration, which it would secure through taxation, with the Church itself exempted from paying tax. The basic tax to be assigned and collected was the *haradji* (Michael 2005: 96) but also the *miri*,[40] the tax covering payment of the salaries of administrative officials, taxes on animals, vineyards and other products. Various types of taxation could also be subleased to third parties (Michael and Kokkinoftas, n.d: 662). This situation was peculiar to Cyprus because in the other regions of the Ottoman Empire the Church collected only the ecclesiastical taxes sanctioned by the state. It did not get involved in collecting state taxes. The extent of political power of the Cypriot Church is also evident, beyond the fact that it was responsible for the education of the Orthodox and was empowered to issue judgements in matters involving the Christian residents of the island, in the way the clerical leadership as authorized agents of the power to tax were able to influence selection of the person to be appointed Ottoman administrator, given that although the consent of the Archbishop was not required in deciding this appointment, it was necessary for the person appointed to preserve harmonious relations with the Orthodox Church, given that the collection of taxes and their surrender to the public treasury by the prescribed time was the responsibility of the Hierarchy (Michael 2005: 97).

So, there are two very important specificities of the Cypriot Church which would set the seal on further developments within the Cypriot

[40] A tax paid by people cultivating *miri* lands, that is to say expanses of state property whose utilization had been ceded for a specific period of time to a timariot.

social formation. One has to do with the political role of the representative of the Orthodox, to the disadvantage of the notables and with the additional right of immediate access to the Porte without the obligatory mediation of the Ecumenical Patriarch. The second pertained to the collection of taxes, a practice which did not recede with the passage of time, but on the contrary was intensified (Dionysiou 1988: 135).

9 The Role of the Church as Landowner and Economic Agent

The special position of the Cypriot Church as a political and administrative institution contributed to its transformation into one of the most important economic factors in Cyprus, with the amount of property in its possession growing uninterruptedly throughout the duration of Ottoman rule.

One important factor in that increase was the market in the right to cultivation of farming land, the *tasarruf*. It was through this that monasteries succeeded in generating very large quantities of agricultural products, creating the necessary capital for expansion of their economic activities. They had already achieved self-sufficiency in most types of food consumed by the brotherhoods and their visitors (Michael 2003: 36–37).

Another mode of wealth generation and acquisition of land was the protection method. In this case the owner donated his property to a monastery which undertook the provisioning, maintenance, payment of taxes and protection for the person in question for the entirety of his life. The people concerned were either cultivators who sought in this way to avoid taxation and usurers, continuing however to cultivate their land and provide to the Church certain forms of payment (Katsouridis 2009: 128) or cases of elderly people without offspring who resorted to the monasteries when they were no longer in a position to provide for themselves.

Finally, there were also the instances where the faithful donated its landed property to monasteries (Michael 2003: 38).

Apart from this there was other ecclesiastical income which further strengthened the economic position of the Church. It included the so-called "dosimata" or contributions from the congregation, above and beyond those that were voluntary. They were mandatory in character precisely because the Church had become an institution of State which, as mentioned, had previously transformed the obligations of the faithful towards the Church into obligations of the faithful towards Ottoman State power.

The outcome of all the above was that an exceptionally well-developed economic activity was developed by the Church which secured its great benefits. Specifically, by the nineteenth century the Orthodox monasteries had emerged as a very important producer of farming and stockbreeding products, with its surpluses being marketed both domestically and abroad. The manufacture of such large quantities of products presupposed the existence of considerable capital, on the basis of which the infrastructures for the crops were generated, the cultivators and the rest of the workforce were paid, and installations were purchased and brought into operation which helped foster the overall economic activity, such as windmills, water mills and olive presses (Michael 2005: 202).

An additional parameter for financial enrichment of the Church was created by the absence of banks, something which enabled monasteries to issue loans on both an individual and a collective basis. The coffers of an Orthodox monastery fulfilled precisely this function. The Kykkos Monastery is a characteristic example. It is Cyprus's prosperous monastery *par excellence*. At the beginning of the nineteenth century it provided loans to Christians and Muslims who were resorting to it in their endeavour to cope with the economic difficulties they were facing (Michael 2003: 43).

10 Insurrections in the Eighteenth and Nineteenth Centuries

The second cycle of insurrections, which erupted approximately a century after the Boyacioglou uprising, but also the preceding "pro-Western" revolts, were prompted by the harsh taxation and exploitation suffered by the farming populations. This, yet again, supplemented more general changes occurring in the Ottoman Empire. It was, on the terrain of landed property, the displacement of the *Sipahis* by the *Ayan*, that is to say the shift from a regime of military power to the advantage of economically more affluent beneficiaries from tax farming, that created an entirely new situation on the island, and particularly for the Muslim population that was surrendering tax revenues to them. It was for this reason, apart from whatever the Orthodox were doing, that there was vigorous Muslim participation in these revolts.

One indicative instance is that of the time when Chil Asman Aga (1764) became Muhassil. In order to be able to bid for appointment to the position he had taken out massive loans in Constantinople (Myrianthopoulos 1973: 90). The heaviest taxes he imposed on Christians and Muslims provoked furious reactions (it is characteristically mentioned that the poll tax increased by 21 kurus to 47[41] (!) while other under-the-counter payments brought in an additional 350,000 kurus, enabling him to recoup the sum he had expended to secure the post) (Zannetos 1910: 1117). And all this in a Cyprus which had only just recovered from an epidemic of plague which had taken a toll of 22,000 victims. In fact the population had initially paid the taxes but after a certain point the inflow had slowed down and the Muhassil's agents had resorted to violence to oblige even the most obstreperous to pay. This triggered a flood of complaints to the religious authorities, Christians and Muslims alike. The latter appealed to the Muhassil but he in turn referred them to the Porte. In the event, after conclusion of a relevant agreement it was decided that representatives of the Church should be sent to Constantinople.

The result was that, having been briefed by the delegation, the Sultan himself decreed through a ferman that the additional taxes be cancelled, the further sums of money that had been collected be returned and a stern censure be published of these initiatives of the Muhassil (Zannetos 1910: 1118). To implement the ferman on 5th November 1764 the representative of the Grand Vizier (Vezirchoqadar) arrived in Nicosia and visited Chil Asman Aga in his palatial residence to announce to him the decisions of the Sultan. Chil Asman there attempted unsuccessfully to murder the Sultan's representative, with the result that the crowd had gathered and was waiting to hear the Sultan's decisions revolted, attacked the Muhassil's residence and set fire to it, killing Chil Asman together with eighteen of his soldiers (Mariti 1994: 875; Sakellarios 1890: 573–575).

In Constantinople when the Grand Vizier was informed of these unprecedented events he persuaded the Sultan that the seriousness of the situation precluded resort to harsh measures. A new Muhassil, Hafez Mehmet, was installed, who did not take any measure against the insurgents or even try to find the murderers of his predecessor, but payment of compensation was demanded both for repairs to the palace and for the relatives of the victims. 500,000 kurus were required to be paid

[41] According to another source the sum was 44½ kurus for Greeks and half of that sum for Ottomans (Mariti 1994: 874).

by Cypriots as a whole, corresponding to 14 kurus per person for the Orthodox and 7 for the Ottomans[42] (Zannetos 1910: 121).

After much hesitation the Christians started to pay. The Muslims, by contrast, refused, and revolted. The argumentation they employed was that they should be recognized by the Porte as men that had rid the Empire of a tyrant who had been bent on the destruction of its provinces. The imposition of a fine, in contrast, stigmatized them as troublemakers (Martiti 1994: 876). Specifically, the residents of Mesaoria went to Kythrea and occupied the flour mills there that supplied Nicosia, thus threatening the capital with a food shortage (Zannetos 1910: 1122). Then the authorities decided to waive the taxation for the Muslims and calm was restored, temporarily. But when a little later the tax collectors went back to work a new movement sprang up. On 27th July 1765 in Myrtou a revolt broke out headed by the Administrator of Kyrenia Castle Halil Aga, with both Orthodox and Muslims participating.[43] Halil Aga declared himself General Administrator of Cyprus and ordered that not so much as an *obol* should be expended on paying fines and that tax revenue should be remitted to him. And indeed he appointed officials for that purpose (Zannetos 1910: 1123). He also pressured the Agas and the church leadership to send a report to the Porte and request that he be recognized as hegemon of the island (Myrianthopoulos 1973: 91). The insurgents then occupied nearly the whole island and ordered the people not to pay tax. They went so far as to mount a siege against Nicosia. On 28th August the Muhassil Hafez Mehmet promised not to insist on collection of tax revenues and Halil Aga returned to Kyrenia.

Meanwhile the delegation of church leaders, headed by Archbishop Paisios, which had travelled to Constantinople, not only did not support Halil and the rebels but condemned them for having staged the revolt, accusing them of tyrannizing the countryside. This was the reaction because, operating as the long arm of Ottoman power and thus enraging the Cypriot people (Pavlidis 1993: 118), the Church had accepted the imposition of the new taxes. Perceiving that the situation was serious, the

[42] But Martiti says that the amount was the same (14 kurus for everyone) (Martiti 1994: 876).

[43] According to certain sources, among the Muslims there were Islamised Greeks who were complaining because the authorities treated them as Christians on questions of taxation despite the fact that they had changed their religion (Hadjidemetriou 2002: 292).

Porte decided to dispatch soldiers to the island together with another new Muhassil, Souleiman Efendi. Immediately on taking office the latter again demanded payment of the fine and then, in January 1766, Halil Aga again besieged Nicosia, claiming recognition as the island's governor (Zanettos 1910: 1124).

After this development, at the beginning of February, the situation on the island was out of control: trade had been discontinued, the fields were not being cared for, many houses had been abandoned and the insurrectionaries were forcing even civil servants to join their ranks. To find an exit from the impasse, Muslim dignitaries from Larnaca, merchants and officials sought the intervention of the European consuls of England, France and Venice. The British consul Turner agreed to mediate, summarizing the demands: (a) issuance of a general amnesty (b) a written declaration from the Muhassil that he would not collect any tax beyond those which will be imposed by the Sultan (c) the Ziamets and the Janissaries who had joined the rebels would keep their positions (d) a statement from all the residents of Nicosia that they would accept Halil as Muhassil if he was properly appointed by the Porte.

The administrator of Larnaca replied to Turner that the Muhassil would not have any objection to accepting all four of these conditions and Halil Aga declared that he was ready to commence negotiations. But the response of the Muhassil himself, on 15th February, was dismissive. But the response of the Muhassil himself, on 15th February, was dismissive. He said that the Sultan had entrusted him with the responsibility for the whole island and that he could not go beyond the brief he had been given, unless he received different orders from the Sultan himself. All that he could offer was a general amnesty for the insurgents. The next day Turner transmitted the Muhassil's position, but the rebels were intransigent in their insistence that the last two conditions should be observed (Mariti 1994: 878).

After this there was no significant change in the situation until June 1766 when new expeditionary forces arrived on the island, dispatched by the Porte. They were headed by Pasha Kior Mehmet, who sent a letter via Turner to Halil's camp in which he said he was proposing that each party should withdraw to its respective home and then he, Kior Mehmet, would examine the issue in the spirit of finding a solution that would be satisfactory for everyone.

The conciliatory content of the letter, in conjunction with fatigue from the protracted military confrontation, had a disorganizing effect on the camp of Halil Aga who, retaining only 200 loyal fighters (from the 5,000[44] he had prior to dispatch of the letter) retreated to Kyrenia (Mariti 1994: 880). Then Kior Mehmet launched a siege of the city and, inviting Halil Aga ostensibly for negotiations, took him hostage, with the result that the next day the insurgents were forced to surrender the town's fortress. Halil Aga was strangled and 200 rebels beheaded (Mariti 1994: 881).

After that order was restored (Hadjidemetriou 2002: 289–291), the taxes were collected that had been established by both Orthodox and Muslims, and to them was added the bill for the 500,000 piastres that the expedition to defeat Halil had cost. Thus, the overall cost to Cyprus amounted to a million kurus, a sum which had to be paid by the 10,000 Christians and 5000–6,000 Muslims.

Some are of the view that the next revolt occurred at the end of the eighteenth century when Hadjibaki was appointed Muhassil. However, despite their undoubted interest the events in question fall far short of being classifiable as a revolt because what is absent is the most basic characteristic of revolt, namely the intervention and mobilization of the popular strata. The reason that the case of Hadjibaki is mentioned is that it serves to highlight the way political ties operated at that time, and not because what is involved was some kind of uprising.

Himself a Cypriot Muslim, Hadjibaki managed to stake out a gradually rising trajectory in the provincial administration and establish a network of entrepreneurial and commercial relationships with consuls from European countries (Hadjikyriakou 2014: 236). This is how he came to win the favour of the Kapudan Pasha and be appointed Muhassil of Cyprus (Myrianthopoulos 1973: 93). The problem is that after some time had passed since his commencement of duties, Hadjibaki started to demand more money in tax than had been prescribed.[45] At the same time numerous accusations came to be levelled against him for corruption: appropriation of inheritances, bribery of false witnesses, forgery, illegal

[44] This number reflects the influence the insurrectionary movement had on the Cypriots. From this viewpoint it is characteristic that when at the beginning of June a military corps of 200 men headed by Tzafar Bey occupied the fortress of Alykes his soldiers proceeded to behave so badly that the residents considered themselves fortunate when the next day the fortress was retaken by the soldiers of Halil (Zannetos 1910: 1125).

[45] Philippou says that he imposed an additional tax of 8 piastres per person (Philippou 1975: 194).

grain exports, imprisonment of the Dragoman Hadjigeorgakis Kornesios and other complaints (Hadjikyriakou 2014: 437).[46]

This lawlessness and arbitrary rule met with intense opposition and a delegation headed by Archbishop Chrysanthos with the Metropolitans of Paphos Panaretos, Kitio Meletios and Kyrenia Sophronios, in August 1783 left for Constantinople with a view to condemning the behaviour of Hadjibaki (Philippou 1975: 117). The clerical leaders in fact handed a document to the Sultan and the Grand Vizier Halil Hamid Pasha in which they had recorded all the demands they were making of the Muhassil. Knowing that Hadjibaki was a protégé of the Kapudan Hasan Pasha, with whom his relations were extremely antagonistic, the Grand Vizier immediately appointed a new Muhassil, taking advantage of the fact that the Kapudan Pasha had suddenly fallen ill. But Hadjibaki made use of his connections in the Porte and still enjoyed the support of the Kapudan Pasha, who, as it turned out, recovered from his illness. Against this backdrop, Hadjibaki not only managed to get himself reappointed as Muhassil (Anagnostopoulou 2002: 275), but also succeeded in having an Imperial Decree issued, according to which, the four archpriests would be exiled to Mount Athos. Learning of this development, the religious leaders took refuge in Smyrna but the Kapudan Pasha managed to extract a decree from the Ecumenical Patriarch requiring the people of Cyprus to elect a new Church hierarchy. Obviously, this order for banishment and also for interdiction was not the result just of Hadjibaki's good personal connections but also of the activation of mechanisms of bribery and corruption. Probably it was also an opportunity for the Patriarch to assert control over the Cypriot Church, which had acquired a significantly enhanced role after the institutional reforms of 1754.

In any case a new hierarchy was elected in Cyprus: the Hegumen Mahaira Ioannikios as archbishop, the Hegumen Pallouriotis as Metropolitan of Paphos, the Hegumen of Agios Lazaros Chrysanthos as Hegumen of Kition and the Exarchos of Kyrenia Ioannikios as Hegumen of Kyrenia. Immediately after the election the problem of ordainment arose and the Grand Vizier ordered the Ecumenical Patriarch[47] to have

[46] Hadjikyriakou maintains that the entire period of government by Hadjibaki was characterized by intense antagonism against Hadjigeorgakis Kornesios (Hadjikyriakou 2014).

[47] As the Patriarch of Constantinople mentions in his letter on the subject, "[...] we were ordered by the Grand Vicar of the Glorious Crown (i.e. the

the Patriarch of Antioch Daniel send advisory bishops to Cyprus to conduct the ordainment of the newly elected Church officials. The Ecumenical Patriarch did indeed send the required letter, signed by the candidates to the episcopacy, and by senior clerics and dignitaries of Cyprus (Philippou 1975: 118). My view is that such a great mobilization cannot be interpreted as just the product of Ottoman pressures and we think it very likely that there was collusion between the Greek Cypriot élite and Ottoman officials to change the ecclesiastical hierarchy in Cyprus. The role of the Ecumenical Patriarch is obvious.

Antioch, for its part, regarded the election of the new leadership as irregular because their predecessors had neither been deposed nor had they submitted their resignation. Nor, indeed was Cyprus under the authority of the throne of Antioch, and its Patriarch accordingly refused to intervene. Nevertheless, the four newly elected officials assumed their posts in Cyprus, after which Hadjibaki demanded 100,000 kurus to legalize them as bishops. To find that very large sum, the high priests started selling off Church property, disposing even of the Church's sacred vessels, but they managed only to raise, with difficulty, 16,943 kurus (Philippou 1975: 120). Thus, to satisfy Hadjibaki they were forced to issue two promissory notes.

Faced with this worsening situation, the Cypriots sent a new mission to the Patriarch of Constantinople, requesting that he intervene and recall Hadjibaki to the Porte to explain his behaviour in the presence of the Cypriot representatives (Philippou 1975: 121). At the same time, the exiled high priests also sent to Constantinople the Cypriot teacher Gerassimos Kritikos to present the corresponding argumentation. Kritikos managed in fact to meet with the Grand Vizier Halil Hamid Pasha and persuaded him to recall Hadjibaki (Philippou 1975: 122).

Following this meeting, Meletios of Kition succeeded in getting away from Smyrna and reaching Constantinople where he managed to have the high priests' exile rescinded, employing the following arguments: (a) The Muhassil raised 30,000 kurus to prepare Cyprus for the Russo-Turkish war, which however was not used, but neither was it returned, (b) he increased taxation on *miri* lands from 412 to 772 *pougkia* (pouches)

Grand Vizier) that he should regard it as a precious duty to write to him that he might send through his own mandate the three holy fathers under his authority to the island of Cyprus to ordain the new Archbishop of Cyprus […]". For Gabriel's letter see *Kypriaka Chronika Vol. III*, 1925: 183.

and in that way succeeded in appropriating 360 *pougkia*, (c) he obliged Cypriots to lend him 180 *pougkia*, to find which he forced them to take out loans with Frankish merchants active in Cyprus (Philippou 1975: 122–123).

So Hadjibaki was made to return to Constantinople and in July 1784 the Ecumenical Patriarch dismissed the four high priests who had in the meantime been elected. Hadjibaki was finally to return the sums that had been credited to him[48] but they didn't go to the Cypriots but instead were sequestered as part payment of the tax on the *miri* lands, and he succeeded in having himself appointed again as Muhassil in Cyprus! This apparently paradoxical development must be due to the fact that in 1785 the Grand Vizier Halil Hamid Pasha was replaced by Sahin Ali Pasha and Hadjinaki had managed to establish close relations with the *Seyhul islam* (head of the Islamic jurisprudence). This triggered new protests by the Cypriots: letters of protest were sent to the Mufti, the ulema, the landed gentry, and others left the island in fear of the revenge of Hadjibaki (Hadjikyriakou 2014: 438). These reactions had their effect and the Grand Vizier Sahin Ali Pasha ultimately cashiered Hadjibaki and sent him to Jaffa as a customs official, where he died.

After this although the island remained under the administration of the Kapudan Pasha there was a shift in the balance of power, with the Dragoman Kornesios transformed into a powerful political and economic factor. At the same time the role of the Muhassil was downgraded (Anagnostopoulou 2002: 276) and the responsibility for collecting taxes was withdrawn from the Archbishop and the Metropolitans, as they had been found guilty of over-taxation and other misconduct (Hadjikyriakou 2014: 432).

The last revolt that took place before the revolution was that of 1804. It targeted the policy of the Dragoman Hadjigeorgakis Kornesios[49] and was linked to the taxation increase of March 1804, although it had been

[48] The official inquiry on Hadjibaki revealed that in his nine years in government he had amassed more than 8 million kurus at a time when the annual revenue of the Ottoman state for 1787–1788 was 13.25 million! (Hadjikyriakou 2014: 439).

[49] Who at that time bore the appellation *Mukatadji* precisely because he had the lease on the taxation of Christians, as well as the role of intermediary between consuls and the Administrator (Theoharidis 1987: 71–72).

preceded by a food shortage that had resulted in famine.[50] The consequence of this was that protests were held culminating in disturbances in which considerable numbers of Muslims were killed. There was a spiralling of conflicts, which spread to cover the whole island. The main body of the rebels were Muslim peasant farmers, with the addition of most of the soldiers of the island's garrison, together with *linovamvakoi* (canvas-cottons- Islamized Greeks secretly following the Christian religion) and a handful of Orthodox Christians. A certain Ismail Aga became leader of the insurgents and led them to Nicosia. There they asked the Governor of Cyprus Suleiman Aga to show them the Ottoman firmans on the basis of which the increase in taxation had been decided. Suleiman then answered them that it wasn't right for them to turn against the Ottoman administration but that they should address their complaint to the Dragoman Kornesios, who was in charge of taxation. The crowd did indeed go to the Dragoman's house but he told them that he did not have authorization from the Porte to show them the firmans. The next day the enraged crowd ransacked the Dragoman's house and also attacked the Archbishopric on the grounds of the opulence and flaunting of wealth which they thought characteristic of the Orthodox religious hierarchy.

In the meantime, the Dragoman, who had succeeded in escaping from the rage of the crowd, had arrived in Constantinople and denounced the insurgents. The Sultan sent troops who managed to suppress the revolt (Pavlidis 1993: 134–135). But it should be noted that the dispatch of troops took place following the intervention not only of Kornesios but also of the Archbishop, and according to some sources the church leadership borrowed 30,000 piastres from the European consuls to pay for the ships that transported these soldiers (Anagnostopoulou 2002: 277; Koumoulides 1971: 59).

[50] The food shortage seems to have been attributable to the fact that in 1802 the Dragoman had concentrated the whole production so as to be able to export to Spain, at high prices, where, because of the Napoleonic wars, there were huge opportunities for profit (Michael 2016: 38; Hadjikyriakou 2014: 435). The result was that grain prices quadrupled. The exorbitant tax was a by-product of the Muslims' obligation to pay their share of the expenses for the expedition in Egypt against that country's occupation by Napoleon (Dionysiou 1988: 41). Initially, Kornesios borrowed almost all the relevant amount and then recouped it from the island's Muslims and non-Muslims alike. Ultimately the amount to be raised included both the interest payable to the lenders and very probably a surreptitious profit for Kornesios himself (2011: 266, 2014: 434).

Seen as a whole, these events have certain implications which may help to understand better the developments that followed. For a start, this revolt was clearly more Muslim in character and was directed against the economic, and not the political, governance of the island, with the consequence of the death of dozens of Muslim dissidents.[51] The fact that the key role in what happened is regarded as having been played by the then assistant to the Archbishop and later Archbishop (1810) Kyprianos[52] was something that the Muslims would not forget, and that would become evident in the massacre of 1821 (see below). To put it somewhat differently there had already been an upgrading of the position of the Church within the Ottoman power system from the time that the right to collect taxes had been ceded to its mechanisms. This promotion had been discontinued because of the demotion suffered by the hierarchy when the right to collect tax was taken away from them due to strengthening of the role of the Dragoman. But this was something ephemeral and would be checked by the events of 1804. Specifically, Kornesios' escape[53] had contributed to reducing the institutional power

[51] According to Dionysiou they must have numbered about forty (Dionysiou 1988: 201), on the basis of the relevant archives Kyrris estimates them to have been *at least* 40, but there is credible evidence that there were more (Kyrris 1970–1971: 317). What is interesting is that in these official documents the victims of execution are called "apostates" and among them there is not even one Christian, something which must be due to all the people executed being soldiers who sided with the revolt (Kyrris 1970–1971: 320).

[52] Due to the absence of Hadjigeorgakis in Constantinople, Kyprianos assumed responsibility for the collection and deposit in the public coffers of the special taxes owed by the Muslims (Dionysiou 1988: 118). This close collaboration between the Orthodox hierarchy and Ottoman power is something that was to continue in the years immediately following. Thus in 1809 Archbishop Chrysanthos issues an order to the Alabey of Paphos on questions of taxation quest, the Alabey drafts a justificatory report to the Archbishop on his actions and communicates with him for prosecution of a Muslim tax collector (Dionysiou 1988: 276). Correspondingly, in 1817/1818 Kyprianos as Archbishop has to raise 89,304 piastres as the remaining *saillanet* tax, a sum which the Alabey of Nicosia undertakes to collect (Dionysiou 1988: 118–119).

[53] The dethronement of Sultan Selim II (1789–1808) and his execution a year later would leave Kornesios without a powerful protector, with the result that he himself was executed in 1809 (Michael 2006: 62). Koumoulides reports that French diplomats played a significant role in having Kornesios executed, on account of their own very bad relations with the Dragoman, and also with the Archbishop, whom they regarded as committed partisans of Russia, which on account of the Napoleonic wars was at that time in conflict with France. In any case with the Treaty of Kuchuk Kainartji in 1774 the Sublime Porte granted the Russians the right to represent the Orthodox Christians within the Ottoman Empire (Koumoulides 1971: 62–63).

of the Dragoman and correspondingly strengthened the position of the Church, fostering its (re)emergence as a very significant economic force on the island. According to Henry Light the income of the Archbishop in 1814 came to 40,000 dollars (Pavlidis 1993: 148) and the testimony of the British official Turner in 1815 asserts that "Although nominally under the power of a Bey appointed under the Kaputan Pasha, Cyprus is in fact governed by the Greek Archbishop and his clerical subordinates" (quoted in Philippou 1975: 201).

The economic prosperity of the Orthodox Church grew further when in 1811 or early 1812 it regained the right to collect taxes and manage the island's economy (Philippou 1975: 201–202) and through a special economic relationship it had established with the Consuls had managed to acquire significant reserves of liquidity. Specifically, the consul-lenders would give the hierarchy credit notes by means of which the Church received their salaries through the embassy of the diplomat's state in Constantinople and would reimburse those sums to the Sublime Porte as part payment of the taxes owed by Cyprus to the State. It was thus in debt to the consuls in Cyprus, but it delayed depositing the money owed in order to have liquid cash, something which in a non-monetary economy gave to Church multiplier advantages. For their part, the consuls agreed to lend money to the clerical hierarchy because, on the one hand, they secured high rates of interest and, on the other, they enjoyed the favour of high-ranking clerics, which could potentially mean the lifting of various obstacles in the exercise of their duties. It is perhaps worth noting also that the consuls, having embarked on commercial activities on the island (see below) did not immediately need to be paid their salaries (Dionysiou 1988: 127–128).

11 The Events of 1821, the Emergence of Greek National Identity and the Participation of Cypriots in the Greek Revolution

The effect of the Greek revolution of 1821, which was to result in the creation of an independent Greek state, in Cyprus must be seen from a twofold perspective: on the one hand there were the events of the summer of 1821 on the island, which led to the execution of dozens of senior

Christian clergy and dignitaries, and on the other there was the participation of Cypriots in the revolution in Greece. But the latter also highlights the question of the reasons why there was this participation, and by extension the question of the Hellenic national identity of Orthodox Christian Cypriots. But let us take matters one at a time.

The Events of 1821 in Cyprus

In October 1818 Demetrios Hypatros arrived in Cyprus as emissary of the Philiki Etaireia[54] and proceeded to elucidate for Archbishop Kyprianos the objectives of the Etaireia (Koumoulides 1971: 69–70). Kyprianos replied that he could provide material and moral support[55] but that Cyprus could not participate in the revolution. For the Archbishop, the island was very distant from Greece and very close to the Ottoman power centres and the danger of a large-scale massacre of Cypriots was acute. For this stance Kyprianos has been criticized that as someone integrated into the Ottoman power system, he was not in any way inclined to become embroiled in dangerous adventures. But the problematic he developed seems quite coherent. In this sense it seems that the Archbishop's hesitancy was well grounded. By contrast, in the event that Cyprus had been closer I think that the Archbishop would have taken seriously into consideration the likelihood of his being politically dominant in a Cyprus without the Ottoman presence.

But in any case, when the revolution began in Greece the Muhassil Kucuk Mehmed sent reports to the Sultan initially demanding the dispatch of troops. And in fact, a few detachments of Albanians were shifted from Syria to Cyprus, and at the same time the disarmament of the Cypriots was implemented, a measure imposed pre-emptively throughout the Ottoman territory. But the Muhassil then proceeded to formulate a request for execution of the most prominent Orthodox Cypriots. It was a good opportunity for the Ottoman administration in Cyprus to appropriate the wealth of the Orthodox Christians. In other words, Kucuk used the pretext of the Greek revolt in other parts of the Empire to secure

[54] The Philiki Etaireia was the secret organization which in 1821 organized the Greek revolution for independence from Ottoman rule.

[55] The promised funds were finally delivered by the Archbishop in early 1821 to the then representative of the Philiki Etaireia in Cyprus A. Pelopidas (Koumoulides 1971: 71).

the consent of the Sultan to his proceeding with executions and expropriations of Orthodox property.[56] This amounted to an endeavour to terminate the very active role of the Greek Orthodox élite in political and economic power on the island. It is very probable that the overall stance of Mehmed did not reflect just the steadily mounting anger of the Muslims with the Orthodox élite, given that the Agas of Nikosia had also expressed agreement with him (Michael 2016: 75) but also the plans of the Empire's upper echelons. Specifically, as argued by Anagnostopoulou, the fact of a new Kapudan Pasha being appointed in 1818 must have played a significant part in developments. The reason for this is that the Kapudan Pasha was determined to proceed with centralization of his power and so wanted a governor in Cyprus with greater power. His relative Kucuk Mehmed was exactly in that category (Anagnostopoulou 2002: 279).[57]

In fact, the Sultan was initially against carrying out executions, with the argument that since Cyprus had become an Ottoman possession the Orthodox had not challenged the rule of the Sultan and when there had been Muslim revolts they had helped the Ottoman army to defeat the rebels. But another letter from Mehmed then followed in which it was mentioned that ammunition had been found in houses and monasteries (Michael 2016: 102). Then the Sultan, aware of the dimensions of the Greek revolution that was in progress on the mainland, believed the reports and ordered the execution of the dignitaries, the confiscation of their property and the sale of their families into slavery.[58] The proscribed individuals assembled in Nicosia without knowing what awaited them and

[56] As the French consul characteristically says of Mehmed: "He imagined a conspiracy and himself produced incriminating letters and in that way succeeded in portraying the people as revolutionary and extracted from his government the order severely to punish those responsible" (quoted in Michael 2016: 65).

[57] According to Kepiades Mehmed was chosen by the Admiral of the Ottoman Fleet to "[…] destroy the influence of the supreme religious leader […] who exercised almost the entirety of the administrative power and was not only independent of the governors that are sent to the island but also decided their appointment and departure" (Kepiades, quoted by Michael 2016: 74).

[58] As mentioned in the relevant directive: "[…] you informed us that ammunition was found in a church and you wrote and informed me that day by day treachery, trickery and game-playing by the bad element in the Romioi against the state of Mohammed were on the increase. The aforementioned executions are therefore proper" (quoted in Michael 2016: 103).

the ferman ordering their execution was read to them. Finally, dozens were executed,[59] among them the Archbishop and three Metropolitans. In parallel with the executions there was also confiscation of property and looting, including of people not mentioned in the ferman.[60] It seems that a great part of the wealth was appropriated by Mehmed himself. The churches and monasteries were ransacked, the houses of the proscribed were seized and their families expelled (Richter 2007: 64–65).[61] With other houses the upper storey was demolished (Michael 2016: 107). The elders, the priests and the rich Orthodox who managed to escape the Janissaries sought refuge in the consulates, which were in Larnaca, and finally considerable numbers left Cyprus.[62] Last but not least, there was the additional consequences of changes in the allocation of taxing. Thus, on the one hand there was a shift in taxation from those who had left the island to the remaining rayah and on the other an overturn in the balance of taxation between Orthodox and Muslims from 2/3 as against to 1/3 to 4/5 as against 1/5 between 1823 and 1827, and from 1827 onwards to 7/8 as against 1/8 (Theoharidis and Andreev 1996: 151).

[59] Ioannis Filimonas raises the number of those executed to 400 but no other source confirms this. Two Ottoman documents mention 16 and 50 people, respectively. Theoharidis records 74 (Theocharidis 1995: 97), Kepiades 68 (Michael 2016: 109) and Zannetos mentions "more than seventy martyrs" (Zannetos 1910: 1155). Note that the executions began with the high priests on 9th June and continued until 17th August (Michael 2016: 106–107). From 20th July the Grand Vizier issued an order that there should be no more executions but the Kapudan Pasha concealed the existence of this order for forty days, obviously for the reasons as those he choose Kucum Mehmed as Muhassil (Anagnostopoulou 2002: 280).

[60] As the consul for the Netherlands Lorenzo Giovanni Santi says of Mehmed: "all the prosperous merchants, industrialists or farmers in each city are seen as deserving the death penalty" (quoted in Michael 2016: 105).

[61] According to the Imperial Decree of Sultan Mahmud "because it is confirmed that the infidel rayah of the island of Cyprus have been accused of complicity with the revolutions of the Romaioi nation and punished by his supreme command, for that reason the portable property and real estate and the rights of those who have fled are confiscated and rescinded by Imperial decree to the advantage of public finances" (quote in Philippou 1975: 208).

[62] It is estimated that between 1821 and 1825 20,000–25,000 Orthodox Christians left Cyprus (Koumoulides 1973: 150).

Questions of National Identity

The Issue of National Identity of Orthodox Cypriots

Up until this point the book has deliberately not mentioned the question of national identity of a part or all of the Cypriot population. This has been because the historical narrative so far has pertained to a premodernistic context in which there was no projection of national identities in the way that has become prevalent in the modernist nation state. From the beginning of Ottoman rule, life for the two most populous religious communities in Cyprus evolved through changes in the population balance,[63] probably as a result of Islamized Christians wanting to avoid the poll tax, with a clear awareness of their separate and different linguistic, religious and cultural characteristics but without all this leading to the development of national, in the modernistic sense of the term, identities. For the Orthodox Christians of Cyprus the acquisition of Greek identity would begin to emerge gradually from the end of the eighteenth century as a consequence of the Greek enlightenment but would become a mass phenomenon in the first phase by virtue of the Greek revolution (see below) and then in consequence of the creation of the Greek state. But the demand for *enosis* or union with Greece would be raised for the first time only when the British took over the government of the island (see below). The reasons for this are related to both the difficulties the Greek Cypriots would have making this demand to the Sublime Porte on their own and the fact that their status as citizens of the pre-modern Ottoman Empire inhibited their wholehearted embrace of a national identity, given the organic integration of the Orthodox Church into the Ottoman administrative system. In contrast the assumption of power on the island by an old-established modernist state had a catalytic effect for adoption by the totality of the population of the Greek identity and projection of the demand for *Enosis*. The Muslims, for their part, saw themselves as subjects of the Ottoman state and as a consequence until 1878 for them it was difficult for there to be any discussion of shaping a different *national* identity. That was set in motion through the British presence in *contradistinction* to the demand for *enosis* and

[63] According to the various historical testimonies presented in a compilation by Papadopoulos, although at the beginning of the Ottoman presence the overwhelming majority of citizens were Christian Orthodox, at the end of the eighteenth century this had been overturned and the majority were Muslim. This did not last long and in 1821 the Orthodox would again be in the majority (Papadopoulos 1965: 48–58).

doubtless through fear of the possibility of ethnic cleansing (see below). So essentially the national sentiment in the Muslims is shaped from the beginning of the British presence, initially taking the form of opposition of Ottomans to Greeks and then, given the influence of the Young Turk movement, as Turks against Greeks.

The Overall Issue of Greek National Identity and Its Elaboration

If the self-determination of Orthodox Cypriots as "Hellenes" is to become comprehensible as an issue, the genesis of the Greek nation must be examined from an overall perspective.

The term "Hellene" was for many centuries identified with idolatry and the gods of Olympus and for that reason was not in use, or was employed only pejoratively, in the period of the Byzantine Empire. But the passage to Ottoman rule would lend a positive connotation to the term, evoking a popular mythology which however was not seen as plausibly related to the familiar humble Greek-speaking peasant farmers whereas the Greek-speaking élite of the Phanar was satisfied with the fact that they occupied high positions in the Ottoman administration (Pizanias 2015: 198–199). Of course, from certain cases of Greek-speaking intellectuals, who however lived in the West, there was some use of the term "modern Greeks" (Pizanias 2015: 75) but this on the one hand involved a marginal phenomenon and on the other remained indeterminate in content. The situation began to change when in 1675 Georgios Kontaris and in 1686 Ioannis Makolas not only spoke of New Hellenes but also counterposed them to the Byzantines (Romioi, which is a corruption of "Romans", because the Byzantine Empire was officially called the Eastern Roman Empire) and also to the Christian *rayah*. The New Hellenes were not *rayah*. They recognized themselves in the ancient Hellenic past (Pizanias 2015: 204–205). This spiritual production was the outcome of communication between prosperous Greek-speaking Orthodox Christian merchants amd intellectuals who gradually began to declare themselves Hellenes, in that way differentiating themselves from the rest of their social environment. Thus, by the end of the eighteenth century an increase was observed in the number of affluent and educated Greek Orthodox people who saw themselves as belonging to the race known as Hellenes, making systematic references to Orthodox religion, the Greek language and ancient Hellenic culture. At the turn of the century there was a shift from "belonging to the race" to "belonging to the nation", with consequent emergence of the demand for creation of an independent Greek state (Dertilis 2018: 235–236). The role of Katartzis was important in this connection. He maintained that Greeks have their own native land and emphasized the continuity of Hellenism which starts from Ancient Greece, continues through Byzantium and ends up with the Romioi (Dimaras 2002: 143). At the dawn of the nineteenth century Korais in one of his texts presents the possibilities for action by Greeks, who should—he said—take advantage of the expansion of the French Empire (Pizanias 2015: 463–464). A little later an unknown author wrote the book *O Rossoanglos (The Russian-Englishman),* which puts forward the idea of an alliance between France, Russia and England for the liberation of the Greeks (Pizanias 2015: 463–466). There would follow in 1806 the volume *Elliniki Nomarchia* ("Greek Prefecture"), also written by an unknown author, with its explicit raising of the question of an uprising of the enslaved Greeks against Ottoman power (Pizanias 2015: 463–466).

The abovementioned positions were facilitated by the proliferation of publishing ventures, the founding of Greek Orthodox schools, the tightening of links between Greek Orthodox communities via trade networks, the development of archaeology.

In this context, and of course under the rubric of the more general neo-romanticism prevailing in Western Europe but also influenced by the evolving structures of the modernist nation states the demand grew in various regions, inside and outside the Ottoman Empire, for an independent Greek state, culminating in the revolution of 1821. The creation of the Greek identity, which was something that initially preoccupied an intellectual and economic élite, came to coalesce with the fact that a section of the population of the Ottoman Empire that spoke Greek and was Orthodox by religion, at the same time suffering economic hardship at the hands of the Ottoman oppressive apparatus saw in the demand for creation of an independent Greek state the prospect for improvement of its own social position, and accordingly participated in the Revolution.

The Participation of Cypriots in the Greek Revolution

As we have seen, a few years prior to 1821 the abovementioned schema was transposed to Cyprus, with personal contacts between Philiki Etaireia members and Archbishop Kyprianos but there was no direct involvement of Cypriot territory in the Revolution. Nevertheless, the fact of the executions of the elders in the summer of 1821 but also the spread of the revolution through the Greek lands would function as detonators, with the result that the Greeks of Cyprus would attempt in various ways to strengthen the Greek liberation struggle. One of those was the conclusion of a loan, guaranteed by the Greek state, to finance a corresponding revolution in Cyprus. But for a number of reasons which it is not possible to enumerate here,[64] this did not become possible. Another was the plan for simultaneous occupation of Cyprus and Lebanon by Greek soldiers. The instigators of these plans thought that in this way Cyprus would be liberated and in addition the Ottoman Empire would be dealt a heavy blow with the loss of Lebanon, which would generally facilitate the endeavour to establish a Greek state. But this scheme did not go forward either (Kyrris, n.d: 6–8; Protopsaltis 1954: 16; Louis 2006, vol. 1: 36). The third way, which was the only one that actually proceeded, was the participation of Greeks from Cyprus in the war for Greek independence. According to the comprehensive records of Rodiona P. Georgiadi more than 600 Cypriots are listed as having fought in the Greek Revolution (Papapolyviou 2020).[65] In my view it was precisely during this phase that Greek national consciousness crystallized in the mass of Cypriot Orthodox Christians, who from Romioi became Greeks of Cyprus.

That said, as far as the process of the new Greek state's construction is concerned, the first Governor of Greece I. Capodistrias, in response to a question from the British diplomat Wilmot-Horton who asked what the boundaries of the new Greek state would be replied "Those borders of 1821 were forged through the blood shed in the massacres of Kydonia, Cyprus, Chios, Crete, Psara and Messolonghi…" (quote in Georgis 2010: 41). This encouraged the Greeks of Cyprus to send a delegation to Greece in August 1828 to submit a series of questions to Capodistrias. It is interesting that in one of his answers the Governor of Greece appears, in this phase at least, not to be including Cyprus in his immediate plans for incorporation in Greek territory. "As for the islands, both history and monuments from antiquity, everything in a word, testifies that Rhodes, Cyprus and numerous other (islands) are parts of Greece. But the present

[64] For the relevant literature see (Conomos 1972–1973; Koumoulides 1973; Kyrris, n.d.: 7).

[65] A very large number given that the total population of the island at that time was no more than 100,000, with the non-Muslims numbering 60–70 thousand (Papadopoulos 1965: 56–58).

provisional government, following the decisions of the three National Assemblies, is obliged to consider as comprising Greece all the provinces which were, or are still, under Turkish domination, and took up arms in 1821, or thereafter [...]" (quoted in Protopsaltis 1971: 90). As is obvious, in the strategic planning of the Greek government what predominated was realism concerning the political and military power balance, taking into account the fact that in Cyprus there was no military force that could support the incorporation of the island into Greece.

12 Administrative Changes and Social Reactions in the 1830–1839 Period

Irrespective of the events of 1821 (both in Greece proper and in Cyprus) from the beginning of the nineteenth century it had become clear that only with specific and radical reforms would it be possible for the Ottoman Empire to survive. Emphasis was placed on the endeavour to have the central state functioning in a more organized and co-ordinated way so as to eliminate phenomena of administrative deterioration and place limits on centrifugal tendencies. Sultan Mahmud II (1808–1839) accordingly adopted a range of institutional changes to the central and regional administration. The specific goals of these actions were on the one hand secularization of the state and on the other more rational organization of the tax system given that phenomena of serious misappropriation and corruption had emerged.

The Sublime Porte wanted to see some degree of consent to the desired reforms. They therefore asked the Orthodox of Cyprus to send to Constantinople a four-member delegation of laymen for discussion of such questions of local character. It is interesting that although the Ottoman Administration asked that lay people should come, their selection—always on the basis of Ottoman directives—was to take place after a conference of clerical leaders and dignitaries which would be convened by the Archbishop, showing what efforts were being made not only to have Orthodox Cypriots represented by lay people (and not priests) *but also to make sure that such lay people remained under the supervision of the Church* (Louis 2006, Vol. 1:43). The reforms which finally took place in Cyprus in 1830 for the first time introduced the popular element into the public affairs of the Greek community. A decision was made for a (central) Council of Elders to be created ("Demogeron" (elder) is the Greek equivalent of kocabasi) along with six local councils of elders whose duties would be to involve themselves in the public affairs of the Orthodox, supervise collection of taxes and conduct regular checks of the public finances. The central Council of Elders played an executive role, appointed the tax collection bodies and was charged with management of taxation questions, but it was the Archbishop and the three Metropolitans that were answerable to the Ottoman administration for collection of tax revenues; this is why the Council of Elders was subject to control by the Church hierarchy when it came to determination and effectiveness of taxation. It seems, therefore, that the powerful presence of the Orthodox Church continued in matters of tax collection, even if now this took place within a broader administrative system. There was also a decision for a seven-member "committee of the public" to be established for supervision of the central and local councils of elders. The committee was comprised of commissioners elected by Orthodox males. It had the role of legislature, auditing committee and information body. The Commission had the right, together with the Church hierarchy, to depose the members of the central Council of Elders and the bodies for implementation of tax collection. It also ratified the budget and "reviewed" the annual report (Louis 2006, Vol. 1: 49–50). Finally, a general assembly was also established. It was convened once a year by the Archbishop and consisted of him personally, the three Metropolitans (these four senior clerics were recognized by the Porte as lifelong protectors of the *rayah*), along with the 24 elders, four for each of the six councils of elders. The annual general assembly elected the four-member council of elders and the 24-member committee of the public (Michael 2015a: 109). The provincial councils of elders, which were elected by the general assembly, taking into account—however—the opinion of the district, were chaired by the Archbishops or one of the Metropolitans. Finally, the secretaries of the kazas of Cyprus, that is to say the people who had the duty of collecting the ecclesiastical donations but also the taxes from the community, were appointed following consultation between the Archbishop and the central Council of Elders (Michael 2005: 256).

Our position is that the concession of rights to lay people on the part of the Ottoman state was linked to a number of different factors: on the one hand to the pressures being exerted by the rising bourgeois strata[66] for participation in the administration and on the other to the protests that

[66] See Sect. 13 of the present chapter.

were being registered against bad financial management and the trends towards mass emigration. The Church accepted the new reality and tried to ensure that the popular representatives would be people in its broader circle of influence. In any case the decisions that were taken were arrived at through common agreement between the triad of the Church hierarchy, the committee of the public and the central Council of Elders (Michael 2005: 145; Konstantinidis 1995: 23–24). In 1838 there were to be certain important changes to that power structure, following a relevant visit by a Cypriot delegation to Constantinople. To begin with, for the first time the senior priests of the Church of Cyprus, as an institution and not as individuals, were recognized as the protectors of the Orthodox population. At the same time, it was decided that the provincial elders would be elected by the residents of the provincial capital, but the consent of the local bishop was also required (Michael 2015a: 110; Dionyssiou 2009: 42). If initially there was an absence of clarity over whether, and to what extent, the role of the Orthodox Church was downgraded in Cyprus, subsequently it became clear that the Church retained the upper hand, albeit within a different framework, conjoining further state regulation as a structure, rather than as an aggregation of individuals, and recognizing the necessity for consensual processes.

Nevertheless, what is to be noted is that notwithstanding the changes of 1830 there was no visible lightening of the burdens for poor farmers and there were joint revolts of Christians and Muslims in 1833. The Orthodox Church hierarchy was *also* targeted by the dissidents, who considered that it bore significant responsibility for the imposition of a new tax (Michael 2005: 259). In reality it was not a single movement but three, which unfolded more or less simultaneously. There were the movements of Nikolaos Thiseas centred on Larnaca, of the monk Ioannikiou with Karpasia at its centre and the third had Paphos as its epicentre and it was led by an Imam, the so-called Gavur Imam. Apart from Ottomans there were also Greeks participating, and *linobambaki,* and the accusation was heard that it had been instigated by the Sultan of Egypt Muhammad Ali.

But to take matters one by one: in 1833 the island's administrator Said Mehmet asked the Cypriots to pay the remainder of the tax they owed from 1831, when the administrator had been the late Halil Said. The Archbishop had given his consent to this. Then, first in Larnaca and then in Nicosia, protests started up and headed for the Archiepiscopate, demanding of the Archbishop that he intervene for a waiver of the tax and threatening that otherwise they would demolish the Cathedral (Michael 2016: 119). Finally, the Archbishop sought refuge in the *saray* as a demonstration was held outside the Bishopric of Citium. A few days after this event, numerous inhabitants of Nicosia went down to Larnaca and joined ranks with the demonstrators (Michael 2015b: 128). The movement as a whole, in which Nikolaos Thiseas had been recognized as leader, had mobilized between 7,000 and 8,000 Cypriots (Greeks, *linobambaki*, Ottomans, even non-privileged Europeans). After the rally in Larnaca, and following intervention by the French consul Bottu, guarantees were given that the tax would be cancelled. Following this development Thiseas agreed to disband the movement, having extracted the promise of general amnesty. But the Ottoman administrator didn't keep his promise and imposed harsh punishment on those who had participated in the movement. Thiseas had to flee to Rhodes. Probably this stance of the Ottoman administration was due to the fact that not long after the final rally in Larnaca there was a new mobilization in Nicosia with 5,000 people participating, among whom, according to the Ottoman authorities, some were armed (Michael 2015b: 128).

Ioannikios was not discouraged by Thiseas' failure. The two of them must have been in some kind of communication,[67] and a little later he proceeded with his own movement, which had more the character of a national liberation movement, in contrast to that of Thiseas which was more social in content. Ioannikios wanted to liberate his country from the Ottoman yoke[68] and not just cancel the imposition of an unjust tax. The Archbishop of Cyprus did not agree with this aim of Ioannikios and denounced him to the Patriarch of Constantinople, charging that his activity was due to the powerful influence of the French Consul in Larnaca. In any case Ioannikios in the first phase left Larnaca with his Albanian allies (Michail 2015b: 133) and established himself in the village of Trikomo near Famagusta with a view to occupying the city and subsequently extending his operations to the rest of the island, overturning Ottoman rule. But the Sultan's peace agreement with Muhammad Ali

[67] It seems that there was also a collusion between Ioannikios and Gavur Imam for a joint attack in Nicosia (Sakellarios 1890: 587–588; Papapolyviou 2019: 14).

[68] According to the testimony of the English consul "The priest promised them freedom and independence and with this vain slogan flattered them that they [...] would achieve his aim, which was total and riotous revolution" (quoted in Michael 2016: 140).

made available Ottoman troops with the result that this movement too was crushed and its adherents were executed (Pavlidis 1993: 195–196).

Gavur Imam's movement was also social in orientation, breaking out when imposition of tax was imposed, provoking—as we have seen—corresponding unrest in Larnaca and Nicosia. The Imam's activity at first was limited in scope, with its range not extending beyond his village when he and his supporters refused to supply a specific quantity of "paximadi" crackers for consumption by the Turkish army. But after the imposition of the tax that had triggered Thiseas' revolt the Imam expanded his operations and along with his supporters arrested tax collectors, from whom he extracted payment of the *miri* tax (Michail 2016: 129). Soon the Imam had succeeded in gathering considerable forces around himself, mostly Muslims but with lesser numbers of Greeks, and imposing his rule on the entirety of the province of Paphos. He managed to keep control for about three months, recruiting troops with a view to gradual occupation of the whole island. Finally, the forces of the Sultan, who just before had defeated Ioannikios, strengthened by forces which had come from Karamania, broke up the army of Gavur Imam, who fled to Egypt but there he was arrested and sent back to Cyprus, where he was executed.

Despite the real differences between these three movements the fact that they unfolded in the same year should not pass unnoticed and, apart from the tension generated by the taxation measures, they should be seen as linked to the war between the Ottoman Empire and Egypt, a development which aroused hopes in a section of the Cypriot population that they could secede from the Ottoman Empire (Michael 2016: 147). It is interesting that although there was already the example of establishing the newly formed Greek state, it was primarily Muslims and not Orthodox Cypriots, as one would probably expect, that were lured by the relevant prospects. This is probably interpretable on the one hand as reflecting the disappointment experienced by the Greeks of Cyprus is at the negative stance adopted by Capodistrias vis à vis their demand for *enosis* with Greece, and on the other to the fact that the Church, the official political representative of the *rayah*, had not throughout all the time from 1821 onwards, shown any such inclination, and had opposed the uprisings of 1833.

13 The Nineteenth Century Reforms in the Ottoman Empire (*Tanzimat*, *Hatt-i Humayun*) as By-product of the Severe Economic Crisis

The Economic and Geomilitary Crisis

The overall transformations that would be ushered in by the great institutional reforms of the *Tanzimat* and the *Hatt-i Humayun* must be seen from within the perspective of acceleration of the rate of disintegration of the Ottoman Empire. A key element in the chronic *crisis* to which they are the prelude is, after a certain point, the Empire's inability to expand further. As very succinctly indicated by Sugar: "The Ottoman Empire was first and foremost a military state that paid very little attention to trade, commerce, and production and relied on loot as its major source of income. This loot came from the conquest of large territories that were also used to satisfy the military's economic needs by being parceled out as timars. As long as large scale expansion was possible the system worked, but once expansion came to an end problems became unavoidable. Given the nature of Ottoman warfare-the army had to be under the sultan's personal command, and the soldiers had to be released around harvest time to return to their fiefs to collect their incomethe campaign season was limited. It began in the Spring when the roads became passable and ended around harvest time. Only a certain distance could be covered within the time available for military operations, and once the empire's borders reached from the doors of Vienna to Azerbaijan and Iraq movements of armies had reached their limits [...] The Ottoman world was rigid while the West was constantly changing and adapting to the socioeconomic and political requirements of a steadily expanding world whose center it became" (Sugar 1996: 191, 193). Stavrianos aptly observes that the Ottoman economic economy remained at the stage of cottage industry from the technological viewpoint and of the guild from the organizational, at a time when in the West the industrial organization of production was under construction, technology was being deployed and guilds marginalized (Stavrianos 1958: 127).

One consequence of the inability of the Ottoman Empire to expand further was that candidate *timariots* were obliged to wait for the death of incumbent timariots (Itzkowitz 2008: 204). Moreover, the economic crisis ensuing from the "Long War" (1593–1606) between the Ottomans and Austria, the perennial battles with Persia and the sudden increase in the number of *vakifs* exempted from taxation led to great deficits in the state budget (Sugar 1996: 190).[69] To cover the debt lifelong leases had to be taken out in a new form of leasehold, *Ayan*. This marked the emergence of a new social stratum who were gradually transformed into proprietors of state land with the consequence that although up to the mid-seventeenth century more than half of the overall appropriated product had gone to the central state, in the course of the nineteenth century this had fallen to a figure of 30–45% (Vergopoulos 1975: 93). Ignoring the issue of the irregular and non-linear way that this occurred, the result was weakening of the power of the Porte, with the agricultural production carried out on the ciftlicks[70] (the transformed *Ayan* property) to a significant extent linked to the Western capitalist economies, in this way marking the incursion of capitalist pressures into the Ottoman Empire, with concomitant decline of local manufacturing production.

The transformation of state property *Hass* into ciftlicks was characterized by (a) inheritability of the right of possession of ciftlicks (b) concession by cultivators to the ciftlicks of a proportion (from 1/3 to 1/2) of their product—above and beyond their other obligations to the state (c) step-by-step independence of the ciftlicks from the central power (Vergopoulos 1975: 72) (d) the rising monetarization of the economy[71] generated both by increase in the number of transactions between the city and the countryside (owing to specialization in professions and in production and to the growth of cottage industry and handicrafts) and to the proliferation of commercial links with the countries of the West,

[69] Other individual factors can be added to this. For example, the fact that in the first half of the seventeenth century the Dutch reached the West Indies and blocked trade from the Ottoman Empire (Stavrianos 1958: 127).

[70] According to L. Mile: "The ciflick is the means for overcoming timariot inertia. It corresponds to the need for central government to raise new tax revenue and is a means for redistributing for the benefit of the dominant social stratum the increased agricultural product of the eighteenth and nineteenth centuries. The fact that the overwhelming majority of ciflicks are in the hands of the Ottomans indicates that the phenomenon is not result of the free functioning of a market in land but is a process linked to the financial and tax practices of the state and in any case situated in the realm of the dominant national-religious grouping" (Mile as quoted in Louis 2006, Vol. III: 397).

[71] A Panagiotopoulos notes: "Monetisation of the timariot's income in conditions of steady devaluation of currency and an upward trend in the price of agricultural products, the need to finance the dominant stratum in Ottoman society, both tended to favour commercial cropping in agriculture and opened the road that led to the ciflick" (quoted in Louis 2006, Vol III: 391).

one important feature being the export of Ottoman agricultural products because of the population increase in the West (Inalcik 1985: 115; Stavrianos 1958: 140). The *ciflickades* (owners of the *ciflick*) were therefore a hybrid-transitional social stratum in a course towards capitalism which caused problems for reproduction of the classical form of Ottoman rule and this explains how it developed in tandem, and not in competition, up to a certain historical point, with other strata in emergent capitalism (merchants, artisans, shipowners, brokers) (Vergopoulos 1975: 74). In any case the destabilization caused by the appearance of the ciflicks was not so much *quantitative* as, first and foremost, *qualitative* in character. This was because beyond a specific conjuncture ciflick relations of land ownership encountered capitalist social relations, laying the basis for predominance of the capitalist mode of production on the territory of the Ottoman Empire. They were the response to international market demand, prioritizing provision of products on the (internal and external) market, which induced the *ciflickades* to turn to the cultivation of crops for which there was a strong demand. These were commodities (cereals, olive oil, cotton, wine) conducive to an intensive labour economy. This, taken together with the transformation of free cultivators into sharecroppers (*koligoi*), led to them working twice as much, in terms of both time and intensity. The reason for this is that once the cultivator was obliged to hand half of the gross product of a field over to a *ciflickas* he had to work twice as many hours as a free farming family (Stoianovich 1980: 180–181).

In any case, the strengthening of the Ayan and emergence of ciflick relations in land ownership were just one aspect of the destabilization of the central state (Karpat 1972: 251). To it must be added sale to contractors of the right to collect taxes, the growing refusal of the *Sipahi* to join the expeditionary corps, the peasant insurrections of the seventeenth century which in various forms continued into the eighteenth and nineteenth, leading to concession, on a case-by-case basis, of rights to the rural population,[72] but also developments of geostrategic character: throughout all the period extending from the second siege

[72] Just in the Greek lands Constantinos Sathas mentions that between 1565 and 1821 more than twenty big agrarian uprisings were recorded, meaning at least one significant revolt every 12 or 13 years. In parallel in the forms of resistance there should be included the generalization of the phenomenon of the mountain bandits, who many times participated actively in the rural insurrections (Vergopoulos 1975: 83; 85).

of Vienna (1683) to the Treaty of Jassy (1792) the Ottoman state suffered major losses, including territory in Hungary, Greece, Transylvania, Bukovina, the northern shores of the Black Sea and Crimea. Finally, national independence struggles broke within the Ottoman Empire, overturning internal power balances (Berberoglu 1982: 2). One important factor that contributed to these military reverses has to do with the Ottoman Empire's decision to establish its capital in Constantinople. This meant objectively that its potential for expansion went as far as Vienna at most because owing to existing production needs the Ottoman cavalry was disbanded each October and the Ottoman army was not fast enough to cover the distances in less time. On the other hand, the decision to portray itself as defender of Islam precluded the Ottomans from moving their capital westwards because such a move would complicate the defence of Mecca, which was under threat not only from the Portuguese but also from the Safavides of Persia (Itzkowitz 2008: 208).

As regards the economy, the basic problem was that the increased volume of trade between Europe and the Ottoman Empire had a negative impact on the latter's manufacturing industry. Faced with high production costs because of the absence of a capitalization process,[73] and with strict price fixing rules, the Ottoman guilds could not compete with clearly cheaper European products. Because of the capitulations these products were imported without tariffs and the situation was worsened by the constant devaluation of the Ottoman currency.[74] At the same time expansion of the activities of European capital led to its delinkage from imports of Ottoman manufactured products, with resultant significant change in trade relations. Specifically, England had until recently been an importer of textile products from the East, but it was subsequently itself transformed into an exporter of these commodities. In 1828 the value of cotton fabrics exported from England to the Ottoman Empire was only £10,834 sterling. In 1829 it went to £39,920, in 1830 to £95,355 and in 1831 to £105,615. In other words, the value of imports from

[73] A fact largely attributable to the "closed" and conservative character of the Ottoman Empire, which appeared hostile towards every kind of innovation (Itzkowitz 2008: 205–206).

[74] Characteristically in 1697 a Venetian sequin was the equivalent of 2.5 piastres but 100 years later (1797) it was worth 7.5 piastres. That is to say, in the course of a century it had been devalued by 200% (Ioannou 1996: 189).

Britain increased tenfold in four years. The tendency for European expansion into the interior of the Ottoman Empire was increased even further after the Anglo-Ottoman Treaty of 1838, which conceded the right of extra-territoriality to foreign merchants and abolished state protectionism and state monopolies. So, from a position of supplying almost all British textile imports in 1825, thirty years later Ottoman exports comprised no more than an infinitesimal fraction of them (1,506 kilos) (Berberoglu 1982: 3). In contrast, British exports of cotton fabrics increased from 15,846,678 metres in 1835 to 121,254,439 metres in 1855, imports of silken fabrics increased from 20,898 kilos in 1835 to 599,148 kilos in 1855 and imports of woollen fabrics increased from 52,819 kilos in 1835 to 906,602 kilos in 1855. At the same time production at the Ottoman spinning mills and textile plant went into a rapid decline: In Albania, the number of looms in operation fell from 600 in 1812 to 40 in 1821, in Tirnova from 2,000 in 1812 to 200 in 1830, in Bursa from 1,000 to 75, with a reduction in the use of raw silk from 25,000 okkas to 4,000 okkas. As indicated by Berberoglu, from whom the remaining data is also extracted, according to the Report of the Industrial Improvement Commission published in 1868, the number of cloth-producing looms in Constantinople and Uskudar in the preceding 30 or 40 years had contracted from 2,750 to 25, the number of braced looms from 350 to 4 and the number of upholstery silk looms from 60 to 8.

The final conclusion is that the process of disintegration of Ottoman manufacturing had started in the sector of textiles from the early nineteenth century; this had a catalytic effect on other sectors through a number of decades with the result that at the end of the nineteenth century the Ottoman Empire had reached the verge of economic collapse (Berberoglu 1982: 3). The solution that was chosen for rescuing the Ottoman economy was a resort to borrowing from abroad. The first loan was negotiated in 1854 and by 1877 the nominal public debt was £190,977,980 sterling (plus interest, which came to £61,803,905) with annual outlay for repayment of interest and capital amounting to £12 million, or more than half of national income. By 1877 the Ottoman state was not in a position to service this excessive debt and was obliged to declare bankruptcy. An so it was that in 1881, under European tutelage, the Ottoman Public Debt Administration was created to raise money to pay off the loans. As the nineteenth century progressed, by the time all these developments had run their course, the Ottoman "Empire" had been transformed into a semi-protectorate of the European Great Powers (Berberoglu 1982: 4).

On the geostrategic plane the establishment of the independent Greek state (1830) opened a significant rift in the Empire. A little later the Crimean War (1853–1856) served to confirm the fashionable characterization of the Ottoman Empire as "the sick man of Europe". Irrespective of the final outcome—the defeat of the Russians by the alliance of the British, the French and the Austrians—from the beginning of the war the Ottomans saw their Fleet destroyed by the Russians. The Russian defeat led not to the renaissance of the Ottomans' Empire but to the essential custodianship of the victorious powers over them.

All these processes we have just described were the causes of the great institutional rifts of 1839 (*Tanzimat*) and 1856 (*Hatt-i Humayun*) as two attempts at modernizing the Ottoman state, solving its problems and adapting to the new realities being ushered in by capitalism's international spring.

The Reforms of Tanzimat *(Reorganization)*

At the level of the central political scene, the *Tanzimat* reform (1839) signified an attempt to achieve two objectives: on the one hand the overturn of the existing system of taxation and tax collection, and accordingly reduction in the power of the *Ayan*, and on the other the establishment of a uniform mechanisms of political and administrative control based to a considerable extent on institutional reform of the *millet* system in such a way that they would function as mechanisms for integration of its members into political processes (Louis 2013: 97). Concentration of centralized power on the institutional level was based on reorganization of the administrative model: the provinces (eyelet) with the Wāli as governor-general were divided into districts (sanjak) with the muhassil-iemval as administrator and the districts into counties (kaza), and counties into subdistricts (nahiye), in their turn comprised of villages (karye). Each official who undertook to govern these administrative divisions was accountable not only to his superior but also centrally, in Constantinople. In this way the central administration was strengthened and local officials weakened. The establishment of Councils also played an important role in the limiting of local power. Specifically, in the big administrative units there was the administrative council (Meclisi-Iidare), which co-ordinated the activities of the individual areas. The governor participated in this, as did the heads of the provinces and six (three Muslims and three non-Muslims) chosen residents (Shaw and Shaw 1977: 89). At the level of the Sanjaks large councils (buyuk milletmeclisi) were established and at the level of the kaza small councils (kucuk milletmeclisi). The large councils had 13 members, seven of whom were ex officio (among them was a representative of the Orthodox). The small councils had a five-member composition: a representative of the Muhassil in the kaza (the vekil)—who presided over the council, the local Kadi, the local police chief and two notables, one Muslim and the other non-Muslim. The issues submitted by the small to the large councils were required to have the approval of the Muhassil. The shift in the presidency of the small councils from the Kadi to the Vekil epitomizes the attempt to secularize the Ottoman state (Dionyssiou 2009: 62–63) and one significant difference from the previously established local councils (divans) is that in the latter there was not always representation of non-Muslims and they were also of quite limited political and administrative importance (Michael 2015a: 111–112). These local councils held frequent meetings—twice or three times a week—and discussed administrative issues, at the same time submitting proposals for approval to the provincial councils on economic matters for which the provincial councils would make the final decisions. It should also be noted that the provincial councils adjudicated civil, financial and judicial disagreements as well as taxation fraud and other violations of the Tanzimat's institutional framework. Only questions of robbery and murder were referred to the central administration (Inalick 1973a: 100–101). The council of *elders* (ihtiyar Meclisi) remained at the lower level of local self-government, that of the community. There each millet elected its own council of elders and its head (muhtar). The electorate was comprised of men who were Ottoman subjects, above the age of 18, and having paid a specific sum in direct tax (Shaw and Shaw 1977: 90).

Another dimension of the effort to concentrate power and weaken every species of provincial notable was the transference of administration of the local Evakf away from the local ulema and their submission to the control of a secular administration answerable to the Evakf Ministry (Nevzat-Hatay 2009: 913–914). Finally, one important aspect of the reforms was abolition of the leasing out of taxation. Tax collection, but also the dispatch of tax revenues to the Ottoman administration, was now undertaken by a state instrumentality, which channelled the entirety of the proceeds to the state coffers.

But the limits of these reforms were not long in appearing. On the economic plane as early as 1842 Reshid Pasha, who was the architect of the Tanzimat, began to see the difficulties with it. Budget deficits began to increase due to the low level of efficiency of the tax collection mechanism. It was hampered by staff shortages because of the low salary levels being budgeted, but also by reaction from the social layers affected (Inalick 1973a: 107). Reshid was obliged to return to the system of leasing out of taxation (Kostis 1991: 69–70). There were corresponding administrative changes: the governor-general (Wali) re-assumed the powers he had in the pre-*Tanzimat* period; to facilitate execution of their new duties the Muhassil were replaced by military administrators (murif) and the governor of the kaza (vekil) by their subordinates (ferik). The official title of the administrator of the Sanjaks became the Kaymakam, dependent on the Wali, and the kaza governors were named mudurs. In the relatively small Kazas the councils were abolished and in larger places the members were not elected but appointed by the Kaymakam (Dionysiou 2009: 67). On the more strategic level, although with the establishment of the councils initially and subsequently with the law on vilaetia (see below) intervention by the central government seemed to be strengthening (see below), in a second phase it became clear that the situation was inherently contradictory, because it was creating the conditions for cancellation of the goal of the reform, which was reproduction of Ottoman rule, given that it was creating the conditions for legitimation of quasi-nationalities which shortly afterwards would try to transform themselves into state entities.[75]

Specifially on implementation of the *Tanzimat* in Cyprus, in 1838 Sultan Mahmud II issued a ferman in accordance with which Cyprus was transferred from the administration of the Kapudan Pasha to that of the province of the islands of the Archipelago as a separate Sanjak attached to the Pashalik of Rhodes. The new administrator of the island was called the Mutasarrif and presided over the Great Council, in which Christians

[75] From this viewpoint it is interesting to examine the views of two Turkish social scientists, Karpat and Oba. Karpat argues that "The centralization policy pursued through the Tanzimat reforms started as a search for mean to create one unified Ottoman nation and ended by stimulating the national awakening of all religious and ethnic groups, including the Turks and Arabs". In the same vein Oba observes that "In a way the 'Tanzimat' assisted the collapse of the Ottoman State, by failing to satisfy the peasantry and contributing to their development of national consciousness" (cited by Nevzat 2005: 88).

were represented by the Archbishop and the notables (Louis 2006, Vol II: 15). He was a salaried employee of the central administration and did not derive his income from leasing taxation franchises because that system was being terminated. He bore the title of Kaymakam and was paid an annual salary of 120,000 kurus. He was selected for appointment by officers of the army, the administrative services or the ministries. The Porte was attempting in this way to modernize its structures, curbing the abuses that had been seen for many decades, if not centuries. All political, fiscal and administrative questions of the island were placed under the jurisdiction of the administrator.

Above and beyond that, at the level of overall administration on the island, the High Council was established, headquartered in Nicosia, and the District Councils. The High Council met once a week and was comprised of[76] the island's administrator, the Mutasarrif, the Mufti, the Molla (high-ranking judge), the Muhasebeci (responsible for finances), the director of the land registry, the director of waqf property, the Archbishop and the six laymen elected by the communities, three Christians and three Muslims. The 12 district councils[77] were presided over by the local Kaymakam (that is to say the head of the region), the local Kadi, the functionaries in the local land registry and waqf property offices, the Metropolitan of the region, the local Christian *kocabasi* and four laymen elected by the communities: two Christian and two Muslim (Michael 2005: 146). There was provision for establishment of a Juridical council as well in every region, presided over by the Kadi, and provision for election of presidents for small local councils, the Mukhbir for the Christian, and the Mukhtar for the Muslim, communities.[78] Their duties

[76] For a more detailed presentation of the respective changes to the composition of the High Council see (Michael 2015a: 114–115).

[77] For the respective changes to the composition of the district councils see Michael (2015a: 116).

[78] From what we know if a village was inhabited exclusively by one community, or a community didn't include more than 30 people, one mukhtar or mukhbir was elected/nominated. In the event of the village being inhabited by more than 30 people of the other community, a mukhtar or mukhbir was also elected/appointed for the other community (Melamid 1956: 364). This information makes it clear that the division between the two communities was deep and had a history to it. And to it there must be added the different historical conceptions that pervaded the two communities by virtue of their education.

included safeguarding the local seal, collecting certain taxes and finding accommodation for officials visiting the region (Michael 2005: 265–266).

At the level of self-government of the Christian millet it was provided for Cyprus that the Archbishop and the three Metropolitans should summon the most judicious citizens from each town to a general meeting where there would be a discussion of the common problems and corresponding decisions would be taken. A twenty-member Committee of the Public was established, with eight participating members from Nicosia and eight from Larnaca-Skala and four from Limassol. The role of the committee was control of the central and local councils of elders and support for socially beneficial activities (particularly in health and public education). The members of the central council of elders and the provincial councils of elders were elected by the residents of the capital of each province with the consent of the Archbishop for Nicosia and of the Metropolitans for each of the remaining cities. The essential role of all these representative bodies was to function as advisors to the Archbishop or Metropolitan, these being the political representatives of the Greek Cypriots (Maratheftis 1982: 147–148).

Seen as a whole, as far as the position of the Church is concerned, what should be emphasized is that through these reforms the central government was attempting to place limits on the privileges of the church hierarchy in the interests of a mode of state organization more adapted to Western conceptions. The church hierarchy therefore appeared to be losing some of its competences relative to its flock, and above all its authority to collect taxes. Nevertheless, my position is that this was not the primary aspect of the reforms. What is essential is that the Church was recognized as the official organ of dominance, at a secondary level, over the Orthodox subjects of the Ottoman state. In other words, the ecclesiastical structure was incorporated into the Ottoman administrative machinery, investing the hierarchy with the status of official state functionaries, and not each prelate on an individual basis (Louis 2013: 96). To put it somewhat differently, prior to the changes these churchmen were regarded as individuals participating in an administrative mechanism but now they represented an *administrative mechanism of the Ottoman state,* the Church (Michael 2009: 230). The Orthodox Church was transformed into a department of the Ottoman polity (Michael 2005: 266). At the same time there was also extensive involvement of church mechanisms in the election of laymen. Because of their influence they could have a significant effect on the relevant selection of persons. What should be underlined is that the overall transformation of the Ottoman economy contributed to the consummation during the same period of more comprehensive changes to the economic role of the Orthodox Church. Thus the beginnings, for the reasons indicated, of liberalization of the Ottoman economy had the consequence of enabling Ottoman subjects who were Christians to lease and to exploit, i.e. to be allotted, ciftliks. The result was that the Orthodox Church, but also Cypriot Christian private citizens, became very actively involved in leasing and farming great expanses of land, and after a certain point, around 1860, foreign economic actors would take up the same activity (Louis 2006, Vol. III: 402–403).

The Hatt-i Humayun (Autonomy Charter)

The deepening of the elements of crisis already described, in conjunction with the exposure of military weakness, as became evident in the Crimean War, generated the need for new institutional reform. So the decree of 1856, *Hatt-i Humayun*, merely served to confirm the changes in the international balance of power brought about by the attempt to modernize and westernize aspects of Ottoman state functioning. On the one hand these changes expanded the rights of non-Ottoman citizens to pursue economic activity inside the Empire, permits the foundation of banks, there was codification of penal and commercial law and elements were introduced of French commercial and maritime law. At the same time strict monitoring was imposed of budget expenditures and change was promoted in the existing regime for the functioning of prisons. On the other hand recognition was accorded to the protection of Christian populations; more opportunities were provided for them to embark on activities of development and improvement of their living standards, the poll tax was abolished and provision was made for appointment of non-Muslims also in public administration and the judicial sector, not to mention military service so that it would be clear that a regime of equal treatment was in force on questions of justice and education (Karpat 1972: 259).

In terms of administration, the Empire was divided into provinces which were called vilayets, instead of eyalets, and were governed by the valis. The provinces were subdivided into regions called sanjaks and they were administered by mutassarifs. The regions were further divided into kazas, administered by kaymakams. The kazas were divided into nahiyes, which were administered by mudurs, with towns and villages administered by councils of elders (ihtiyarmeclisi), presided over by mukhtars. The vali, the kaymakam and the mudurs were appointed by the Sultan but the mukhtars were popularly elected. At the same time a number of councils were established at the three basic levels of administration. The administrative councils (meclis-iidare) were attached to the vilayet. Sanjak and kaza governors dealt with political, fiscal and economic questions. These councils were comprised of ex officio members who were Muslim, state officials and intellectual leaders of the non-Muslims at the sanjak and kaza level. These intellectual leaders ceased to be members of the vilaet council. Two Muslims and two non-Muslims were elected to the vilaet and kaza councils. Finally, a general meeting (meclis-Iumumi) was convened in the capital of every vilayet, to which the four elected members, two Muslims and two non-Muslims, were elected by the sanjaks of the vilayet (Dionyssiou 2009: 82–83).

From 1872 onwards Cyprus was divided into 5 kaymakamliks, each with two councils, the administrative (meclis-iidare) and the judicial (meclis-idava). The administrative council of Nicosia was comprised of the governor, the Kadi, the Mufti, the Muhasebeci, the evkaf-inaziri (director of evkaf properties), the catib (the director of the real estate registry), three Muslims, three Christians and the Archbishop as ex officio member. In 1876 there would be a change and it would now be comprised of 8 Muslims and 3 Christians, and the councils in each kaymakamlik were comprised of 5 Muslims and three Christians (Dionyssiou 2009: 84–85).

At about the same time we have the establishment of mayoralties in Nicosia and other cities. The mayoralty of Nicosia was comprised of a Muslim president who was appointed by the governor, and six members, three Christians and three Muslims, elected separately by the two communities. In the other towns there was a Muslim president and four members, two Christians and two Muslims elected in the same way (Maratheftis 1982: 149). In the villages, in those inhabited by the Christian community they continued to elect a small council with a president who was called the Mukhbir and in those inhabited by the Muslim community the Mukhtar presided (Louis 2013: 96).

14 The Shaping of the Emergent Cypriot Bourgeois Class[79]

The transition of the Cypriot social formation to the capitalist mode of production is inseparably linked to the more general developments taking place in the European continent with the emergence of the industrial revolution and the appearance of a new economic relationship between East and West. What happened was a proliferation of economic channels from and to the East. Raw materials were transported to the West, subjected to industrial processing and then sold back to the East in the form of industrial commodities. Cyprus, in parallel, was an important transfer point towards Europe for products from the Ottoman Empire (Rizopoulou-Egoumenidou 1996: 196). To illustrate the dimension of the phenomenon I merely mention that from the mid-eighteenth century approximately 600 merchant ships, mainly from France, England and Holland, but also from other European countries, entered Cypriot ports with cargoes of agricultural and stockbreeding products (Michael 2005: 203–204).

The situation intensified at the turn of the nineteenth century when Western trading companies competed to maximize their penetration in trade between East and West. A key role in this competition was played by the consulates, something which should not seem strange. The European states had as official policy the operation of their consulates for the facilitation of commercial transactions with the Ottoman Empire. It is characteristic that by 1872 there were 13 consulates in Larnaca,[80] with 73 diplomats working at them, as well as local staff. These diplomats were not there to protect the interests of their fellow citizens who lived

[79] Let it be noted here that obviously there can be no comparison with the evolution of the bourgeoisie in the countries of the West. The bourgeois strata in nineteenth century Cyprus were mostly merchants and small-scale producers, with social categories with a reproductive role in the social relations of capitalism (lawyers, engineers) as participants in the system of domination. The contribution of the latter was decisive for the shaping of a precocious framework of capitalist productive relations (legitimation/promotion through imposition of a capitalist character on various economic sectors) and should not be confused with the clearly subordinate role such strata played in the developed form of capitalism.

[80] These 13 consulates represented Austria, the USA, Belgium, Denmark, France, Britain, Greece, Holland, Italy, Prussia, Russia, Spain and Sweden. Of them seven were headed by consuls and six by sub-consuls (Konstantinides 2011: 53).

in Cyprus, who in any case were very few in number. The decisive reason was the development of trade.

The great expansion of trade can be seen in the Cypriot trade balance: between 1854 and 1858 exports amounted to £131,110 and imports £57,939. A few years later, in 1877. £93,803 worth of exports £41,290 of imports went through the harbour of Limossol alone. The same year total exports from Larnaca were £150,918 λίρες and total imports £105,277 λίρες (Aristeidou 1984: 59–60). For Larnaca in particular the existing data indicates that the total number of ships' arrivals in its harbour went from 320 in 1854 to reach 715 in 1858, signifying a 65% rise. The significant role of Cypriot trade is evident from the fact that European merchants could obtain Cypriot products, which were much in demand in the European states, from the markets of Smyrna, Alexandria, Constantinople and Thessaloniki. This notable European demand has to do with the qualitative advantage of Mediterranean farming and stockbreeding products, which were called upon to cover the needs of the West, left uncovered through the growth of industrial capitalism (Michael 2003: 59–60).

The Levant Company, which made available Cypriot products on European markets and imported industrial products to the island: felt, coffee, paper, iron, steel, tin, and everyday household items, was particularly influential in the Cypriot economy. The English consuls were themselves representatives of the Company in Cyprus (Konstantinides 2011: 54). In the Company's regulations, which were published in 1800, it stipulated that the consuls of Great Britain in Cyprus who were involved in commerce could keep up to 2% of the value of all products marketed (Michael 2003: 59). At the same time, they were also active as moneylenders. According to what is reported by Konstantinides, a characteristic example is one of the British consuls lending at 20% and appropriating the interest in silk, wine, cotton, corn and other products. They then sold these products, reaping profits of at least 30% and if they didn't receive the money on the prescribed date they were able to confiscate the property of the debtor (Konstantinides 2011: 54). Other activities of the consuls were to lease from the state the right to collect taxes, which they then deposited, either as bills of exchange or in kind, or in cash. In the first case they enjoyed the advantage of being able to channel the cash into other more profitable activities, in the second they handed over a proportion of the quantities of products they had received from taxpayers and marketed the rest.[81]

The products that are produced in Cyprus and were later sold abroad by the merchants were mostly wine, cotton, silk, oil, but also salt, wool, fabrics, tar, legumes, cereals, animal skins, animals. An important role in agricultural development was played by the fact of transition from the classical timariot system, dominated by fragmented individualized production, to the time when ciflicks made their appearance, these being essentially large farming and stockbreeding units (Michael 2003: 56–57). The greater part of the exports was destined for the Ottoman Empire, France, England, Russia, Austria, Italy and Greece. But in tandem with the increase in exports went an increase in imports of finished industrial products mostly manufactured in Western countries: tools, cooking utensils, nails, maps, fabrics and certain types of food. All of these were imported from England, France, Italy and Austria, but also from Turkey and Greece (Aristeidou 1984: 60).

The entrepreneurial consuls were aided and abetted by Greek Cypriots who initially worked as translators but subsequently because of their involvement with trading circles succeeded in embarking on independent business activity. As employees of the foreign consular agencies within the institutional framework determined by the Capitulations they enjoyed privileges and special treatment from the Ottoman authorities (Michael 2003: 61). It is characteristic that while in the period between 1744 and 1756 there was no Cypriot presence at all, between 1776 and 1781 38.33% of trade was in the hands of locals and 61.67% owned by foreigners (Ioannou 1996: 266, 312, 316). So, a new social category was created, in which merchants living in cities with harbours were participants (Larnaca, Limassol). Unlike the situation on the coast, trade in the hinterland of Cyprus was decidedly underdeveloped because of the non-existence of a transportation network, given that until the end of the nineteenth century the only carriage road was that between Nicosia and Larnaca (Aristeidou 1984: 60).

[81] But on the other hand the absence of an organized banking system was particularly noticeable because for their transactions with Europe, merchants were obliged to resort to Beirut, which meant delays, additional expenses and numerous dangers (Aristeidou 1984: 60).

In this context the rise of the social stratum of Greek-speaking Christian merchants became increasingly clear as they continued their steady economic ascent. In the nineteenth century the Christian merchants would have reached the position of having the entirety of the Cyprus export trade under their control, with cotton, wine and sesame as their chief products, in that way achieving clear economic superiority over the Muslims.

This development was not, of course, attributable to some metaphysical supremacy of the Christian population but to the fact that the more educated elements in the Muslim population were oriented more towards occupying a position in the state machine, thereby leaving a space in the economy to the advantage of Christians. The reason for this was that initially appointment of non-Muslims was forbidden and subsequently, after the lifting of the ban, there continued to be a preference for Muslims in manning the army and staffing the administration and the judicial institutions (it is indicative that in 1872 there were only 26 Greek Cypriots in public administration, and they were in subordinate positions). On the other hand, Christians were not subjected to moral and religious stigma in relation to managing money, comparable to those applying with Muslims, who regarded such activities as undignified (Milios 2000: 248; Polis 1979: 57; Irakleidis 2006: 257). This was a typical cultural stance of Muslims when co-existing with entrepreneurially more active non-Muslim communities, one characteristic example being that of Malaysia, with the lifestyle of the Muslim Malaysians in contrast to that of their Indian and Chinese compatriots (Irakleidis 2006: 269).

An important role in that economic supremacy was played by the fact of difference in educational level[82] vis à vis the Muslim element—a difference in part due to the priority set by the Orthodox Church with its funding of education but also to the fact that Muslims were suspicious of educational issues as providing an opening for the demons of innovation (Irakleidis 2006: 257). A contribution to this was also made by the Ottoman administration's policy of non-interference in such issues, which they saw as internal matters of the Christian community. And so it was that from the mid-eighteenth century, with the permission of the authorities, that Christian schools were established; in fact, the authorities allowed the entry of teachers from what was to be Greece proper in order

[82] The subjects taught at the Greek schools were Ancient Greek, mathematics, geography, religion, history, physics, French and Turkish (Papadopoulos 2011: 390).

to improve the educational level of the island (Gazioglou 1990: 196). And this in contrast to the education provided for the Muslim population, which was confined to the elementary level or oriented towards education for administrative employees—at a time when the emphasis in education of the Orthodox was on developing skills for later engagement in trade or the liberal professions (Attalides 1979: 42).

That said, the Church which is involved in all the previous activities, undoubtedly played a promotional role in the development of capitalism in Cyprus. It traded in precious metals, primarily for manufacturing sacred vessels, and exporting products produced on its lands, with the Common Funds functioning as credit reserves and a part of its capital being invested in leasing real estate (Michael 2005: 210–211).

Another section of the indigenous bourgeoisie was the section connected with managing monastery property, such as the representatives of the wealthy monasteries in the cities and countryside and those collecting tax following the assignment of this task to the Church.

Other sections of the bourgeoisie were money changers-jewellers, landowners who cultivated grain or bred livestock, and capitalists who lent their capital as an investment or for the leasing of shops and mills (Michael 2005: 210).

The ultimate social outcome was creation of a commercial bourgeoisie which successfully eroded the traditional structures of the Cypriot economy, breaking up the regime of own-consumption, establishing fiscal circles which elaborated the conditions for transition to a monetized economy (Michael 2005: 210).

15 The Emergence and the Transformation of the Differences between the Two Communities

From what has been mentioned already, up until the early nineteenth century three institutional factors appear to have paved the way for the later national differences. One has to do with the existence of taxes which were paid only by Christians and amounted to one third of total taxation. It is only natural that this situation would generate growing dissatisfaction, the more so because changing one's religion (a practice adopted by certain Christians) led to exemption from these taxes.[83] Secondly the fact that until the mid-nineteenth century Muslim officials bought their positions led to practices of overexploitation of Christians of every layer, for whom there was no such possibility for making this type of "investment" seem feasible. This situation reinforced the differences which, although ostensibly attributable to religion, in reality had more to do with relations of exploitation and domination, and were conducive, albeit secondarily, to impelling the Christian social strata towards adopting different economic practices (trade) which proved more lucrative (Pavlides 1993: 16–17). Thirdly there were also specific legal differences: Until 1878 in the administration of every region there was a Muslim majority, the Muslims had the upper hand in the composition of the courts and the Orthodox, for most of the Ottoman period, could not even testify as a witness. Moreover Christians could not bear arms and were legally obliged to behave with respect towards Muslims (Apeyitou 2003: 69, 90–91; Attalides 1979: 38–39).

Despite all this, until at least the beginning of the nineteenth century there was no active strife between the two communities, precisely because there had been no convergence of the factors that would trigger an explosion of the already existing conflicts. Moreover, the absence of a stable reference point (the existence of a concrete state entity) for the Christian element inhibited the emergence of national differentiation.

But in the course of the nineteenth century the appearance of three new factors would lead events onto a different course. To be specific, this has to do with (a) the adoption of a common national identity by the Greek-speaking Christians of the Ottoman Empire, which was initially a result of the Greek Enlightenment and consequently of formulating the demand for an independent Greek state. This prospect was the basis for the Greek Revolution, which was supported by the rural population too, above and beyond the intellectuals and the merchants. The peasant cultivators on the one hand were experiencing serious economic exploitation, from which they wished to be freed, and on the other thought that this could be achieved by overthrowing Ottoman power and creating a new state with fellow-religionists speaking the same language (b) establishment of the independent Greek state together with its continual extension

[83] According to another source the tax differences between Christians and Muslims were much greater than a third. Kyrris mentions that in 1806 wealthy Greeks *paid* 70 Kurus tax per capita, the poor paid 40 and Muslims only 7.5 (Kyrris 1985: 279).

through annexation of the Ionian islands (1862) and Thessaly (1881) and elaboration of the ideology of the *Megali Idea* (Great Scope). The latter involved the strategy of creating a Greater Greece incorporating all the Greek-speaking Orthodox populations of the Ottoman Empire and the territories inhabited by them (c) elimination of the Asiatic mode of production and transition to the capitalist system—a development which consigned the Muslim element to an economically disadvantaged position, given their non-involvement in commercial activities (d) the assignment of Cyprus to the British, a change which had the following consequences for relations between the two communities: (i) for the first time in three centuries the Muslims found themselves without the clear support of central government, unlike the Orthodox, who even before 1878 were in the position of not enjoying such support (ii) in their efforts to tame the Greek element, which was beginning to demand *Enosis* with Greece and by extension the end of British rule, the British proceeded to create an internal regime which disproportionately privileged the Muslim minority.

16 Conclusion

The conquest of Cyprus by the Ottomans would mark the transition to the Asiatic mode of production. This development would have one consequence which, though initially of secondary significance, would later become an organic element in the system of domination. This was the upgraded reactivation of the Orthodox Church. Organized in *millet*, the Ottoman Empire would need the church hierarchy in order to be able to administer the island effectively.

The first period of Ottoman rule would be characterized by a plethora of failed uprisings whose aim was to restore the previous regime. But they were merely remnants of a past which in reality had been left behind. The new territories and the appearance of the first elements of capitalist organization turned the attention of the West in new directions.

In any case the Ottoman Empire itself would, after the conquest of Heraklion in 1669, begin to perceive the limits of its power. It was up against two serious problems: on the one hand the proper administration of all this vast empire was becoming impossible, with the result that autonomist movements were breaking out and phenomena of quasi expropriation of state lands were being observed. On the other hand, the first forms of vertical integration of productive processes in the

West led to penetration of Western commodities into the East, causing macro-economic problems.

In the particular case of Cyprus the Sublime Porte tried to solve the problem of tax collection through delegation of those duties to the Cypriot Church. And so it was that integration of the Church into State became an observable reality.

It was in this context of crisis of Ottoman power that the Vogiatzoglou insurrection came as the first of the revolts of the new period. It did not aim at restoring a past (Venetian rule) that no longer existed but sought the fulfillment of autonomist tendencies generated by the prevailing bad economic situation on the island. The defeat of Vogiatzoglou would lead to reorganization within the Ottoman regime, with an upgrading of the role of the island's administrator. In this way an alliance was created between administrator and the Orthodox hierarchy with a view to ensuring orderly reproduction of the system, but also the provision of economic benefits for the Church.

Perpetuation of the crisis of the Ottoman Empire had as one of its consequences, in the mid-eighteenth century, a further promotion of the church hierarchy, with Cypriot churchmen recognized as Kodjabashis. This was something significantly different from the situation in mainland Greece, where the Kodjabashis were a separate stratum, secular in character, giving rise to primary relations of popular representation, and it was a difference that proved decisive for further developments. A key factor behind its emergence was the prominent position occupied by the Church, which was without question a much more important factor than the bourgeois newcomers.

One thing to be noted about the Ottoman Empire was the never-ending conspiracies and intrigues within the Palace, with the result that at any given time the filling of the positions of both Muhassil and Archbishop were influenced by them and it was also particularly important whether the island was under the direction of the Grand Vizier or the Kapudan Pasha. In any case the exercise of power quite frequently provoked discontent in the inhabitants, Christian and Muslim alike, the more so when it was accompanied by an increase in taxation. At the same time, the steady weakening of central government because of the underlying and advancing crisis of the Ottoman state (economic as well as geostrategic), multiplied the opportunities for the development of autonomist movement and/or social revolts. For a long period of time both communities participated in these revolts.

But things would begin to change when the Christian community, on the one hand, began to develop economically and on the other, started to create for itself elements of Greek national consciousness influenced by the current of Greek enlightenment. This would lead us to the events of 1804 but also to the massacre of the notables in 1821, events dramatically emphasizing the differences between the two communities. Subsequently, with the development of the Greek revolution and the creation of the independent Greek state the acquisition of a Greek national identity by the Greek-speaking Cypriots would greatly intensify.

But apart from the local developments, from the 1830s onwards there would be an attempt centrally by the Ottoman Empire to secularize and to modernize political institutions and relations of representation, to be systematized in the *Tanzimat* and *aHatt-iHumayun* reforms. In Cyprus, in particular, there would be specialized policies aimed at eradicating the abuses perennially visited upon the Cypriots, while at same time an attempt was made to put a brake on the privileges of the church hierarchy in the interests of a more Western type of organization. But in my opinion this is not what is important. The important thing about these reforms is that for the first time the church hierarchy was seen as part of the official State functioning. One caveat, however: it did not simply have State-relevant duties as in the past: it was a sector of the State with ex officio participation in the administrative institutions of the State.

These changes proceeded in tandem with extension of the dynamic of a rising Greek Cypriot bourgeoisie. The geographic position of Cyprus facilitated its use as a commercial hub and a significant role in that was played by the foreign diplomatic delegations, which conducted openly commercial operations. At their side linguistically educated Greek Cypriots began to acquire expertise. In a subsequent phase the Greek Cypriots began themselves to occupy consular and sub-consular positions and as a result to become active participants in trade circles. The Muslims were unable to follow suit. They were impelled more towards farming activity and staffing the public sector and their education did not make things easy for them, because it was centred on studying the Koran.

My position is that by the time of Cyprus' being ceded to the British the conditions had been created that later dictated the emergence of two different and separate communities. Differences had existed since the beginnings of the Ottoman occupation given that the Christians were obliged to pay the *jizye* and were subjected to certain other forms of discrimination. Subsequently the fact of the Church hierarchy's being accorded special favour and playing a clearly economic role had an alienating effect on the feelings of the Muslims, who experienced Orthodox economic oppression in a regime of Ottoman rule. But the real breach would come with the Greek Enlightenment and the gradual emergence of the Greek national identity in areas inhabited by Greek-speaking Christians. The outbreak of the Greek Revolution and the prospect of an independent Greek state within which the compulsions of the Ottoman administration would not apply made a decisive contribution to the mass adoption of the *ανήκειν* (belonging) to the Greek nation by the Greek-speaking farming strata also. It is in this way that the mass participation of Cypriot Christians in the Greek Revolution becomes explicable. Essentially with the Greek Revolution and the establishment of the Greek state the separate national character of the Cypriot Orthodox Christians is consolidated. But it was a development that did not lead to formulation of the demand for *Enosis* until the arrival on the island of the British. This was attributable firstly to the integrative effectiveness of the Ottoman administrative system, which was exercised by the Orthodox Church, secondly because the military presence of the Ottomans on the island precluded such aspirations and thirdly because the bourgeois strata that might lead such a strategy had not yet sufficiently emerged.

References

Anagnostopoulou, S. 2002. Les rapports de l' Eglise Orthodoxe avec le Kapudan Pacha (fin du XVIIIeme debut XIXeme siècle). In *The Kapudhna Pasha, His Office and His Domain*, ed. E. Zachariadou, 265–289. Rethymnon: Crete University Press.

Apeyitou, E. 2003. Turkish-Cypriot Nationalism: Its History and Development (1571–1960). *The Cyprus Review* 15 (1): 67–98.

Aristeidou, A. 1980. *Unpublished Documents on Cypriot History from the Archives of Ragusa (16th century).* Nicosia: Cyprus Centre of Scientific Research (in Greek).

Aristeidou, A. 1984. Production and Commerce in Cyprus in the 18th-19th Centuries. In *Life in Cyprus in the 18th and 19th Centuries*, 33–62. Nicosia: Municipality of Nicosia (in Greek).

Asdrahas, S. 2003. The Political Terms of the Economic. The Conquests and Their Economic Logic. In *Greek Economic History 15th-16th*, vol. 1, ed. S. Asdrahas, et al., 249–288. Athens: Piraeus Bank Group Cultural Foundation (in Greek).

Attalides, M. 1979. *Cyprus. Nationalism and International Politics*. Edinburg: Q Press.

Aymes, M. 2004. 'Position Delicate' ou ile sans Histoiries? L' integration de Chypre a l' Etat Ottoman des Premieres Tanzimat. In *Insularites Ottomanes*, ed. N. Vatin and G. Veinstein, 241–275. Paris: Maisonneuve & Larose.

Barkan, O.L. 1975. The Price Revolution of the Sixteenth Century: A Turning Point in the Exconomic History of the Near East. *International Journal of Middle East Studies* 6 (1): 3–28.

Berberoglu, B. 1982. *Turkey in Crisis*. London: Zed Press.

Conomos, N. 1972–1973. Moves Towards Contracting of a Cypriot Loan During the Greek Uprising. *Yearbook of the Scientific Research Centre*, VI: 237–268 (in Greek).

Coureas. N. 2009. Stunted Growth: The Latin Clergy of Cyprus During the Ottoman Period. In *The Minorities of Cyprus: Development and the Identity of the Internal-Exclusion*, ed. A. Varnava, N. Coureas, and M. Elia, 92–110. Newcastle: Cambridge Scholars Publishing.

Cvetkova, B. 1978. *Les Institutions Ottomanes en Europe*. Wiesbaden: Franz Steiner Verlag GMB.

Cvetkova, B. 1979. The Evolution of the Turkish Feudal Regime from the End of the 16th to the Mid-18th Century. In *The Economic Structure of the Balkan Countries in the Years of Ottoman rule*, ed. S. Asdrahas, 89–112. Athens: Melissa (in Greek).

Dertilis, G. 2018. *History of Modern and Contemporary Greece*. Heraklion: University Editions of Crete (in Greek).

Dimaras, K.T. 2002. *Modern Greek Enlightenment*. Athens: Ermis (in Greek).

Dionysiou, G. 1988. *Church and Terminology in Cyprus in the Last Century of Turkish Rule (1779–1856)*. Doctoral thesis, University of Athens (in Greek).

Dionyssiou, G. 2009. *The Implementation of the Tanzimat Reforms in Cyprus (1839–1878)*. Nicosia: MAM.

Divtcioglou, S. 1979. Economic Model of Ottoman Society (14th and 15th Century). In *The Economic Structure of the Balkan Countries*, ed. S. Asdrahas, 115–131. Athens: Melissa (in Greek).

Gazioglou, A. 1990. *The Turks in Cyprus. A Province of the Ottoman Empire (1571-1878)*. London: K. Rustem & Brother.

Georgis, G. 2010. The Contribution of Cyprus to the Revolution of 1821. *Pergamini* 5: 31–43 (in Greek).

Giannopoulos, G. 1975. The Decline of the Ottoman State. The Adaptation of Institutions to the New Reality. In *History of the Greek Nation*, vol. XI, 98–110. Athens: Ekdotiki Athinon (in Greek).

Grivaud, G. 1983. L' ile de Chypre en 1697 d' après un memoire du consul Francois Luce. *Yearbook of Cyprus Research Centre*, XII: 171–183.

Hadjianastasis, M. 2004. *Bishops, Agas and Dragomans: A Social and Economic History of Ottoman Cyprus 1640–1704*. Ph.D. thesis, University of Birmingham.

Hadjianastasis, M. 2011. Crossing the Line in the Sand: National Officials, Monopolization of State Power and 'Rebellion'. The Case of Mehmed Aga Boyacioglu in Cyprus, 1685–1690. *Turkish Historical Review* 2: 155–176.

Hadjianastasis, M. 2015. Between the Porte and the Lion: Identity, Politics and Opportunism in Seventeenth Century Cyprus. In *Frontiers of the Ottoman Imagination*, ed. M. Hadjianastasis, 139–167. Leiden/Boston: Brill.

Hadjidemetriou, K. 2002. *A History of Cyprus*. Nicosia: Hermes Media Press.

Hadjiioannou, K. 1976. The Origins of Turkish Cypriots and the Cyprus Question. http://www.lykionellinidon.org.cy/likeio/userfiles/documents/kiriakos_Xatziioannou_i_katagogi_ton_tourkokiprion.pdf. Accessed on 5 May 2017 (in Greek).

Hadjikyriakou, A. 2011. *Society and Economy on an Ottoman Island: Cyprus in the Eighteenth Century*. Doctoral thesis, University of London.

Hadjikyriakou, A. 2014. Local Intermediaries and Insular Space in late-18th Century Ottoman Cyprus. *The Journal of Ottoman Studies*, XLIV: 427–456.

Hadjikyriakou, A. 2019. Beyond the *Millet* Dabate: Communal Representation in Pre-Tanzimat-Era Cyprus. In *Poltical Thought and Practice in the Ottoman Empire*, ed. M. Sariyannis, 71–96. Rethymno: Crete University Press.

Hidiroglou, P. 1975. Some Administrative Institutions of Turkish Rule in Cyprus. *Kypriakai Spoudai*, XXXVIII–XXXIX: 91–110 (in Greek).

Historical Encyclopedia of Cyprus. 1979–1980. Ed. P. Papadimitris. Nicosia: Epiphaniou Publications (in Greek).

History of Cyprus. 2010. Vol. II. Nicosia: Odysseia (in Greek).

Inalcik, H. 1973a. Application of the Tanzimat and Its Social Effects. *Archivum Ottomaticum* 5: 97–127.

Inalcik, H. 1973b. Ottoman Policy and Administration in Cyprus After the Conquest. In *Proceedings of the First International Cypriological Congress*, ed. T. Papadopoulos and M. Christodoulou, vol. III, first part, 119–136. Nicosia: Association of Cypriot Studies.

Inalcik, H. 1985. The Emergence of Big Farms, ciftlicks: State, Landlords and Tenants. In *Studies in Ottoman Social and Economic History*, ed. H. Inalcik, 105–126. London: Valorium Reprints.

Inalcik, H. 1997. Introduction: Empire and Population. In *An Economic and Social History of the Ottoman Empire*, ed. H. Inalick and D. Quataert, vol. I: 1300–1660, 11–43. Cambridge: Cambridge University Press.

Indianos, A. 1938. The Dragoman regime and Dragomans in Cyprus. *Kypriakai Spoudai* 2: 141–195 (in Greek).

Ioannou, T. 1996. *Commercial Relations Between Cyprus and France in the 18th Century*. Doctoral thesis, National and Capodistrian University of Athens (in Greek).

Irakleidis, A. 2006. *The Cyprus Problem 1947-2004. From Enosi to Partition*. Athens: Sideris (in Greek).

Islamoglou, H., and C. Keyder. 1977. Agenda for Ottoman History. *Review (fernard Braudel Center)* 1 (1): 31–55.

Itzkowitz, N. 2008. *Ottoman Empire and Islamic Tradition*. Athens: Papazisis (in Greek).

Jennings, R. 1993. *Christians and Muslim in Ottoman Cyprus and the Mediterranean World 1571-1640*. New York: New York University Press.

Karouzis, G. 1977. *Land Ownership in Cyprus-Past and Present* (with special reference to Greek and Turkish ownerships). Nicosia: "Strabo".

Karpat, K. 1972. The Transformation of the Ottoman State, 1789–1908. *International Journal of Middle East Studies* 3 (3): 243–281.

Katsouridis, Y. 2009. *The Party System in Cyprus 1878–1931: Construction and Peculiarities*. Doctoral thesis, Nicosia: University of Cyprus (in Greek).

Kizilyurek, N. 2009. *Turkish Cypriots, Turkey and the Cyprus Question*. Athens: Papazisis (in Greek).

Konstantinidis, S. 1995. *The Cyprus Problem, Structures of Cypriot Society and the National Question*. Montreal-Nicosia: Metoikos (in Greek).

Konstantinidis, S. 2011. *Review of Modern Cypriot History, Social Structures, Institutions, and Ideology. From Ottoman Rule and British Rule to Independence*. Athens: Taxideftis (in Greek).

Kostis, K. 1991. Communities, Church and Millet in "Greek" Areas of the Ottoman Empire in the Period of Reforms. *Mnimon* 13: 57–76 (in Greek).

Koumoulides, J. 1971. *Cyprus and the War of Greek Independence 1821–1829*. Athens: National Centre of Social Research.

Koumoulides, J. 1973. An Attempt for the Liberation of Cyprus During the Struggle for Greek Independence. In *Proceedings of the First International Cypriological Congress*, ed. T. Papadopoulos and M. Christodoulou, vol. III, first part, 149–154. Nicosia: Association of Cypriot Studies.

Kyrris, K. n.d. Diplomatic Background to the Revolution of 1821 in Relation to Cyprus. *Morphosis*, part IV, 6–8 (in Greek).

Kyrris, K. 1964. *The Dispute Between Dragomans Markoullis and Georgis (1669–1674) and the Relations Between Greek and Turkish Cypriots at That Time*. Nicosia (in Greek).

Kyrris, K. 1970–1971. Unpublished Accounts of Hatzigeorgakis Kornessios. *Yearbook of the Scientific Research Centre*, IV: 283–328 (in Greek).

Kyrris, K. 1973. The Role of the Greeks in the Ottoman Administration of Cyprus. In *Proceedings of the First International Cypriological Congress*, ed. T.

Papadopoulos and M. Christodoulou, vol. III, first part, 155–179. Nicosia: Association of Cypriot Studies.

Kyrris, K. 1984. Anatomy of the Ottoman Regime in Cyprus 1570–1878. In the collective *Life in Cyprus in the 18th and 19th Centuries*, 65–82. Nicosia: Municipality of Nicosia (in Greek).

Kyrris, K. 1985. *History of Cyprus*. Nicosia: Nicocles Publishing House.

Louis, K. 2006. *Forms of Economic relations in Cyprus (1817–1839)*, vol. 1. Nicosia (in Greek).

Louis, K. 2013. Makarios I, The Tanzimat and the Role of the Archbishop-Ethnarch. In *The Archbishops of Cyprus in the Modern Age*, ed. A. Varnava and M. Michael, 88–105. Newcastle: Cambridge Scholars Publishing.

Mandel, E. 1996. The Asiatic Mode of Production and the Historical Prerequisites for Capital Growth. *Theseis*, 57. http://www.theseis.com/1-75/theseis/t57/t57f/mandel.htm. Accessed on 13 September 2012 (in Greek).

Mantran, R. 1989. L' Etat ottoman au XVIIIe siècle: la pression européenne. In *Histoire de l' Empire Ottoman*, ed. R. Mantran, 265–286. Paris: Fayard.

Maratheftis, F. 1982. The Growth of Cities in Cyprus in the 18th and 19th Centuries. In *Life in Cyprus in the 18th and 19th Century*, 135–152. Nicosia: Municipality of Nicosia (in Greek).

Mariti, T. 1994. On an Uprising Which Took Place a Short Time Ago on the Island of Cyprus. In *Cyprus Through the Centuries in Texts of Visitors from Abroad. From the 1st Century to the 20th*, ed. Andros Pavlides, vol. II, 874–881. Nicosia: Filokypros (in Greek).

Melamid, A. 1956. The Geographical Distribution of Communities in Cyprus. *Geographical Review* 46 (3): 355–374.

Michael, M. 2003. *The Kykkos Monastery in the Ottoman Economic Context on the Basis of Code 56 (1844 1890)*. Nicosia: Kykkos Monastery Research Centre (in Greek).

Michael, M. 2005. *The Church of Cyprus in the Ottoman Period (1571–1878). Its Step-by-Step Formation as an Institution of Political Power.* Nicosia: Cyprus Scientific Research Centre (in Greek).

Michael, M. 2006. Mouchasilis, the Dragoman, the Archbishop and Claims on Political Power in the Cyprus of the Ottoman Regions, 1789–1810. *Yearbook of the Scientific Research Centre*, XXXII: 209–240 (in Greek).

Michael, M., 2009. An Orthodox Institution of Ottoman Polititical Authority: The Church of Cyprus. In *Ottoman Cyprus. A Collection of Studies on History and Culture*, ed. M. Michael, M. Kappler, and E. Gavriel, 209–230. Wiesbaden: Harrassowitz Verlg.

Michael, M. 2010. History, Myth and Nationalism: The Retrospective Force of National Roles within a Myth-Constructed Past. In *Nationalism in the Troubled Triangle*, ed. A. Aktar, N. Kizilyurek, and U. Ozkirimli, 149–159. London: Palgrave Macmillan.

Michael, M. 2015a. From the Ottoman Meclis-I Idare to the British Legislative Council. In *Religious Communities and Modern Statehood*, ed. M. Michael, T. Anastassiadis, and C. Verdeil, 105–130. Berlin: Klaus Schwarz Verlag.

Michael, M. 2015b. Revolts and Power Negotiating in Ottoman Cyprus During the First Half of the Nineteenth Century. In *Archivium Ottomanum*, ed. G. Xazia, vol. 32, 117–138. Gottingen: Hubert & Co.

Michael, M. 2016. *Insurrections as Terrain for Negotiation with Power. Ottoman Cyprus, 1804–1841.* Athens: Alexandria (in Greek).

Michael, M., and K. Kokkinoftas. n.d. The Church of Cyprus. In the collective *Cyprus*, 646–705. Athens: Domi A.E. (in Greek).

Milios, G. 1996. The Asiatic Mode of Production. *Theseis*, 57. http://www.theseis.com/1-75/theseis/t57/t57f/asiati.htm. Accessed 4 September 2020 (in Greek).

Milios, G. 2000. *The Greek Social Formation. From Expansionism to Capitalist Growth.* Athens: Kritiki (in Greek).

Myrianthopoulos Konstantinos. 1973. Cyprus Under Turkish Rule (1570–1878). *Kypriakai Spoudai*, XXXVII: 85–102 (in Greek).

Nevzat, A. 2005. *Nationalism Amongst the Turks of Cyprus: The First Wave.* University of ULU. https://herkules.oulu.fi/isbn9514277511/isbn9514277511.pdf. Accessed on 3 June 2012.

Nevzat, A., and M. Hatay. 2009. Politics, Society and the Decline of Islam in Cyprus: From the Ottoman Era to the Twenty-First Century. *Middle Eastern Studies* 45 (6): 911–933.

Orhonlu, C. 1973. The Ottoman Turks Settle in Cyprus (1570-1580). In *Proceedings of the First International Cypriological Congress*, ed. T. Papadopoulos and M. Christodoulou, vol. III, first part, 257–261. Nicosia: Association of Cypriot Studies.

Pampalos, C., and I. Theoharides. 2008. *The Turkish Press on Cyprus (1928–1945).* Nicosia: Holly Monastery Research Centre of Cyprus (in Greek).

Papadopoullos, T. 1965. *Social and Historical Data on Population (1570–1881).* Nicosia: Cyprus Research Centre.

Papadopoulos, T. 2011. Hellenic Education in Cyprus Under the Ottomans. In *History of Cyprus*, ed. T. Papadopoulos, vol. VI, 379–468. Nicosia: Makarios III Institute (in Greek).

Papageorgiou, S. 1990. *Kapodistrias and the Roots of the Cyprus Question.* Nicosia: K. Epiphaniou Publications (in Greek).

Papapolyviou, P. 2019. An Unknown Text on the Cypriot Revolts of 1833. *Yearbook of the Kykkos Monastery Research Centre* 12: 365–374 (in Greek).

Papapolyviou, P. 2020. Cypriot Fighters of 1821. https://papapolyviou.com/2020/03/25/kiprioi-agonistes-tou-1821/. Accessed on 12 September 2020 (in Greek).

Pavlidis, A. 1993. *History of the Island of Cyprus*, vol. 4: From 1571 to 1964. Nicosia: Filokypros (in Greek).

Philippou, L. 1975. *The Church of Cyprus Under Turkish Rule*. Nicosia: Cyprological Library (in Greek).

Pizanias, P. 2015. *The History of the Modern Greeks. From 1400 to 1800*. Athens: Estia (in Greek).

Polis, A. 1979. Colonialism and Neo-colonialism: Determinants of Ethnic Conflict in Cyprus. In *Small States in the Modern World. The Conditions of Survival*, ed. P. Worsley and P. Kitromilides, 45–80. Nicosia: New Cyprus Association.

Protopsaltis, E. 1954. Plans for an Expedition from Lebanon and the Liberation of Cyprus, in 1827. *Elliniki Kypros*, January: 16 (in Greek).

Protopsaltis, E. 1971. *Cyprus in the Struggle of 1821*. Athens: Publication of the Cypriot Union of Greece (in Greek).

Richter, H. 2007. *History of Cyprus*, vol. 1 (1878–1949). Athens: Estia (in Greek).

Rizopoulou-Egoumenidou, E. 1996. The Economy of Cyprus Under Ottoman Rule with Special Emphasis on the Late 18th and Early 19th Centuries. In *The Development of the Cypriot Economy. From the Prehistoric Period to the Present Day*, ed. V. Karageorghis and D. Michaelides, 193–208. Nicosia: University of Cyprus-Bank of Cyprus.

Sakellarios, A.A. 1890. *The Cypriot Question, i.e. Geography, History and Language of the Island of Cyprus from Antiquity Until Today*, vol. 1. Athens (in Greek).

Sarris, N. 1990. *Ottoman Reality. Systemic Juxtaposition of Structures and Functions. Vol. 2, Administration Dose by Dose*. Athens: Arsenidis (in Greek).

Shaw, J.S., and E.K. Shaw. 1977. *History of the Ottoman Empire and Modern Turkey*, vol. II. Cambridge: Cambridge University Press.

Stavrianos, L.S. 1958. *The Balkans Since 1953*. New York: Rinehart & Company Inc.

Stavridis, T. 2003. The Defection of Mehmed Boyacioglou (1683–1690). *Yearbook of the Scientific Research Centre*, XXIX: 115–143 (in Greek).

Stojanovitc, T. 1980. Balkan Farmers and Landowners and the Ottoman State: Family Economy, Market Economy and Modernization. In collective volume *Modernization and Industrial Revolution in Balkans During the 19th Century*, 157–198. Athens: Themelio (in Greek).

Stylianou, P. 1975. The Cypriot Revolution of 1606 Under Petros Aventanios. *Kypriakos Logos* 41–42: 337–341 (in Greek).

Stylianou, P. 1976. The 1609 Cypriot Appeal to the Spanish King Philip III for Liberation of Cyprus, Examined Historically. *Kypriakos Logos* 43: 3–13 (in Greek).

Sugar, P. 1996. *Southeastern Europe Under Ottoman Rule, 1354–1804*. Seattle: University of Washington Press.
Theoharidis, I. 1987. On the Institution of the Dragoman in Cyprus Under Turkish Rule. In *Proceedings of the Second International Cyprological Congress*, vol. III (modern section), 65–75 (in Greek).
Theoharidis, I. 1995. The Cypriot Forerunners of 1821 According to an Unknown Ottoman Source. *Dodoni* 24: 67–109 (in Greek).
Theoharidis, I., and S. Andreev. 1996. *Sequel to the 1821 Tragedy. Ottoman Source on Cyprus 1822–1832*. Nicosia: Kykkos Monastery Research Centre (in Greek).
Vergopoulos, K. 1975. *The Agrarian Question in Greece*. Athens: Exantas (in Greek).
Zachariadou, E. 1997. *Cyprus in the First Century of Ottoman Occupation (1570-1670)*. Nicosia: Leventis Foundation (in Greek).
Zanettos, F. 1910. *History of the Island of Cyprus*, vol. I. Larnaca (in Greek).
Zanettos, F. 1911. *History of the Island of Cyprus*, vol. II. Larnaca (in Greek).

CHAPTER 4

The First Period of British Administration: 1878–1939

1 On the Act of Cession of Cyprus from the Ottomans to the British

If the factors that led to the cession of Cyprus to the British Empire in 1878 are to become comprehensible, one must take into account the more general geographical and military context of the time. Essentially the period is characterized by the rivalry between Britain and Russia on the territory of the "sick man of Europe", i.e. the Ottoman Empire. The Russian side was focussed on Constantinople and its straits and thus the opening of an exit to the Aegean and the Mediterranean, but also Kars, Ardahan, Erzurum and accordingly access to the Persian Gulf, the Arabian Sea and the Indian Ocean. A further goal was to force the Ottomans to accept the proposals of the Constantinople Conference[1] which would restore the balance between the Great Powers within the

[1] The Constantinople Conference was held between 23rd December 1876 and 20th January 1877. The conference was called after the uprising in Bosnia (1875) and Bulgaria (1876). There the Great Powers came out in support of creation of an autonomous province of Bosnia and a corresponding grant of autonomy to Bulgaria. The Ottoman Empire rejected these proposals, with the result of war breaking out between the Ottomans and Russia (the Russia-Ottoman war of 1877–1878). But this time Britain and France, in contradistinction to their stance in the Crimean War, did not side with the Sublime Porte.

S. Sakellaropoulos, *The Evolution of the Political, Social and Economic Life of Cyprus, 1191–1950*, Palgrave Studies in Economic History,
https://doi.org/10.1007/978-3-030-91839-2_4

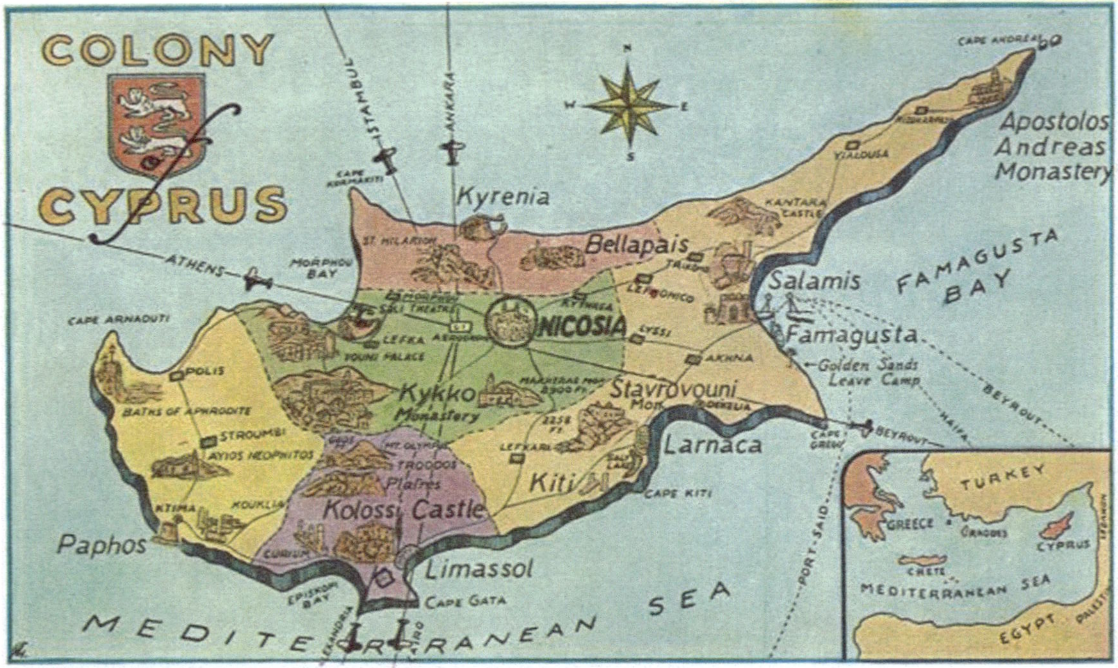

Map 1 The Ottomans cede Cyprus to the British (1878) (*Source* https://tfrnorthcyprus.wordpress.com/2015/04/05/nicosia-to-kyrenia-the-convoy-memories-of-the-1960s/)

Ottoman Empire (Pavlidis 1993: 227). All the above, reaching its zenith with the Russian occupation of Kars and a great part of Armenia in 1877, would provoke serious unease in London, where the assessment would be that there was now a distinct possibility of Persia coming under the control of Russia, placing in danger the route to India (Map 1).

The situation would be further aggravated when the Ottoman fleet retreated in the face of the advance of the Russian fleet, resulting in the signing of the Treaty of San Stefano on 3rd March 1878[2] creating a powerful Bulgaria, acknowledging Russia as patron of all the Orthodox subjects of the Sultan and regulating a range of issues (Bosnia, Herzegovina, Romania) to the disadvantage of the Ottoman Empire (Pavlidis 1993: 228). Britain took advantage of this opportunity to pressure the Sultan into accepting the cession of Cyprus to its Empire in exchange for military aid and economic compensation. The Ottomans were obliged to consent and the agreement was signed secretly on 4th June 1878 (Economides 1993: 58–59).

Britain for its part would decide for the occupation of Cyprus with a view to making it the Gibraltar of the Eastern Mediterranean and securing control of the coasts of Syria and the entrance to the Dardanelles, not to mention the continuation of the monitoring of traffic in the Suez Canal, which had been opened in 1869 (Britain had acquired control of it as early as 1875, buying out the shares of the Egyptian Prince Regent Ismail Pasha) (Richter 2007: 31). At the same time it was a secure military post for operations both in Asia Minor and in North Africa (Psyroukis 1983: 181) while also facilitating control of the Ionian Islands, the Balearic Islands and Souda in Crete and creating the prerequisites for ultimate occupation of Suez and Egypt, the southern coast of the Arabian Peninsula, the island of Socotra and the African coasts of Somalia (Kitromilides 1977: 387). In that way they opened the way for exploitation of the resources of Syria, Mesopotamia and Asia Minor.

Another question which preoccupied the British was the acquisition of a second access route to India through the construction of a railway line in the Euphrates Valley, in that way defending the Asian part of the Ottoman Empire and the Indies from the Russian threat (Lee 1934: 129–130). To be precise, British control of the Euphrates could be of decisive

[2] Agios Stefanos (San Stefano) is a suburb of Constantinople and the russian advance was halted only after intervention by the British—indicating the degree to which Constantinople itself was in danger of falling into the hands of the Russians.

importance against the Russians' attempt on the one hand to expand in the Southern Caucasus and on the other the attempt to launch an attack through the Dardanelles on Suez. In this contingency the existence of a naval base in Cyprus would be to its strategic advantage (Hill 1952: 270). At the same time, from the military viewpoint, Cyprus possessed the asset of not being an easy staging point for foreign troops and being able to be controlled by a relatively small garrison (Lee 1931: 241).[3]

The final text of the Cyprus concession agreement was signed on 4th June 1878; in accordance with its content[4] Britain undertook to protect the Ottoman Empire from Russian ambitions and the Sultan in return accepted the obligation to cede the administration of Cyprus to the British, which however would formally remain Ottoman territory but would also proceed with reforms to the benefit of Christians and other minorities.

In parallel with these developments the English entered negotiations with the Russians and the latter were persuaded to consent to contraction of the borders of Bulgaria and evacuation of the Alashkert Valley and Beyazid, but they did not agree to leave Kars and Batumi. They nevertheless affirmed that they had no other claims in Asia (Richter 2007: 36). So, everything was prepared for the signing of the final agreements at the Berlin Conference which got under way on 13th July 1878 and would set its stamp on the new order in the Balkans.

Encouraged by the recent developments, the Porte tried to renegotiate the Cyprus concession treaty, raising matters such as the retention of the Islamic court, the non-compensation of Britain in the event of Cyprus'

[3] Holland and Markides mention that initially Crete had been proposed in the place of Cyprus, but this was rejected because of the "problematic" character of the island. But Cyprus too was not unanimously accepted as a potential colony (Holland and Markides 2007: 310–311). In the debate that took place in the British parliament in July 1878 the Prime Minister Disraeli defended the content of the Cyprus annexation agreement with the argument that it checked the further expansion of Russia in Asia, supported the Ottoman Empire and secured British interests in the East. The opposition questioned how suitable Cyprus was for defence of the Asian possessions of the Porte and it was also raised the issue of the cost entailed by occupation and administration of Cyprus. Finally, it was argued that it would be difficult to halt the Russian advance into Ottoman territory given that it was difficult for the British, unlike Russians, to ensure continuity of supplies. For a presentation of the relevant debate see Georgalis (2016: 58–63), Lee (1934: 128–129), and Richter 2007: 45–46.

[4] For the full text of the agreement between Great Britain and the Ottoman Empire see Zannetos (1911: 13).

return to the Ottoman Empire, and finally the appointment directly from Constantinople of the manager of muslim foundations (Evkaf). The English were to accept the first two demands and reject the third. And so, it was that on 1st July an additional text was signed in the form of an appendix to the treaty.

"[…] It is understood between the two High Contracting Parties that England agrees to the following conditions relating to her occupation and administration of the Island of Cyprus:

I. That a Mussulman Religious Tribunal (Mecheme-i-Sheri) shall continue to exist in the Island, which will take exclusive cognizance of religious matters, and no others concerning the Mussulman population of the Island.
II. That a Mussulman resident in the Island shall be named by the Board of Pious Foundations in Turkey (Evqaf) to superintend, in conjunction with a Delegate to be appointed by the British Authorities, the administration of the property, funds and lands belonging to mosques, cemeteries, Mussulman schools, and other religious establishments existing in Cyprus
III. That England will pay the Porte whatever is the present excess of revenue over expenditure in the Island; this excess to be calculated upon and determined by the average of the last five years, stated to be 22,936 purses, to be duly verified hereafter, and to the exclusion of the produce of State and Crown lands let or sold during that period.
IV. That the Sublime Porte may freely sell and lease lands and other property in Cyprus belonging to the Ottoman Crown and State (Arazi-i-Mirieve Emplaq-i-Humayun), the produce of which does not form part of the revenue of the Island referred to in the Article III.
V. That the English Government, through their competent authorities, may purchase compulsorily, at a fair price, land required for public improvements, or for other public purposes, and land which is not cultivated
VI. That if Russia restores to Turkey Kars and the other conquests by her in Armenia during the last war, the Island of Cyprus will be evacuated by England, and the Convention of the 4th June, 1878, will be at end" (cited by Luke 1969: 260–262).

What emerges from the above text? For a start that the English confirmed the achievement of their basic objective, which was control of Cyprus. But such an important acquisition demanded numerous concessions: Ottoman interventions on questions related to religion (the Islamic court, Evkaf management), recovery of the fiscal surplus, a possible expiration date and return of Cyprus to the Ottomans. In this context a preliminary reading leads to the conclusion that the agreement exemplifies what in diplomacy is called win–win: everyone gains something. But a more attentive approach yields different conclusions. The Ottoman Empire saw only too clearly that Russia was *ante portas* and that the only hope for survival was through agreeing to concessions to England. But when a State gets to this point, it is very difficult, at least in the medium term, for it to be able to restore its powers, with the result that it remains in a subordinate position. This subordinate position also conditions its—limited—ability to control the terms of its implementation of the agreement. This is evident, as it will be seen, among other things also from the fact that the Ottomans never received the "present excess of revenue". At the same time, the prospect of the return of Cyprus, given Russia's explicit position on remaining in Armenia, looked like wishful thinking. And England was succeeding in keeping the Russians out of the Balkans and confining them to Transcaucasia. The process of transforming the Mediterranean into a British lake had been brought to fruition (Pantelis 1986: 65). Finally, England was acquiring an important economic resource: it is characteristic that whereas prior to the concession commercial transactions between Cyprus and the United Kingdom had not developed to any significant extent, in the course of the next eighty years and up until independence, trade with England and its possessions would amount to around 2/3 of the total (Psyroukis 1987: 61–62).

In conclusion, the real winner was England. For the Ottoman Empire the treaty in question was just a pause in the process of its collapse and the only people who were not asked were the Cypriots.

But very soon the occupation of Egypt also by British troops (1882) was to reduce the importance of Cyprus, with the result that the British Empire's interest in it at the end of the nineteenth century would correspondingly diminish. This happened because for the Royal Navy the fall of Egypt secured access to the harbour of Alexandria, next to the Canal. The lack of deep-water harbours made Cyprus unsuitable as a base for the new battleships that began to be constructed in the 1880s (Hadjivasileiou 2009: 229). But for a number of reasons the choice that was made was for the island to remain under the control of the English. The Colonial Office, and a portion of politicians, economists and the military had it as a basic principle not to consent to any reduction of Imperial territory. This was even truer of Cyprus, where occupation by another power could threaten British control of the Mediterranean route to India (Hadjivasileiou 2009: 229–230). Intellectual circles, too, were opposed to territory inhabited by a majority of Christians passing back under Ottoman rule. On the other hand, it was by no means certain that the island would with the passage of time reacquire geopolitical value (Papageorgiou 1996: 87–88.)

2 The Institutional and Political Context of Governing Cyprus Prior to the Revolt of 1931

In September 1878 the Queen of England through a relevant decree, that of 14/9, established the structure of political power in Cyprus: the basic office-bearer was the High Commissioner, who had decision-making powers and was flanked by two other bodies appointed by himself, with advisory competences. They were the eight-member Legislative Council (comprised of four English public functionaries and four Cypriots) and the Executive Council, in which four British officials, two Christians and one Muslim participated, and which was convened as a body for the first time only in 1897 (Crouzet 1973: 55). This form of organization of political power, where absolute control was retained by the colonial authority through one person and a given political balance,[5] met with substantial reactions from the Greek Cypriot community, the more so because—as historical research has shown, among the objectives of the rulers (irrespective of whether or not it was ever achieved) was the plan for altering the demographic composition of the population through the transportation of Ottoman Muslims from East Rumelia, but also Latins from Malta (Hadjivasileiou 1998: 43–45).

[5] For the reasoning on the basis of which the first form of political power in Cyprus was formulated, the position of the Under-Secretary of State for Colonies Edward Wingfield was very characteristic: "What we need for the moment is a legislative council in which we shall have the upper hand in voting. We could at the same time allow a reasonable presence of unofficial members on the Legislative Council, to be elected through universal (male) suffrage, with which the people seem to be familiar" (cited in Katsiaounis 1994: 317).

The attempt to undermine the position of the Greek Cypriots should be seen, *inter alia*, in the context of their desire for *Enosis* with Greece, a development attributable: (a) to the fact that the great majority of inhabitants regarded themselves as belonging to the Greek nation[6] (b) to the already achieved partial realization of the *Megali Idea* plan, which had been devised by the Greek state, through the annexation of the Ionian islands (1864) and Thessaly (1881) (c) The precedent of the cession of the Ionian islands by the British to Greece strengthened corresponding aspirations of the Greek Cypriots (d) moreover the withdrawal of the Sublime Porte from Cyprus reduced the likelihood of a military confrontation between Greece and the Ottoman Empire in the event that the Greek Cypriots raised the demand for *Enosis*.

In any case, and beyond the question of *Enosis*, Greek Cypriot dissatisfaction over the way the political institutions were being established resulted in the organizing of pan-Cypriot rallies in 1881 in which it was decided that "the people should refuse to co-operate with the government", following which the Greek Cypriots participating in the Legislative Council should resign,[7] along with an appreciable number of municipal councillors. Under this pressure the Royal Decree issued on November 30, 1882, would state that that the Legislative Council would now comprise 18 members, of whom six would be English civil servants to be appointed by the Crown and the remaining 12 would be elected. Of those nine would be non-Muslims and the other three would be Muslims. The island would be divided into three districts, each of which would elect four members, one Muslim and three non-Muslims (Orr 1972: 100). In this way an attempt would be made to curb the dissatisfaction of the Greek Cypriots, not through *Enosis*, of course,

[6] The first official census of the Cypriot population was carried out by the Ottoman official Talaat Efendi in 1841 and indicated that in a population of 108,600 inhabitants there were 73,200 Greeks, 33,330 Ottomans and 21,000 Catholics, Armenians and Maronites (Papadopoulos 1965: 62). The first census by the British was conducted in 1881 and recorded that 73.9% were members of the Greek Orthodox Church and 24.4% Mohammedans. The next census was carried out in 1891 and recorded that 75.8% were members of the Greek Orthodox Church and 22.9% were Mohammedans and the census of 1901 would record 77.1% as being members of the Greek Orthodox Church and 21.7% Mohammedans.

[7] As will be evident from what follows, the resignation of the Greek Cypriot members of the Legislative Council was not only a reaction to the way the body was functioning but was also the result of pressures from the Church because for the first time no provision was made for *ex officcio* participation by clerics.

but through the establishment of a more democratic functioning of the colonial institutions.

But even this reform cannot be regarded as having led to the acquisition of real powers[8]: in any eventuality the Crown was able to override the decisions of the Legislative Council and impose legislation without the approval of the latter—which indeed was done in the few instances where the British lost their majority (see below). Apart from that it was only on the initiative of the High Commissioner that laws could be passed on the subject of public finances, and particularly taxation, and he was the only one who was able to defer a meeting of the Council or dissolve it. At the same time, the balance between the two national groups generated a framework which revealed the more general orientations of the colonizers. Aware that the Greek majority wanted *Enosis* with Greece, the British instituted a balance where, voting together with the English, the Ottomans could block any initiative of the Greek Cypriot side, the more so because in the event of a tie the High Commissioner had the casting vote. Even in his absence, the appointed member who chaired had, in addition to his own, the casting vote of the High Commissioner (Orr 1972: 101).

It is worth underlining the fact that the British were not wrong to support an institutional approach in the certainty of an alliance with the Cypriot Muslims. The events of 1881 had elicited a vehement reaction from Muslims, who on 5th April 1881 submitted to the Secretary of State

[8] It is interesting that the English justified their absolute domination by the fact that formally Cyprus was still an Ottoman possession. As remarked characteristically by the Secretary of State for the Colonies Lord Kimberley: "As the island of Cyprus is not part of the Queens' possessions, but is administered by Her Majesty under a Treaty with the Sultan, which is terminable in certain events, it is impossible for the Queen to finally surrender any part of the powers and responsibilities of Government. For this and other reasons power will be reserved to her Majesty to amend or revoke the Instrument creating the Constitution if she thinks fit" (cited by Orr 1972: 96). In any case the remark made by Georghalides should be noted that even under these assumptions, the establishment of a Legislative Council for a dominion which had been in its possession for only four years, without British inhabitants and with a majority of elected members on it, was a progressive action (Georghalides 1979: 42). The Cypriot inhabitants were in this way given a form of subordinate and partial, but real, participation in the administration of their island.

for Colonies Lord Kimberley a memorandum in which they declared their total opposition to any prospect of *Enosis* of Cyprus with Greece.[9]

In conclusion, what emerges from all the above is that the British had opted for a politics of Divide and Rule[10] whereby they would legitimate their own rule by sharpening the existing conflicts between greeks and muslims and transforming the Cypriot Muslims into idiosyncratic partners of the colonial administration and the Greek Cypriots into a permanent opposition (Crouzet 1973: 52–53). It was for this reason that the election of the members of the Legislative Council took place with separate electoral catalogues so that on the one hand on a symbolic/institutional plane the fact would be underlined that these are two separate populations and on the other that the Greek Cypriots would not be able to elect the Muslim of their choice but also correspondingly the Muslims would be prevented from supporting the Greek Cypriots they desired.

Characteristic of the above situation is the fact that from time to time the Greek Cypriots proposed resolutions for *Enosis* of Cyprus with Greece. which would be rejected by the English-Muslim alliance. The only exception was on 7th May 1903 when, where due to an absence of a muslim, a resolution was adopted seeking "greater participation of the

[9] For the complete content of this memorandum see Papageorgiou (1996: 259). It had been preceded by two calm memoranda from the Cypriot Muslims a few days before but in response to relevant encouragement from the Ottoman Empire the third had been more aggressive. The Porte, for its part, also exerted corresponding pressure on London through a representation on 6th April 1882 and a verbal note on 1st July, see Georgallis (2016: 155–159).

[10] There is extensive archival material to document this intention. In a memorandum drafted in August 1881 by the Under-Secretary for Colonies L. Courtney on the structure of the Legislative Council there is emphasis on the need for future collaboration between the British and the Muslim representatives to forestall any injustice against them, while at the same time he considered it more or less impossible that there should be any future alliance between Greeks and Muslims (Kyriakidis 2016: 80). A similar co-operative spirit between Britons and Muslims in the Legislative Council is to be seen in the answers given by British diplomacy to the Ottoman Ambassador in London when the latter raises the question of equal representation of the two communities in the Legislative Council (Kyriakidis 2016: 93). The same orientation is also visible in two British documents quoted by Kafkarides. The first includes the remark: "In the Legislative Council, at that time, the elected members were in the permanent majority. For that reason, the practical functioning of the Constitution depended on exploitation of the national difference between Greeks and Turks. "In the second it is asserted that: "Rule over the Crown colony must be continued in some way under the cover of a free constitution. The simplest way seems to be the policy of 'divide and rule'" (Kafkarides 2010: 32–33).

representatives of the Cypriot people in the administration of the island, pending national restoration through *Enosis* with the Greek motherland". Shortly afterwards, the Muslims returned to the question and proposed a resolution, which was in fact accepted, in which it was asserted that "if Britain ever abandons Cyprus, the island must be returned to Turkey".

The next change in the form of the Legislative Council would come in 1925, following the proclamation of Cyprus as a Crown Colony on 10th March of the same year (see below). The most important change was that the Commissioner was designated Governor and the non-Muslim population acquired an additional three seats, but the number of English appointed public functionaries was similarly increased (Tsalakos 1981: 146). Five of the nine British public officials were directly appointed by the Governor and another four were *ex officio* members of the Council by virtue of the position they already occupied: the Colonial Secretary, the Attorney General, the Treasurer of the Island and the Chief Commander of the Police. These four people were also the British representatives on the Executive Council, in which two Greek Cypriots and one Turkish Cypriot also participated (Choisi 1995: 41).

This was a change that did not affect the general balance of power because the British with the Turkish Cypriots had the majority and there was no extension of the competences of the two Councils.

As regards staffing of public administration, here too discrimination can be seen at the expense of the Greek Cypriot population, although it comprised a large majority and was distinguished by a high educational level. At the end of the nineteenth century there were 472 Cypriot civil servants, of whom only 237 (50%) were Greek Cypriot, as against 198 Muslims (42%) and there was a distinct preference for Armenians and Maronites[11] who, although they comprised only 2% of the population,

[11] In Cyprus there are not only Greek Cypriots and Turkish Cypriots but also three small communities of Armenians, Maronites and Latins. The Maronites come from the Maronite community of Syria and Lebanon and from there settled in waves in Cyprus. The first arrival took place in the seventh century A.D. in the wake of the Arab invasions and the second immediately after the occupation of Cyprus by the Franks. Given the special privileges they enjoyed, they multiplied quickly, but the Venetian occupation and then the advent of the Ottomans would have the effect of abruptly reducing their numbers. The Maronites are Catholic Christians by religion and are fall under the Maronite Archiepiscopate of Lebanon. The Armenians in their first phase were descendants of immigrants who arrived in Cyprus in the sixth century A.D. as hostages of the Byzantine army. In the following centuries more Armenians came either for economic reasons or as officials in the service of the Byzantines. Their presence was strengthened under Frankish rule but

occupied 37 of the positions (8%). These disproportions were even more conspicuous in the police force, where in 1919 of the 763 policemen 420 (55%) were Muslims (Katsiaounis 1996: 81). By 1928 this disproportion had moderated slightly, with the Turkish Cypriots occupying 36% of the positions in public administration *in toto,* Greek Cypriots 56% and the remaining 8% Britons, Latins and Maronites (Nevzat 2005: 401).

3 Education

As already mentioned, up until the cession of the island to the British, the Christians had pursued an education which oriented them more towards trade and the liberal professions. Apart from religion they were taught arithmetic, geography and modern Greek. In contrast, the education of the Muslims aimed at making them good Muslims. It prepared them for access to positions in the public sector. Finally, with the coming of the British, on the terrain of administration what was imposed was that in May each year the Mukhtar (president of the community) of every village with a school called a meeting of all the taxpayers. This meeting elected the school committee, which was comprised of between three and seven members and was responsible for hiring and firing the teacher, determining his salary, calculating the general expenses of the school and deciding for all residents the amount they were required to pay, depending on their economic situation. The school fees were collected by tax officials. If the school expenses exceeded the local income, the government recouped the deficit. Accordingly, from 1882 onwards the British contributed to the funding of education, providing £2,250 sterling annually for the Greek Cypriots and £750 for the Turkish Cypriots (Richter 2007: 123).

A little later the educational council was founded. The council itself decided the curriculum and the schoolbooks and attended to educational

Ottoman mobilization also recruited many thousands of Ottoman-Armenian artisans, some of whom remained permanently in Cyprus. The coming of the British attracted numerous Armenians who worked either as interpreters or as civil servants. The last phase of arrivals dates from after the persecutions by the Young Turks in 1915 and the incorporation of Armenia into the USSR. They are Christian Orthodox by religion (Armeno-Gregorians). The Latins are Roman Catholic residents of Cyprus and are descendants of the Franks, Venetians and Genoans. They live mainly in Nicosia, Larnaca and Limassol (Sophokleous 1993: 525–526).

issues. It was also responsible for hiring and firing of teachers (Richter 2007: 123).

What should be underlined is that in the new situation the differences in the curricula between the two communities not only were not reduced but were reinforced. In the Muslim curriculum the teaching of religion was central and was followed by Turkish language, Ottoman history and geography, the basics of arithmetic and elements of the Persian and Arabic languages.[12] In the Greek schools, by contrast, apart from religion, emphasis was placed on the Greek language, with ancient Greek taught in the larger schools, and mathematics included geometry. The curriculum was supplemented by natural history, philosophy, history, geography, music, calligraphy and gymnastics (Richter 2007: 123–124).

The general conclusion which emerges is that the educational curricula were copies of the corresponding Greek or Ottoman, the schoolbooks were imported from Greece and the Ottoman Empire and the teachers were either citizens from the motherlands or Cypriot graduates from their institutions.

Higher education received minimal support from the British. The Muslims maintained the Idadi school with a curriculum including Persian, Arabic, English, Modern Greek and mathematics. The Greek Cypriots had six high schools in the country whose purpose was to prepare students for their admission into the University of Athens but also to train primary school teachers (Richter 2007: 127).

It is obvious that this specific educational structure did nothing other than reproduce two separate, and potentially conflicting, realities. The Ottoman narrative, which corresponded to a State in collapse and the Greek narrative, which corresponded to a State in continual expansion with the *Megali Idea* as its basic strategy, a demand which appeared entirely feasible in Cyprus, given the composition of the population.

The end of the First World War, the multiplication of Greek pressures for *Enosis* (see below) but also the establishment of the Kemalist state led to the emergence of the danger of intensified divergence between the two communities and a greater challenge to British rule. For this reason, in 1929 all decisions concerning educational personnel (hiring, discontinuation, promotion, transfer) and their remuneration were assigned to the Governor, and a six-member educational council was appointed

[12] For a detailed description of the content of Turkish Cypriot education see Weir (1952: 69–74).

with responsibility for curricula and schoolbooks (Papapolyviou 2004: 328). The 1931 revolt (see below) induced the British to harden their stance. The law of 1st April 1933 on primary schools transferred to the Governor's responsibility for elementary education. He made the decisions on schoolbooks and teaching programmes., appointed the members of the educational councils and regulated the finances of the educational system. Through the system of issuing decrees, it became possible to intervene in what was being taught.[13] By this means the teaching of Greek history was banned, along with education in Greek poetry and demotic songs (Richter 2007: 554).

4 The Institutional Context for Local Government

The Cities

As far as municipalities are concerned,[14] the law of 1882 amended the institutional framework existing from the time of the *Hatt-i Humayun*. A reminder is perhaps needed that the *Hatt-i Humayun* (Charter of Autonomy) provided that every municipal council was comprised of the President, who was required to be a Muslim and was appointed by the Governor, and of six councillors (three Christians and three Muslims) who were elected by the residents. The basic change introduced by the law of 1882 was that the president of the Council (the Mayor) was elected by the other members of that body and was not appointed by the authorities and the number of members of the municipal council varied between eight and twelve with corresponding representation by population. Each community voted its candidates from a separate list but until 1889 was also able to vote for candidates from the other community (Koupanou 2017: 38–40).[15] In 1907 the Legislative Council adopted alterations to the functioning of the municipalities. The minimum number of municipal councillors was increased to nine. The municipal councillors elected

[13] For a more detailed presentation of the measures in question see Chapter 5 Sect. 10.

[14] The British had progressed to the establishment of rural municipalities in ten farming towns above and beyond the urban municipalities in operation in the cities of Cyprus (Nicosia. Kyrenia, Larnaca, Limassol, Paphos, Famagusta).

[15] This possibility was abolished following a proposal from Rashid Effendi, which received joint support from Britons and Muslims.

the President and Vice-President (Mayor and deputy-Mayor) for a three-year term. A session of the Council was regarded as legal if 1/3 of its members were present, as opposed to 2/3 hitherto. This development favoured the Greek side, which was in a position, given that it held the majority of seats, to conduct the session even if not all the Greek members were participating. The change was met with protests from the Muslim councillors (Katsouridis 2009: 186–187; Koupanou 2017: 41–42).

In any case, what should be noted is that the institutional framework for municipal councils which had been introduced by the British established a system of limited democratic freedoms, since various actions of the Municipal Council were not deemed valid unless adopted by the Administrator or the Governor. The Governor was also entitled to examine appeals against decisions of the Municipal Council and in cases of dereliction of duty by the Municipal Council had the right to declare it deposed and appoint a Municipal Commission (Loukaidis 1986: 69).

The existence of the institution of Municipal Commissions makes it clear that elected municipal authorities were not the only self-governing bodies able to be present in a municipality. The phenomenon came into being when the British administration judged that the Councils were unable to operate and so they were duly replaced by Commissions appointed by the British. As is natural, the Greek Cypriots preferred the existence of the Councils given that they themselves were able to control the majority of the municipal councillors and the election of the President. On the contrary, the Turkish Cypriots sought to have the Commissions operating, which had a membership of three: a Greek Cypriot, a Turkish Cypriot and the president, who was usually British. The conflict had indeed reached such a point that in Paphos and Nicosia, where the Turkish Cypriot community was a significant presence, the Turkish Cypriots exploited the relevant legislation providing that if 1/3 of the members of the Council submitted their resignation the Council ceased to exist. The Turkish Cypriots accordingly resigned and the British appointed Commissions. Quite a few years had to pass and the composition of the population to change in order to be an end to this situation (Katsiaounis 1996: 83–84).

The Villages

As far as self-government at the village level is concerned, up until 1891 the British respected the Cypriots' acquired right to elect their own local leaders. In accordance with it every community was administered by the Mukhtar, his substitute and a council of elders elected annually in which the imam and priest of the village participated *ex officio*. In mixed-population villages each population group had its own community leader. The mukhtar was usually the richest person in the village and his voters were most times in his debt. It was consequently very difficult for there to be an alternative candidate (Katsouridis 2009: 185). The District Council—Mejlis Idare)[16] nominated four people, from among whom the High Commissioner appointed the mukhtar of the village. If the majority of villagers were Christians, the mukhtar was required to be a Christian and vice versa if the majority was Muslim. Appointment was for a year (Loukaidis 1986: 71).

Between 1907 and 1923 the British again accepted a system of electing local leaders. For the 617 villages a corresponding 617 local committees were established, elected every two years and with five members. The mukhtar presided and there was participation from 4 azas (dignitaries). If the community was of mixed population and included more than thirty residents, each nationality elected its own mukhtar. If there were fewer than thirty inhabitants, only one mukhtar was elected (Katsouridis 2009: 186). The relationship between the mukhtar and the elected representatives differed from village to village. Sometimes he played the role of mouthpiece of the colonial administration and sometimes he was an authentic representative of local interests and accordingly did not enjoy the confidence of the colonial authorities (Crouzet 1973: 59). The duties of mukhtars were limited compared to in the Ottoman period given that they were no longer involved with tax collection: they included setting the price of wine, recording the community's finances and issuing warrants for confiscation and selling off of property following non-payment of taxes.

In 1923, in its endeavour to acquire greater control over the (Greek) mukhtars, who in a number of cases had played a leading role in raising the demand for *Enosis*, the British administration changed the system

[16] The District Councils were comprised of the incumbent prefect, a Muslim judge, a local bishop, the superintendent of finances and two Greek Cypriots and Turkish Cypriots who were chosen and appointed by the High Commissioner following an indirect vote. It was conducted as follows: in each of the six provinces the Greek and Muslim inhabitants of each parish or village elected representatives, from whom the prefect chose 4 Greeks and 4 Muslims. From among these the High Commissioner selected two from each community (Richter 2007: 285; Georghallides 1979: 245).

for electing them. Under the new law, in a first phase, the local population appointed or elected a list of people which it then submitted to the Provincial Council, who selected two names from this list. The members of the Legislative Council participating in the local Provincial Council chose another three individuals besides those proposed. And then the High Commissioner decided which of these five persons would become the mukhtar. In the villages where there was no majority from the Christian or Muslim communities, the Governor was able to appoint members of his own choice. Finally, in cases where there was a mixed population and the members of one community did not exceed 30 in number a local committee was appointed of people belonging to the majority community (Loukaidis 1986: 71–72). This complicated system, which was invented so that the British could intervene in the choice of community leader, also assumed another dimension: the establishment of clientelistic links between mukhtars and parliamentarians, given that the mukhtars voted on which deputy would go to the Provincial Council but also because parliamentary members of the Provincial Council chose three of the five candidates for the position of mukhtar.

5 The Initial Forms of Capitalist Economic Growth

The transfer of power to the British Empire would strengthen the economic dynamic of the new bourgeois strata. Within the first year of the British presence carriage roads were linking Nicosia with Famagusta and Kyrenia, Larnaca with Mathiatis, Limassol with the Troodos. All in all in the first years of British rule 356 miles of roads were constructed, though some of them were of poor quality. The works continued into the following years, with the result that at the turn of the twentieth century there were 628 miles of public roads in Cyprus. The ratio between road network and geographical area was one to 57, meaning that Cyprus had one of the best road networks in the possessions of the United Kingdom (Katsiaounis 1996: 175). Apart from the construction of new roads one important development was the relative improvement of the harbours. Thus between 1903 and 1906 works were carried out at the harbour of Famagusta and construction went forward of the railway to link Nicosia with Famagusta and Morphou in support of the operation of that harbour (Moustaka 2010: 49). This plan of action facilitated the expansion of internal economic activity, which was also fostered by the establishment of a stable currency, the pound (Katsiaounis 1996: 175), as well as contributing to an increase in employment.

In a very brief space of time the effectiveness of these measures became evident: In 1900 external trade (exports + imports) had risen by 27.3% over the figure for 1879. At the same time there was a strengthening of the internal economic life of the island. According to the existing data for 1880 there were three tanneries, three tobacco factories, two distilleries and ten mills (steam mills and flour mills). By 1900 the number of tanneries had risen to 13, the number of tobacco factories to eight, the number of steam mills to 26 and distilleries to 21. There were also 42 steam-driven cotton gins, ten machines of non-specific purpose, ten printing presses, along with factories manufacturing bricks, soap, plaster, mineral water and pasta. The growth of the wine trade alone had resulted in the installation of approximately 400 wine presses. One significant difference from the recent past is that the centre of economic activity had shifted to Limassol where the whole process was facilitated by the stationing of British troops in the area (Katsiaounis 1996: 176).

Finally, as regards agricultural production, it could be seen as significant that at the end of Ottoman rule, precisely because of the overall decline of the "Sick Man of Europe", free property in cultivated land began to make its appearance, together with a more extensive presence of ciflicks (Louis 2006, Vol. III: 402).

6 The Internal Conflicts Within the Hegemonic Groups of Greek Cypriots

The Overall Context

The rise of the new bourgeois strata a considerable time prior to cession of the island, in conjunction with of the establishment and development of the Greek state, resulted in the formation of two opposing groups within the Greek Cypriot elite. The conflict came to light around the question of the finances of the Kition Monastery. The so-called Kitiako was in the forefront between 1855 and 1870. Ostensibly it had to do with the Metropolitan of Kition's budgetary management and the criticisms levelled at each successive Metropolitan for excessively conciliatory relations with lay people, explicable largely by the Metropolitans' debts to the up-and-coming bourgeoisie. But in reality this was merely a pretext. Essentially it was a question with deeper ramifications but interconnected causes: on the one hand the rising bourgeoisie was trying to have a say in the management of the assets so as to acquire a share of the power held by the Church; on the other the conflict between the Metropolitan of Kition and the Archiepiscopate reflected the ongoing struggle between those seeking a different way to activate the leaders of the Orthodox Community by adding to their perspective the demand for *Enosis* and those who persisted in traditional handling of affairs within the parameters of the Ottoman Empire (Michael 2005: 315–316).

This controversy was to persist into the following years when the British established themselves on the island. Attempting to pursue a process of capitalist modernization of the island's antiquated structure, the latter would make it one of their priorities to reverse the state-centred character of the Church, a policy which would have significant economic and political dimensions to it.

On the economic plane: (a) there was abolition both of exemption of the Church from property tax and of its legal rights in issues of family law,(b) church taxes were no longer regarded as forms of state taxation so and accordingly the state did not secure their collection (Kalantzopoulos 2015: 37). The state was prohibited from being present at their payment, with the result that the income to the Church diminished by one third. But the British continued to provide tax collection services for the Muslim Evkaf (c) A third dimension concerned the church lands, for the distribution of which the Church had hitherto been responsible, without possessing rights of ownership. In these cases the British administration treated them as belonging to the State (Michael 2008: 357).

As for the political dimension, the central British thesis was one of denying recognition to the Church as representative of the Greek Orthodox, with corresponding privileges of the Church hierarchy in the management of Greek affairs. In terms of measures, what followed was abolition of the *ex officio* representation of the Church in the various governing councils (Meclis-Iidare). The institution of equal treatment of lay and clerical persons, particularly in the law courts, would be of particular symbolic significance (Michael 2008: 339–341). The upshot was that in order to retain their political role, the Church hierarchy was forced to start competing in elections with secular politicians (Katsouridis 2009: 135–136).

This development would have contradictory repercussions within the Church hierarchy. One section was taken by surprise by the turn of events and, accustomed to its long-standing organic relationship with the Ottoman authorities, was not able to adapt to the new reality. To begin with they would proceed with a series of reflex reactions where, apart from letters of protest, etc. they would urge all Orthodox members (clerical and secular) to resign from the Administrative Councils (Large and District) which, as indicated, for a time continued in operation even under British rule (Kalantzopoulos 2015: 38). But the fact that there were some lay people who did not resign shows that an unequivocal trajectory of independence of Greek Cypriot political personnel from the Church was already under way (Michael 2008: 344–345). This development was linked to the fact that there had been an increase in the number of lay people whose wealth was increasing without their being involved in any joint economic activity with the Church (Michael 2008: 347).[17]

By contrast, a more dynamic section followed a different path. They would come to the conclusion that the Church must adjust to a new reality where a state institution was changing into a spiritual institution in a course parallel with that of the State. Accordingly, it was required to choose a course of transformation from being a state institution to being the institutional representative of the Greek Cypriots, given that it was no longer able to demand a role equivalent to that which it had played in the Ottoman governing system. British rule was after all entirely different in content, institutionally, economically and politically. So, the Church should perceive itself to be the central agency for formulation of the demand of *Enosis*. As before its role would be perceived to be that of leader of the Nation, but not in the sense of representative of the Christian *millet* within the multinational Ottoman Empire but rather as a catalytic factor contributing to the shaping of Hellenic national integration in a world dominated by sovereign nation states. For *Enosis* to be achieved, an alliance with the new bourgeois strata was indispensable.

These new strata were pursuing capitalist enterprises, albeit with low-intensity capital, such as the tobacco factory and the iron foundry. The traditional side of the Hierarchy regarded them with intense disdain, persuaded that certain individuals of low origin were attempting to overthrow the established order of rule by old families and their connections (Katsianounis 1996: 180–81). As argued by Englezakis: "It was a clash

[17] Another characteristic example of non-conformity with the urgings of the Church hierarchy was that Archbishop Sophronios requested participation by the flock for establishment of an Assembly that would raise the question of Church property but encountered generalized indifference from the Orthodox citizenry (Zannetos 1911: 391).

between two classes, the old and the new, two ideologies: the liberal conservatism of Nicosia deriving from Turkish-occupied Cyprus and the conservative liberalism of Limassos and Larnaca, which appeared with the new generation that essentially had not known Turkish rule [...] Automatically it was the conflict between two stances and programmes vis à vis England (quoted in Katsouridis 2010: 47–48).

There were a number of parameters contributing to this development. As already mentioned, from the end of the eighteenth century but above all in the nineteenth century a significant growth of trade was observable in Cyprus. The undertaking of the administration of Cyprus by Britain and the institutional and social changes that this brought with it accelerated the modernizing tendencies in the Cypriot community. Of course, the education in Greece of the children of the neophyte Greek Cypriot bourgeoisie and the transmission to the island of the image of the motherland and by extension the vision of *Enosis* contributed to this. The latter endeavoured to penetrate the Cypriot elite, making itself into the technocratic component of the new society under construction. Through their presence the British operated objectively in the interests of the modernizers as both symbolically and on the material plane they represented the new, which was capitalism and the division of the world into capitalist nation states. Of course the element of contradiction was conspicuous: on the one side were the modernizing forces seeking an extension of capitalist productive relations and fusion with the Greek nation state, on the other were the conservatives who were being overtaken by the new forms of organization of production and for that reason remained attached to the existing situation of colonized government—which however favoured capitalist development within a colonial framework! At the political level all of this focussed on control of the Church, i.e. the recognized national representative of all Greek Cypriots.

It was in this way that a political, ideological and social division was created, depending on the stance being adopted by each party, each bishop and each politician in relation to the colonial authorities. The "Kitiakoi" (followers of the Metropolitan of Kition) wanted *Enosis* without any compromise whereas the Kyrenians (corresponding followers of the Metropolitan of Kyrenia) accepted collaboration with the British with a view to effecting a number of reforms. Thus, on the one hand one had the intransigent "nationalists" and on the other the conservative "moderates".

The stakes were political, but also ideological. On one side were the more traditional strata who owed their leading role to the traditional religious organization of the community, on the other the new more dynamic economic circles who aimed at *Enosis* and who, unable radically to overturn the relations of representation enjoyed by the Church with the popular classes, infiltrated this partnership with a view to making it more national. In reality the new ideas brought a dualism into the hierarchy but made it impossible for them to be expressed by unequivocally political spokespersons. For this reason, although in the first elections, in 1883, the demand was made for non-participation of the church hierarchy and for involvement of lay persons in management of Metropolitans' finances, finally the Metropolitan *were* candidates. The fact, too, that the Metropolitan of Kition was elected to Legislative Council in two electoral precincts (Larnaca-Famagusta and Limassol-Paphos), i.e. in the areas that were bastions of the circles seeking immediate *Enosis* of Cyprus with Greece, demonstrates that this section of the electorate *too* accepted a church official as its representative. This must have happened because the new bourgeois strata did not possess the credibility that the Church could project in its representation of the poorer popular classes—a function that the religious elite had exercised for centuries (Anagnostopoulou 1999: 203). As a result, any conflict that arose was internalized within the Church. As pointed out by Anagnostopoulou, the old guard party consolidated around the Metropolitan of Kyrenia and as its leading figures had the Metropolitan of Kyrenia, the local archimandrites, the abbot of the Kykkos monastery and the lay persons Liasidis and Konstantinidis. The modernizing party congregated around the Metropolitan of Kition (Larnaca) and had as its leaders the Metropolitan of Kition, the Metropolitan of Paphos and a number of lay persons, with Katalanos a prominent figure.

The clash which followed had a pronounced geographical component to it: the conservatives were more influential in the provinces of Kyrenia, Nicosia and Famagusta, which were under the ecclesiastical jurisdiction of the Archiepiscopate and the Metropolitan of Kyrenia. On the other hand in the provinces of Larnaca, Limassol and Paphos the predominance of the "Kitiakoi" was near absolute (Katsouridis 2010: 50).

There was ambiguous conflict between the two sides until 1900 when the position of Archbishop of Cyprus fell vacant, as Sophronios, Archbishop until that time, had been under the influence of the conservatives (see below). The need to fill the vacant position would trigger vehement confrontation between the two sides, culminating in the emergence of an Archiepiscopal Question, which would continue for ten years and end finally with the victory of the "Kitiakoi" through the ascent of the Metropolitan of Kition Kyrillos to the archiepiscopal throne.

Emphasis on the importance of the conflict around political representation of the Greek Cypriots and highlighting of the question of *Enosis* should not overshadow a second determinant in the whole controversy. This is the securing of control as such of the Cypriot Church, which was safeguarded through access to the archiepiscopal throne. Acquisition of this office led to access to the Church property and to the ability to represent indirectly Greek Cypriots which the church hierarchy was granted under British rule. In this context, as quite correctly observed by Y. Katsouridis, it is understandable that a section of the Greek Cypriots should demand democratization of the Church. The modernizers lacked access to the upper echelons of the Orthodox hierarchy and for that reason their faction sought "the most active participation of lay people, through democratic procedures, in the management of church funds, as a lever by means of which the bourgeois class, which it represented, might intervene and have a say in the management of ecclesiastical property but also participation in the community's decision-making" (Katsouridis 2010: 49).

On the basis of this orientation a political discourse developed on the side of the modernizers centred on the need for change in the regulations for management of ecclesiastical revenues and more direct participation of lay people in church finances. To put it somewhat differently, the modernizers did not seek a diminution of the role of the Church as political representative of the Cypriot nationality. They were not proponents of a radically different rebellious ideology which would challenge the power of the Church as a whole: they sought a different role for the Cypriot Church. They wanted a body that would be subject to control from the flock and would take the lead in demanding *Enosis*, in that way articulating the desires of the newly formed bourgeois strata. It was for this reason that they accepted continuation of the hegemonic position of the Church vis à vis the Greek population and characterized it as "the safest and most certain centre for the nation" (Katsouridis 2010: 56). Arguably an important role in this was played by awareness of common interest at the social level. On the one hand the emergent bourgeois strata and on the other the Church, which quite apart from politics was also a powerful economic force.[18] Through this protracted but real process of capitalist integration of Cypriot society it was to be expected that these two aspects from a certain point onwards would come together.

Historical Development

The first time that the dispute acquired distinct features was in 1889 when the question arose of sending a delegation to London where the demand for *Enosis* would be put forward. The "nationalistic" side wanted something along these lines whereas the "conservative" side, with Archbishop Sophronios as the dominant figure, was opposed (Katsouridis 2010: 48), though finally, given the majority that was at the disposal of the other side, he was obliged to participate (Katsiaounis 1996: 186–187).

The next time was in 1895 with the drafting of a memorandum addressed to the British administration and formulating certain economic and organizational demands. Taking their lead from this, a number of young professionals, mostly lawyers, who had studied in Greece, thought that what had to be prioritized was not secondary issues but *Enosis*. The "moderate" side, in contrast, thought that demands around certain immediate problems, and the elaboration of solutions to them, should not be hindered by the framing of a strategic goal. This division found expression in the schism within the Press also. According to Varnava, Archbishop Sophronios, representative of the "moderates", had accepted the "*Enosis*" outcome in the event that the British abandoned the island, not because he regarded himself as a Hellene but because after the massacres of the Armenians in 1894 by the Ottoman state, he preferred the prospect of living in the corresponding Greek state (Varnava 2013: 194).

The legislative elections of 1896, where the conservative side won an easy victory, provided the backdrop for the next showdown. But the mood had become acrimonious—intensely so—something that was to be repeated in the following confrontations. Harsh expressions were to be heard from both sides. The "Kitiakoi" called the Kyrenians "ravening

[18] In an essay published by the *Eleftheria* (Freedom) newspaper on 23rd December 1923 it says that the assets of the church organizations amounted to £1,125,000 sterling (at a time when the annual levy to Britain was £92,000) and that included cash (£3,000), deposits (£6,000), loans to villagers (£3,000), portable property (£44,000) and fixed assets of the Thrones and the Metropolitans (£200,000), of the Kykkos Monastery (£160,000) and other monasteries (£300,000) (Katsouridis 2009: 129).

wolves", "hell hounds", "a pack of scoundrels", "venomous snakes", "a murderous cabal", "insatiable leeches"; the Kyrenians for their part accused the "Kitiakoi" of being "anti-Greek, working against the national interests" (Katsouridis 2010: 51).

The supporters of the conservatives included old Nicosia politicians, the most important merchants and lenders from Nicosia, Kyrenia and Famagusta and the totality of those having dealings with the schools, the monasteries and the Archiepiscopate. This is why a basic element in the programme of the hardliners was control of the Church finances. Most of the lower-ranking clergy, particularly in the monasteries, had sided with the moderates, as had the bigger shop owners and master craftsmen. What is interesting is that a large number of indebted farmers had also lined up with the moderates, and the poorer elements among the workers had done the same. The explanation for this is that through the client networks generated by the money lending mechanisms of the Church these people were politically dependent on their creditors (Katsouridis 2010: 52–53).

The "Kitiakoi" side included some of the affluent urban strata (lawyers, doctors, educators and rather fewer merchants and landowners) as well as the section of the intellectuals that supported *Enosis*. Their social support were the lower strata, the small producers and breadwinners who took up residence in the urban centres at the turn of the twentieth century, wage-earning artisans and unskilled labourers and sections of the farming population who lived close to cities (Katsouridis 2010: 54).

As one enters the twentieth century the continuing opposition, in contrast to the 1896 result, is compounded by the social transformations introduced by Cypriot economic development, with the consequence of a change in the balance of forces and the beginnings of a clear lead by the modernizers in the public opinion of the Greek Cypriots. Faced by this development the Kyrenian party attempted throughout the decade of the Archiepiscopal Question to resolve it without the involvement of the people, with continual attempts to have a new Archbishop elected through a convening of the Great Synod of Orthodoxy, a tactic in which they also had as their ally the Ecumenical Patriarch who, Ottoman subject as he was, wished to see the election of the Metropolitan of Kyrenia (Katsouridis 2010: 62). But it would be the dynamic of the movement of the modernizers that would impose the institution of a system of electors, some of whom would be elected by the people of Cyprus (Panayiotou 1999: 144–145).

The next phase of the conflict, the first for the Archiepiscopal Question as such,[19] would come on 3rd September 1900 with the process of election of the special representatives, from which it was the "Kitiakoi" who emerged victorious. Their orientation was towards a nationally aligned Church whose finances would be subject to public auditing: they elected 47 of the total of 66 general representatives (Katsiaounis 1996: 229). But the Kyrenians refused to accept the result and tempers flared further when they organized a meeting in Nicosia and a protest march towards the Archiepiscopate where they submitted a resolution challenging the result and signed by prominent personalities.[20] These contestations would lead to an impasse in the proceedings for election of the Archbishop which would continue for around eight years.

The new round of confrontation will take place in the elections for the Legislative Council in 1901, where there will be an impressive increase in numbers of registered voters from 12,093 in 1896 to 24,952! This is evidence that both parties had begun to attach great importance to mobilizing their supporters. It was the reason, also, that they called upon the people to vote for the organized lists of each side. The final outcome was a great victory for the "Kitiakoi", who elected all nine deputies (Katsouridis 2010: 64).

The tension would be even greater around the November 1906 elections, and the High Commissioner Charles King Harman accordingly determined, for the first time, that the elections would be conducted by secret ballot. Registered voter numbers increased again by 33%. But the same was not true for the numbers actually voting, where there was a slight fall by comparison with 1901: 17,166 as against 17,816, a development which translates as 51.65% participation in the elections compared to 71.4%. Probably the significantly reduced participation was attributable the fact of the secrecy of the ballot. The political patrons would have been anxious about how their clients would vote and would accordingly have been less determined to have them go to the polls. In any case the "Kitiakoi" were declared winners again only in the Limassol-Paphos region and this time a Kyrenian was also elected (Katsouridis 2010: 64).

[19] Archbishop Sophronios had died on 9th May 1900.

[20] Passions had so greatly intensified at that time that there was fighting in the streets between supporters of the contending parties (Katsianounis 1996: 232–233).

As for the central Archiepiscopal Question, in December 1907, the Kyrenian side would try to put an end to the issue, calling for convening of the Holy Synod of the Church of Cyprus. Finally, at the beginning of 1908 the High Commissioner Charles King Harman in his speech in the Legislative Council allowed it to be understood that the need for legislative intervention was now undeniable. On 19th February 1908, in response, the Patriarch of Constantinople Ioakim III appointed the Metropolitan of Kyrenia to the position of Archbishop. As a result, on 28th March there were clashes and incidents all over the island and a state of emergency was declared.[21] After all this, the British were prompted to table a bill prescribing election procedures on the basis, chiefly, of the provisions of the Holy Synod's encyclical of 1900.

The 1908 municipal elections were conducted in this gloomy climate. The conflicts came to a head and as a result of them in Nicosia a muslim mayor was elected. Under British rule it was the first time this had happened. This happened because the two Greek Cypriot sides could not agree on a candidate of common acceptance. Specifically, on 12th March municipal elections were held and in Nicosia 6 Greek Cypriots and 5 Turkish Cypriots were elected and together comprised the municipal council. The point is that of the 6 Greek Cypriots three were "Kitiakoi" and the other three were Kyrenians. On 19th March the Administrator of Nicosia invited the 11 municipal councillors to elect a mayor, who on 1st April would take up his duties (Lympouridis 1985: 96). But the Greek Cypriots did not put in an appearance because they had not agreed on the person they would support, so only the 5 Turkish Cypriots turned up, and they proposed Mehmet Shevket Bey for Mayor. Because they did not have a quorum the election did not take place finally and the process was adjourned until 21st March. But even then, the Greek Cypriots did not show up. Finally, at the third session the Greek Cypriots came and the three "Kitiakoi" proposed Nikolaos Dervis and the three Kyrenians Paschalis Konstantinidis. The Turkish Cypriots persisted with Mehmet Shevket Bey who, having the requisite majority, was proclaimed Mayor of Nicosia (Lympouridis 1997: 62–63).

The bill for the election of the Archbishop finally went to the vote on 6th May 1908 and was published in the governmental gazette on 25th

[21] The Metropolitan of Kyrenia, proclaimed Archbishop, recognized the seriousness of the situation and did not accept his election, sending a telegram to the Ecumenical Patriarch to this effect (Lympouridis 1985: 96).

May 1908. The authorities would ignore the protests of the Kyrenians and would nominate 10th February 1909 as the date for the election of the special representatives. A total of 993 special representatives elected the 60 general representatives who, together with the Holy Synod, on 21st April 1909, elected the Metropolitan of Kition as the new Archbishop. The Kyrenians abstained in the elections and the representatives who were elected were all "Kitiakoi" (Katsouridis 2010: 62–63). On 18th February 1910, a public reconciliation was achieved between the Metropolitan of Kyrenia Kyrillos and the former Metropolitan of Kition and incumbent Archbishop of Cyprus Kyrillos.

After this turn of events the Cypriot Church adopted the orientation of *Enosis* (Anagnostopoulou 1999: 204). In this way the Church was detached from the past of centuries-long collaboration with the Ottoman occupation authorities as social demands associated with poverty and economic constraints were regarded, indirectly, as being soluble through the achievement of *Enosis*. It was a twofold development of great significance. On the one hand the Church acquired an entirely different role from the one it had adopted in the past, because for the first time it was emerging as a pole of opposition to state power, and on the other a uniform strategy was being elaborated, again for the first time, within the context of self-recognition of a national totality.

The extent to which disagreement was being effaced and the Greek Cypriots were homogenized was evidenced in the result of the 1911 elections to the Legislative Council. In them the number of voters was drastically reduced to less than half (8,241 as opposed to 17,166 in 1906). It is characteristic that in the Limassol-Paphos precinct elections were not held because the number of candidates was identical to the number of seats (Katsouridis 2010: 65).

7 The First Phase in the Emergence of the Turkish National Identity (1878–1912)

A significant proportion of the Greek-language literature on Cyprus takes the position that Turkish nationalism was an important factor in developments on the island in the 1950s when the armed insurgency commenced with the establishment of EOKA (National Organization of Cypriot Struggle). There are of course views that centre on its role in the interwar period. Without questioning the idea that in both these periods Turkish nationalism did make a tangible contribution to the course of events, the fact remains that it is crucial to take into account the factor of Turkish nationalism as manifested in the period prior to the First World War. Indeed, the existing evidence points to the appearance of this tendency as early as the first years of British rule.

The phenomenon is linked to the fact that the Muslims of Cyprus were in a state of twofold subordination, both on the political plane on account of the newly established British rule and on the economic, with the continuing growth in the economic prosperity of Greek Cypriots. Prior to the arrival of the British, the economic backwardness was counterbalanced by political domination, but now not only was this changing but at the same time the Greek side was positing, for the first time, the demand of *Enosis*. The anxiety of the Muslims increased after the annexation of Thessaly by Greece (1881), indicating that unequivocally Ottoman territory could become Greek—the more so that Britain had proceeded to assign the Ionian Islands to Greece in 1864. The fear that from being 24% of the Cypriot population the Muslims would be transformed into 2.5% of the Greek population made a decisive contribution to stimulating the sense of a common Muslim identity. The common religious and cultural elements gave a shared sense of belonging to a nationality, but they fell short of comprising a national identity. The change in Cyprus but also the international recognition of independence in Serbia, Bulgaria and Romania made it clear that the Ottoman Empire was ceasing to be what it had been, and continual border changes were coming to the fore. So, the entry of modernity into the former Ottoman Empire was raising the issue of national identity for the Muslims of Cyprus also.

It was in this context that in the 1880s the Ottoman society (Kiraathane) was founded in Nicosia in the form of a reading room, coffee shop and discussion centre. The Society would acquire its own print shop and begin to publish periodicals and from 1891 to 1900 the newspaper *Kir'ati Zaman*, which was influenced by the ideas of the Young Turk movement (Perikleous 2007: 283). Turkish Cypriot education contributed to this orientation. The secondary teachers had studied at Turkish universities, which facilitated transmission of the ideas of the Young Turk movement. The same was true of the primary schools because the teachers, graduates of the Lycee[22] became preachers of Turkish nationalism (Perikleous 2007: 284).

[22] Turkish Cypriot high school in Nicosia which was regarded as a bastion of the ideas of the Young Turks.

The events of the 1890s but also of the first decade of the twentieth century would be stamped by the way that Cyprus was affected by the events in Crete. As Niyazi Kızılyürek has aptly noted, the similarity between Crete and Cyprus (size, position, geopolitical significance, connection with the Ottoman Empire, duality of population. existence of a unity movement, involvement of Western powers) is noteworthy. Just as the Greek Cypriots saw the massacres and persecutions of the Greeks of Crete as a likely fate for themselves in the event of the island returning to the Ottoman Empire, so the Turkish Cypriots were afraid that this was what Turkish Cypriots could expect also if Cyprus was united with Greece.[23] This became particularly clear with the outbreak of the Greco-Turkish war of 1897.[24] So much tension was generated at that time that the High Commissioner issued a ban on public meetings, marches and articles in the press on the subject in question. What became obvious is that seeing the tendency of the Greek state to incorporate parts of the Ottoman Empire, the Muslims identified more and more with the latter. This led to them declaring their desire for Cyprus to remain a British possession and in the event of the English withdrawing for the island to be ruled again by Ottoman Empire (Perikleous 2007: 288).

Subsequently, when in April 1906 Greek Cypriots demonstrated in Famagusta in favour of *Enosis* and intruded, according to some accounts, into the precinct of a mosque, Muslims reacted by holding a meeting in Nicosia and shouting the slogan "Long live the Sultan!" In October 1907, a delegation of Muslims, including two of the three Muslim deputies, Shevket Bey and Mehmet Zei, visited Constantinople and in a series of contacts with Ottoman officials presented the problems of the

[23] When in 1910 the Greek Cypriot proposal was submitted for demographically proportionate representation of Greeks and Muslims on the Legislative Council, Sevket Bey reacted by referring to the "bitter example of Crete" and demanded that each community have an equal number of representatives. A few years later, in 1915, when Crete had been integrated officially into the Greek state and the question of *Enosis* of Cyprus had been posed following the relevant British offer (see below), Irfan Moussa Bey would say: "[...] The Muslim population of Cyprus fears the union of Cyprus with Greece and reacts against it intensely because they have seen the annihilation of Muslim populations in regions that have passed under Greek rule [...]. In 1878 there were 100,000 Muslims in Thessaly, (whereas) today there are hardly any. In Crete in 1897 there were 90,000 Muslims and today there are only 30,000 of them" (quoted in Ktoris 2013: 84–85).

[24] In 1897 Greece attempted to invade over Thessaly in the territories o the Ottoman Empire. The Ottomans will counterattack, and the war will end with a great defeat for Greece.

community and indirectly raised the issue of the return of Cyprus to the Ottoman state (Perikleous 2007: 286).

In this context in 1907 Mustafa Hami, member of the Legislative Council, tabled a proposal to the assembly for rotating occupation of the mayoral position for a time period proportionate to the population of each city and where the mayor would be a Greek Cypriot and the deputy mayor a Turkish Cypriot and vice versa. In 1908, the Turkish Cypriots of Famagusta sought to have their area declared a separate municipality (Perikleous 2007: 287).

In parallel in 1907 in Nicosia an authorized branch was established of the "Unification and Progress" Committee, which was the official name for the Young Turks and a few months later a second branch in Larnaca, which on account of the enrolment of a great number of members would be recognized in January 1908 as the headquarters of the Young Turk movement in Cyprus. In this way within the Turkish Cypriot elite central issues in the Young Turk ideology were placed on the agenda. The turn to science and education but also the projection of Turkish national identity[25] would be basic elements of the Young Turk movement in Cyprus (Perikleous 2007: 285).

All this would be intensified after the revolution of the Young Turks in Turkey in June 1908. It was thought then by Muslims that the movement in question could save the minority from the prospect of *Enosis* but also secure its rights in relation to British rule.

At this point it should be emphasized that above and beyond questions of language, religion, cultural identity but also fear of the likelihood

[25] At this point there is an important observation to be made. The articulation of every national identity undoubtedly includes an imaginary element that contributes to the sense of collective belonging. But common material elements are always the primary factor. In the case of the Turkish Cypriot community this means first of all common religion and language with metropolitan Turkey. But it does not mean only that. Anthropological studies have revealed a whole host of customs and practices shared by the Turkish Cypriots and the Turks of Anatolia: the mode of construction of the houses, the social behaviour associated with kinship, family and the community. Corresponding similarities can be seen in dietary habits but also in their traditional moral principles: respect for elders, specific behaviour between spouses, the sons of affluent families remaining in the paternal residence, the bride going to her husband's house, the son undertaking management of the land and the daughter care of the household (Erdentug 1973: 127). For a more comprehensive account of all the similarities between Turkish Cypriots and the Turks of Anatolia see all the relevant article of Erdentug.

of *Enosis*, an additional reason for assembling a Turkish national identity could be considered to be the demoting of the Muslim community from a superior social unit (Millet-iHakime) to a minority religious group obliged to operate on the basis of British rules. Essentially, as already mentioned, Muslims suffered a twofold shock. On the one hand they lost their primacy as a community and on the other they were henceforth obliged to follow the secularist course promoted by the British, something which led, for their community as well, to an overturning of the character of their religious/societal institutions. This development periodically caused tension in the relations between Muslims and Britons, contributing to the forging of a different national identity for the Muslims of Cyprus. The first conflict with the British took place when the Muslims vehemently criticized the introduction of proportionality for the election of members of the Legislative Council, proposing equal participation for the two communities (Kalantzopoulos 2015: 38).[26] The next controversy concerned the great number of changes the British instituted in their attempt to achieve secularization of the Evkaf—that is to say the fund for management of Muslim property. The first move was that they placed it under the joint management of a British official and a Muslim appointed by the Ottoman Ministry for Evkaf (Nevzat and Hatay 2009: 916), in that way implementing the relevant provisions of the Treaty of 1878. After that they began to limit the role of the religious courts supervising the Evkaf and placed Evkaf matters under the jurisdiction of the civil courts,

[26] The Muslims' protests were based on the fact that in its first version in the Legislative Council the proposal provided for appointment and not election of "representatives of the communities", with participation of an Orthodox Christian, G. Glykys, the Muslim M. Fuad Bey and a Franco-Levantine R. Mattel. The remaining three members were British officials. It is clear that not only were the Greek Cypriots equated with the Muslims but also that they were a minority among the members who were not British (Kyriakidis 2016: 45–46) This would change with the form assumed by the Legislative Council in 1881, which will provoke the protests of the muslims. Their argument was that from the moment that equal participation applied in the rest of the Ottoman Empire, the same be done in Cyprus because formally it was still Ottoman territory. The British counter-argument was that in the Ottoman Empire proper where locally elected representation was conceded, population balance was taken into account (Kyriakidis 2016: 93). When similar protests were also put forward by the Ottoman ambassador in London, the British side responded that in the 1878 Treaty no relevant condition was included covering the organization of the administration in Cyprus (Kyriakidis 2016: 93). The Ottoman side insisted that it could not be foreseen by the Ottoman Government that the British would consciously downgrade the status of the island's Muslims, but the British view was not about to change (Kyriakidis 2016: 94).

with the office of the Kadi deprived of many of its essential competences—though the Kadi continued to be appointed by the Sublime Porte and to preside over the *sharia* courts.[27] At the same time, in order to simplify the functioning of the Evkaf, the British abolished numerous small *vakif* properties. The *mutevellis* who had been running them were dismissed, receiving a one-off compensation payment. All this generated discontent in the Muslim elite, a situation compounded in 1907 when Muslim notables called for the ouster of Irfan Moussa Bey Muhasebeci from Evkaf, something which he accepted but the British did not (Bouleti 2011: 51–53). So, there were issues that caused tension in the relations between Britons and Muslims, a fact which contributed to the development of Turkish nationalism.

That said, an important role in the evolution of Turkish identity for the Muslims was played by the changes in the international environment. The war waged in 1911–1912 in North Africa between the Ottoman Empire and Italy ended in the defeat of the Ottomans and the loss of the Dodecanese. Almost simultaneously came the loss of Balkan territory in the first Balkan wars. The Turkish Cypriots saw that there were now considerably fewer areas inhabited by Orthodox Christians that were under the control of the Empire. They judged that this would encourage the Greek Cypriots to insist on the demand of *Enosis* (Kızılyürek 2009: 37). And indeed in 1912 the Greek Cypriot deputies resigned from the Legislative Council following the emergence of a serious political crisis centred on calls for an increase in political freedoms, abolition of the tribute (see below) and projection of the demand for *Enosis* with Greece (Koupanou 2017: 327).

This sharpening of the mood contributed decisively to the provocation of bloody incidents. The trigger was an excursion by fifteen pupils and two teachers from the Pancyprian Gymnasium where on their way back from the outing, according to the Greek version of events, they were attacked by Muslim shepherds, with one teacher being beaten up and a number of frightened pupils wandering for hours on the slopes of the Pentadaktylos. The Turkish Cypriot newspaper *Vatan* says that the pupils were singing Greek nationalistic songs and holding military exercises that extended to the houses of Muslims. The Muslims took three of them

[27] Correspondingly the Mufti, who was spiritual leader of the Muslim community, also continued to be appointed by the Sultan. It is obvious that the British were trying to preserve some elements of continuity with the previous regime, without that negating their basic goal of secularization.

hostage and escorted the others out of the village (Koupanou 2017: 333). In any case the incident was inflated out of all proportion with the result that skirmishes broke out in many villages on the island and intervention by the police (in which as indicated there were more Muslim Cypriots than Greek Cypriots) only heightened the tension even more. The conflict reached a climax on 14th May in Limassol where hundreds (or thousands according to some sources) of residents participated in a clash, leaving six dead (four Greek Cypriots and two Muslims) and hundreds injured (Papapolyviou 1997: 238). The police were obliged to call for reinforcements from a company of infantry to put down the unrest (Asmussen 2004: 87) and the Greek side denounced the killing of two Greeks by police, who had fired, according to the greeks, only in one direction.

After these developments, the mood between the two communities grew uglier. There were beatings of Muslims by Christians (Koupanou 2017: 337–338) and a proliferation of divisive actions. As Dudley-Huxton indicates in his 1913 study of Cyprus, most Greeks did not have dealing with Turks and there was a deep division between the two communities, linked to differences in language, religion and customs (cited in Nevzat 2005: 212). Indicative of the shaping of a different national consciousness is the fact that Turkish Cypriots enlisted in the Ottoman army during the Balkan wars and the 1st World War as well as in the war for Turkish national independence, whereas Greek Cypriots throughout the nineteenth century enlisted in Greek military forces and in the twentieth century fought alongside the Greek army in the Balkan wars (Papapolyviou 2010).

8 The Debate on *Enosis* Between Greeks and Turks Inside the Legislative Council: The General and Specific Context

During the nineteenth century there was not a relevant debate on the subject of *Enosis* inside the Legislative Council, on the one hand because the Greek community had opted for other modes of exerting pressure (demonstrations, memoranda, referenda) and on the other because there were serious disagreements, as already indicated, over the issue within that community. In contrast, throughout the twentieth century the subject of *Enosis* was raised many times directly in debates in the Legislative

Council,[28] taking the form of expression of a clear demand on the British that it should be implemented. In these cases the reaction of the Turks of Cyprus was always emphatically negative (Sakellaropoulos 2019: 69).

In the deliberation over implementation versus non-implementation of *Enosis* there were, both for the Greek and for the Turk deputies, arguments perennially used throughout the period from 1903 to 1931 and arguments linked to the specific conjuncture within which, on each occasion, the discussion was proceeding.

From the recurrent arguments put forward by the Greeks the following narrative emerges: Cyprus is inhabited by a 4/5 majority who are Greeks and have lived on the island for thousands of years (Kyriakidis 2016: 431). Despite the successive conquests, by Franks, Venetians, Turks, Britons, the Greeks have managed to survive by virtue of their specific characteristics and their civilization. Given this, and in the light of their demographic superiority but also of the liberal character of the British polity, they ask that, as was done with the Ionian islands,[29] Britain should consent to *Enosis* of Cyprus with Greece. As for the question of the fate of the Muslims of Cyprus, if they desired to remain in what would now be a Greek Cyprus, they would enjoy the same rights as the other Greek citizens, and those who left would be leaving not because of the policies of the Greek state but because of the inability of the Muslims to accept living as a minority.

In relation to the financial situation of Greece, the point would be made that despite its years-long involvement in wars, its economic growth has been noteworthy, as expressed in the development of its infrastructures, and there would be emphasis on the fact that *per capita* taxation is lower in Greece than in France or Great Britain. Also mentioned would

[28] Above all in the course of the responses of the Greek side to the annual speech of the Governor where in various years (1903, 1904, 1905, 1906, 1907, 1909, 1911, 1914, 1915, 1916, 1917, 1918, 1920, 1931) the demand was that a paragraph should be appended referring to the desire of the Greeks of Cyprus for union with Greece. In 1928 and 1930 the question was raised of ceding more powers up until the achievement of "national independence". These responses were part of the ceremonial following the delivery of the annual speech of the High Commissioner and Governor from 1924 onwards in which, sometimes, various demands of the elected deputies, were aired.

[29] The argument of the precedent of the Ionian islands is mentioned, *inter alia,* by N. Rossos in 1903 (Minutes of the Legislative Council 1903: 41), by T. Theodotou (Minutes of the Legislative Council 1915: 25–26) but also by L. Loizou (Minutes of the Legislative Council 1917: 27).

be the very powerful presence of its merchant fleet and the fact would be underlined that in a very brief space of time it managed to house and settle one and a half million refugees after the defeat in Asia Minor in 1922.[30] Economic development in Cyprus under British rule, in contrast, was characterized by stagnation when it came to covering the social needs of the inhabitants. Whatever had been achieved was attributable to the hard work of the Cypriot people. Moreover, *Enosis* would have the effect of eliminating customs duties with Greece whereas rival products from other countries would face the high tariffs of the Greek state (Sakellaropoulos 2019: 70).

The Muslims for their part, as they projected their counter-arguments, were constructing an altogether different narrative. Cyprus had never been Greek,[31] the coming to power of the Ottomans had been to the benefit of the Greeks. The agreement ceding the island to the British provided that in the event that the British decided to leave Cyprus, it would be returned to Turkey (Koupanou 2017: 260–261). Evocation of the Ionian case was inappropriate for two reasons: the first was that the Ionian islands belonged to England whereas Cyprus at least until 1925 did not. The second was because the geographical position of Cyprus is much more important than that of the Ionian islands. Beyond that they responded negatively to the—rhetorical—question of whether Greek was capable economically and militarily of protecting Cyprus (Kyriakidis 2016: 451). In any case they were opposed to the prospect of *Enosis* because they feared that it would be followed by practices of their deracination from Cyprus, something that had already happened with the Muslims in Greece.

But most interesting are the arguments elaborated in response to the historical conjuncture, which can be divided into following four phases.

The first phase extends from the turn of the twentieth century up to the outbreak of the First World War and it is characterized by limited exposure of the issue. This can be attributed to the fact that on the one hand Greece had had numerous other open fronts (Crete, Macedonia, Thrace) and on the other Britain was arguing that Cyprus did not belong

[30] In 1922 Greece was defeated by Turkey in the war waged for the conquest of Asia Minor. The result was that about 1,500,000 Greeks living in Turkey were forced to emigrate to Greece.

[31] Irfan Moussa Bey (Minutes of Legislative Council 1916: 7), Nejati Bey (Minutes of Legislative Council 1931: 22).

to it so that it was unqualified to conduct any discussion on *Enosis*. In any case the Muslims of Cyprus were altogether opposed to the prospect of *Enosis*, maintaining that in the event of British withdrawal from the island it should return to the Ottoman Empire (Sakellaropoulos 2019: 85).

In the second phase, which includes the entirety of the First World War, the scene is modified for two reasons: the first is that after the end of the Balkan wars Greece has annexed the greater part of Macedonia, South Epirus, Western Thrace and Crete, and accordingly is now able to set its sights on Asia Minor, Constantinople, Northern Epirus, and also Cyprus. The second has to do with the state of war between Britain and the Ottoman Empire, which enabled Britain to declare the island a Crown possession (1914) and accordingly to assume responsibility themselves for its subsequent fate. In this situation the Greek parliamentarians in the Legislative Council pressured the British to carry out *Enosis* on the basis of the argument that (i) it no longer belongs to the Sultan and (ii) Britain's involvement in the war can be presented as participation in the struggle for freedom of the peoples. Particularly after the 1915 offer (see below) the Greek side stepped up its pressures, judging that the momentum for *Enosis* had arrived. The argumentation of the Muslim deputies was based on three axes: The first was that from the moment that the Ottoman Empire had not consented to the island's being declared a British colony, the question of Cyprus's status remained undetermined and would have to be clarified when the war had ended. The second was that hearing of *Enosis* would provoke very intense reactions among Muslims living in the British Empire. The third was that ultimately the British and the Ottomans would find a way to achieve a rapprochement.

The third phase covers the period from 1918 to 1930. The end of the First World War would find Cyprus outside the priorities of the Greek government. Moreover, the British side had decided to keep it under its own rule (see below). Because of this the Greek deputies' posture was defensive (whereas throughout the First World War it could be argued that they had been on the offensive). The efforts for *Enosis* were perfunctory because of the international balance of forces, which became even more unfavourable after the defeat of Greece's Asia Minor campaign. Realizing that they were in the stronger position, the Turkish deputies in their interventions in the Legislative Council persisted in highlighting the benefits for Britain of continued occupation of Cyprus. The conclusion drawn from all this by the Greek side was initially that they should adopt a stance of abstention from the proceedings in the Council and subsequently that they should project, as they did in two years (1928 and 1930), the issue of national independence but not *Enosis*.

The fourth phase includes the watershed year of 1931, when the question of *Enosis* was posited by the Greek Cypriots in a most intense manner. At that time, a range of current issues (an increase in taxation through the budget, advent of the consequences of the global crisis in the Cypriot economy) would come to be added to the pre-existing factors for discontent (payment for around 50 years of the Tribute of Cyprus—see below, extreme social inequality, uncontrolled action of the creditor stratum) so resulting in profound discontent with the regime of British rule (see below). It came to be assumed that the achievement of *Enosis* would free the Greeks of Cyprus from these woes, so that the demand was raised again for the first time in ten years inside the Legislative Council. Within this body the conflict assumed harsh tones. Essentially the British were accused by the Greeks of pursuing a violent colonialistic policy (Onurkan-Samani 2018: 84) which had to be terminated forthwith. At the same time Greeks and Turks were exchanging recriminations over who was the foreigner on the island. Beyond that, both sides were attempting to persuade the British what solution would be in the best interests of Britain. The Turkish arguments centred on the vested interests which remained applicable for the British in Cyprus, while at the same time they kept issuing reminders of Cyprus's proximity to Turkey, a fact which in their opinion put Turkey in the lead when it came to discussing the island's future. The Greek side focussed on the provision of military facilities to the British in the event of *Enosis* (Sakellaropoulos 2019: 86).

What is important is that in reality the discussion was taking place within a given international balance of power which there was no prospect of overturning. The Turks were well aware of this situation and for this reason made mention of the fact that not even the Greek state was any longer insisting on *Enosis* (Kyriakidis 2016: 547).[32] It would be precisely this unfavourable power balance internationally that would preclude the 1931 movement from achieving its objectives, experiencing not only liquidation from the British machinery of repression but also censure from the Venizelos government (see below).

[32] The stance of the Greek government on *Enosis* in the 1930–1931 period is presented in Chapter 5.

9 The British Offers of Cession of Cyprus to Greece in 1912 and 1915

Irrespective of what happened in Cyprus, the more general developments occurring on the international terrain in the decade after 1910 would induce the British to initiate negotiations with the Greek state with a view to the possible cession of the island in exchange for the conclusion of a military alliance with Greece.

The 1912 Offer

The issue was first tabled for negotiation in 1912. The Italo-Turkish war and the outbreak of the Balkan wars appeared to be introducing significant changes into the European power balance. Italy was emerging as an evidently powerful presence in the Mediterranean and Austria was promoting a policy of entry and presence in the Mediterranean, eliciting a notably anxious response from Britain. The final phase of the Italo-Turkish war of 1911–1912 did indeed aggravate relations between Britain and Italy. Contributing to this were factors such as the likelihood of establishment of Italian naval bases near Suez, the friction between the Entente and Italy during the Italo-Turkish war, the disputes between Italy and Britain as exemplified by the surrender to the British of the Italian-occupied fortified Libyan town of Sallum. The British were apprehensive that the Italians, but also the Austro-Hungarians, might proceed with construction of dreadnought-type battleships.[33] The Italians were exhausted from war with the Ottomans and this made the British uneasy about the prospect of them allying themselves with the Austro-Hungarians in a possible war against the forces of the Entente. This would mean equality if not the supremacy of the fleet of the two powers against that of England. The British therefore decided in July 1912 to launch a large enough naval force to be able to face the Austrians on their own. But pending that, which they estimated they would manage in 1915, there would have to be a stopgap solution (Fotakis 2008: 93–93).

It was for this reason that they chose Greece, which had a strong navy, which in certain circumstances was in a position to operate in a supplementary role to the corresponding British fleet, but which also had an extensive coastline and natural harbours. Also of great significance was

[33] This was the predominant model of battleship at the turn of the twentieth century.

the possibility of establishing British bases in the Ionian Sea because this would make it possible for the Strait of Otranto to be monitored effectively so that confronting the Austrian fleet would become feasible. (Hadjivasileiou 2009: 230).

Unofficial contacts were employed, in November 1912, to pursue this collaboration, namely between Sir John Stavridis, Greek Consul general in London, Lloyd George, Chancellor of the Exchequer, and Winston Churchill, who was at that time First Lord of the Admiralty. Churchill[34] proposed utilization of the harbour of Argostoli by the British fleet and in return promised cession of Cyprus. And indeed, on 17th December of the same year an agreement was reached on Cyprus and Argostoli. Greek Prime Minister E. Venizelos consented, judging that not even King George would have any objection. His only fear was that in the event that Britain used Argostoli for military actions Greece would be infringing its neutral status. Accordingly, the agreement would have to remain secret (Varnava 2009: 255–256).

But from the beginning of the next year, it started to become evident that following relevant pressure from the French, the English were coming to prefer an overall settlement, that is to say adoption of an open Anglo-Hellenic treaty with secret clauses covering sensitive aspects of military collaboration (Christodoulou 1999: 93–96). The main reason for this was that they felt stronger as a naval power in the Mediterranean and the North Sea and were not so much in need of Argostoli. That is also evident from the fact that on 6th February 1913 the German announced that they would be proceeding with a limitation of spending on military equipment on account of the economic and diplomatic impasses they were facing as a result of soaring defence expenditures. At the same time, with its conquest of Libya Italy found itself obliged to stay on good terms with England and France, who retained powerful military forces in the region—the British in Egypt and the French in their North African possessions (Fotakis 2008: 94–95).

Of course, there were also reasons of secondary importance for the final cancellation of this offer. Churchill ascertained that Greece was not following the advice of the Admiralty in its naval policy. The withdrawal of the British fleet and the undertaking by Greece of responsibility for the security of the Aegean islands and the waters around Cyprus was

[34] Churchill was quite well-informed on the question because in 1907 when he was Under-Secretary of State for the Colonies he had visited Cyprus (see below).

a gamble which depended on the mobility of the Greek navy and the establishment of defensive flotillas. The policy was not adopted by Greece (Varnava 2009: 260). This in conjunction with the upheaval introduced by the conflicts between the victors of the first Balkan wars[35] and the commencement of the second Balkan wars, not to mention the internal discord that was visited upon Britain by the crisis around the Irish question[36] would all contribute to Churchill's proposal being taken offstage (Richter 2007: 163–164).[37]

The 1915 Offer

The outbreak of the First World War and Britain's apprehension of a general attack of the Central powers on Serbia, not to mention the appeal for help from the Russians, who were under great pressure from the Ottomans on the Caucasus front, would highlight the need for Greece's participation on the side of the Entente.

In the interest of achieving this objective from as early as the end of 1914 Britain was in search of a suitable inducement that could be offered. Venizelos himself had mentioned that an appropriate recompense could energize public opinion and help to bring Greece into the war. On 11th January 1915 the British Foreign Office official Sir Lancelot Oliphant said that the inducement could be Smyrna and perhaps Cyprus,[38] and

[35] It is a fact that Britain feared the dissatisfaction of the Ottoman Empire precisely because it sought to keep it far away from Germany (Pikros 1980: 8).

[36] The aggravation of the Irish question and the discussion within the British elite on military intervention made it impossible for any loss of British territory, even of limited extent, to be countenanced (Varnava 2009: 261).

[37] It is worth noting the reaction of the Turkish Cypriots to this prospect (overlooking the fact that they were not fully informed of the plan): in December 1912 the Turkish Cypriots participating in the Legislative Council Mehmet Sevkey, Mustafa Hami and Mehmet Ziyai, sent a protest to Britain Home Secretary in which *inter alia* they indicated that in the event that Britain could not continue to have Cyprus under its occupation, it was prefereable for the island to be ceded to Egypt than to be transferred over to Greece (Nevzat 2005: 209).

[38] The fact of the outbreak of the First World War in August 1914 and the participation of the Ottoman Empire in the camp opposing the British, along with the Austro-Hungarians, resulted in the issuance of a Royal Decree on 5th November 1914 by which Britain declared null and void the Treaty of 1878 and annexed Cyprus. Immediately after the annexation the Greek Cypriot side started pushing towards *Enosis*. Thus, on 8th November, only three days after the official British annexation, the Greek Cypriot

the Cyprus option was aired on 11/1/1915 by another senior official. On 18/1 in a telegram to the British ambassador in Paris F. Bertie, the Foreign Secretary Grey said that Greek participation in the war was so important that "we too will be considering ceding Cyprus to Greece". One day later Grey indicated that he would be raising the issue of cession of Cyprus at the next Cabinet meeting.

It should of course be noted that above and beyond the importance of implicating Greece in the war, Cyprus itself, according to a section of the British Establishment, was not of much consequence for the British, given that the basic priority was to deal with the threat of German's high seas fleet. It was for this reason that at the beginning of 1913 they had allowed France to take the lead in maintaining a naval presence in the Mediterranean. As Prime Minister Asquith puts it in a letter: "It is not worth much to us—now that I mention it, it is not worth anything". Remarks in the same vein were made by George V who, having accepted the possibility of the island's being ceded would emphasize through his private secretary Stamfordham: "Financially Cyprus is, I suppose, a loss to this country. Strategically His Majesty understands that it has proved a failure: the harbours impracticable and ships obliged to lie six miles from the coast. So far as this war is concerned its strategic value would be the same to us if in the possession of the Greeks" (cited by Georghallides 1979: 95). But the objections raised by Kitchener, Secretary of State for War, according to which Cyprus was necessary for penetration through Alexandretta into Mesopotamia and the Persian Gulf, resulted in no decision being taken by the Cabinet.

Shortly afterwards, as negotiations continued with various proposed trade-offs (division of Albania between Greece and Serbia, cession of Smyrna) the Greek Consul General in London Sir John Stavridis, in a personal initiative, would propose an overall package of proposals, among which were included—once again—the cession of Cyprus, but also of Northern Epirus, Smyrna and the Dodecanese. The English would have accepted everything apart from ceding the Dodecanese, given that they thought the Italians would be willing to come in on the side of the Entente. However, the Greek Government, where Venizelos has resigned due to disagreements with King Constantine in favour of entering the war on the side of thee Entente, did not want to abandon the neutral

deputies and Archbishop Kyrillos visited the British Commissioner, submitting to him the demand for *Enosis*.

position and rejected the British proposal in an official communique of 28/3/1915 (Richter 2007: 182).

The occupation of Belgrade on 9th October 1915 by the army of Mackensen would induce the British to proceed even further with concessions to the Greeks on the basis of an entirely new logic: they would offer Cyprus in direct exchange for Greek participation in the war. In a telegram sent on 16th October by Grey to the British Ambassador in Athens Sir Francis Elliot it was asserted that Britain was willing immediately to cede Cyprus to Greece on the precondition that the latter would join the war on the side of the forces of the Entente.[39] At the same time through Bonar Law—Secretary of State for the Colonies, a telegram was sent to the High Commissioner of Cyprus Sir John Clauson by means of which not only was he told of the decision but he was also asked to inform the Greek Cypriot political elite so that pressure could begin to be exerted on Athens (Richter 2007: 188–189).

The British strategy had clearly undergone many changes. On the one hand they were ceding Cyprus as a direct trade-off and on the other for attainment of the goal of Greek entry into the war with the incentive of Cyprus they had decided to mobilize Cypriot Hellenism themselves. That the British were in a difficult position in this conjuncture was obvious. The more so when, as acknowledged by Lord Robert Cecil, Assistant Secretary of Foreign Affairs, the aim was to have the Archbishop approach Athens with the British proposal in his hands and that he should inform the King and the Parliament so that the popular enthusiasm generated would have a catalytic effect (Pikros 1980: 20). But the plan came to nothing because Clauson raised objections, fearing the reactions of the Muslims, who had hitherto been the Crown's basic ally on the island.[40] On the other hand, in Athens the King, briefed on the issue by the Prime Minister Zaimis,[41] rejected the proposal on 18th October, insisting on the view that Greece should maintain a neutral stance. In reality. this development represented a clear victory for the Germanophile circles in Athens,

[39] For the text of the telegram see Koumoulides (1987: 96).

[40] Informed of the developments, the Cypriot Muslims indeed submitted a memorandum in which they declared their total opposition to the plan being elaborated and their desire that Cyprus should remain under British rule (Richter 2007: 192–193).

[41] Zaimis maintained later in an unpublished letter of his to Dimitrios Gatopoulos that it was Constantine himself who made the decision: "unfortunately I was persuaded from higher up" (quoted in Woodhouse 1985: 88).

who had reached the point of disseminating the idea that with their ultimate victory the Germans would cede Cyprus to Greece in response to the stance of neutrality (Georghallides 1979: 101).

What should be noted is that despite the disappointment that predominated on the British side over the failure of this plan, there were those who saw the outcome as favourable, judging that Cyprus's geostrategic status would gradually rise. At the Secretariat for Colonies, for example, a sanguine mood prevailed: "The issue of ceding Cyprus has collapsed, hopefully forever" (quoted in Richter 2007: 192). Shortly before the end of the First World War the English General Staff would put it even more succinctly: "the value of Cyprus has tended to increase rather than being likely to decline in future". The reason for this is because the invention and use of aircraft, apart from ships, as a weapon of war, has made it possible to establish military bases with a view to "controlling the regions of Asia Minor, Syria, Egypt and a considerable section of the Berlin-Baghdad railway" (cited in Tsalakos 1981: 165). As a reading it gained traction when the First World War ended and other powers made their entry into the Eastern Mediterranean: France in Syria and Lebanon, Italy in the Dodecanese, Libya and later Albania (Hadjivasileiou 2009: 230).

For these reasons the negotiations which followed the First World War (Paris Peace Conference) did not include any ceding of Cyprus given the assessment that anything like that would diminish the naval and air supremacy of Great Britain in the Near East and Middle East (Klapsis 2013: 768–771)[42] and there were voices that spoke of the need for preserving equilibrium with the Ottoman Empire and others who expressed doubts as to how far in future Greece would be an ally of Britain (Varnava 2019: 170–171). Apart from this the revolts that broke out more or less simultaneously in India, Egypt and Malta in 1919

[42] For the importance Cyprus had for London in that conjuncture also see the British documents in Svolopoulos (1985: 240–241) and Georghallides (1971–1972: 227). The truth is that for Britain to arrive at the decision not to cede Cyprus a very intense internal dialogue was needed beforehand. Even some of those who during the war had favoured cession of Cyprus were at the same time in favour of ceding Kavalla to Bulgaria (Varnava 2019: 163). On the other hand, more than a few who rejected *Enosis* used other arguments apart from the geopolitical: Most Greek Cypriots supported the ex-King Constantine who did not want Greece embroiled in the First World War; Greece went into the war at the last minute; there was vehement opposition from the Muslims; the movement for *Enosis* did not attract the support of the majority of Greek Cypriots etc. (Varnava 2019: 169–170).

further reinforced the perception of a need for the British presence to be retained in Cyprus (Varnava 2019: 173). The French position also had an inhibiting effect.[43] Moreover, the Treasury opposed any such alteration, judging that the cession of Cyprus would mean that British citizens would be obliged to undertake servicing of the loans that the City's money markets had made to the Sultan (Varnava 2019: 167). When the Ottoman Empire had been declared bankrupt and the island had been ceded to the British this loan had been serviced through appropriation by the British of the budget surplus recorded by Cyprus[44] (Richter 2007: 216). At the same time considerable numbers of British business people with interests in Cyprus were pressuring for Britain to remain ((Varnava 2019: 168). Also, to be noted was the reaction of the Muslims of Cyprus, who in a relevant resolution of their national council (Meclis-iMillet) in December 1918 asked for the return of Cyprus to the Ottoman Empire (Moutsis 2014: 133). But the *Enosis* issue would not be raised by the Greek government either, having as they did the priority of securing support from the allies for the occupation of Smyrna by the Greek army, which was carried out in May 1919 (Holland-Markides 2007: 329; Varnava 2019: 177).

10 The *Enosis* demand in the 1920s

The failure of their demands for *Enosis* did not daunt the Greek Cypriots, who were determined to keep struggling for accomplishment of their vision, even without clear support from Greece. Thus, on 9th December 1920 the nine Greek Cypriot deputies resigned in protest at Britain's refusal to cede Cyprus to Greece, through this action initiating

[43] On 23rd December 1920 France signed an agreement with Britain where in article 4 it states that owing to the geographical and strategic position of Cyprus just outside the Gulf of Alexandretta, the British government agrees not to engage in negotiations for cession of Cyprus without the prior consent of the French government. The agreement was concluded just before the return to Greece of the deposed, for a time, King Constantine, because on the one hand the French side, but also the British, feared the possibility of Cyprus coming under the control of a hostile power but on the other because having already occupied Syria, the French were interested in annexing Alexandretta. The latter goal was accomplished a little later, in October 1921, when France with the Treaty of Ankara recognized the government of Kemal Ataturk and withdrew from Cilicia but retained control of Alexandretta (Pikros 1980: 50–52).

[44] For a more thorough presentation of this question see Sect. 4 of Chapter 5.

a campaign of rejection of all co-operation with the British authorities. In the repeat elections that were held subsequently the same people were elected[45] only to resign again, submitting a memorandum, on 8th March 1921, in which they demanded that a referendum be held on the question of *Enosis* with Greece. The British government refused in response and at the next elections, which were held on 3rd November 1921, the National Council of the Political Organization of Cyprus, which had been established a short time previously with a view to achieving *Enosis*,[46] decided on a stance of abstention.

The abstention line would be continued in the repeat elections also, which were held on 4th January 1923 to fill the seven[47] vacant places for non-Muslims. Finally, there were 14 Greek candidacies, but they received very few votes.[48] This result showed that the National Council retained significant influence. In any case the elected Greek Cypriots differed a great deal ideologically in their views from those of the great majority of their compatriots, which did not bestow great legitimacy on them.

Nevertheless, on the one hand the continued failures to secure acceptance from the British authorities of the demand for Enosis and on the other the hope that Cyprus would be proclaimed a British colony,[49] with resultant coming into force of the new Constitution, would generate some favourable momentum for the Greek Cypriots and lead to a change

[45] To be precise elections were not held on 21st January 1921 as programmed, given that there were no rival candidacies so the government considered the candidates elected (Richter 2007: 256).

[46] The National Council was the supreme body of the Political Organization of Cyprus, with 46 members. 41 of them were elected and 5 were *ex officcio*: the Archbishop, the Metropolitans of Paphos, Kitio, Kyrenia and the abbot of the Kykkos Monastery (Choisi 1995: 44).

[47] There were seven vacant positions and not nine, which was the total, because in the 1921 elections, on British encouragement, two Maronites stood as candidates for elections, and were elected.

[48] The level of participation was very low: 6% in the Nicosia-Kyrenia region, 8% in the Paphos-Limassol region, and there were more votes against than for in the case of many of those elected. That happened because for each candidate the voter had the right to submit either a positive or a negative vote (Richter 2007: 282).

[49] Adoption of the Treaty of Lausanne (1923) paved the way for Cyprus to join the British Commonwealth, with Turkey stating that it could no longer claim any right over Cyprus. Turkey gave this acknowledgement in return for abolition of the Capitulations for British subjects (Kaukaridis 2010: 20). On 10th March 1925 Cyprus accordingly became a member of the British Commonwealth.

of course. Thus in June 1923 when the 3rd Pancyprian National Assembly was convened, it decided in a majority vote that the demand for constitutional reforms should have precedence as an intermediate step towards *Enosis*, and the claim was postponed for a time when things were more straightfoward. But for a vote on constitutional changes to pass there would have to be Greek Cypriot deputies to vote for it (Konstantinidis 2011: 115). Thus, in mid-May 1925 the National Council resolved that: "Faced with the situation created under this government and its agencies the Council has decided that the people should not abstain from the coming parliamentary elections" (quoted in Christodoulou 1999: 138). Certain additional factors contributed to this decision—for example, the ideological consequences of the recent defeat of Greece by Turkey in Asia Minor but also the sidelining of the National Council by the Authorities' recognizing as representatives of the Greek Cypriots the elected deputies, that is to say the individuals who had submitted candidacies in defiance of the line of the Council.

Among the interesting details of the elections of 1925 was the election of C. Hadjiprokopis who had served as a deputy in the period of abstention by the National Council (a development which may be interpreted on the one hand as a reflection of the significant clientelistic networks of that time but also as a result of the active support he enjoyed from the High Commissioner Sir Malcolm Stevenson) (Protopapas 2012: 251), the election of the Metropolitan of Kition Nicodemos—for the first time in many years a priest was elected to parliament, the election of Rossides, who appeared now on the scene as leader of the newly founded Agrarian Party[50] and the election of three deputies from the likewise newly founded People's Party (Hadjipavlou, Stavrinakis, Ioannides). In terms of political programmes, Nicodemos placed the subject of *Enosis* at the centre of his campaigning and the group of Hadjipavlou launched attacks on the Church and the existing "political aristocracy" (*Historical Encyclopedia of Cyprus* 1979–1980 No. 5: 121–124).[51]

The new deputies emerging after the elections of 13th October sought to advance four basic demands: abolition of the Tribute of Cyprus (they acquired the majority on this, together with the Turkish Cypriots but the

[50] The Agrarian Party was founded in April 1924 with the objective of defending the interests of the rural population.

[51] For the brief career of the Popular Party see Katsourides (2014: 82–84).

Governor too would impose it with an Order in council—see below), the abolition of the tithe in grain production (in co-operation with the Turkish Cypriots it was abolished in 1926), reimbursement of the sums withheld through the budget in the form of the Tribute of Cyprus (notwithstanding the alliance with the Turkish Cypriots they did not succeed in obtaining this), the granting of a liberal Constitution.

To achieve the change in the Constitution the Greek Cypriot deputies submitted the relevant memorandum demanding the institution of a regime of self-government. The Turkish Cypriots submitted their own memorandum at the same time in which they asserted "We are opposed to the demands of the Greek deputies both for *Enosis* and for Autonomy under the British Crown. Through the demand for autonomy the Greeks seek to expel from the Colony all the British governmental employees other than 5–6 in the top positions so as to assume control themselves, leaving just a few crumbs for the Muslim elements" (cited in Economides 1993: 16). The following answer was given by the Secretary of State for the Colonies on 23rd February 1926: "The question of *Enosis* with Greece has been definitively closed and cannot be reopened, and as for demand for self-government, the Secretary does not think that Cyprus has reached such a stage of political development as to justify, for the moment, the concession of broader constitutional powers" (cited in Economides 1993: 16).

The factors that brought the British to this stance had to do with the more general geostrategic interests of the United Kingdom on account of the growth of French and Italian influence in the Mediterranean[52] and the corresponding strategic significance acquired by Cyprus, particularly after the coming into use of aircraft. Britain accordingly continued to have a particular interest in retaining possession of the island and it was on the basis of that interest that it framed its policies throughout the 1920s.

Not realizing the above, the Greek Cypriot side attached importance to issues of secondary significance. For example, the coming to office of the Labour Party in June 1929 rekindled the hopes of the Greek Cypriots given the declaration of the party's leader Ramsay MacDonald at the International Socialist Conference in Bern that "the Labour Party will implement self-determination in Cyprus when it comes to power". On the basis of this position the Greek Cypriot deputies presented a

[52] For a full presentation of the related British apprehensions see Svolopoulos (1985: 239–240).

relevant memorandum to the Labour government's Secretary of State for the Colonies Lord Passfield.[53] With the memorandum in question they demanded a more liberal constitution which would provide a framework for autonomy in government. But on 28th November 1929 Lord Passfield issued yet another negative response to the Greek Cypriots, employing exactly the same argumentation as his predecessors[54] (Richter 2007: 383–384).

11 Conclusion

The continual retreats of the Ottoman army after the mid-nineteenth century and the emergence of the Russian danger would provide a significant opportunity to the British Empire. Henceforth it would undertake the protection of the Sublime Porte from the Russians and in exchange Cyprus would be ceded to it, this being considered a strategically important place for control of the Mediterranean, at the same time opening the terrain for exploitation of the wealth-generating resources of Syria, Mesopotamia and Asia Minor.

The institutional framework for government imposed by the British colonialists included attempted modernization of some of the country's structures, without in any sense compromising the essence of English rule. The Legislative and Executive councils were instituted in this way, bodies controlled by the British sometimes directly and sometimes through the alliance they had with the Turkish Cypriot representatives, sometimes through the casting vote of the Governor, sometimes through referral to London of the controversial issue of the moment. But what was most important was the consolidation of the existence of two different national entities in a state of rivalry. This would become even more intense from the moment that the Greek Cypriot side would begin with some urgency to pose the question of *Enosis,* believing that this could be attained as occurred in the case of the Ionian Islands. On this point the Turkish Cypriots would be under pressure because they could not counter-propose entry into the disintegrating Ottoman Empire, the more so because the island had just withdrawn from Ottoman occupation. An attempt would be made to fill the gap through an upsurge in Turkish

[53] For the content of the memorandum see Alastos (1976: 326).

[54] Passfield's response is presented in (Richter 2007: 383–384).

Cypriot nationalism, the unfolding of a unified, national, religious and cultural identity. The bottom line was to avoid *Enosis* with Greece and to avert that it had to be abundantly clear that there was another entirely different national community on the island.

Thus, the parallel coexistence of two different communities became ever more conspicuous. The role of education was decisive in this. Each community followed its own curriculum, which appeared to have been transplanted from the corresponding motherland. The British encouraged the split precisely so as not to have to face co-ordinated moves by the two communities which might challenge their power.

The question of *Enosis* was unequivocally the dominant strategy of the Greek Cypriot element throughout the period. But it was no easy matter to impose it and adopt it. Continuing what had preceded vis à vis control of the coffers of the Kition Monastery, the conflict between the traditional wing of the Hierarchy and the alliance forged between the rising bourgeois strata and the "modernizing" tendency in the Church would continue throughout the last fifth of the nineteenth century. The "modernizers" were an expression of the rising bourgeois and petty bourgeois class and believed that their material interests would be served within a broader capitalist context that *Enosis* with Greece would provide for them. For that reason, they became supporters of such a scheme. In contrast, the "traditionalists" accepted that the Church should continue as a constituent element in the Ottoman power structure. Socially, apart from certain sectors of the religious hierarchy, they represented those rural strata who had become involved in usurious practices with the farming population, along with the borrowers themselves who under the threats of the usurers were obliged to support the "traditionalists". What is interesting is the contradiction this entails: on the one side was the colonial administration which sought modernization of the traditional structures of Cypriot society, in alliance with a coalition of non-capitalist forces, and on the other the modernizing alliance of up-and-coming bourgeois strata working for the overturn of the colonialist framework. It is interesting that both camps recognized sections of the ecclesiastical hierarchy as their political representatives. This reveals the continued presence of the established relations of representation that the Church had forged with the Greek Cypriots from the period of the Ottoman Empire, and on the other hand explains why the Ethnarchy would play such an important role in the twentieth century. Essentially the inherently contradictory character of this situation, where the traditional side is more closely linked with the colonialist forces, who are attempting to make the country more capitalist, whereas the pro-capitalist forces are in conflict with the British, contributes to the process of nationalization of the Church, precisely because capitalism as a system of social relations can be equated with the development of the national state.

Accordingly, at the turn of the twentieth century and henceforth, when the "modernizers" had emerged victorious, the Church would become consolidated as the political representative of the Greek Cypriots around the strategy of "*Enosis*". Through the coming years, in all the moves that would be made by the Greek Cypriots, the role of the Hierarchy would be that of a protagonist and would be decisive in the course of events. This is so because the modernizing side was never anti-clerical. It did not seek limitation of the role of the Church but a reformulation of the content of that role.

The vehement reactions of the Turkish Cypriots against the prospect of *Enosis* would not prevent the British from exploring it twice as a possibility in the second decade of the twentieth century. The first time was in 1912 when, seeking through an alliance with Greece and the securing of bases in Ionia to prevent the emergence of Austria into the Adriatic, the British offered cession of Cyprus in exchange. But the outbreak of the second Balkan wars, the crisis around the Irish question and the pressures from France for a more comprehensive settlement, scuppered that prospect. The second offer came in 1915 when the British proposed to cede Cyprus in exchange for Greek entry into the First World War. But the acquisition of governmental power by the forces that did not desire participation by Greece on the side of the Entente led to the cancellation of this proposal. But it should be noted that above and beyond the requirement that Greece should go with the Entente. a section of the British establishment believed that Cyprus no longer had the importance for the Empire that it had had in the past. Nevertheless, it was the opposite view from another section of the British elite that would prevail finally and determine British policy in the following years. It would be considered that the invention of the aircraft and its utilization as a weapon of war would make it possible for military bases to be established with a view to controlling a wider geographical area, upgrading the position of Cyprus in overall British planning.

In the 1920s the Greek Cypriots would many times bring back the subject of *Enosis* and the newly established National Council which co-ordinated the struggle for *Enosis* decided on abstention from the elections for the Legislative Council. Although this line enjoyed mass support, it did not prevail over the British decisiveness not to discuss cession of Cyprus. From the 1925 elections and after the Council would abandon the line of abstention and would attempt, through its elected deputies, to change the Constitution in a progressive direction. But this demand was also rejected given the continual upgrading of the importance of Cyprus in British planning. The situation would not change even when the Labour Party came to government. This development indicated that it had not been understood by the Greek Cypriots that the times had changed and the line of the bourgeois-colonialist British establishment was uniform and tightness.

References

Alastos, D. 1976. *Cyprus in History. A Survey of 5000 Years*. London: Zeno.

Anagnostopoulou, S. 1999. The Church of Cyprus and Its Role as Ethnarch: 1878–1960. The 'religiofication' of 'Cypriot' Political Activity: *Enosis. Synchrona Themata*, 68–69–70: 198–227.

Asmussen, J. 2004. Early Conflicts Between the Greek and Turkish Cypriot Communities in Cyprus. *Cyprus Review* 16 (1): 87–106.

Bouleti, E. 2011. The Muslin Community on Cyprus and British Colonial Policy 1878–1915. *Cyprus Review* 23 (2): 39–56.

Choisi, J. 1995. The Greek Cypriot Elite- Its Social Function and Legitimization. *The Cyprus Review* 7 (1): 32–68.

Christodoulou, M. 1999. *Relations Between Athens and Nicosia. Rise and Fall, Emergence and Regeneration*. Nicosia: Proodos (in Greek).

Crouzet, F. 1973. *Le Conflit en Chypre 1946-1959*. Tome Premier-Tome Deuxième, Bruxelles: Etablissements Emile Bruylant.

Dwight, Lee. 1931. A Memorandum Concerning Cyprus, 1878. *The Journal of Modern History* 3 (2): 235–241.

Economides, C. 1993. *Demythologized History of the Cyprus Issue in the Last 50 Years*. Nicosia: Economides Publishing House (in Greek).

Erdentug, N. 1973. The Cultural Unity of the Turkish Traditional Societies of Cyprus and Turkey. In *Proceedings of the First International Cypriological Congress*, ed. T. Papadopoulos and M. Christodoulou, vol. III, second part, 125–130. Nicosia: Association of Cypriot Studies.

Fotakis, Z. 2008. The Naval Policy of Great Britain and the Prospect of Ceding Cyprus to Greece, 1912-1914. In *Eleftherios Venizelos and Cyprus*, ed. G. Kazakias and P. Papapolyviou, 88–97. Athens: Kastaniotis (in Greek).

Historical Encyclopedia of Cyprus. 1979–1980. Ed. P. Papadimitris. Nicosia (in Greek).

Georgalis, K. 2016. *The British in Cyprus. Taxation and Politics in the First Period of British Rule and the Question of Tribute*. Athens: Kastanioris (in Greek).

Georghallides, G.S. 1971–1972. Memorandum by Mr. Headlam-Morley and Mr. Childs Respectinf Cyprus. *Yearbook of Cyprus Research Centre*, V: 189–240.

Georghallides, G.S. 1979. *A Political and Administrative History of Cyprus 1918-1926*. Nicosia: Cyprus Research Centre.

Hadjivasileiou, E. 1998. *The Cyprus Question, 1878–1960: The Constitutional Aspect*. Athens: Ellinika Grammata (in Greek).

Hadjivasileiou, E. 2009. Britain, Mediterranean Geopolitics and Cyprus (1878–1960). In *Cyprus, Geopolitical Developments in the 21st Century*, ed. V. Horafas and L. Rizas, 229–233. Athens: Monthly Review (in Greek).

Hill, G. Sir. 1952. *A History of Cyprus, vol. 4, The Ottoman Province, The British Colony 1571-1948*. Cambridge: Cambridge University Press.

Holland, R., and D. Markides. 2007. *The British and the Greeks*. Athens: Patakis (in Greek).

Kafkarides, C. 2010. *Turkey and Cyprus 1923–1960*. Athens: Amorgos (in Greek).

Kalantzopoulos, D. 2015. *Competing Political Spaces in Colonial Cyprus, 1931-1950*. Doctoral thesis, University of London.

Katsiaounis, R. 1994. Electing and Being Elected in the First Parliamentary Elections Under British Rule in 1883. *Yearbook of the Centre of Scientific Research*, XX: 309–345 (in Greek).

Katsiaounis, R. 1996. *Labour, Society and Politics in Cyprus During the Second Half of the Nineteenth Century*. Nicosia: Cyprus Research Centre.

Katsouridis, Y. 2009. *The Party System in Cyprus 1878–1931: Construction and Peculiarities*. Doctoral thesis, Nicosia: University of Cyprus (in Greek).

Katsouridis, Y. 2010. The Church as a Vehicle for Ideological and Political Processes. *Elliniki Epitherisi Politikis Epistimis* 36: 37–71.

Katsourides, Y. 2014. *The History of the Communist Party of Cyprus*. London: I.B. Tauris.

Kitromilides, Paschalis. 1977. "Cyprus" Entry. *History of the Greek Nation*, XIV: 387–395 (in Greek).

Kizilyurek, N. 2009. *Turkish Cypriots, Turkey and the Cyprus Question*. Athens: Papazisis (in Greek).

Klapsis, A. 2013. The Strategic Importance of Cyprus and the Prospect of Union with Greece 1919–1931. The Greek Perspective. *The Journal of Imperial and Commonwealth History* 41 (5): 765–782.

Konstantinidis, S. 2011. *Review of Modern Cypriot History, Social Structures, Institutions, and Ideology. From Ottoman Rule and British Rule to Independence*. Athens: Taxideftis (in Greek).

Koumoulides, J. 1987. Sir John Stavridi and British Offer of 1915. *Journal of Modern Hellenism* 4: 93–119.

Koupanou, A. 2017. *The Shaping of Relations Between Christians and Muslims in Cyprus During the First Period of Colonial Government (1878–1914)*. Doctoral thesis, University of Cyprus (in Greek).

Ktoris, S. 2013. *Turkish Cypriots, From the Margins to Association (1923–1960)*. Athens: Papazisis (in Greek).

Kyriakidis, H. 2016. *The Legislative Council of Cyprus (1878–1931)*. Nicosia: House of Representatives.

Lee, D. 1934. *Great Britain and the Cyprus Convention Policy of 1878*. Cambridge: Harvard University Press.

Louis, K. 2006. *Forms of Economic relations in Cyprus (1817–1839)*, vol. 1. Nicosia (in Greek).

Loukaidis, L. 1986. The History of Local Self-Government. In *Kypriaka 1878-1955*, 63–76. Nicosia: Publication of the Municipality of Nicosia (in Greek).

Sir, Luke H. 1969. *Cyprus Under the Turks, 1571–1878*. London: C. Hurst and Co.

Lympouridis, A. 1985. *British Rule in Cyprus. From the Occupation to the End of the First World War*. Nicosia (in Greek).

Lympouridis A., 1997, *Cyprus' Contentious Archiepiscopal Question and the l Ten Years Adventured Course of 1900 -1910*, Nicosia: Fakos, (in Greek).

Michael, M. 2005. *The Church of Cyprus in the Ottoman Period (1571–1878). Its Step-by-Step Formation as an Institution of Political Power*. Nicosia: Cyprus Scientific Research Centre (in Greek).

Michael, M. 2008. Ottoman Rights of the Senior Clergy of the Church of Cyprus and the British Administration. *Yearbook of the Scientific Research Centre*, XXXIV: 333–367 (in Greek).

Minutes of Legislative Council. 1903.

Minutes of Legislative Council. 1915.

Minutes of Legislative Council. 1916.

Minutes of Legislative Council. 1917.

Minutes of Legislative Council. 1931.

Moutsis, I. 2014. *The Turkish Cypriots (1918–1931): From a Religious Community to an Ethnic Minority*. Doctoral thesis, University of London (in Greek).

Moustaka, S. 2010. *The Workers' Movement in Cyprus During the Period of British Rule 1878–1955*. Doctoral thesis, Athens: Panteion University (in Greek).

Nevzat, A., and M. Hatay. 2009. Politics, Society and the Decline of Islam in Cyprus: From the Ottoman Era to the Twenty-First Century. *Middle Eastern Studies* 45 (6): 911–933.

Onurkan-Samani, M. 2018. The Legislative Council and Its Historical/Political Implications in Cyprus (1882-1931). In *Cypriot Nationalisms in Context. History, Identity and Politics*, ed. T. Kyritsi and N. Christofis, 75–92. London: Palgrave.

Orr, C.W.J. 1972. *Cyprus Under British Rule*. London: Zeno Publishers.

Panayiotou, A. 1999. *Island Radicals: The Emergence and Consolidation of the Cypriot Left, 1920-1960*. Doctoral thesis, University of California.

Pantelis, S. 1986. *The Modern History of Cyprus*. Athens: I. Floros Publications (in Greek).

Papadopoullos, T. 1965. *Social and Historical Data on Population (1570–1881)*. Nicosia: Cyprus Research Centre.

Papageorgiou, S. 1996. *The First Period of British Rule in Cyprus [1878–1914]. Political Modernization and Social Inertia*. Athens: Papazisis (in Greek).

Papapolyviou, P. 1997. *Cyprus and the Balkan Wars. Contribution to the History of Cypriot Voluntary Service*. Nicosia: Scientific Research Centre, Sources and Studies of Cypriot History XXVI (in Greek).

Papapolyviou, P. 2004. Cyprus 1922–1940. The 1931 Revolt and the Colonialist Counter-Revolution. In *History of Modern Hellenism*, vol. 7, 325–336. Athens: Ellinika Grammata (in Greek).

Papapolyviou, P. 2010. Cypriot Voluntary Service in Greek Wars, 1866–1945. In the volume of the National and Capodistrian University of Athens. Committee for Cyprus, ed. Andreas I. Voskos, 204–229. Cyprus: Freedom Struggles in Greek History. Athens (in Greek).

Pavlidis, A. 1993. *History of the Island of Cyprus*, fourth volume: From 1571 to 1964. Nicosia: Filokypros (in Greek).

Perikleous, C. 2007. *The 2004 Referendum. The Regional and International Environment. The Conception of a Solution and the Conjuncture*. Athens: Papazisis (in Greek).

Pikros, G. 1980. *Venizelos and the Cyprus Question*. Athens: Philippotis (in Greek).

Protopapas, V. 2012. *Electoral History of Cyprus. Politicians, Parties and Elections Under British Rule 1878-1960*. Athens: Themelio (in Greek).

Psyroukis, N. 1983. *History of Contemporary Greece (1940–1967)*, vol. II. Athens: Epikairotita (in Greek).

Psyroukis, N. 1987. *The Cypriot Drama (1958–1986)*. Athens: Epikairotita (in Greek).

Richter, H. 2007. *History of Cyprus*, vol. 1 (1878–1949). Athens: Estia (in Greek).

Sakellaropoulos, S. 2019. The Debate on *Enosis* Between Greeks and Turks of Cyprus in the Legislative Council. *Deltos* 4: 67–86 (in Greek).

Sophokleous, A. 1993. Geographical Determinism in the Future Development of Cyprus. In *The New International Order, Greece and Turkey and the Cyprus Problem*, ed. C. Giallouridis and P. Tsakonas, 515–546. Athens: I. Sideris (in Greek).

Svolopoulos, C. 1985. The Lausanne Peace Treaty and the Cyprus Problem. In Proceedings of the International Symposium, *Greece and Great Britain During World War I*, 233–245. Thessaloniki: Institute for Balkan Studies.

Tsalakos, G. 1981. Brief Review of Certain Aspects of British Rule in Cyprus. In *Cyprus, History, Problems and Struggles of Its People*, ed. G. Tenekidis and G. Kranidiotis, 137–166. Athens: Estia (in Greek).

Varnava, A. 2009. *British Imperialism in Cyprus, 1878–1915. The Inconsequential Possession*. Manchester: Manchester University Press.

Varnava, A. 2013. Sophronios III, 1865–1900: The Last of the 'Old' and the First of the 'New' Archbishop-Ethnarchs? In *The Archbishops of Cyprus in the Modern Age*, ed. A. Varnava and M. Michael, 106–147. Newcastle: Cambridge Scholars Publishing.

Varnava, A. 2019. *British Cyprus and the Long Great War, 1914–1925*. London: Routledge.

Weir, W.W. 1952. *Education in Cyprus. Some Theories and Practices in Education in the Island of Cyprus Since 1878*. Cyprus.

Woodhouse, C.M. 1985. The Offer of Cyprus: October 1915. In Proceedings of the International Symposium, *Greece and Great Britain During World War I*, 77–97. Thessaloniki: Institute for Balkan Studies.

Zanettos, F. 1911. *History of the Island of Cyprus*, vol. II. Larnaca (in Greek).

CHAPTER 5

The 1931 Revolt and Its Consequences

1 The Overall Context

The decisive issue influencing the Cypriot question in the 1930s was the 1931 revolt. But in relation to what happened during the revolt of the Greek Cypriots through October 1931 we should underline the importance of a host of social factors in what followed. They include: (a) the social and economic disparities entailed in British rule which, despite their profoundly class-based character, the hegemony of the bourgeois strata would induce the popular classes to see as exclusively a product of colonialist domination, which only *Enosis* would resolve (b) the serious consequences stemming, for decades, from payment of the Tribute of Cyprus, (c) the effects of the global economic crisis, (d) realization on the part of the Greek Cypriot element that there was little to be expected from the diplomatic route towards the objective of *Enosis,* (e) the attempt by the British to interfere in the administration of education, (f) the aforementioned refusal in September 1929 of the Secretary for the Colonies Lord Passfield to introduce further representative institutions and, of course, (g) the refusal of the Governor to accept the Legislative Council's resolution on economic issues in September 1931, which refusal was motivated by the fact that the Turkish Cypriots did not vote with the British. Let us examine all this in more detail.

S. Sakellaropoulos, *The Evolution of the Political, Social and Economic Life of Cyprus, 1191–1950*, Palgrave Studies in Economic History,
https://doi.org/10.1007/978-3-030-91839-2_5

2 The Issue of the Socio-Economic Inequalities in Rural Areas and the Special Role of the Creditors

The advent of the British did not serve to mitigate existing structures of inequality and exploitation. What is observed in the first years of British rule is a great increase in the cost of living, introducing significant difficulties of day-to-day subsistence whose effects were felt first and foremost by the peasant farmers and the poorer strata in the cities.

Serious problems that the Cypriot farmer had to deal with were protracted droughts, the perennial problem of irrigation, antiquated methods of sowing and harvesting, fragmentation of inherited land holdings into small widely separated plots, non-intensive cultivation of land, a limited internal market, the absence of organized exports for agricultural products. Moreover, the greater part of the most fertile lands belonged either to the Church or to Muslim religious foundations or to ciflicks (Papapolyviou 2004: 335).

All this testifies to the existence of a society afflicted with the over-indebtedness of a great majority of cultivators. The transference of Cyprus to the British would find four percent of the population of Limassol to be sued for compensation because of indebtedness and the prisons filled with people unable to pay their debts (Loizos 1977: 116; Hadjidemetriou 2002: 351). The fact that the British would ban personal detentions for debts did provide some relief for small cultivators but did not solve the problem, which was reproduced as before. It is characteristic that between 50 and 60% of the cases tried in provincial courtrooms concerned promissory notes and mortgages due to agricultural debts (Georghallides 1985: 163). It has been said that the Cyprus peasant (with the exception of a small minority) "is born in debt and dies in debt" (Surridge 1930: 36).

As for the factors generating the debts, what should be noted is that in very few cases they were the outcome of investments for improvement in the productivity of cultivation. In a significant proportion of cases, around 30%, some inherited land was burdened with debt and two successive bad harvests sufficed to oblige the heir to take out a new loan and incur new debts. Another category was those peasant farmers who had purchased land on credit and were unable to repay the debt (Surridge 1930: 44). Finally, all the above was exacerbated by the institutional framework governing inheritance. On the basis of the law "On Wills and Inheritance" (1895) up to two-third of the landed property of the deceased is distributed between all the relatives starting from the spouse, the siblings and the children and extending to relatives ten degrees removed (!). This law self-evidently led to very great fragmentation of land ownership (Kondylis 2009: 103).

In this situation when peasant farmer was obliged to borrow money, the usurer typically lent it to him on the following terms: the average rate of interest was as high as 24%, payments were made in kind with a 15% discount on current prices and had to be remitted within the specified deadlines even if the time was approaching for harvesting of the crop in question. But even these onerous terms were not enough to satisfy the lenders. To increase their profit, given that they were mostly dealing with illiterate people, they resorted to additional subterfuges such as forgery through adding an extra zero to the sum owed, erroneous methods of calculating the interest, underweight payments in kind, etc.

It was a state of affairs which continued for as long as the tithe was in existence, that is to say from the nineteenth century until 1926, when it was abolished. During this time cash payment of the tax in question had been required. The farmers had to prepay the taxes on the basis of estimates of their volume of production and because they did not have savings they went to moneylenders. In the event that the estimates exceeded the ultimate real volume of production the producers were obliged to place their products on the market to pay off their debts but there the buyers were often moneylenders, who forced down the prices (Richter 2007: 67).

On the basis of this whole system, it has been estimated that between 1919 and 1939 there were 18,000 foreclosures on mortgaged properties and another 19,500 court decisions were made for forced sale of mortgaged land. All in all, in this 20-year period there were forced sales of 600,000 skales (donums)[1] of fields, one million trees and 8,000 houses. Apart from that a very large number of holdings were sold "voluntarily" to pay off debt. In total during this period approximately two-fifth of the farmland and trees of all Cyprus and around one-sixth of the housing changed hands (Konstantinidis 1995: 39). The total sum of farm debt at the end of the nineteenth century reached a figure of £150,000; at the end of the 20s Surridge estimated it at £1,800,000; in the mid-30s

[1] One skala (donum) is equivalent to 1,340 m^2.

Oakden estimated it at £2,000,000, and in 1940 Lanitis estimated it at £2,329,000 (Faustmann 1998: 68).

At the same time, it should be emphasized that for the two lowest income categories, for those, in other words, who had property up to £50 in value, the level of indebtedness was 33%; 25% for those with property up to £100 in value. The percentage was perceptibly lower (between 19 and 21%) for the other categories. In other words, the poorest were unequally burdened if one compares them with the more affluent (Lanitis 1944: 26–27).

In his very interesting book *Rural Indebtedness and Agricultural Co-operation in Cyprus* Lanitis mentions three basic categories of lender: the locals, the city merchants and the professional city lenders. The local lenders were usually the mukhtars of the village who at the same time owned the local shop, but also some farmers who had a production surplus which they put at the disposal of their fellow villagers,[2] charging the corresponding interest. The city merchant had embarked on his career from being a shop owner selling commodities not produced by peasant farmers. Given that the farmers generally did not have money, they obtained the products in exchange for wheat, a transaction which transformed the lender into a grain merchant and in a subsequent phase into a trader in potatoes and fertilizers. If that was the situation the merchant did not plan on becoming a cultivator: what interested him was to be able to market agricultural products at high prices. The third category comprised lenders who were at the same time landowners and worked on the basis of mortgages. The borrower mortgaged a plot of farmland so as to be able to secure the cash loan and undertook to pay off the loan in instalments. Late payment of one instalment sufficed to put the land in the possession of the lender. The objective of the lenders was

[2] As the British commissioner for the Larnaca province Surridge put it in a related report: "[...] money- lending is not confined to the capitalist of towns. The more well to do peasant with a little money to spare is equally insistent on his pound of flesh and, since he is often the only source of credit open to the poorest peasant, his demands are usually greater and more unconscionable. After a few years of profitable money-lending in a village he opens a small shop and while continuing to farm his own land he also acts as an agent for a town merchant. He is thus enabled to extend his operations and gradually to bring into his clutches a large number of his fellow villagers. Then when they fail to meet their obligations he sells them up, takes over their land, and allows them to cultivate it on terms which at most allow them a bare living" (Surridge 1930: 46).

to profit from the high interest and acquire land cheaply (Lanitis 1944: 41–43).

The two financial crises of the 1920s (1923 and 1929) would contribute decisively to creating the situation described, at the same time highlighting new dimensions to the problem. The outbreak of the crisis of 1923 which was to lead to an increase in the number of auctions—in 1923, 4,197 hectares of land was put up for auction and in 1924, 7,608 hectares—would have the effect of pushing small producers into the cities in search of work. The global economic crisis of 1929, together with a long period of drought, multiplied the existing problems. The price of barley fell from three shillings per kilo to one; carob from 26 shillings per kantar[3] to nine, wine from 21 shillings per gomari[4] to ten and potatoes from two kurus per okka to half a kurus (Graikos 1994: 6).

At the same time, the inadequacies of the laws of 1919[5] would become evident. To cite Surridge: "The immediate result of the 1919 laws was restriction for credit which in its turn led to the selling up by the creditors of the immovable property of their debtors, an increase in the number of landless peasants and a general lowering of commercial morality" (Surridge 1930: 46). In other words, formally the peasant farmers were protected but they did not have any way to borrow money other than by recourse to their familiar creditors. They were not in a position to jeopardize their ability to acquire credit by denouncing to the authorities the people who reliably lent them money (Faustmann 2006: 200).

In the aforementioned report, which was compiled in 1927 and 1928, Surridge calculated that 52% of the peasant farmers owned 2.7 hectares *per capita,* 21% 12 hectares and 27% 20 hectares. At the same time, according to the calculations, he himself had made a family with three children had to cultivate an area of nine hectares to ensure subsistence

[3] A kantar was the equivalent of 44 okkas or 56.408 kilos.

[4] Gomari was the loading that could be transported on an animal.

[5] At that time the government tried to intervene by exempting from the auctions holdings less than 20 pounds in value, but this move was pointless because it concerned only very small plots which could not support a family. At the same time a maximum limit of 12% was imposed for interest rates on borrowing, which meant that there could be indictment of exorbitant interest charges. Lenders would have to keep records of their transactions, monitorable by British officials. For a time, there was discussion of the possibility of establishing an Agricultural Bank, but this plan, despite the elaboration of a relevant demand by all deputies in the Legislative Council, was delayed for some years owing to the impossibility of finding the necessary capital.

(Surridge 1930: 57–58). And all of this was from prior to the coming of the drought and the outbreak of the financial crisis. The consequence was initiation of a wave of forced auctioning, for the poorest cultivators were yet again unable to pay the interest on their loans. The problem could not be solved by the (in 1925) newly founded Agricultural Bank because it lent money at very high interest rates, in the order of eight percent, when farmers could only afford four to five percent payments. At the same time, the Agricultural Bank only granted long-term loans to the co-operatives, and the lack of concern for provision of short-term loans meant, particularly in the period of financial crisis between 1930 and 1933, that many cultivators were (again) turning to private lenders and losing their land (Faustmann 2006: 202–203; Tsekouras 1984: 92). The result was a perpetuation of the situation whereby the usurer was kept busy lending the villager commodities he needed such as fertilizers, animals and fodder. Very often the village shop owner agreed to sell consumer items in return for payment in kind but the exchange rates were much lower than normal (Tsekouras 1984: 93).

To these adversities, there must be added factors such as the great difficulty with irrigation that was faced by 15–20% of cultivators (Pikros 1980: 73–74) and the lack of hygienic condition. It is indicative that people slept together with the animals and there was stagnant water, resulting in an explosion of malaria, intestinal disorders, influenza, tuberculosis, eyesight problems and high infant mortality (163.3 per 1,000 infants) (Hadjidemetriou 2002: 354–355).

It would be necessary to wait until the mid-1930s for there to begin to be implemented, for reasons we shall examine subsequently, a policy that might contribute to relief from such problems. Thus, in 1935, the register of co-operatives was created with a view to promoting the co-operative idea and helping co-ordinate existing co-operatives. As a result, there was an increase in the number of peasant farmers participating in co-operatives from the 16,000 existing at that time to 29,000 in 1942. In parallel with this, the problem of the inability of the Agricultural Bank to issue short-term loans to the cultivators prompted the establishment in 1937 of the Central Co-operative Bank, which was financed by deposits from the co-operatives and by Britain's Barclay's Bank. A further measure that greatly improved the situation, contributing to the financial downfall of the money lenders, was the establishment, in 1940, of the Debt Settlement Board and the creation of Rural Debtors' Courts. These institutions helped to relieve cultivators from the burden of old debts, adjusting interest rates with a view to reach a fair settlement. Some debts were reduced by 30% and a maximum repayment period of 15 years was initiated, with delivery to be phased in annual instalments. In the whole period between 1940 and 1945 around one-third of the farmers saw a reduction in their indebtedness and from 1940 onwards interest on lending was not allowed to exceed nine percent (Faustmann 1998: 57).

3 Socio-Economic Inequalities Between Workers in the Urban Centres

The difficult situation in the countryside would lead to an oversupply of labour in the urban centres, with the result, also, that wages were kept at low levels. Specifically, the daily wage in the interwar period varied between one and two shillings for 12 to 14 hours work. In print shops, minors between 14 and 18 years of age worked 9.5 hours a day for between four and eight shillings a week, and adults for ten to 17 shillings. Workers in shoe factories worked 13 hours a day for two shillings, workers on public works projects for 1.5 shillings a day, workers in restaurants for half a shilling plus their food and in mines workers were paid two to 2.5 shillings per day (*Historical essay* ..., 1968, Part 1: 45–46).

Food prices at that time were as follows: bread cost 4.5 kurus per okka (nine kurus were the equivalent of a shilling), potatoes two kurus, onions two, beans two, broad beans six, sugar six, oil 28 kurus and soap 12 kurus. The daily wage barely sufficed to feed a five-member family just on beans, oil and bread. But money was also needed for rent, clothing and hygiene. And to get by on this one worked 12 hours a day in winter and 14 in summer (Pancyprian Syndicalist Committee-Pancyprian Federation of Labour 1991: 28). So workers, like peasant farmers, lived beneath the threshold of poverty.

This is an interesting contrast to the income of the British personnel serving in Cyprus. The family of a British official had the following monthly expenses: for food £10 to £13 sterling, for the pay of a cook and servant £5 to £9 sterling, for rent £3 to £7 sterling and for laundry one pound sterling. To these expenses, there must be added the expenses for the children, which are estimated *per capita* at around £3 sterling. It is also estimated that apart from the remaining family expenses, there were a number of other costs for an official: entertainment, furniture, clothing, etc. (Richter 2007: 613).

4 The Burdens of Taxation and the Particular Significance of the Tribute of Cyprus

My position is that beyond the extreme disparities of class which played their role, albeit refracted and misdirected, in the 1931 revolt, an important role was also played by the economic burden, entitled Tribute of Cyprus, which for around a half-century had weighed on the shoulders of the Cypriots. Note that from certain perspectives, it was not exclusively the geomilitary importance of Cyprus that contributed to the island's being ceded to England. Also relevant was the endeavour being made by the British side to recover the debt owed by the Ottoman government and to do this by passing on the cost to Cypriot taxpayers.

* * *

To be specific, it was a loan from 1855 to the amount of £3,815,200 sterling with annual interest of £81,752 sterling which had been guaranteed by the British government. In the year in question, in fact, the Sultan took out a loan of five million English pounds, mostly from the London money market, for the purpose of meeting the cost of the weaponry and other military material supplied by England and France for the war he was waging in Crimea against Russia. There was interest due on that loan and it was being repaid with an amortization of one percent per year. The governments of England and France had guaranteed payment of the interest to the bondholders. As collateral, the Sultan had mortgaged the Tribute he received from the Regent of Egypt and the import duties from Smyrna and Syria.

Up until 1874, the interest was duly paid but on 6th October 1875, the Sultan declared bankruptcy with the result that the bondholders could expect to be paid only 72,000 English pounds a year from the Egyptian Tribute and the governments of England and France, as guarantors, were obliged to pay 81,752 English pounds to cover the interest, along with the bank charges. It was for this reason that Article 3 of the cession agreement for Cyprus included a provision that Britain would surrender to the Sultan the surplus that would emerge following subtraction of the expenses from the income. Of course, this was all entirely in the realm of public relations. In reality, what the British were interested in was instituting a Tribute that the Cypriots would have to pay to the Sultan, which the British would appropriate as *quid pro quo* for the delay in payments on the loan instalments, a sum which would come to £92,800 annually (£81,000 for servicing of the debt plus £11,000 to be paid into a special account to cover future amortization of the debt).

Of course, numerous strategems were employed to accomplish forced payment of this sum. In principle, Cyprus never paid Tribute to the Sultan. The latter simply seized the island's budget surplus. This meant that in drought years like 1871 and 1872 he received almost nothing. Apart from that, the final sum that it was calculated the British should receive, based on the Sultan's income in the last five years of occupation of Cyprus, was conspicuously overvalued (between 28 and 39%), for the following reasons: (a) the years 1871 and 1872, when nothing was produced, were not counted, (b) between 1873 and 1877 the harvest in one year was exceptionally poor but in two other years exceptionally good (Georghallides 1969–1970: 168–169). The upshot was that in 1907 the Cypriots had paid £1,799,860 sterling to Great Britain (Richter 2007: 104–106) and total British subsidies came to £857,085.[6]

So, the issue of the Tribute of Cyprus was a permanent irritant in relations between the British and the Cypriots. On 22nd February 1887, the parliamentary deputy N. Rossos tabled a motion in the Legislative Council[7] which was supported by the Greeks but also by two of the three Ottoman deputies (Hussein and Rashid, with Naim voting against[8]) which required in the event of an agreement not being possible

[6] The British subsidies were paid precisely because on account of the extremely high demands of the Tribute of Cyprus, the Cypriots in the period between 1878 and 1907 only managed three times to raise the sum of £92,800. So, the British public sector was called upon to cover the "deficit" for which it was itself responsible, and the Cypriot tax contribution was managed in the same way.

[7] It had been preceded by two resolutions, on 6th March 1885 and 17th April 1886, tabled by deputy Z. D. Pieridis, which had met with unanimous support from the Christian and Muslim parliamentarians (Bouleti 2008: 133). There were certain other cases of similar collaboration between representatives of the two communities. For example, in 1888–1889 there was the formulation of the demand for abolition of the High Representative's casting vote, and opposition to the introduction of new taxes. The same occurred in 1910 against the reduction in the British contribution from £50,000 to £40,000, and in 1892, 1899 and 1902 Greek and Muslim deputies together opposed change in the law on protection of antiquities (Bouleti 2008: 135–136; Kizilyurek: 121–122).

[8] As indicated by Bouleti, the British administration attempted to exploit the divided loyalties vis-à-vis this subject that was characteristic of the Muslim community, arguing that the tax represented an obligation towards the Ottoman Empire and for as long as it continued to exist the Sublime Porte's link with the island would similarly continue

between the Sublime Porte and the United Kingdom that the latter should undertake payment of the sum in question (Economidis 1999: 63).

The climate of reaction which had been generated against British taxation would lead to the entirety of deputies in 1888 voting against the annual budget, with the result that that year income from taxation fell by £7,962 (Bouleti 2008: 135).

There would be a renewed reaction in 1892 when the Council presented a unanimous demand for payment of the tax by the British Exchequer, but beyond that the Turkish Cypriots' fear of the Greek Cypriot demand for *Enosis*, which as mentioned was also raised from 1902 onwards in the Legislative Council, would induce them to abstain from supporting the demand for abolition of the Tribute of Cyprus, until 1923, the year of the breakup of the Ottoman Empire.[9]

* * *

So, abolition of the tax would now be a demand only of the Greeks. In 1907 an opportunity arose to change things for the better, at least as regards payment of the Tribute of Cyprus, when Winston Churchill became Under-Secretary of State for the Colonial Office and in the summer of the same year visited Cyprus. There he met with the members of the Legislative Council and the Metropolitan of Kition handed him a memorandum with the assertion that the Tribute of Cyprus represented a "completely heartless tactic" and that Cyprus was being obliged to bear the weight of an "entirely foreign obligation", which was clearly a matter for the British administration (Richter 2007: 109). In his response Churchill left open the possibility of an increase in support for Cyprus (Georghallides 1969–1970: 212–213) but returning to Britain he saw

(Bouleti 2008: 133–134). The first—and for the nineteenth century only—British success along these lines occurred in 1889 when the first Cypriot delegation to go to London to raise economic issues was comprised exclusively of Greek Cypriots, given that the Turkish Cypriots did not accept any reference to abolition of the Tribute of Cyprus (Anagnostopoulou 1999: 23).

[9] For the relevant debate in the Legislative Council in the 1902–1911 period see Kyriakidis (2016: 395–403) and for the 1923–1924 period see Kyriakidis (2016: 480–481). There was to be only one instance of collaboration: in 1909 the deputies of the two communities together proposed that the Tribute of Cyprus be used for transportation works (Kizilyurek 2007: 121).

the question from an even more positive perspective and compiling the relevant memorandum to the Government accepted that Britain has no right to take even a penny from the Cypriots for the purpose of meeting its own obligations (Hill 1952: 468). But Treasury rejected Churchill's memorandum, characterizing it as absurd. In April 1908, Churchill left the Colonial Office and the dispute ended there (Richter 2007: 112). It is interesting that the overall problem remained even in 1914 when Cyprus was taken over by England because the British redefined the Tribute of Cyprus as Cyprus' share of the Ottoman debt.

In 1926, the total sum paid by the Cypriots had reached the level of around £2,650,000 sterling. At that time, given the recent proclamation of Cyprus as a British colony, the Turkish Cypriot deputy Djelaleddin Efendi at the 24th November session of the Legislative Council felt obliged to speak "with the voice of revolution" against the tax which "like a viper is sucking the blood of the Cypriots". So that day the Greek Cypriots and the Turkish Cypriots together voted against the 1927 budget tabled by the Governor (Kyriakidis 2016: 502–503). This humiliating defeat led the British government, through the governor of Cyprus Sir Ronald Storrs, on 31st August 1927, to announce the abolition of the relevant tax and its replacement by a £10,000 tax as a contribution to the defence of the Empire. But what did not become known for a long time was how the abolition of the tax was linked to the relinquishing of every right over the £2,650,000 paid up to that time (Georgallides 1969–1970: 190–191).

It should be noted also that apart from being the heavy economic burden that it was for Cypriots, the Tribute of Cyprus had an inhibiting effect on approval for expenditure in several sectors. For example, in 1895 the annual income from taxation increased from £113,000 sterling that it was in the Ottoman period to £188,000, representing a 66% increase. But given that about half was channelled into the Tribute of Cyprus and £8,000–£10,000 used for road works, only £4,000 sterling was available for health and £22,600 sterling for education. As a result, that year Greek Cypriots and Muslims protested together, arguing that taxation consumed 25% of the island's income. And this was due chiefly to the Tribute of Cyprus, but not exclusively, given that other taxes had also been introduced. So, the British may have abolished the taxes paid by the Orthodox in return for their exemption from military service, for the right to engage in trade or practise a profession or for real estate rental but these taxes were replaced by indirect taxation on necessities, taxation on land ownership and property transfer was continued and a school tax was added, calculated on the basis of land ownership. Another tax was also added for control of locusts. The locusts were quickly exterminated but the tax lived on (Hadjidemetriou 2002: 368).

After all this, it should come as no surprise that prior to the First World War Cyprus was the only British colony to surrender 27% of its gross revenue to the British State state. The Ministry of the Colonies was forced to acknowledge in 1904 that Cyprus was the country with the highest rate of taxation in the world (Richter 2007: 108). Taxation was undoubtedly very heavy, and it made even more unbearable the fact that Cyprus was an agricultural community significantly dependent on the ups and downs of the harvest.

The high taxation was not only a reflection of the Tribute of Cyprus but was produced by the overall framework of taxation instituted by the British. At the same time, it should be noted that the British administration provided generous funding to pay the salaries of an inflated number of highly paid personnel. It is characteristic that between 1913 and 1929 the salaries of the British civil sevants increased by 200%. The internal structuring of taxation was another serious problem: 67% of the country's income came from indirect taxation and only 12% from direct taxation (Katsouridis 2009: 75–77).

In any case the result would be that the consequences of this altogether exorbitant taxation for around a half-century would weigh heavily in the climate that was to lead to the revolt of 1931.

* * *

5 The Consequences of the Economic Crisis of 1929

Beyond the chronic economic problems which had for years accumulated to burden the people of Cyprus there should be added the specific problems imported into Cyprus by the global crisis of 1929. The existing data indicate that between 1920 and 1930 exports fell by 25% (from £1,635,736 to £1,218,321) and there was a 28% reduction in imports (from £1,983,833 to £1,419,989). There were also serious consequences for employment. From as early as November 1930 it was estimated that 8,000 jobs had been lost due to the closing of the asbestos mines (Georghallides 1985: 432). In 1929 the Cyprus Asbestos Company employed 3,538 people daily and expended more than £156,000. In 1939 the same enterprise employed only 1,017 workers and expended £70,000 on salaries. The outcome of all this was that a significant number of workers lost their jobs and by extension saw their purchasing power reduced. Things had deteriorated so much that in August there were 100 applications for a position as secretary-typist in the Ionian Bank (Georghallides 1985: 293).

6 The Fiscal Question

Another question that also had the effect of exacerbating residents' chronic profound exasperation was fiscal management. The 1931 budget which the Government put up for discussion showed income of £739,000 and expenditure of £801,000, i.e. a deficit in the order of £62,000. This difference is calculated to have been covered by the £21,000 which was the surplus from 1930 and £41,000 deducted from the island's reserve, which totalled £90,000.

The reaction of the Greek Cypriots was notably vehement, given that they thought the funds in the reserve should be used for situations of emergency, the more so because at that time Cyprus was again going through a period of drought and the decision to reduce civil servants' salaries by five percent was to lead to a saving of only £2,500 for 1931, which was regarded as derisory by the Greek Cypriot side. At the same time, they estimated that despite the severe cuts in public works funding provided for in the new budget, the deficit finally would be over £100,000. The Greek counterproposal was for revision of the salary scale for civil servants[10] with abolition of superflous positions, reorganization of services and axing of unproductive expenditures. Their calculation was that by adopting such measures they would not only cover the deficit but would leave room for an increase in expenditure on health, agriculture and public works (Stylianou 1984: 38).

[10] It is characteristic that although the British comprised four percent of governmental officials they received 19% of the total expenditure on salaries whereas the Greeks, who comprised 56%, received 48.1% and the Turks, who comprised 36% received 27.5% (Katsouridis 2009: 102).

Finally, the budget was voted by nine Britons, the three Turkish Cypriots[11] and the Governor against the 12 votes of the Greek Cypriots.

7 The Political Representation of the Two Communities

On the internal Cypriot front, the political collectivities which would represent the two communities began to take shape slightly before the 1931 revolt. For the Greek Cypriots, it was the founding of the National Organization of Cyprus (Ethniki Organosis Kyprou-EOK) and for the Turkish Cypriots the emergence of Kemalism and the Turkish National Council of Cyprus.

The Creation of the EOK (National Organization of Cyprus)

The National Organization of Cyprus (EOK) was founded on 26th January 1930 because of the refusal of Lord Passfield, on 28th November 1929, to consent to the Greek Cypriot demand for *Enosis*. Archbishop Kyrillos III was placed at the head of the organization and its 37-member leadership included members of the Holy Synod, the abbot of Kykkos Monastery, representatives of other monasteries, the Greek Cypriot parliamentary deputies and other personalities. Its purpose was mentioned in Article 2 of its statute and was "achievement of this national restoration through the unification of available forces and co-ordination of the feasible efforts of the Greek population of Cyprus achievement of this national restoration through its unification with the Hellenic Motherland, sought for ever through every means judged by the Organization as promising and instrumental for that purpose" (cited by Pavlidis 1993: 294). Note the reference to the need for utilization of every means and thus non-exclusion even of armed struggle.

[11] Note that Necati, the Turkish Cypriot parliamentary deputy whose vigorous activism will be mentioned below, had expressed certain thoughts on the bill, foreshadowing his later stance in the bill on customs duties, but finally he voted for it. But the misgivings of Governor Storrs as expressed in the letter he sent on 26th November to his friend Philip Graves, journalist at the *Times*, are revealing: "You find me dragging my budget with rough strife through the iron gates of a newly elected and unusually crapulous Legislative Council. The Greeks have purchased one of the three Turkish members upon whose vote I ultimately rely for the passing of any legislation" (cited by Georghallides 1985: 438).

The first action was organization, on a pan-Cyprian scale, in favour of *Enosis* on 25th March 1930[12] and the dispatch to London of relevant resolutions. In the Legislative Council's elections of October 1930, the EOK supported such candidates as stood with the slogan "*Enosis* and only *Enosis*", who were all elected.

But it soon became evident that the issue of *Enosis* was not finding receptive ears in the British administration given that the relevant efforts that were undertaken proved fruitless. The last time was when, in October 1930, the Under-Secretary of State for the Colonies Drummond Shiels, on a visit to Cyprus, excluded that prospect. But in August 1931, a section of the Greek Cypriot press was to assert that secret discussions were being conducted between Britain and Greece with a view to *Enosis*. When it turned out that these were merely figments of someone's imagination, disillusion began to grow among the Greek Cypriots (Georghallides 1985: 655–657). On the other hand, the bad economic situation continued, the damaging economic measures had, in one way or another, been institutionalized and the future seemed most unpropitious.

All this was reflected at the level of politics, generating transformations *both* in political practices *and* in relations of representation. The first very large mass demonstrations demanding *Enosis* had already been seen: on 25th March 1931 around 15,000 Greek Cypriots headed for the Nicosia Stadium where patriotic speeches were delivered and on 24th April 3,000 people marched on the Legislative Council demanding *Enosis* (Richter 2007: 469–477). This was something unprecedented for Cyprus society, which had not been used to such dynamic reactions. But on the other hand, the position of the National Organization of Cyprus, which was co-ordinating action for *Enosis*, was deteriorating due to its inability to secure tangible results. A popular discontent was growing which was not confined to the subject of *Enosis* but was spreading from the issue of exorbitant taxation. Serious internal frictions developed within the National Organisation of Cyprus, in the weeks preceding the revolt focussing on the tax issue. A more intransigent tendency was emerging, headed by the Metropolitan of Kyrenia, who demanded the collective resignation of the Greek Cypriot deputies in the Legislative Council and all others participating in the bodies created by the colonial regime. The roots of this tendency dated from prior to the 1931

[12] For Greeks 25th March is the national day because it has been established as the date of commencement of the revolution which led to the creation of the Greek state.

budget events, and specifically from 1929 when the clandestine organization EREK (National Radical Union of Cyprus) was established. Initially the National Radical Union operated in secret and in a second phase aimed at founding a political party (openly) which would seek the imposition of *Enosis*[13] through the use of more dynamic measures than submitting memoranda (the so-called "memorandum industry") (Katsourides 2017: 161) which it had been adopted until then.[14] On the other hand, inside the National Organisation of Cyprus there was a more moderate tendency which, while it accepted the need for the parliamentary deputies to resign, did not agree with resignation of the Greek Cypriots from all the colonialist institutions, placing emphasis of broadening the competences of the Legislative Council and abolishing the Orders in Council. This tendency, represented by the *Paphos* newspaper and its owner L. Philippou, thought that if the Greek Cypriot parliamentarians resigned, elections were called and the same candidates were re-elected, and resigned again, etc., this would place significant pressure on the British to proceed with constitutional changes.[15] Finally, there was the tendency, chiefly among the parliamentarians, which did not find the weapon of resignation appropriate (Sophokleous 2003: 107–108). This difference between parliamentary deputies and the National Organisation of Cyprus was evident at the conference of parliamentarians held in Saita on 12th September 1931. Even though whatever decisions were

[13] According to the testimony of its legal adviser S. Loizidis, the EPEK oath read as follows: "I swear [...] that I will struggle with all my might, not sparing even my life, for the unification of my particular homeland Cyprus with the Hellenic mother country" (Loizidis 1983: 31).

[14] These measures included resignations of parliamentary deputies, refusal to submit candidacies in new elections, the creation of chaotic situations with obstructions and sabotage, the boycotting of British products (Chrysanthis 1983: 86; Katsiaounis 2004: 32). Essentially in this case, the objective was not to exert pressure for more political freedoms to be granted (increasing competences of the Legislative Assembly, an upgrading of the Greek Cypriots' role in it) but to display the illegitimacy of the British presence and by extension to increase the pressure for cession of Cyprus to Greece.

[15] The importance acquired in the most recent years by the need for democratic functioning of the representative institutions was great precisely because of the sudden use of Orders in council. It is characteristic that whereas in 1920, 28 laws and 18 Orders in council had been issued, in 1931, there were 21 laws and Orders in council. The observation of Rappas was interesting when he said that beyond the discontent caused by the increasing resort to Orders in council, it is worth noting the more general British stance of refusal to be accountable to their colonial subjects (Rappas 2014: 16–17).

taken were supposed to be submitted for ratification by the National Organisation of Cyprus, the parliamentary deputies had decided that they would be implemented anyway. Finally, resignation of the parliamentarians was not decided on at that conference. The proposal was rejected by a nine–three majority in favour of refusal of payment of taxes, the so-called "forostasio" or tax resistance (Sophokleous 2003: 109–110). Of course, implementation of the "forostasio" had the problem that only the poor remained as tax refusers because the wealthy had already paid their taxes. But given that their refusal would be ineffectual because existing legislation provided for confiscation of their property, the colonial administration would anyway collect what they had legislated for. After all this, discussions were held inside the National Organisation of Cyprus without leading anywhere in particular, with the result that several cadres resigned, disagreeing with the choice of non-resignation of parliamentarians. Finally, after a month had been spent in discussions, on 10th October those remaining in the National Organisation of Cyprus leadership, most of whom were parliamentary deputies, affirmed the decision for non-resignation and tried to find replacements for the officials who had resigned, but this did not prove possible (Sophokleous 2003: 111–113). The last meeting of the National Organisation of Cyprus before the revolt took place on 17th October at the Great Synod of the Archiepiscopate. There was a discussion there of a moratorium on repayments and it became clear that tax evasion would have the consequence either of the people affected being compensated from confiscations of National Organisation of Cyprus property or of those who had evaded the tax being obliged to pay it or losing what had been confiscated. In any case the English would not lose. Faced with the looming impasse the Metropolitan of Kition proposed a collective resignation of the deputies and proclamation of *Enosis* with Greece. Finally, it was decided that the session should be resumed on 24th October (Stylianou 2013: 115–116).

Nevertheless, on the morning of the next day (18th October) with a letter to the British administration Kition submitted his resignation from parliament, posing the question of *Enosis*. In this way, he was essentially attempting as an individual to gain the initiative of movement, on the one hand to outflank in radicalism the demonstration in Larnaca announced for the same day where the subject of parliamentary resignations would be raised by the organizers and on the other to pre-empt the founding conference of EREK, the National Radical Union of Cyprus, which had been programmed for 18th October and where the subject of *Enosis* would be highlighted. The political theses of the National Radical Union of Cyprus had been ready since September 1931 and the first number of its newspaper, characteristically entitled *Adiallaktos* (Intransigent) had been programmed to start circulating on 24th October (Loizidis 1983: 32).[16] And indeed, on 18th October the founding declaration of the National Radical Union of Cyprus was made public, signed by 20 personalities from the Greek Cypriot population, but everything had now been overshadowed by the initiatives of Nicodemos.[17]

It was in this connection that on 19th October three more deputies resigned: Lanitis, Kyriakidis and Arapidiotis. But the other eight deputies not only did not resign but on the same day issued a joint statement in which they specified the reasons for their decision, directing stern criticism at Nicodemos Mylonas for his initiative (*Historical Encyclopedia of Cyprus* 1979–1980, Vol. 6: 21). But the pressure generated by the positive responses of the Greek Cypriots to Kition's stance led just one day later (on 20th October) to there being two new resignations (Siakkalis and Rosidis) and on 21st October to the resignation of Stavrianakis, Theodotou, Hadjipavlou and Severis. Finally, and after the events of the first day of the revolt (21st October) (see below) Galatopoulos and Koundouros would also resign (Sophokleous 2003: 128–129).

The Position of the Turkish Cypriots in the Overall Conjuncture and the Creation of the Turkish National Council of Cyprus

The realignments within the Turkish Cypriot community in this specific conjuncture are developments of the utmost importance not only for

[16] From 14th August 1931 E. Papanikolaou had requested official permission to publish a weekly newspaper with that title, and on 3rd October P. Ioannou had submitted the two hundred British pound deposit prescribed by law (Georghallides 1985: 659).

[17] A perusal of the programmatic theses of the National Radical Union of Cyprus reveals that nowhere is any other issue posed other than that of *Enosis*, e.g. an increase in the number of Greek Cypriot deputies in the Legislative Council or the moratorium. The primacy of this issue is indeed strengthened by the content of Article 5 where the National Radical Union of Cyprus' opposition is displayed not only towards those Greek Cypriots who are against *Enosis* (i.e. the Communist Party of Cyprus—see below) but also towards those moderate nationalists who are considered to be "weakening the national struggle".

comprehension of the context of the 1931 revolt but because they set in motion more comprehensive changes that were to have a decisive influence on the evolution of the Cyprus issue.

* * *

Concretely the formation of the Kemalist state from a certain point and beyond began to have significant politico-ideological effects on the Turkish Cypriots as well. The reforms that Kemal began to implement, which aimed at sidelining Islam and creating a secular state, began to have resonance in ever wider circles of Turkish Cypriots. With the help of the Turkish Chargé d'Affaires the Turkish Cypriot Kemalists organized themselves around the newspapers *Soz* (Word) and *Ses* (Sound) and also initiated a campaign for secular reforms in Cyprus: closure of the religious orders, a change in traditional Ottoman attire and adoption of the Western equivalent, institution of the Latin alphabet, introduction of civil marriage, election of the administration of Evkaf (Holy Land Foundation) and not appointment by the British. Apprehensive that the activity of the Turkish Cypriot modernizers might encourage national awakening of the Turkish Cypriots, the British rejected all the proposed reforms with the exception of the change of alphabet and that was because it suited them that the British and the Turkish Cypriots should have the same alphabet (Kizilyurek 2009: 42–43).

The first forms of opposition to the British administration from a section of the Cypriot Muslims associated with the consolidation of Kemalism were to be noted in 1922, when a Turkish Cypriot report was compiled which proposed several changes in the way Evkaf was administered. Let us point out here that Evkaf dealt with the greater part of the economic, social and religious life of the Muslim community and the remaining institutions (religious courts, education system, religious officials and local government) were closely linked to it (Bouleti 2008: 10). The Evkaf was responsible for repairs and renovations at schools, mosques, teachers' houses, cemeteries, historical monuments, financial support for schools, extension of the road network and the water supply network, economic assistance for poor Muslims, etc. The question of electing the administration resurfaced in 1924 when the recently established Muslim Organisation of Cyprus (Cemaat-IIslamiye) proposed the

Evkaf should be administered by a committee elected by Turkish Cypriots (McHenry 1981: 125). Essentially, and apart from the confrontation between the Kemalists and the British administration, what started at this time was a conflict inside the Turkish Cypriots where on the one side were the modernizing Kemalists who sought direct control and accountability through an elected Evkaf administration and on the other the traditionalist Turkish Cypriots who for years had been collaborating with the British, who were appointing them to the administration of Evkaf.[18] This is why the conservative Turkish Cypriots were henceforth called "Evkafcilar" (supporters of the colonial administration) whereas the Kemalists were known as "Muarizlar" (oppositionists). Beyond the subject of the manner of administration of Evkaf as such, the hostility between Kemalists and Britons was linked to the fact that the institutional changes being imposed at that time by the British involved transference to the jurisdiction Evkaf of a range of competences that had until then been exercised by the Mufti (McHenry 1981: 128). Accordingly, by the end of the 1920s, eliminating the office of the Kadi (Kadilik), Sharia court judges would henceforth oversee and administer *sharia* jurisprudence as appendages of the Evkaf, from whose funding they were to be paid. In addition, the British abolished the office of Mufti and created a new office which was under the authority of the British- appointed Evkaf Directorate. And they also abolished the office of the Mufti. It was precisely in this context that Evkaf found itself gaining strength, albeit amidst significant differentiations, in both form and function (Bouleti 2008: 123). This means that Evkaf decisions were now being determined by the British administration and not by the religious courts and the provincial Kadis, as now the Governor had the power to select both delegates of the Evkaf, given that Evkaf was now deemed to be a Government Department (Nevzat and Hatay 2009: 910). The delegates of the Evkaf passed under the direction of the Governor, and the Evcaf accounts now operated under the control of the Government (Kalantzopoulos 2015: 131). At the same time, many of the social services made available by the waqfs through Evkaf were

[18] Bryant says that a first dispute between a more conservative and a more modernising tendency within the Muslim community was noted in 1890 with the death of the Mufti of Cyprus Esseid Efendi. There was a clash in which a significant number of Muslim citizens asked through a petition that Mehmet Raif Efendi become the new Mufti, whereas the notables of Nicosia wanted Ali Rifki Efendi to be appointed, as indeed was to happen despite the protests of a large section of the Muslim population (Bryant 2004: 29–31).

terminated and the institution of the flat-rate compensation award overturned the long-standing practice of paying dividends to Muslims which in the past had had the effect of expropriating them of their property (Bouleti 2008: 254). What is important is that these reforms, which "normally" would have had to face opposition from proponents of "tradition", met with wholehearted acceptance from them precisely because they were an inseparable part of the administrative system and for that reason were appointed to the relevant key posts. And Munir Bey, the Turkish Evkaf delegate, was able to impose wide-ranging control over the functioning of the Sharia judges because with the reforms their erstwhile independence was abolished (Kalantzopoulos 2015: 123).

The Kemalists, for their part, were totally opposed to these changes. They demanded the abolition of the Sharia courts and their replacement through implementation in Cyprus of the Swiss Civil Code, along with reform of the existing Muslim Inheritance Law, as they did not consider that it provided equal rights for both sexes (Kalantzopoulos 2015: 124–125). Essentially by articulating this opposition, motivated by real problems, the Kemalists aimed at creating a parallel (as regards the role of the Archbishop) institutional reality where there Mufti would also function as a legitimate political representative of the Turkish Cypriots. From the viewpoint of history what is interesting is on the one hand the Cypriot peculiarity of secular participation in the election of religious leaders, something not customary either in Muslim or in Christian tradition (Bouleti 2008: 13), and on the other the fact that the Kemalists, for whom secularism was a basic element in their ideology, could be found supporting the *raison d'être* of a religious leader (Kalantzopoulos 2015: 120).

As for the British, they would advance as an argument for abolishing the office of Mufti the fact that Turkey had in March 1924 abolished the Caliphate.[19] But given that Cyprus was not part of Turkish territory, the Cypriot Muslims perceived religion as an element in their collective identity. This was because although the Mufti in the years of Ottoman domination never acquired the institutional and political influence that

[19] That is to say, that form of politico-religious state where the fundamental components of central government were the imposition of the law (*sharia*), the defence and expansion of the rule of Islam and overall supervision of economic matters. The institution of the caliphate was imbued with political and religious symbolism, particularly in what concerned the unity of the Muslim world.

the Archbishop exercised, after the transition of the island to British rule his role was to change. So, the Mufti twice, in 1917 and 1918, summoned pan-Cypriot assemblies to discuss the future of the Muslims in the context of the disintegration of the Ottoman Empire, but also of the probability of *Enosis* of Cyprus with Greece (Ktoris 2013: 315). Moreover, the Muslims protested because corresponding reforms were not being carried out with the Greeks, who continued freely to manage their church property, elect their religious leader and, without much British interference, shape the content of Greek Cypriot education (Ktoris 2013: 52–51).

* * *

Year 1928 would be a watershed year for these questions because Evkaf by Order in Council was to be treated as a part of the government and subjected legally and financially to its control. It would now be the Governor who would appoint the two commissioners, their appointment would subsequently have to be ratified by the Colonial Secretary and these commissioners, although civil servants, would have their salaries paid out of foundation funds (Bouleti 2008: 399). In this same year, the disputes between the two Turkish Cypriot sides would be conducted between clearly distinct political groupings. The opportunity was provided with the preparations being made by the authorities to celebrate 50 years of the British administration in Cyprus. Then at the initiative of Fadil Niyazi Korkut, he himself and Dr. Pertev, Necmi (Avkiran) Bey and Sevekt Bahce—all Nicosia municipal councillors—jointly signed a declaration on the basis of which they explained why the Turkish Cypriots should not participate in the British celebrations. It was characteristically titled "The 50th anniversary is a day of mourning for the Turks of Cyprus".[20]

There was a great deal of reaction to the text in question, particularly within the Turkish Cypriots. One of the signatories, Sevket Bahce Bey, distanced himself from it, saying that he had been ill throughout the time that the text was being written and so had not been able to exercise proper oversight of the content.

Subsequently, it was the *Hakikat* (Truth) newspaper that would undertake to answer on behalf of the "traditionalists" in an article entitled "Is

[20] The text is to be found in Nevzat (2005: 362–363).

oppositional politics and the hostility that has emerged perhaps doing more harm to our parent country than it is to the Government here?".[21]

The next round of conflict would come a little later and would be about the demand put forward by the "conservative" side on 8th November 1928 concerning abolition of the position of the Mufti. The anti-Kemalist side was afraid that even if the Mufti was appointed by the British, and even if his competences were very limited there would still be the possibility of him operating as leader of the Turkish Cypriots who were against the British. Characteristically they said that the Kemalists were "troublemakers who are impatient to find a leader for their illegal activity in various circumstances and every now and then presented themselves to the Mufti to misrepresent the duties of his position and turn him into the leader of a gang" and subsequently maintained that the Kemalists were trying to obtain access to the heads of the foundation and disrupt its power (Bouleti 2008: 402).

The British side accepted the censure of the anti-Kemalists and in their endeavour to maintain the *status quo* proceeded a step further. Accordingly, by governmental resolution of 8th November 1929 the independent functioning of the religious judges was abolished. They now had the status of salaried government employees, albeit funded by Evkaf. This meant that the government could control them without the economic burden of paying for it (Bouleti 2008: 404).

All the above on the personal level had its reflection in the criticism directed at the Turkish Cypriot representative Mehmet Munir Bey during the 1930 pre-electoral campaign for the Legislative Council. He thought of himself as representing the old Ottoman idea of collaboration between Britons and Turkish Cypriots in the context of an alliance aimed at institutional marginalization of the Greek Cypriots. But the modernizing spirit that characterized the Kemalists prompted the young lawyer Ahmed Said to denounce Munir for multiple office-holding and uncritical support of the British. And indeed over the years Munir had concentrated considerable power in his hands[22]: He was a member of the Legislative and

[21] *Hakikat* of 17th Mach 1928. The full text is to be found in Nevzat (2005: 364).

[22] One interpretation of the central role acquired by Munir in the representation and management of Turkish Cypriot affairs up to the end of the 20s is given by Raif Bey (father of Rauf Denktash). Raif Bey believed that an important role in the construction of a network of clientelistic relations friendly to the "traditionalists" had been played on the one hand by the existence of significant loan obligations for many Turkish

Executive councils, a member of the Education Council, President of the Religious Court, director of the Foundation for the Management of Public-Benefit Foundations and senior Mufti. The criticism of him made by Said, which he sent in the form of a memorandum to the Colonial Office, was that it was inappropriate for Munir as director of the Waqf and as such a public functionary and official of the executive branch to be at the same time an elected member of the Legislative and Executive councils. His criticism of the "traditionalists" also focussed on the view of their having tolerated a number of measures that downgraded the position of the minority: abolition of the position of the Kadi, abolition of the position of the Mufti, abolition of the relative autonomy of Evkaf through appointment of its representatives, abolition of the mandatory position for a Turkish Cypriot judge in every district court—these were seen as acts of favouritism towards the Greek Cypriots (Nevzat 2005: 376). Even though the measures in question from a certain viewpoint might be characterizable as modernizing, they were regarded by the majority of Turkish Cypriots as acts of abolition of their autonomy at the religious and cultural level (Perikleous 2007: 208). On the part of the Kemalists, it was asserted that the provision in the new system that Evkaf pay judges' salaries, whereas in the past they had come from colony's general budget, jeopardized the integrity of judges, transforming them into instruments of Evkaf, downgrading their dignity in the eyes of people whose lives would be affected by the decisions of these judges. Moreover, the already overstretched Evkaf was called upon to accept yet another significant burden, which in turn would contribute to further restriction of the potential to protect religious and educational institutions (MacHenry 1981: 129).

At the electoral level the harch criticisms of the Kemalists in conjunction with the vigorous activity of the Kemalist Turkish consul Assafbey[23] would, despite the vehement criticism coming from the conservative[24]

Cypriots to Evkaf, the Turkish Commercial Bank and the Turkish Orphans' Fund—institutions controlled by Munir, and on the other hand by Turkish Cypriots' expectations of appointment to the public sector (Ktoris 2013: 147).

[23] In his letter of 7th May 1930 to Passfield, Storrs writes that from the moment the Turkish consulate recommenced operations and Assaf returned to Cyprus, the latter involved himself with awakening the national consciousness of Turkish Cypriots (Georghallides 1985: 465).

[24] See the article published in *Hakikat* on 11th August 1930 in which the Kemalists are described as failed professionals and beggars who seek to sow division between Turkish Cypriots (Bouleti 2008: 411–412).

side also, lead to significant regroupment. Of the Turkish Cypriot old guard only Eyyub[25] was re-elected, by a margin of 24 votes.[26] Munir received only 1,533 votes, as against the 1,993 of Mehmed Necati Ozkan,[27] and Celaleddin withdrew his candicacy when he concluded that he had no chance against Mehmed Zekia. Necati Ozkan's securing the position of parliamentary deputy enabled him to embark on forceful political activity, promoting the ideas of Kemalism for the purpose of generating a Turkish national consciousness in Turkish Cypriots in addition to developing organizational structures in the Muslim community. And so it was that on 1st May 1931, 140 people gathered at his home and founded a Constituent Assembly, corresponding to the Turkish National Council established by Mustapha Kemal in 1919 and named the Turkish National Council of Cyprus. At this meeting, in which the opposing Muslim side did not participate (Moutsis 2014: 169),[28] the following decisions were taken:

* * *

[25] Who had also condemned Assafbey for egregious interference during the pre-election period in support of Kemalist candidates (Georghallides 1985: 467).

[26] But it should be noted that Eyioub cannot be described exactly as an anti-Kemalist. Until 1920 he was the most prominent exponent of Kemalism but his excessive debts to Evkaf reduced him to dependence on the options of Munir (Ktoris 2013: 152). It is characteristic that in 1924 he would agree with Greek Cypriot parliamentary deputies about abolishing the Tribute of Cyprus and also would vote together with them on a number of other issues, most notably voting against the budget. His stance reflects the position that more support should be given to Muslim interests by exerting pressure on the British administration, a line that would being him into conflict with the Turkish Cypriot deputy Irfan Efendi (Kyriakidis 2016: 481–482).

[27] The defeat of the British favourite greatly disconcerted them. As elegantly expressed by the then Greek consul Alexandros Kyrou (10th November 1930) "the English circles did not conceal their surprised displeasure at the unexpected failure of Munir, and in the immediate aftermath of the election reappointed him as auxiliary member of the island's Executive Council, in spite of the thirty-year established custom of parliamentary deputies being nominated for this Council so that there should be popular representation in the executive authority, even if merely formal, for the sake of appearances" (quoted by Kondylis 2009: 298).

[28] The anti-Kemalist newpaper *Hakikat* denounced the Conference, judging that it had not been legitimated and was contrary to the interests of the Turkish Cypriots (Moutsis 2014: 170).

(a) A demand for autonomous middle-school education has been instituted for Greeks and Armenians.
(b) Restoration of the office of Mufti as a spiritual leader, to be elected by the Turkish community.
(c) Securing of autonomy or religious courts or, alternatively, family law cases of Turkish Cypriots to be adjudicated by Turkish Cypriot judges.
(d) Securing of autonomy for Evkaf, to be administered by a six-member committee elected by the National Council.
(e) Proclamation of the Kemalist Ahmed Said as Mufti of Cyprus (Perikleous 2007: 300; Moutsis 2014: 164–165).

Note that the British government did not recognize either the Turkish National Council or the election of Ahmed Said, whom the Kemalist side sought to promote as adversary to the Orthodox Archbishop. The "Evcafcilar", for their part, besides challenging the ability of "130 people to decide for the 70,000 of the island" also refused to recognize the new Mufti. And the *Hakikat* newspaper in an article (23rd May 1931) condemned the Kemalists for collaboration with the Greeks seeking *Enosis*, when only stable co-operation of Muslims[29] with the British could avert such an outcome (Moutsis 2014: 171–172).

During the same period, i.e. the first half of 1931, at the initiative of Necati Ozkan the subject of directorship of the Turkish high school was raised. The new Kemalist majority wanted to detach it from the control of Evkaf and the government, demanding appointment of a Turk in the place of the British director that had been the rule hitherto (Richter 2007: 440–443; Moutsis 2014: 122–124).

The Kemalist centre was pursuing a threefold objective with these moves. On the one hand, it sought to forge a Turkish consciousness in the Turkish Cypriots. On the other, it was important in a difficult economic conjuncture to impress upon the Turkish Cypriots that it was able to improve their lives through the effective political activity of their Kemalist representatives (Apeyitou 2003: 79). Finally, an attempt was initiated to make it clear to the British that the alliance between Britons and Turkish

[29] It is typical that the article in question refers to the community as Muslim (Cemmat-i Islamiye) and not as Turks of Cyprus (Kibris Turku) (Moutsis 2014: 173).

Cypriots could not be maintained forever just on the basis of some traditional links.[30] There had to be specific material advantage also from the part of the British Empire. The first tangible form of differentiation of the Kemalists was to come on 11th April 1931 with the joint submission of a resolution by the parliamentary deputies Theodotou and Necati Ozkan who, in the field of education, demanded abolition of the positions of the British Director and the British Assistant Director and their replacement by a Greek Education Director, responsible for Greek education and a Muslim education director responsible for Turkish education (Andreou 2007: 64).[31] A few weeks later at the end of April, the bill came to the Legislative Council which provided for expanded taxation and the introduction of new customs duties on essentials. Necati strongly opposed the imposition of higher taxes, arguing that under the prevailing economic conditions taxation should be reduced not increased (Stylianou 1984: 42). Eyyub, by contrast, as representative of the conservative side, came out in support because he thought that it would benefit the local silk industry, and went on to propose that the matter be referred to a sub-committee of the Council. Finally, when the matter came to the vote, both Necati and Eyyub stayed away. The third Turkish Cypriot Zekia Bey was out of Cyprus, with the result that for the first time, with 11 votes[32] against nine, the initial British proposal was defeated (Nevzat 2005: 404). What ensued was panic on the part of the British, who saw a central pillar of their power in Cyprus being challenged, and so were obliged to exert themselves to recreate the Divide and Rule framework.[33] It was precisely in that direction that the British would henceforth move, up until the end of the 1950s.[34]

[30] For the relevant information, see the Turkish Cypriot newspaper *Soz* of 16th July 1931 (Ktoris 2013: 158).

[31] During this period, there was also mutual support through the Press of the two communities on educational questions (Kalantzopoulos 2015: 135).

[32] One Greek Cypriot position was vacant on account of cancellation of the election of the deputy Triantafyllidis in the Morphou-Lefka district.

[33] For relevant details in relation to Storr in his memoirs (Storrs 1937: 588). The Colonial Office for its part a few days after the relevant negative vote began to discuss to the possibility of elaborating a new constitution which would give the Governor total control over legislation on the island's finances (Kalantzopoulos 2015: 140).

[34] Also see relevant British documents from 1937 compiled by the Colonial Office but also by the then Governor Palmer (Apeyitou 2003: 80).

It should be noted that this ephemeral alliance between Greek Cypriots and Turkish Cypriots would not last, precisely because the strategies of the two communities were entirely different. One typical point is that on 20th April, only a few days prior to the rejection of approval for the British bill on customs duties and during a committee session preparing the Parliament's response to the Governor's greeting speech, the Metropolitan of Kition and the parliamentarian Nicodemos Mylonas proposed that a paragraph should be added declaring Cypriots' desire for *Enosis* with Greece. Necati took the floor and argued that given Cyprus' proximity to Turkey, it was an extension and a part of Turkey. Greece, he continued, was very far off and had never governed Cyprus, unlike Turkey, which had liberated the island from foreign occupation, giving its inhabitants many privileges. That said, he asserted, ceding Cyprus to Britain represented an interruption in the development of the island, but the Turkish Cypriots were nevertheless entirely satisfied with the British administration. He finished by saying that Cyprus is a part of Asia Minor and those who are foreign to the island should go to Greece (Richter 2007: 466–467).

So, opposition to the bill for higher taxation was not an action aiming at political convergence of the two communities, but a stance dictated by the need to champion the fellow-nationals who had voted for him. And even the aforementioned joint resolution of Greek Cypriots and Turkish Cypriots on education directors was merely a conjunctural compact for the purpose of underlining the differences in national characteristics in the field of education also.

Mention should be made finally that the changes in customs duties were to be adopted despite the vote against them in the Legislative Council on 11th August 1931 following the issuance of a relevant imperial Order in Council (Stylianou 1984: 41).

8 Details of the Revolt

As already mentioned, on 18th October the Metropolitan of Kition Nicodemos submitted his resignation as a deputy in the Legislative Council, declaring that all Greek Cypriots should resist unjust laws, raising the banner of *Enosis*.[35] Immediately afterwards, he embarked on a series of addresses to the Greek Cypriot people: on 18th October he gave a

[35] For the full text see Stylianou (1984: 54).

speech in Larnaca urging that Cyprus and Greece proceed with *Enosis* and on 20th October he spoke in Limassol.

Publication of the telegram announcing the Limassol meeting, which the ex-deputy Lanitis (he had resigned) sent as a report to the Athenian newspaper *Elefthero Vima*, in Ledra St. near the church of Faneromeni, attracted a crowd which gathered to hear news of developments, as others began to ring the bells with the result that the numbers present increased even further (Rappas 2014: 1–2). This spontaneous gathering was quickly transformed into a demonstration and people there were asked to speak, which some did. The deputies Hadjipavlou, Theodotou, Stavrinakis and Siakkalis spoke, Klytidis spoke on behalf of the National Radical Union of Cyprus and the steward of the church of the Faneromeni Kykkotis also spoke. After the speeches, the slogan "to Government House" was heard and irrespective of the objections of the parliamentarians a march began to Government House, with the Greek flag at the head held by Kykkotis and the Greek Cypriot deputies (Georghallides 1985). The march was joined by ever more people as it proceeded. When the crowd reached Government House, they attempted to break through the police cordon and enter, with the result that clashes started with the police, which soon took the form of stone-throwing and lowering of the Union Jack and simultaneous raising of the Greek flag. Then the parliamentary deputies attempted to persuade the crowd to leave but people were adamant and insisted that Storrs should accept in Government House a delegation which would present the demands of the crowd which had gathered. Storrs said that he would accept a small delegation on the condition that the demonstrators withdrew (Stylianou 1984: 69). But despite the related urgings of the deputies Theodotou and Hadjipavlou, and of Kykkotis also, the crowd continued as before to insist on staying there (*Historical Encyclopedia of Cyprus* 1979–1980, Vol. 6: 42). After that, the British administration sent a detachment of troops and the first shots were heard. The crowd then began to break into Government House, which not long after went up in flames. Governor Storrs left the premises and the police started firing indiscriminately, with the result that one person lost his life and another fourteen were injured. Late in the evening, the situation stabilized but as a precaution against every eventuality Storrs requested, and received, military reinforcements from Egypt, which were flown in because of the urgency of the situation.[36] The next day, 22nd October, the British administration will give the order that the walls would be adorned with posters announcing the imposition of martial law, in English, Greek and Turkish. But these developments did not prevent other protests from being organized in the capital in the immediately following days.

News about the events in Nicosia fomented unrest in Famagusta also. Demonstrations were held on 23rd and 24th October and on 25th October demonstrators attacked police stations with the result that one demonstrator was killed, and many were injured. The agitation continued until 29th October. It is perhaps worth noting how fear of immediate military intervention induced the Greek Cypriot political elite to attempt a measured manipulation of the social dynamic. At a meeting called by the city's deputy administrator Wilson, with participation from Bittleston, commander of the warship Achates, Bittleston threatened the city's Greek Cypriot political leaders (Emfietzis, Louizidis, Mylonas, Saveriades, Alexandritis and Hadjidimitriou) with the use of violence if he deemed it necessary. The Greek Cypriots promised to exert all their influence to preserve the peace and the same assurances were given subsequently by the parliamentary deputies who were resigning, Siakallis and Rossidis. A little later, following a complaint from Wilson to the mayor Emfietzis about the raising of Greek flags on Greek houses, the latter promised that they would be taken down after the programmed rally. It is perhaps not surprising that Emfietzis spoke very little at the rally and Rossidis and Siakallis asked people after the rally to disperse peacefully, which however did not happen because many participants subsequently staged a march (Stylianou 1984: 89–93). The non-dissipation of the dynamic would become obvious in the actualization of the rally the next day but also in the conflicts up until 29th October.

Larnaca, where Nicodemos had delivered his revolutionary oration, had been in a state of ferment since 18th October. Demonstrations were held on 22nd and 25th October and the following days there would be clashes despite the speakers' appeals at the second rally that participants should show restraint (Stylianou 1984: 106). The city would remain in turmoil until 1st November.

[36] At that time, the headquarters of the British armed forces in the Mediterranean were in Egypt. Apart from the troops that came by air, four warships were moved from Souda (in Crete) to Cyprus (Sophokleous 2003: 133).

There were no demonstrations in Kyrenia until 25th October. On that day, the Metropolitan Makarios was forbidden to go to Nicosia. On his return, he addressed the crowd which had already gathered at the church of the Archangel and denounced the British tyranny. This was followed by a march on the Residency where the Greek flag was raised despite the intervention of the mayor C. Dimitriadis, who asked the crowd to preserve order and disperse. In the evening of the same day, there was a rally with participation from residents of the surrounding villages, and clashes took place, with injuries and one person killed. Finally, the Army occupied the bishopric and arrested Makarios.

In Paphos on 22nd October and 24th October, there were big demonstrations with the result that on 25th October martial law was declared. Incidents followed on 25th October and arrests were made. Unrest continued until Saturday 31st October.

In Limassol, the public meeting that was held on 22nd October led to a siege and the occupation and torching of the house of the British administrator. After two days the British succeeded in arresting the Metropolitan of Kition Nicodemos Mylonas but when the Greek Cypriots heard the news, the next day there were clashes, leaving one person dead and many injured. House arrest was imposed on the city's residents and arrests were carried out, which continued until 1st November. The arrest of Mylonas was accompanied by arrests of another five Greek Cypriots in Nicosia (G. Hadjipavlou, D. Kykkotis, O. Tsangaridis, T. Theodotou and T. Kolokasidis), who were regarded as the instigators of the unrest and a few days later, along with another four people (S. Loizidis, the Metropolitan of Kyrenia Makarios and the leading cadres of the Communist Party of Cyprus C. Vatyliotis and K. Skeleas) were banished from Cyprus. The truth is that when the first arrests became known in Nicosia on 24th October a crowd gathered at the archbishopric demanding the release of those arrested but after urging from mayor T. Dervis and from Dr. Kalavros, the gathering dispersed (Stylianou 1984: 82–83).

There were serious incidents in the countryside also, where police stations were occupied, ransacked and torched (Komi Kepir, Rizokarpaso, Limnia and Paralimni), governmental installations were attacked (telegraph and telephone communications were cut), bridges were destroyed, tax collectors and governmental employees (Apaisia) were beaten up and kicked out, policemen were disarmed (Vasa, Omodos, Zoopigi and Lofou), forests were burnt, troop concentrations were stoned (Kato Zodia and Argaki Morphou), state property was destroyed (public salterns and nurseries) in Gialousa, Bogazi, Agios Theodoros of Famagusta, Koma, Proastio and Amvrosio, forestry authority houses were burned (Koronia and Dafni) and mayors resigned (Limassol province) (Stylianou 1984: 146–150; 2013: 101).

What can be seen is that there were certain differences between how revolt was conceptualized in the cities and in the countryside. For a start, the uprising quickly spread in all six of the big cities of Cyprus (Nicosia, Paphos, Famagusta, Larnaca, Kyrenia and Limassol). In contrast, according to the report by Governor Storrs the same is not true of the provinces. There, of the 598 villages that there were in total, 200 particicipated actively in the revolt and 307 were not involved at all (cited in *Historical Encyclopedia of Cyprus* 1979–1980, Vol. 6: 126). This must be due on the one hand to the impossibility at that time of direct contact between the villages of Cyprus and on the other to the presence of Turkish Cypriots in many of those villages. That said, there were differences in relation to the content of demands: in the cities, there is a clear predominance of the demand for *Enosis*[37] and the impossibility, in many cases, of parliamentarians being able to determine developments. In the villages, there was no presence of parliamentary deputies but the practices that were adopted tended more towards those of insurrection against state symbols and state power.

9 The Stance of the Communist Party of Cyprus (KKK)

For the role of the Communist Party of Cyprus (KKK) throughout the revolt to become comprehensible, it is necessary that there should be a reference to its previous activity.

The workers' movement in Cyprus developed somewhat slowly because of the island's economic backwardness: a particularly oversized agricultural economy, small capitalist enterprises, great political and ideological influence of big landowners, including the Church. At the same time, the question of *Enosis* imposed certain limits on the possibilities for

[37] Characteristically, we mention the parading of the Greek flag on the march to Government House on 21st October, the raising of the Greek flag and lowering of the Union Jack at Government House, the fact that in all the speeches by politicians in all the cities the question of *Enosis* held centre stage, the display of Greek flags on many houses, etc.

joint action of Greek Cypriot and Turkish Cypriot workers. The Russian Revolution and the slow, but real, movement towards a capitalist economy gave the necessary stimulus for the founding of the Communist Party of Cyprus. It was preceded by the creation of Marxist clubs, within which the first Communist cadres became active: primarily employees in mercantile enterprises and working artisans. The newly formed Communist Party Cyprus was particularly strong in the working class of Limassol, to an extent in Famagusta and in a more limited sense in the other urban centres but not in farming areas. It also had influenced in intellectual circles. There were about 35 members in 1923, a number which rose to 180 at the end of the 1930s and 365 during the uprising. The founding Congress took place in August 1926, with the Cypriot C. Vatikiotis playing a central role. He lived at that time in Greece and came to Cyprus as an emissary of the KKE, his mission being to prepare the theses and organize the Congress. The programme of the Cypriot Communist Party sought to rally workers and peasant farmers (of both nationalities) against the capitalists, the landowners, and the Orthodox Church, proclaiming its opposition to the prospect of *Enosis* with Greece, supporting independence from colonial ties within the framework of establishing a Soviet Cypriot workers' democracy as an integral element of the Socialist Balkan Federation. Its vehicle of preference was the united front against the British, which from 1928 onwards included, above and beyond the Greek Cypriot and Turkish Cypriot workers and farmers, the bourgeois parliamentarians, and petty bourgeois political activists. But this came up against, on the one hand, the refusal of the Greek Cypriot Right to ally itself with the Communists and on the other the very serious disagreements between Right and Left over the subject of *Enosis* (Katsouridis 2009: 395–396).

What should be noted is that its position on Independence did not prevent the Cyprus Communist Party from exerting a certain electoral influence among the working-class strata of some cities. The three Cyprus Communist Party candidates would receive 15.7% of the votes in the 1926 municpal elections in Limassol. In the repeat elections held in the same city in 1927 the Communist candidates won 14% and in the corresponding elections in 1929 they took 14.3% (Protopapas 2012: 275–276). In the March 1930 municipal elections in Limassol the Cyprus Communist Party also won 15% but note that this time they stood as an autonomous political force and not under the aegis of the Workers' Centre, which had broadened their audience. All this is undoubtedly clear evidence that there was penetration of Cyprus Communist Party influence into sections of the working class, the more so because only owners of fixed property and people paying rent had the right to vote and there were many pressures not to vote Communist (Lefkis 1984: 139). Nevertheless, as already indicated, the influence of the Cyprus Communist Party was confined to Limassol and to some extent Famagusta, leaving out the other urban centres and the countryside, where a large proportion of the population lived.

The return of Vatis to Cyprus at the end of 1930 gave the Cyprus Communist Party a new lease of life. Vatis become general secretary of the party—a position occupied until then by K. Skeleas—and he would contribute to reorganizing it, placing emphasis on mass recruitment, highlighting the question of unemployment and enlightening the masses through publication of a range of pamphlets.

But the question that was to be definitive for the politics of Vatis but also for the overall stance of the Cyprus Communist Party was the national problem. Following the line of Independence, members and followers of the party decided to act on 25th March 1931. So it was that in Nicosia an attempt was made to circulate a handout denouncing *Enosis*, leading ultimately to the arrest of eight workers promoting the line of the Cyprus Communist Party. In Limassol, the situation became even more serious. In the course of an anniversary function in the premises of the high school members of the Cyprus Communist Party raised a red flag and proceeded to shout slogans such as "down with *Enosis*", "long live the Soviet republic of Cyprus". Clashes followed with proponents of *Enosis* and the police arrested 22 members and friends of the Cyprus Communist Party (*Historical Encyclopedia of Cyprus* 1979–1980, Vol. 6: 150–151).

It was again the national question that was to determine the initial stance of the Cyprus Communist Party towards the revolt, where only after the torching of the Governor's residence was it induced to participate officially in the events whereas until then participation by members had been the result of individual initiative. That was because the attitude hitherto had been that the mobilizations were being conducted in a reactionary framework under the hegemony of the Church and the Greek Cypriot bourgeoisie.

There would have to be further developments before the party's Central Committee would be able to issue an announcement on 23rd October that the differences between the nationalists who wanted *Enosis* with Greece and the Communists agitating for a Soviet republic in Cyprus would not necessarily comprise an impediment to the formation of a united anti-imperialist front. The existing disagreements could be resolved after the departure of the Imperialists from the Cypriot political scene. The announcement went on to re-evaluate the preceding policy of abstention, a rethinking which was pursued by the local party cells during the popular protests. Carrying out a kind of self-criticism, the Central Committee concluded that the line of non-involvement was to be condemned. Neutrality had proved damaging to the anti-imperialist struggles of the labouring masses.[38] After this decision of 24th October, the leader of the Cyprus Communist Party Haralambos Vatyliotis, together with T. Anthias and K. Kononas, following intervention by the lawyer A. Aimilianidis, met together with the Archbishop and there was discussion of the idea of forming a united anti-colonial front, without an agreement being reached finally, however.

After the failed meeting in the Archbishopric, Vatis had a meeting at the party's club with Mustafa Houlousi, a member of the central committee of the Cyprus Communist Party, where they discussed the way in which they might publish a bilingual declaration with a view to inducing the Turkish Cypriots to participate in the revolt and the strikes. Mustapha Houlousi said that it was dangerous to publish a declaration of that kind before making it known to the British government. Vatis replied that it was useless to publish a declaration which had been censored in advance by the British. Houlousi said in response that he would agree to publication of the declaration only if they accepted his proposal and finally Vatis did so (Stylianou 1984: 311–312). But there is no testimony to a Greek-Turkish declaration having been published.

10 The Stance of the Turkish Cypriots

As far as the Turkish Cypriots are concerned, there does not seem to have been any active participation in the events of the revolt. This is interpreted by some as a stance of neutrality (Pantelis: 174). But a relevant statement by Necati presents the events in a different light: "[…] the recent activities in Nicosia of our Greek compatriots […] are not directed to our community but are events which occurred between Greeks and the

[38] For the full text see History of the Cyprus Communist Party—AKEL (Progressive Party of Working People), Vol. I, 1926–1941 (pp. 171–173).

Government. Therefore, our duty in such an excited and extraordinary time is to maintain our perfect quietness and impartiality [...] and to leave the matter entirely to be dealt with by the responsible authorities [...]" (cited by Nevzat 2005: 408). These remarks reveal an extreme punctiliousness and preoccupation with legality in everything affecting their relations with the British and an apprehension that any Turkish Cypriot involvement could prejudice their position. The Turkish Cypriot pro-Kemalist newspaper *Soz*, for its part, in its editorial of 29th October 1931, having condemned "Greek Cypriot extremism", expressed its sympathy for the British administration and Governor Storrs and expressed regret that the Turkish Cypriot community was not able to help the administration impose order and ultimately declared—yet again—the community's faith in British rule (Bouleti 2008: 425). We see that *Soz* took a step further, openly supporting the British side, on the one hand, apprehensive about the prospect of *Enosis* with Greece and, on the other, fearing that hardening of the stance of the regime would have consequences not only for oppositional Greek Cypriots but also for oppositional Kemalist Turkish Cypriots. The traditionalist Turkish Cypriot side did indeed see the revolt as an opportunity to impose its priorities on its intra-communal opponents. In an article in *Hakkikat* of 30th December 1931, the newspaper asserted that the recent unrest was due to the action of the Orthodox clergy who instead of performing their spiritual duties got mixed up in politics, to the nationalistic activity of Greek educators in the schools, and to the mobilizations of Greek Cypriot mayors and Greek Cypriots who had been appointed to high-level public positions. These latter, according to *Hakkikat*, should be removed from their positions, and the situation in the Church and in education necessitated the introduction of laws which would prohibit the people concerned from proceeding with nationalistic harangues, confining themselves to performance of their duties. Finally, there was support for the British decision to suspend the functioning of the Legislative Council and their wish to see revision of the Constitution (Bouleti 2008: 428). As is obvious, *Hakkikat's* proposals affected the Kemalists *also* because the ban on elections abolished the direct relations of representation enjoyed by Kemalist deputies, leaving British appointee Munir Bey[39] as sole representative of the Turkish Cypriot community,

[39] Who in statements he made on the revolt said that there was a necessity for a permanent presence of the Army on the island, and control of education because of the active role of schoolteachers in the events (Theoharidis 2010: 317).

and the passage of new laws on education and religion placed these two institutions, which were a basic pole of contention between Kemalists and conservatives, even more under the control of the British.

And indeed, shortly after the conclusion of the revolt, the upper hand would be obtained by the conservatives, exploiting the traditional relations they had cultivated with the British. Centre stage would be occupied once again by Munir, who on 15th January 1932 submitted through the Cypriot government a document to Sir Philip Cunliffe-Liste, Secretary of State for the Collonies, emhasizing the opposition of the Turkish Cypriots to any change in the Cypriot *status quo*. This document bore the signatures of Turkish Cypriots from 218 villages of Cyprus which were either entirely Turkish Cypriot or of mixed population. It included the assertion that "the established representatives and interested parties among the Mohammedans of Cyprus emphatically stress their opposition to the recent unrest in Cyprus". The Turkish Cypriots also declared their total opposition not only to any form of autonomy or self-determination of Cyprus but also towards any thought of broadening the powers of local government (Stylianou 1984: 176).

11 The Stance of the Greek Government

The Greek government was entirely dismissive of the Greek Cypriot movement. Immediately the events in Cyprus started to become known, the Prime Minister E. Venizelos declared categorically: "As I have stated before, there is no Cyprus issue between the Greek Government and the British Government. It is between the latter and the Cypriots. Until now, however, these struggles have been carried out on behalf of the latter through memoranda, resolutions, rallies, through means which the liberal English character considers perfectly legitimate. But unfortunately, today, according to the news in the press, criminal deviations have also been noted. [...] I cannot but express my deepest regret for these aberrations. [...] But I take this opportunity to state [...]: however deep the impression that the national aspirations of the inhabitants of these islands have on the Greek psyche, *it is not possible* for the Greek state to undertake to support their actualization. [...] Vital, absolutely vital, interests of Greece require it to maintain relations of undisturbed friendship [...] towards Great Britain and towards our neighbouring great Mediterranean power,

Italy[40] [...] Only in the event that Great Britain would assert that Cyprus is not useful to it at all, or that the usefulness it may have can be secured by the retention of only a small part of it, would it be possible for it to heed the national interests of the Cypriots, provided that the relations of the population with the sovereign power were restored so smoothly that it could not be assumed that the latter had succumbed to violence" (cited by Stylianou 1984: 241; Svolopoulos 1978: 504).[41] The declarations of the Greek Foreign Minister Michalakopoulos were in the same vein.[42] The reactions there were inside Greece, demanding that the Government show solidarity with the Greek Cypriots would lead Venizelos to try to cancel the memorial ceremony which had been programmed for 1st November to honour the memory of those killed during the revolt. Finally, instead of at Agiou Konstantinou in the centre of Athens the memorial was held at the Church of the Dormition of the Virgin Mary in the Athenian suburb of Maroussi with the simultaneous announcement of a repetition of the memorial in every district of the country. At the same time, outdoor gatherings in support of the revolt were banned, leading to bloody clashes with the police, which would subside only when the movement in Cyprus had come to an end and Venizelos threatened to hold elections.

How is this stance of Venizelos to be interpreted? Why was the prospect of *Enosis* excluded, leaving only a very narrow margin of possibility for a different development, at a time unspecified, through concession of a British base in Cyprus[43]?

It seems that there was a complex of factors contributing to the Greek government's adoption of such a stance: For a start, account should be taken of the consequences of the serious military defeat suffered by Greece in Asia Minor in 1922. After it, Athens tried to establish neighbourly relations with all the Balkan countries and a stable alliance with Britain. The Greek-Turkish Friendship Treaty signed between Venizelos

[40] Venizelos here implies the occupation of the Dodecanese, where there was a Greek majority, by the Italians.

[41] As early as 13th May 1931 in a confidential document Venizelos was recommending moderation and claims via "legitimate means" (Pikros 1980: 100–101).

[42] For the content of the Michalakopoulos statement see Richter (2007: 513).

[43] In a discussion in 1930 between Venizelos and the British Prime Minister Ramsay MacDonald Venizelos said that in return for *Enosis* Greece could accept the establishment of a British military base in Famagusta with full sovereignty over its harbour (Pikros 1980: 95). Moreover, this is implied in the statement condemning the revolt.

and the Turkish Prime Minister İnönü was jeopardized by potential rekindling of the Cyprus question. Similarly jeopardized were the relations between Greece and Britain—the touchstone of Greek foreign policy—not to mention the fact that the example of the Greek Cypriots could be imitated by the Greek inhabitants of the Dodecanese, torpedoing relations between Greece and Italy.

But there is also another factor that could have contributed to the stance of the Venizelist centre. Only a few years had passed since the Bolshevik Revolution, with the great effect that it had had on the whole world. The founding of the Communist Party of Cyprus and the increase in its influence lent legitimacy to Leftist ideas, something that Venizelos was not inclined to tolerate. To this, there should be added the fact that one feature of the Cypriot insurrection was the spontaneous character of the mass action, very remote from the secure and ready-made aspects of diplomatic discussions. As a quintessentially bourgeois politician had every reason to dislike situations and practices that liberated the social dynamic.

12 The Consequences of the Revolt

Having succeeded in reaffirming their domination, the British implemented several measures to ensure that such actions would not be seen again. On 22nd October the colonial administration brought into force legislative adjustments to which they gave the name "Regulations for the defence of Cyprus": more than 400 Greek Cypriots were arrested, 3,359 prosecuted and 2,606 convicted, with a variety of penalties being imposed (around 2,000 were fined amounts varying from two to ten pounds and some were imprisoned, with sentences from six to 19 months) (Richter 2006: 137) and, as indicated, ten of the most prominent cadres of the anti-colonial struggle were exiled for life. The Colonial Office and the Cypriot authorities concluded on 18th November, at a first calculation, that the costs of restoring the damage came to £28,000, half of which would be paid by the inhabitants of Nicosia; The Law on Expenditure and Restoration, which was ratified on 21st December, decided that damaged property should be replaced and repaired at the expense of the villages and cities responsible (Pantelis 1986: 79). The total sum they paid came to £34,315. That done, on 12th November by royal command the Legislative Council was abolished. Henceforth, the Governor had the power to rule by decree.

On 1st December 1931, three laws were promulgated: the first ruled that from then on the Mukhtars would be appointed by the Governor and would not be elected, the second prohibited the raising, without permission, of flags of a foreign state and the third prohibited the ringing of bells without corresponding permission of the Provincial Administrator—but this measure reminded Greek Cypriots of the period of Ottoman domination, when the silence of bells symbolized the subordination of Christians. Other measures followed: political parties were prohibited from functioning and any propagandizing that challenged British sovereignty on the island became a criminal offence. As regards the Cypriot Communist Party in particular, the possession of Communist material (books, magazines and newpapers) was deemed illegal and punished with two years' imprisonment. In cases where individuals were suspected of reading Communist material, the police had the right to carry out arrests without a warrant to conduct searches of homes and confiscate printed material (Richter 2006: 139).

In October 1932, a new law defined with remarkable strictness the preconditions under which a gathering of more than five persons could be permitted, and there were restrictions on arrivals and departures to and from Cyprus. The police had the right to enter any house and stop any citizen on the street for the purpose of conducting investigation. Censorship was also imposed on publications disseminating inflammatory views, i.e. views challenging British rule, and it was not permitted for Athenian newspapers and certain printed materials from other countries to be imported into Cyprus (Alastos 1976: 356–357). No article could be published dealing with local or international matters if it had not been previously cleared by the censor. Even the republication of letters and articles which had already been published in the Times or speeches in the British parliament were subject to censorship and usually certain paragraphs were omitted (Pantelis 1986: 177). In order for censorship to be effective, there were "innovations": By October 1931 every article had to pass through the censorship prior to publication. But this required a large staff. After the revolt, the following method was accordingly implemented: every newspaper was required to have a publication permit and so was obliged to deposit with the authorities a bond to the value of £500. In cases where the newspaper published something "subversive" or presented the news in a non- "objective" way, the permit could be rescinded, and the deposit lost (Richter 2006: 138). Censorship was imposed even on the post office and telegraph (Pavlidis 1993: 304).

Under a law passed in 1937, the government had the right to refuse entry to a Cypriot "if there are indications deemed adequate by the Governor that he may behave in a manner dangerous for order and peace". Under another law passed in 1939, the Governor gave unlimited power to the police "to arrest or banish any individual who is operating, or is likely to operate, in this manner or who could take advantage of the relative freedom of movement he enjoys to propagate ideas with the potential to hinder defence of the State".

Changes were made in education for the basic purpose of "Britishizing" the students. Power over educational policy was transferred to the competence of the Governor, and the educational council was transformed into a mere advisory committee. The Governor himself was now responsible for teacher appointments[44] and salaries, for determining the syllabus and educational materials so that anti-British propaganda was not disseminated in the schools.[45] In the detailed syllabus, which was common to all students, the English language was introduced into the upper classes of the primary school, along with the British national anthem, the Union Jack and mandatory celebration of the royal anniversaries—this was why those who wished to be teachers were required to follow courses in teacher training institutions in addition to completing Greek or Turkish high school—and the Governor also had the right to appoint the members of the educational councils and control the finances of the educational system (Crouzet 1973: 128–129; Richter 2006: 139). Under this disposition, the emphasis on the subjects of History and Geography shifted from Greece and Turkey to the Middle East, the Mediterranean and the rest of the world (Rappas 2014: 45), with an increase in the teaching of English in high school. The display of photographs of national heroes was not permitted in schoolrooms or public places (Pantelis 1986: 178) and teachers were threatened with punishment "if the national symbols of any foreign country with whom

[44] Under the law of September 1935 in order for a teacher to be appointed, the headmaster of the school had to have judged that "such person is educationally, morally and in all other respects a fit and proper person to be a secondary school teacher" (cited by Heraclidou 2017: 62).

[45] In this connection, the import of books from Turkey was banned in 1935 and an English director was appointed for the Turkish high school, which was renamed a Muslim high school (Ktoris 2013: 165). At the same time, the Director of Education had the right to forbid the use of any book that could be considered seditious and morally harmful (Heraclidou 2017: 62).

insurgent elements in the population are striving to unite [...] are left in the schools" (cited by Papapolyviou 2004: 331). Even the screening of films on the current events of the times was banned, so that the projection of footage from the funeral of Ataturk or from weddings of the Greek Royal family were forbidden, provoking reactions from both communities. The ban on establishing local political associations was in the same vein and lawyers working in Cyprus were obliged under law to be enroled in the registers of British attorneys so that anyone wishing to pursue this profession would have to study at a British university.

Finally, in what concerns the Orthodox Church, from 1933 on it remained without a head. This was because after the 1931 revolt two Metropolitans, those of Kition Nicodemos and of Kyrenia Makarios had been sent into exile and on 16th November 1933 the Archbishop of Cyprus Kyrillos III died, with the result that there remained only the Metropolitan of Paphos Leontios, who was absent in London throughout the disturbances, as *Locum Tenens* for the Throne. The election of the new Archbishop was not able to take place, given that the British forbade the return of the two exiled Metropolitans, so that the competent ecclesiastical synod could not be convened. When after the death of Nicodemos an attempt was made to circumvent this obstacle through convening an elected synod (after relevant consultation of the *Locum Tenens* and the exiled Metropolitan of Kyrenia Makarios) which would be comprised of the *Locum Tenens*, the Metropolitan of Trebizond Chrysanthos, as representative of the Metropolitan of Kyrenia, and the Archbishop of Sinai Porphyrios, the British proceeded to ban the election of the Archbishop of Cyprus. It was done through laws 33 and 34 of 1937, which specified that a candidate could not be elected Archbishop if he had been exiled by the government or convicted of wrongdoing or was not a British subject, and his election had to have the approval of the Governor. So that there could not be any possibility of the case being revived, the British in 1938 condemned Leontios to further time at the Paphos Estate under police surveillance, a regime that was to be maintained until 1940 (Stylianou 2013: 99–100; Yiagou 2013: 113).

13 The Change in the Power Structure and the Schism Within the Two Communities

The abolition of the elections for Legislative Council and local government and the appointment by the British of the new political elite brought about significant changes in the form of political power in Cyprus. A new power system was constituted which was not an expression of the will of Cypriots but rather aimed at controlling them. The collaborators with the British were appointed by the colonial administration and enjoyed a range of privileges precisely so that they could control the activities of their fellow citizens. The entire policy was aimed at de-nationalizing the Cypriots, breaking their links with Greece and Turkey and leading them to acquire a hybrid identity of British subjects with a different civilizational background (Markides and Georghallides 1995: 76).

At the decision-making level, a bureaucracy had been created consisting of the members of the Executive Council, the provincial Administrators, and the mayors. For the depth of the profoundly conservative convictions of the collaborators with the British to be perceptible, suffice it to mention two incidents.[46] In the first, in a meeting he had on 18th October 1938 at the Colonial Office in London with J. B. Williams, an official of the Finance Section, the appointed mayor of Nicosia Themistocles Dervis argued that the present constitutional situation in Cyprus should be maintained and elections not be conducted again, because if there were elections again there would be bribery and corruption again. The second had to do with the prominent merchant and member of the Advisory Council P. Tseriotis, who on 24th October 38 also visited Williams and submitted a request for the term of office of Palmer in Cyprus to be extended (Katsiaounis 2000: 46–47).[47]

That said, the most neuralgic body, the backbone of the system, was that of the Mukhtars. Their role in the small communities of Cyprus was always central because "most times the Mukhtar was also a grocer or a coffee shop owner or both; sometimes he even ran the post office and it was very rare to find a Mukhtar of a large village who was not embroiled in all this, and above all in trade [...] Surrounded by the police, field wardens, provincial overseers, sanitary, agricultural, land registry and

[46] For a period (from 1933 to 1939) the Advisory Council was in operation, with participation from four Greek Cypriots and a Turkish Cypriot as part of an endeavour to have a more government-friendly (appointed) body functioning. But neither was statutory provision made for it nor did it play any role because the recommendations it made were never considered (Markides and Georghallides 1995: 76–77).

[47] These stances should be linked to the fact of the British administration attempting to create a pro-British elite of Greek Cypriot origin. So above and beyond the invitations to distinguished Greek Cypriots to British events, throughout the Palmer administration medals and honorific titles were bestowed upon Greek Cypriots to a much greater extent than in all the previous 55 years together (Katsiaounis 2004: 33–34).

other officials with whom they were linked through close friendship, the Mukhtar office was covered in every way and nobody could touch them [...]".[48]

People appointed to this position developed a mode of behaviour entirely subordinated to the caprices of the British. Characteristic from this viewpoint was a memorandum presented to the British authorities by the mukhtars of 37 villages of Messaria and Karpasia on the occasion of the crowning of the new British King George VI: "that the Lord grant Him a long life to rule the great and mighty Empire and the other subject peoples in it along with our little island of Cyprus. We express loyalty and obedience to our new King". The memorandum in question was, as it were, a diversion from the arrival of a three-member Greek Cypriot mission in London with a view to formulating the petition for restoration of political freedoms.[49] The memorandum went on to deplore "a move on the part of a certain circle of Cypriots who are very far from representing the view of the people and who as we understand are trying to bring back the old arrangements and seek to elect parliamentarians, etc. We ask, however that the opinion of these individuals not be taken very much into account under the Government of His Majesty [...] We are very happy with the present system because first of all the Government has understood that the people have not done anything wrong and today what the Government has done is for the good of our country" (cited by Katsiaounis 2000: 45).

Apart from the Mukhtars, great power was also acquired by the members of the appointed school ephorates who were responsible for

[48] These are extracts from an article written by the Secretary of the Teachers' Co-operative Savings Bank of Cyprus N. Clerides in Eleftheria of 21st March 1937 (quoted in the *Historical Encyclopedia of Cyprus* 1979–1980, Vol. 4, pp. 255–256).

[49] What is interesting is that this move enjoyed the sympathy of Kemalist circles also so that finally this petition to the authorities in London for reinstatement of political life was signed by many Turkish Cypriots, including Necati. Finally, the Colonial Office rejected all the requests. Nevertheless, the collection of signatures for petitions continued all the following years, with the result that between 1939 and 1944 88 petitions were signed, with a total of 19,587 signatures (Rappas 2014: 104). In 1939 there was a resurgence on account of the imminent departure of Palmer from the position of Governor. The initiative was taken then by the lawyer G. Vasileiades and the illegal Communist Party of Cyprus in collaboration with Turkish Cypriots (Katsiaounis 2001: 149). This was the first manifestation of collaboration between the Cyprus Communist Party and progressive bourgeois which two years later was to lead to the establishment of AKEL (the Progressive Party of Working People) (see below).

teacher appointments and promotions. Another social stratum allied with the British were a section of the clergy and the laity who managed church property.

Finally, in relation to the Turkish Cypriots, the British administration tried to implement a "carrot and stick" policy. On the one hand, all the restrictions that had been introduced for the Greek Cypriots remained in force..[50] On the other, an attempt was made to favour the anglophile section of the Turkish Cypriot elite[51] and through that there were several beneficial measures for the Turkish Cypriots. As Katsiaounis puts it: "[...] the tactic of the British was not confined to mere repression of the opposition. There was an attempt to co-opt the traditionally law-abiding Turkish notables [...] at the behest of Governor Palmer Munir Bey toured the Turkish communities of Cyprus, organizing meetings of people of influence at which he attempted to calm the general discontent with government policy. In return for a display of conformity, they were promised relief from agricultural debts, which weighed more oppressively on Turkish peasant farmers than on Greeks (Katsiaounis 2000: 55–57).

And indeed, as Storrs wrote to the Colonial Office in 1932 "Munir Bey is the leader of the Turkish population of this colony. He is 100 percent pro-British [...] and has absorbed himself every office he could (cited by McHenry 1981: 138).[52] But after a certain point the British

[50] Not surprisingly, the pro-Kemalist newspaper *Soz* was suspended in 1937 and placed under censorship from 1938 (Stubbs and Taseli 2014: 288). In an attempt, indeed, to roll back the nationalism of the Turkish Cypriots the government changed the name of the Turkish High School to Islam High School.

[51] Nor is it surprising how difficult it was for the anti-Kemalist ***Hakikat*** to hide its enthusiasm for the abolition of the Legislative Council: "[....] there is no legislative council, and no members of the Legislative Council exist for the Present. This fact will produce good reforms in the Country, and will, no doubt, settle many disputes among the Turks. Because it will give an end to the divisions created by the elections and will settle the question of the Lycee, which was the source of many troubles, as the members of the council will now disappear" (cited by Moutsis 2014: 183).

[52] Characteristically, there was a secret letter from Munir Bey to Sir Philip Cunliffe–Lister, the Secretary of State for Colonies, in which he complains about the behaviour of the Turkish Consul, accusing him of pressurising members of his family. According Munr Bey, the Turkish consul sought the dismissal of his nephew from the Military Veterinary College in Ankara so that Munir Bey would be obliged to pursue a pro-Turk policy (Xypolia 2011: 115). The British partiality towards Munir Bey is evident not only from the fact that he had been appointed a member of the Executive Council while also retaining many other public posts (Kalantzopoulos 2015: 117) but also from his remaining in the position of delegate of the Evkaf until 1948 (Moutsis 2014: 174).

government perceived that "the traditionalists", cut off from Turkey as they were, represented a link with the old, which was on the way out, whereas the Kemalists successfully represented the new reality. This was recorded for the first time in a Colonial Office memorandum in 1935, where there is an assertion that one serious reason for the rise of Kemalism among the Turkish Cypriot was the unpopular character of Munir Bey: "It is beginning to look doubtful whether the support which past Governments have given to that rather unsound person has been politically worthwhile" (cited by Choisi 2010: 289). Receiving the above view, the British government decided to try gradually to improve relations with the Kemalists. Thus, in a telegram of 19th November 1937 to Palmer it argues: "[…] the collapse of the old order of things in Turkey and the founding of Kemalist Turkey has created a new situation, to which the British government in Cyprus must find ways to adapt. It is legitimate for the government to attempt to approach young and more progressive Turkish Cypriots […]" (quoted in Ktoris 2013: 169).[53]) Even Governor Palmer himself had realized that significant changes were occurring within Turkish society and that was having ever greater impact on the Turkish Cypriots also: "the older generation of Turks is gradually disappearing and dwindling, and as the younger generation tend to become Kemalists, we cannot in any case return to the old method of controlling Cyprus for long" (cited by MacHenry 1981: 139). Essentially it was too difficult for the British side to close its eyes not only to the fact that Munir Bey expressed a situation corresponding to an Empire that no longer existed but also to the reality that the secularism embodied by the Kemalists was much closer to the cultural and social model of Britain. This change was facilitated by Turkey's assurance to Britain that any Turkish Cypriot who challenged the existing order in Cyprus became an enemy of Turkey. Towards the end of the 1930s (October 1939), the relations between Britain and Turkey would become even closer with the signing by Britain and France of a Treaty of Defence of Turkey in the event of an attack from Germany (Kalantzopoulos 2015: 143–144). But it should be emphasized that this change in the stance of the British towards the Kemalist Turkish Cypriots, whatever the declarations, pursued a long-protracted course which would be consummated only after the failure of the 1948 Consultative Assembly (see below).

[53] For corresponding documents also see Kalantzopoulos (2015: 143.

That said, the outcome of defeat for the traditionalists in the 1940s owing to loss both confidence of Turkish Cypriots and of British favour does not alter the fact that the conflict between conservatives and Kemalists was an active one throughout the 1930s. In 1931, Munir Bey accused Raif Efendi, District Judge at Nicosia and Kyrenia, of being implicated in political life. In 1932, the Kemalists came out in total opposition to the functioning of a new theological school (Nevzat and Hatay 2009: 920). In 1933, the Kemalist newspaper *Soz* condemned the British-appointed leadership of Evkaf for not being representative of Turkish Cypriots. The Kemalists also launched an indictment against Evkaf for mismanagement of its finances (Xypolia 2011: 114–115).

In relation to the Kemalist current and its relations with Turkey, apart from the fact that the *Soz* newspaper was an abiding link between Turkey and the Turkish Cypriots there were also other newspapers whose columns were replete with news from Turkey—newspapers such as *Hakkikat* and *Vakit* which placed significant emphasis on Turkish foreign policy and particularly its approach to Greece, but also on internal Turkish developments (McHenry 1981: 140). This link with Turkey encouraged further strengthening of the Kemalist movement. The Turkish Cypriots continued to celebrate Turkish Independence Day each October and a customary practice was for people to gather in houses and listen to radio programmes on Turkish stations (McHenry 1981: 141). Characteristic indeed of the sentiments of Turkish Cypriots was the fact that when the training ship Hamidiye of the Turkish fleet visited Famagusta on 29th June 1938, the entire Turkish Cypriot population of the city gathered for the reception, headed by Necati and Zekia, along with another 4,000 people, and pro-Kemal slogans were heard such as "yasasun Ataturk" (long live Ataturk) (Bouleti 2008: 446). This event was evidently encouraging for the Turkish Cypriots and a year later at the anniversary celebrations, on 29th October 1939, Necati led a procession of Turkish Cypriots through the streets of Nicosia to the Turkish consulate to congratulate the consul on the occasion of Turkey's national day. Palmer regarded the conducting of the march as an infringement of the 1932 decree restricting public gatherings and arrested Necati along with six colleagues who were taken to court and fined. Similar repressive measures had been implemented in 1938, as already indicated, when censorship was imposed on *Soz* in response to the charge that it never published anything other than news from Turkey or pro-Kemalist articles denigrating Evkaf. Palmer described the newspaper as egregiously subversive, adding that it was more likely that its publication would be banned completely than that censorship would be lifted on it (McHenry 1981: 148).

14 Beyond the Consequences of the Revolt. Growth of the Cypriot Economy and the Transition from Agrarian Power Coalition to Capitalist Hegemony

At the level of articulation of social (class) power, up until the early 1930s, what could be observed in the Cypriot social formation was the existence, to cite Gramsci, of an "agrarian power coalition"[54] politically expressed through participation of the Cypriot community (Greek Cypriots and Turkish Cypriots) in the Legislative Council: there at level of social composition an over-representation was evident of the stratum of creditors, disproportionate participation of the Church and merchants and under-representation of peasant farmers, characteristic elements of the structure of the agrarian power coalition (Tsekouras 1984: 90).[55]

From an overall perspective the political system displays a transverse cut including a level of concentration of colonial power endeavouring to legitimate itself through the Legislative Council and a second level within which the agrarian power coalition was articulated around two parameters: the presence of the church as a vehicle of political and social representation and the existence of the economic stratum of creditors able to function only in conditions of extensive agricultural production. An important social category in all this, although not the hegemonic faction of the power coalition, are the great landowners, who on the one hand

[54] On the question of the agrarian power coalition, according to Gramsci it comprised three social layers: the great amorphous and disintegrated agrarian mass, the intellectuals of the small and medium rural bourgeoisie, the big landowners, and intellectuals of large-scale landownership. See Gramsci (1978. 454–459).

[55] An important role in this was played by the fact that up until the elections of 1906 the system of the open ballot was in force, undoubtedly working in favour of clientelist relations and local notables. As pointed out very pertinently by Katsouridis "In the course of the election the voter was obliged to announce the name of the candidate he was supporting to a committee made up of the Mukhtars of the villages included in the register of the electoral centre, and of representatives of the candidates" (Katsouridis 2009: 199).

employ farm workers to cultivate their fields and others comprise the most basic moneylenders of the countryside. The accumulation of wealth leads them in a second phase to move to the city and become involved in more authentically capitalistic activities. The key allied stratum for this rural bourgeoisie is the rising lower middle class, with lawyers playing a front-line role. They assume the responsibility for providing "technical guidance" to big landowners. They represent them in litigation against borrowers. They issue legalistic threats to oblige borrowers to accept the demands of lenders.

This social alliance is reflected in the composition of the Greek Cypriot deputies of the Legislative Council. From 1883 to 1931, 88% of them were big landowners, lawyers and merchants, considerable numbers of whom were also lenders (Faustmann 1998: 48). According to the more detailed data presented by Lyssiotis of the 56 people serving as members of the Legislative Council, 36 (64.2% of the total) were graduates from universities and another five (8.9%) from other tertiary institutions (seminaries, pedagogical academies) and 30 had studied law (61.2%). It is interesting that 21 of the lawyers did not have any additional form of employment but the other nine were—some of them—lawyers-big landowners-merchants, some lawyers-big landowners, some lawyers *and* industrialists and one lawyer *and* bank manager. Apart from those having some connection with law there were 11 merchants (three of whom also had a second professional identity). Lyssiotis' conclusion is that the great majority (49 of the 56 members) practised one or more of the professions of lawyer, merchant and landowner (Lyssiotis 1990: 58–64). In the light of all this, as far as the "internal" balance of power is concerned, merchant and money capital seem to be the hegemonic section of the ruling class, on the basis first and foremost of the wealth transfer generated by the exploitation of debtors. It is this accumulation of wealth that in a second phase would establish the prerequisites for the development of industrial capitalism in Cyprus.

Between the 1930s and the end of the war, the situation seems to have changed. The expansion of capitalist elements into the Cypriot economy leads to the dissolution of previous modes of production, strengthening the primary and articulated position of the capitalist mode of production.[56] Specifically, according to the available data, people working on

[56] For the way in which the capitalist mode of production prevails over and articulates the other modes of production, see Poulantzas (1978: 22) and Rey (1973: 111–126).

the land in 1931 comprised 53.6% of the economically active population, down from 67.0% in 1901 and by 1946 the number had fallen to 44.0%. At the same time, people working in secondary production increased from 22.0% of the economically active population in 1901 to 35.3% in 1946. Finally, those employed in administration of trade and services would shift from 8.3% in 1901 to 11.1% in 1931 and 21.2% in 1946. These transformations are due to the fact that slowly, but surely, local industry began to develop: food, drinks and construction (Christodoulou 1995: 16–17). It is characteristic that between 1920 and 1930, the number of industrial installations in Cyprus increased from less than 150 to almost 300 and the volume of industrial production increased from less than 400,000 units in 1920 to more than 1,400,000 units in 1930 (Panagiotou 2016: 223–224). A proportion of those industrial products was export-oriented. It is interesting that a reorientation of exports is to be noted, away from sending them to the countries of the Levant and towards sending them to Britain and other countries, indicating an export potential to more developed states where the competition is more intense over which products will be imported. Specifically, in 1911, 52.35% of Cypriot exports were directed to the countries of the Levant, 24.1% to Great Britain, 0.25% to the British colonies (outside the Levant) and 23.3% to other countries. The corresponding figures for 1931 are 45.64% for the countries of the Levant, 20.41% for Great Britain, one percent for the British colonies (outside the Levant) and 32.95% for other countries, and for 1946, 24.35% for the countries of the Levant, 28.7% for Great Britain, seven percent for the British colonies (outside the Levant) and 39.95% for other countries (Kazamias and Panayiotou 2016: 120).

These developments become even more obvious if we examine them at the level of individual professions. The 1891 census indicated that there were 34,748 landowners in 68,010 residences who had declared an occupation (50.7% of the total). They included 15,605 farmers (22.9%), 8,476 labourers (12.5%), 4,705 shepherds and cowherds (6.9%). Above and beyond that, apart from farming there were the following occupations, comprising more than one percent of working people: 3,685 servants (5.4%), 3,424 weavers (5.0%), 1,840 boot and shoemakers (2.7%), 910 masons (1.3%) and 720 coffee house keepers (1.1%) (Report on the Census of Cyprus 1891: 11; 50).

In the more detailed data of the 1901 census there are references to 86,905 working people, of whom 35,338 are landowners (40.7% of the total), 12,862 are labourers (14.8%), 6,259 (7.2% of the total) are shepherds and cowherds, 6,034 (6.9% of the total) weavers, 4,050 (4.7%) domestic servants, 1,983 (2.3% of the total) boot and shoemakers, 1,252 (1.4% of the total) masons, 1,162 (1.3% of the total) ploughmen and 1,093 (1.2% of the total) coffee house keepers (Report on the Census of Cyprus 1901: 12). We note that in the course of a decade there has been no change in the manifestly agricultural character of the society. But the fact that the other agricultural occupational categories show an increase while the category of landowners moves at clearly lower levels leads us to the conclusion that a still greater concentration of land ownership is beginning.

In 1911 the methodology of the study was modified somewhat through change in the occupational categories but whatever modifications were made they cannot hide the fact of emerging bourgeois and petty bourgeois strata. While the overall workforce comes to 103,352 individuals there is a duality within this figure. The clearly larger part of it comprises people working in agricultural and pre-capitalist activities. There are 29,363 farmers cultivating their land (Farmers and Cultivators) and they comprise 28.4% of the total, 16,080 ploughmen and agricultural labourers (15.6% of the total), 10,121 weavers (9.8% of the total), 7,336 shepherds (7.1% of the total), 2,682 boot and shoemakers (2.6% of the total), 2,532 domestic servants (2.4% of the total), 2,401 embroiderers (2.3% of the total), 2,069 seamstresses and dressmakers (2% of the total), 1,735 masons and stone cutters (1.7% of the total), 1,507 vinegrowers (1.5% of the total), 1,435 coffee house keepers (1.4% of the total), 1,184 cart and carriage drivers (1.2% of the total) and 1,130 gardeners (1.1% of the total). On the other hand, there is the presence of occupations that display elements of early capitalist development or an agrarian power coalition: there are 631 landowners (0.6% of the total), 902 merchants (0.9% of the total), 879 high school and primary school teachers (0.9% of the total), 1,218 clerical and other white-collar employees (1.2% of the total) and for the first time a purely working-class category, makes its appearance, the 2,078 day labourers (2% of the total) (Report on the Census of Cyprus 1911: 13–14).

In 1921, the census indicated that there were 113,372 working people. For the first time, the term "landowners" was not used in the study, perhaps because it was considered that it was too general and obfuscated a complex reality, embracing a variety of occupational categories active in the agricultural sector. That said, 33,417 Cypriots were farmers and cultivators (29.5% of the total), 18,151 were ploughmen and agricultural labourers (16% of the total), 9,749 weavers (8.6% of the total), 7,344 shepherds (6.5% of the total), 3,766 domestic servants (3.3% of the total), 3,442 seamstresses and dressmakers (3% of the total), 3,296 boot and shoemakers (2.9% of the total), 2,466 embroiderers (2.2% of the total), 1,959 cart and carriage drivers (1.7% of the total) 1,864 masons and stone cutters (1.6% of the total), 1,550 coffee house keepers (1.4% of the total), 1,547 carpenters (1.4% of the total) 1,316 gardeners (1.2% of the total), 988 grocers (0.9% of the total) and 603 blacksmiths (0.5% of the total). It is interesting that there are 1,380 merchants (1.2% of the total), 1,318 clerical and other white-collar employees (1.2% of the total) 1,178 high school and primary school teachers (one percent of the total) and 2006 day labourers (1.8% of the total) (Report on the Census of Cyprus 1921*:* 11–12). This shows that slowly but surely a process of transformation towards capitalism is underway, which does not, however, go beyond the framework of the agrarian power coalition.

For 1931, the census data indicate that the economically active population came to 134,279 people. This time the (big) landowners were recorded and numbered 678 or 0.5% of the population, i.e. around the same proportion as was recorded in 1911. Additionally, there were 34,546 farmers and cultivators (25.72% of the total), 22,654 ploughmen and agricultural labourers (16.9% of the total), 8,861 shepherds (6.6% of the total), 6,222 weavers (4.6% of the total), 5,212 domestic servants (3.9% of the total), 3,608 boot and shoemakers (2.7% of the total), 3,079 lace makers, (2.3% of the total), 2,891 dressmakers (2.2% of the total), 2,235 carpenters (1.7% of the total), 2,216 gardeners (1.6% of the total), 2,070 masons (1.5% of the total), 1,671 café proprietors (1.2% of the total), 1,493 grocers and fruiterers (1.1% of the total), 1,261 carters (0.9% of the total), 1,144 barbers (0.9% of the total), 1,066 chauffeurs (0.8% of the total) and 1,027 tailors, (0.8% of the total). On the other hand, there were 3,197 who were classified as other labourers in mines and quarries (2.4% of the total), 1,938 high school and primary school teachers (1.4% of the total), 1,932 builders' labourers (1.4% of the total), 1,334 commission agents and merchants (one percent of the total) 1,254 clerical and other white-collar employees (0.9% of the total) (Census of 1931: 15; 54). The difference from the censuses of 1921 and 1911 is that there are clearly accelerated rates of transformation towards capitalism in social relations. This does not mean that Cyprus is no longer basically agricultural in character. It means that within the existing agrarian power coalition the capitalist elements are strengthening. This becomes obvious if we take it into account that after the First World War light industrial units were established which processed raw materials, whether they were produced on the island (mines, spinning mills, wineries and factories processing agricultural products) or imported from abroad (factories producing buttons or shoes and tanneries) (Papapolyviou 2004: 335).

The most interesting point, of course, is the changes occurring between 1891 and 1931. For a start, we see both the public sector and forces of repression growing. The number of civil servants rose from 500 (0.8% of the total) to 2,204 (1.6% of the total) and the number of police from 623 (0.8% of the total) to 849 (0.6% of the total). What gets underway is elaboration of a growing structure of administrative services, together with contraction of the initially higher number of police which in the first years of the British presence can be attributed to the need to secure smooth transition from one regime to the next. But it is interesting to observe the increase in numbers of primary and secondary school teachers from 554 in 1901 when records start (0.6% of the total) to 1,938 in 1931 (1.4% of the total). As far as doctors and lawyers are concerned, in countries of developed capitalism they belong to the new petty bourgeoisie but in transitional/hybrid societies like pre-war Cyprus they play a role both political (we saw how many lawyers become parliamentary deputies and mayors) and economic (through their involvement with moneylending circles), contributing to the accumulation of capital and extension of capitalist relations of production. So at this specific stage of development, it can be postulated that they comprise part of the agrarian power coalition. In 1901 there were 35 doctors, six dentists, 54 lawyers and 16 engineers, i.e. altogether 111 educated professionals altogether (0.1% of the total) belonging to this faction of the ruling class. In 1931, 138 lawyers were recorded, 121 doctors, 48 dentists and 42 engineers, i.e. 349 educated professionals (0.3% of the total). Our view is that despite the increase they remain a numerically small occupational category with a completely different role from the one the corresponding professions play in developed capitalism, and for this reason remain part of the agrarian power coalition. At the same time, the basic pole of the antithesis in capitalism, wage labour, goes from strength to strength: in 1911 there were 1,218 white-collar workers (1.2% of the total population) and 2,078 day labourers (2% of the total) and in 1931 there were 3,197 other workers in mines and quarries (2.4% of the total), 1,932 builders' labourers (1.4% of the total) and 1,254 white-collar workers (0.9% of the total).

Last but not least, it should be noted that at the community level the evolution of capitalist relations had a much more positive effect on those members of the Greek community that had been involved for decades in accumulating capital. On the other hand, this development aggravated differences, overall, between Greeks and Turks. As already mentioned, there were prior differences which had to do with the involvement of the Orthodox in commerce from as early as the end of the eighteenth century and there were clear differences between the education systems, both in the Ottoman and in the British periods.[57] From a certain point onwards the dynamic that was generated acquired a very significant momentum. This accumulation of capital[58] made it possible for some Greek Cypriots to embark on moneylending activities both with Greek Cypriot and with

[57] In an article published in the Turkish Cypriot newspaper *Kibris* one reads: "it is obvious that the teaching of the skills such as writing and disciplines such as history, arithmetic and the positive sciences is necessary [...] This is why the Christian schools are making more progress than the Muslim schools. For example, within one or two years from when he/she starts school a Christian child will have acquired some knowledge of reading, writing, arithmetic, history, geography. In our schools not even a tenth of that is on offer. We put in one percent of the effort and zeal displayed by the Christians to make their education progress" (cited by Kizilyurek 2019: 67).

[58] In 1897 the Turkish Cypriot newspaper *Zaman* asserts that the Turkish Cypriot community "has failed to assign the necessary importance to the question of commerce and its members have remained behind Greek citizens in terms of wealth. The result is that profits and income derived from trade on the island accrue almost entirely to the Christians. Only 5% of the proceeds from commercial incomes goes to Muslims. The other 95% goes to the Christians" (quoted in Ktoris 2013: 44). Indeed, in a text referring to the econonomic situation of Turkish Cypriots Dr. Hafiz Kemal notes that 95% of Turkish Cypriots are in debt, as against 10–12% of Greek Cypriots (Kizilyurek 2019: 69). The more general backwardness of the Musim community at the dawn of the twentieth century is also evident from the fact that in 1901 there was not one doctor among the island's 37 doctors, there was only one chemist among the 39 Cypriot chemists and only 7 lawyers in a total of 54. Taking into account this reality, *Zaman* argues on 30th November 1908 that "[...] with the end of the attachment to public office and the ambition to become government employees [...] we must place importance on pursuing important occupations such as in agriculture, the technical professions, trade" (quoted in Kizilyurek 2019: 68).

Turkish Cypriot farmers,[59] and this coincided with abolition of the collective payment of tribute to the administration, which existed during the Ottoman rule. The result was that in the mid-1930s, there were 521 Greek Cypriot as against 81 Turkish Cypriot merchants, 34 Greek Cypriot as against four Turkish Cypriot industrialists, 87 Greek Cypriot as against five Turkish Cypriot building contractors, 102 Greek Cyriot as against ten Turkish Cypriot doctors, 72 Greek Cypriot as against eight Turkish Cypriot pharmacists and 55 Greek Cypriot as against 12 Turkish Cypriot lawyers (Ktoris 2013: 48).[60]

15 Conclusion

The 1931 revolt should not be interpreted monocausally but should be seen as the outcome of a whole complex of factors operating from the outset of the British presence and which in combination would have a catalytic effect on subsequent developments.

One basic point that is sometimes overlooked is the extreme social inequalities that are endemic in Cyprus, exerting powerful economic pressure on the farming strata that were overindebted to the moneylending strata. One might expect this fact, together with the emergence of the first blue collar and white-collar layers, to lead to a more straightforward form of class mobilizations (class against class). But the fact is that whatever attempts at action were launched by the Cyprus Communist Party, there were no social mobilizations of any importance prior to the

[59] As noted in 1925 by the British administrator Storrs: "[...] it is true that the political and economic strength of the Muslim community is slowly waning. Powerless to help themselves its members are in many cases in the hands of Greek usurers" (quoted in Ktoris 2013: 46).

[60] This economic and social backwardness of the Turkish Cypriots did not go unnoticed either by the Turkish Cypriot press or by the press of Turkey. *Cumhuriet* was particularly caustic when it said on 4th December 1930: "In Cyprus the Greeks occupy the high economic positions. Day by day the Turks are losing these positions because of their indolence and sloth. Today they are paying the bitter price for it as a punishment, without there being any hope of a change of course.[...] they have sold their most fertile and productive land [...] The erstwhile masters of the island, our fellow nationals, bear sole [...] responsibility for this thoughtless behaviour [...]" (quoted in Pampalos and Theoharidis 2008: 72). In 1933 the veteran Turkish Cypriot parliamentarian Mehmed Zekia Bey reaches similar conclusions in a series of articles in the *Soz* newspaper (Kizilyurek 2015: 175–176) as does the Turkish Cypriot Nevzat Karagil several years later (1945) in a report to the Turkish Prime Minister Sucru Saracoglu (Kizilyurek 2019: 70–71).

revolt. The interpretation that is offered is that such reaction as there was to the conditions of exploitation was channeled into the demand for *Enosis*. The view that prevailed in the popular strata was that only after the incorporation of Cyprus into Greece would they be able to live in a regime of economic and political justice. This was supported by the fact that for about 50 years the payment of the Tribute of Cyprus to the British and the rest of the taxation had transformed Cyprus into the most heavily taxed territory of the British Empire. At the same time, the Cyprus Communist Party's position of Cyprus participating in the establishment of a Balkan Soviet Republic was not tempting for the Greek Cypriots by comparison with the relatively more achievable demand of *Enosis*. Within this dynamic the overall framework had already been established: the class struggle found expression in the anti-colonial struggle, where hegemony was already exercised by the bourgeoisie and the Church.

Given all this, other factors impelling people to revolt in 1931 were the effects of the global economic crisis of 1929: commercial transactions in free fall, increasing unemployment, wage cuts, skyrocketing agricultural debts. It is characteristic that the British government, unable—or rather unwilling—to understand the conditions that had been created, decided on a new tax increase.

Apart from its manifestly economic dimension, taxation had very important political consequences. In its initial form, it encountered active opposition from Turkish Cypriots *also*. The stance of the Turkish Cypriots had similar economic roots to the corresponding Greek Cypriot position but was a part of a different and more authentic orientation. The victory of Kemalism in metropolitan Turkey had started to have repercussions in Cyprus as well. The 1930s began with the emergence of a harsh conflict between the traditional Muslim elite that was the Britons' organically and the Kemalist newcomers who sought an essential upgrading of the position of the Turkish Cypriots. Apprehensive about the potential for collaboration between Greek Cypriots and Kemalists and the tightening of links between Turkish Cypriots and Kemalist Turkey, the British sought in every way to retain control over the Turkish community. Accordingly, they proceeded with a number of institutional changes to make Evkaf a powerful institution for control of the Turkish Cypriots through appointment of individuals loyal to the colonial administration.

Within that context, there would be a transient tactical alliance between Greek Cypriots and Turkish Cypriots against the 1931 budget which would lead to an initial vote against it. But this was a conjunctural meeting of two sides moving in entirely different directions. The Greek Cypriots wanted *Enosis*, the Turkish Cypriots wanted rejection of *Enosis* and the acquisition of greater rights. So however much, conjuncturally, because of the tax hikes and the education reforms, there was a convergence between Greek Cypriot and Turkish Cypriot Kemalists, in reality the emergence of the latter widened the distance between the two communities, for it consummated the process of Turkification of the Cypriot Muslims.

As far as the revolt itself is concerned, what should be underlined is the unprecedented violence of the reactions of the insurrectionists but also the repressiveness of the British practices in response. It is worth pointing out that before 1930 political protest marches were almost unknown in Cyprus. So, the burning of the governor's house, the street fights, the torching of police stations, the person vs person physical combat, marked the entry into a new phase of the anti-colonial struggle in Cyprus. But on the other hand, the arrival of reinforcements from Egypt and Crete showed that the British were determined to maintain their sovereignty over the island by hook or by crook, apprehensive that with the rise of Kemalism the threats to the British Empire were multiplying.

One interesting point is the stance of the Communist Party of Cyprus towards the insurrection where inability to comprehend the importance the demand for *Enosis* had for most Greek Cypriots, led Communist Party of Cyprus to adopting a contradictory position: right up until the torching of the Governor's house the demand for *Enosis* was denounced and a policy of abstention from the events was recommended. Immediately afterwards, under pressure from the social dynamic the line changed and what was supported was the necessity for the formation of a united anti-imperialist front. But in any case, this stance of the Communist Party of Cyprus reflects an inherently contradictory orientation which was not able to be resolved even in the following years. On the one hand, it wished to be identified with the Church and the urban centres but on the other when it took initiatives was inevitably accused by the Greek Cypriot ruling class of not promoting the national cause and being interested only in its own political survival (see following chapter).

Another important consideration is the stance of the Greek government towards the revolt, which Venizelos denounced in every possible register, characterizing it as an irresponsible move. In our view this policy can be explained by the fact that did not wish in any circumstance to come into conflict with the British, particularly after the Asia Minor disaster, but neither did he wish there to be similar developments in the Dodecanese and the friendly relations with Italy to be disturbed. The deeply anti-Communist Venizelos was also afraid of the possibility of the Cyprus Communist Party fellow-travelling with the official bourgeois milieu of Cyprus in the context of anti-colonialist collaboration.

The consequences of the revolt were now very serious for the Greek Cypriots: arrests, imprisonments, banishments, burdening with the costs of the damage, abolition of the Legislative Council, abolition of elected local government, abolition of the functioning of political parties, strict control of public gatherings, imposition of censorship, interventions into education, in general repression of ever action that could bring to the surface the demand for *Enosis*.

But something that is often overlooked is the fact that the same prohibitions were imposed on the Turkish Cypriots. Of course, there was nothing coincidental about this. The British exploited the insurrection to restrict the activity not only of the pro-*Enosis* Cypriot circles but also of the Kemalist Turkish Cypriots, given that both these sides, the Greek Cypriots at a more developed stage, the Turkish Cypriots in a more incipient way, were challenging British domination. It was for precisely that reason that people friendly to the colonial administration were promoted to political power.

Discussion of the events linked to *Enosis*, notwithstanding their paramount importance, should not overshadow presentation of significant socio-economic developments taking place in Cyprus in the 1930s. An agrarian power coalition dominated the island. Big landowners and moneylender made their presence very much felt, in alliance with subordinate and expanding industrial and commercial capital. After a certain point accumulation of the wealth of the rural bourgeoisie would lead to their moving to the urban centres and taking up more "authentic" capitalist occupations. An alliance was then formed with the petty bourgeois strata and in particular the lawyers, who adopted a "technical advisor" in the legal affairs of the lenders, helping them to secure the property of the borrowers. This made possible an accumulation of capital which would come to be interlinked with already existing capitalist activity and contribute to transition to developed industrial and commercial capitalism. This process was brought to fruition in the 1930s, with extension of the operations of capitalist enterprises and accumulated surplus value being produced from intensive exploitation of the working class.

At the level of political and social power, there were essentially two axes: on the one hand, colonialist power concentrated in the Governor and the Legislative Council and, on the other, the agrarian power coalition which was constructed on the one hand around the Church as a factor in the economy representing both the Greek Cypriots politically and the demand for *Enosis*, and on the other around the landowners, creditors and merchants who through their activity contributed to the accumulation of capital.

The result was that the demand for *Enosis* expressed a concretion of different class interests. On the one hand, the popular classes believed that in this way they would free themselves from the political and economic oppression to which they were being subjected. On the other, the bourgeoisie, having long since overtaken the Turkish Cypriots in ability to undertake economic activity and taking advantage of the overall modernization that had been brought by the British administration, sought emancipation from the politically subordinate status to which they had been relegated by the British power system. They judged, given the geographic position of Cyprus, that within the greater Helladic space, which had been significantly enlarged since the time when the demand for *Enosis* had been first articulated, they would be able greatly to expand their field of activities.

References

Alastos, D. 1976. *Cyprus in History. A Survey of 5000 Years*. London: Zeno.

Anagnostopoulou, S. 1999. The Church of Cyprus and Its Role as Ethnarch: 1878–1960. The 'religiofication' of 'Cypriot' Political Activity: *Enosis. Synchrona Themata*, 68–69–70: 198–227.

Antreou, M. 2007. *How Turkish Cypriots Are Represented in the "Eleftheria" Newspaper in the 1930–1958 Period*. Postgraduate dissertation in the Department of Political Science and History. Athens: Panteio University (in Greek).

Apeyitou, E. 2003. Turkish-Cypriot Nationalism: Its History and Development (1571–1960). *The Cyprus Review* 15 (1): 67–98.

Bouleti, E. 2008. *British Policy Against the Turkish Cypriot Community 1878–1950. The Course Towards Nationalization of the Muslim-Cypriot Community.* Doctoral thesis. Athens: Panteion University (in Greek).

Bryant, R. 2004. *Imagining the Modern*. London: Tauris.

Choisi, J. 2010. The Turkish Cypriot Elite-its Social Function and Legitimisation. In *Colonial Cyprus 1878–1960. Selected Readings From the Cyprus Review*, ed. E. Solomou and H. Faustmann, 277–300. Nicosia: University of Nicosia.
Christodoulou, D. 1995. Life Chances in Cyprus: Occupational and Social Structures and Mobility Viewed in Perspective. *Cyprus Review* 7 (1): 7–33.
Chrysanthis, K. 1983. Historical Data on the Movement of the Year 1931. In *Hellenic Cyprus: The Cypriot revolt of 1931*, 84–89. Nicosia: Hellenic Cultural Association of Cyprus (in Greek).
Crouzet, F. 1973. *Le Conflit en Chypre 1946-1959*. Tome Premier-Tome Deuxième, Bruxelles: Etablissements Emile Bruylant.
Faustmann, H. 1998. Clientelism in the Greek Cypriot Community of Cyprus Under British Rule. *The Cyprus Review* 10 (2): 41–77.
Faustmann, H. 2006. Clientelistic Relations in Greek Cypriot Society Under British Colonial Rule. In *The Cyprus Question in Foreign Eyes*, ed. A. Stergiou and H. Richter, 177–229. Athens: Roes (in Greek).
Georghallides, G.S. 1969–1970. Churchill's 1907 Visit to Cyprus: A Political Analysis. *Yearbook of Cyprus Research Centre*, III: 167–220.
Georghallides, G.S. 1985. *Cyprus and the Governorship of Sir Ronald Storrs: The Causes of the 1931 Crisis*. Nicosia: Cyprus Research Centre.
Graikos, K. 1994. *The Movement of October and the Communist Party of Cyprus*. Nicosia (in Greek).
Gramsci, A. 1978. Some Aspects of the Southern Question. In *Selections from Political Writings 1921-1926*, 441–462. London: Lawrence and Wishart.
Hadjidemetriou, K. 2002. *A History of Cyprus*. Nicosia.
Heraclidou, A. 2017. *Imperial Control in Cyprus*. London: I.B. Tauris.
Hill, G. Sir. 1952. *A History of Cyprus, vol. 4, The Ottoman Province, The British Colony 1571-1948*. Cambridge: Cambridge University Press.
Historical Encyclopedia of Cyprus. 1979–1980. Ed. P. Papadimitris. Nicosia (in Greek).
Historical Essay on the Communist Party of Cyprus and AKEL. 1968. Unpublished document (in Greek).
Kalantzopoulos, D. 2015. *Competing Political Spaces in Colonial Cyprus, 1931-1950*. Doctoral thesis, University of London.
Katsiaounis, R. 2000. *The "Diaskeptiki 1946–1948. A Review of the 1878–1945 Period*. Nicosia: Centre of Scientific Research (in Greek).
Katsiaounis, R. 2001. The Cyprus Question and the Discussions for Its Resolution in the 20th Century. In *Our Neighbours the Arabs*. Municipality of Nicosia Editions, 143–162. Nicosia (in Greek).
Katsiaounis, R. 2004. Social, Ethnic and Political Conflicts in Cyprus During the Period of British Rule 1878–1950. In Lectures at the People's University, *British Rule Themes in Cyprus*, pp. 19–43. Nicosia (in Greek).

Katsouridis, Y. 2009. *The Party System in Cyprus 1878–1931: Construction and Peculiarities*. Doctoral thesis, Nicosia: University of Cyprus (in Greek).

Katsourides, Y. 2017. *The Greek Cypriot Nationalist Right in the Era of British Colonialism*. London: Springer.

Kazamias, G., and M. Panayiotou. 2016. Cyprus' Trade with the Levant, 1881–1946/47. In *The Greeks and the British in the Levant, 1800–1960s*, ed. A. Yangou, G. Kazamias, and R. Holland, 111–122. London: Routledge.

Kizilyurek, N. 2007. Relations Between Greek Cypriots and Turkish Cypriots. From the Traditional Ottoman Period to Modernity. In *Cyprus in the 20th Century*, 111–136. Nicosia: Municipality of Nicosia (in Greek).

Kizilyurek, N. 2009. *Turkish Cypriots, Turkey and the Cyprus Question*. Athens: Papazisis (in Greek).

Kizilyurek, N. 2015. Modenrity, Nationalism and Secularization: The Tyrkish Cypriot case. In *Religious Communities and Modern Statehood*, ed. M. Michael, T. Anastassiadis, and C. Verdeil, 173–181. Berlin: Klaus Schwarz Verlag.

Kizilyurek, N. 2019. *A Story of Violence and Resentment, The Origins and Evolution of the Ethnic Dispute in Cyprus*. Nicosia: Heterotopia (in Greek).

Kondylis, T. 2009. *Eleftherios Venizelos and Greece (1928–1932). Diplomatic Policy and Economy*. Athens: Iamvos (in Greek).

Konstantinidis, S. 1995. *The Cyprus Problem, Structures of Cypriot Society and the National Question*. Montreal-Nicosia: Metoikos (in Greek).

Ktoris, S. 2013. *Turkish Cypriots, From the Margins to Association (1923–1960)*. Athens: Papazisis (in Greek).

Kyriakidis, H. 2016. *The Legislative Council of Cyprus (1878–1931)*. Nicosia: House of Representatives.

Lanitis N.-C. 1944 [1992]. *Rural Indebtedness and Agricultural Co-operation in Cyprus*. Limassol: Proodos.

Lefkis, G. 1984. *The Roots. Historical Study*. Limassol (in Greek).

Loizidis, S. 1983. National Radical Union and 1931 Revolt. In *The Cypriot Revolt of 1931*, 30–38. Nicosia: Hellenic Cultural Society of Cyprus (in Greek).

Loizos, P. 1977. Politics and Patronage in a Cypriot Village, 1920–1970. In *Patrons and Clients in Mediterranean Societies*, ed. E. Gellner and J. Waterbury, 115–126. Duckworth: Center for Mediterranean Studies of the American Universities.

Lyssiotis, Marios. 1990. An Analysis of the Cyprus Legislative Council. *Cyprus Review* 2 (2): 55–69.

Markides, D., and G.S. Georghallides. 1995. British Attitudes to Constitution-Making in Post-1931 Cyprus. *Journal of Modern Greek Studies* 13 (1): 63–80.

McHenry, J.-A. 1981. *The Uneasy Partnership on Cyprus, 1919-1939: The Political and Diplomatic Interaction Between Great Britain, Turkey and the Turkish Cypriot Community*. Doctoral thesis, University of Kansas.

Moutsis, I. 2014. *The Turkish Cypriots (1918–1931): From a Religious Community to an Ethnic Minority*. Doctoral thesis, University of London (in Greek).

Nevzat, A. 2005. *Nationalism Amongst the Turks of Cyprus: The first Wave*. University of ULU. herkules.oulu.fi/isbn9514277511/isbn9514277511.pdf. Accessed on 3 June 2012.

Nevzat, A., and M. Hatay. 2009. Politics, Society and the Decline of Islam in Cyprus: From the Ottoman Era to the Twenty-First Century. *Middle Eastern Studies* 45 (6): 911–933.

Pampalos, C., and I. Theoharides. 2008. *The Turkish Press on Cyprus (1928–1945)*. Nicosia: Holly Monastery Research Centre of Cyprus (in Greek).

Pancyprian Trade Union Committee-Pancyprian Federation of Labour. 1991. *History of the Pancyprian Trade Union Committee - Pancyprian Federation of Labour*. Nicosia (in Greek).

Panagiotou, M. 2016. Harbours, *Harbour Works and Foreign Trade in Cyprus, 1878–1927*. Doctoral thesis, University of Cyprus (in Greek).

Pantelis, S. 1986. *The Modern History of Cyprus*. Athens: I. Floros Publications (in Greek).

Papapolyviou, P. 2004. Cyprus 1922–1940. The 1931 Revolt and the Colonialist Counter-Revolution. In *History of Modern Hellenism*, vol. 7, 325–336. Athens: Ellinika Grammata (in Greek).

Pavlidis, A. 1993. *History of the Island of Cyprus*, vol. 4: From 1571 to 1964. Nicosia: Filokypros (in Greek).

Perikleous, C. 2007. *The 2004 Referendum. The Regional and International Environment. The Conception of a Solution and the Conjuncture*. Athens: Papazisis (in Greek).

Pikros, G. 1980. *Venizelos and the Cyprus Question*. Athens: Philippotis (in Greek).

Poulantzas, N. 1978. *Classes in Contemporary Capitalism*. London: New left Books.

Protopapas, V. 2012. *Electoral History of Cyprus. Politicians, Parties and Elections Under British Rule 1878-1960*. Athens: Themelio (in Greek).

Rappas, A. 2014. *Cyprus in the 1930's*. London: I.B. Tauris.

Report and general Abstracts on the Census of Cyprus 1911.

Report and general Abstracts on the Census of Cyprus 1921.

Report on the Census of Cyprus 1891.

Report on the Census of Cyprus 1901.

Report of the Census of 1931.

Rey P.-P. 1973. *Les alliances de classes*. Paris: Maspero.

Richter, H. 2006. Benevolent Aristocracy. In *Britain in Cyprus. Colonialism and Post-colonialism 1878-2006*, ed. H. Faustmann and N. Peristianis, 133–150. Nicosia: University of Nicosia.

Richter, H. 2007. *History of Cyprus*, vol. 1 (1878–1949). Athens: Estia (in Greek).

Sophokleous, K. 2003. *Struggle for Freedom. Internal Conflicts*, vol. I. Nicosia (in Greek).

Storrs, R. 1937. *The Memoirs of Sir Ronald Storrs*. New York: Putnam.

Stubbs, J., and B. Taseli. 2014. New Press, Nationalism and Empire. The Turkish Cypriot Press in the British Colonial Period and Its Aftermath. *Media History* 20 (3): 284–301.

Stylianou, P. 1984. *The Movement of October 1931 in Cyprus*. Doctoral thesis, Nicosia (in Greek).

Stylianou, P. 2013. The Revolt of October 1931 (Oktovriana). In the collective *The Struggles Prior to the Struggle of 1955. Aspects of the Preparation for Organization of the Struggle*, 11–108. Nicosia: Academy of Historical Studies (in Greek).

Surridge, B.J. 1930. *A Survey of Rural Life in Cyprus*. Nicosia: Government Printing Office.

Svolopoulos, K. 1978. The Stance of the Greek Government during the Cypriot Crisis of 1931. *Epistimoniki Epetirida tis Panteiou Anotatis scholis Politikon Epistimon*, 485–511. Athens (in Greek).

Theoharidis, I. 2010. The Turkish Cypriots in the Turkish Press (1928–1945). *Yearbook of the Kykkos Monastery Research Centre* 9: 311–336 (in Greek).

Tsekouras, T. 1984. Cyprus Question: From *Enosis* to Zurich. *Theseis* 7: 83–104 (in Greek).

Xypolia, I. 2011. Cypriot Muslims Among Ottomans, Turks and Two World Wars. *Bogazici Journal* 25 (2): 109–120.

Yiagou, A. 2013. English Policy 1931–1950. In *The Struggles Prior to the Struggle of 1955. Aspects of the Preparation for Organization of the Struggle*, 109–127. Nicosia: Academy of Historical Studies (in Greek).

CHAPTER 6

From the Second World War to the 1950 Referendum on *Enosis*

1 The Second World War

The Second World War strengthened the tendencies towards dismantling the traditional structures of the Cypriot economy both by virtue of the growing demand for commodities because of the increased presence of the British army on the island and because of the initiation of significant infrastructural works (military and agricultural) (Tsekouras 1984: 95). This resulted in changes in the form of the social power coalition whereby usury capital and wealthy landowners no longer constituted the leading faction. Commercial, construction and industrial capital took their place.

As far as the question of *Enosis* is concerned, it came back into prominence from the moment that Greece and Britain found themselves in alliance in this war.[1] The occupation of Greece by the Germans in April 1941 induced the Greek government to move to Crete. But it very soon became obvious that militarily it was not secure either and the Greek political leadership would have to abandon it. The Prime Minister Tsouderos then put forward the idea of the Greek government going to Cyprus: "As encouragement to the Greeks in the present disaster Cyprus should

[1] The more so because in the Second World War 1,000s of Cypriots were enlisted, for the first time, on the side of the British and the Allies (see below).

S. Sakellaropoulos, *The Evolution of the Political, Social and Economic Life of Cyprus, 1191–1950*, Palgrave Studies in Economic History,
https://doi.org/10.1007/978-3-030-91839-2_6

be given as a personal gift to the King of the Hellenes. For the duration of the war His Majesty will govern the island through the existing British administration, and after the war Greek officials will govern" (quoted in Richter 2007: 640). The British were opposed to the Greek government moving to Cyprus because they feared the possibility of a German attack on the island. But apprehensive of the likelihood of the Germans offering Cyprus to Greece after occupying it first, the Foreign Secretary Eden seems to have agreed to the prospect of the island being transferred to Greece when the war was over on the precondition that the Greeks rejected the German offer. The Colonial Office for its part raised vehement objections to this possibility and finally on 6th June 1941 Churchill declared that "it is much better to leave all matters of territorial arrangement for after the war [...] I don't think we should concede even an inch of British territory" (quoted in Richter 2007: 642).

The subject would resurface in the spring of 1943 when various views were exchanged between sections of the British state. The Foreign Office argued that the climate favouring *Enosis* would intensify when the war ended and would be grounded in the principle of self-determination, which was supported by Britain itself. Therefore, what needed to happen was that the island should be ceded to Greece in return for the retention of British military bases and facilities for military aviation or their establishment elsewhere. The Colonial Office, in contrast, insisted that Cyprus should remain in British possession. The stance of the Turkish Cypriots was negative and in April 1943 they declared that in the event of British withdrawal Cyprus should return to Turkey (see below) (Rizas 1998: 213, 214).

2 A Brief Reference to the New Stance of the Communist Party of Cyprus (KKK) on the Question of *Enosis*

The resumption of the *Enosis*' demand, apart from its connection with the Second World War, is also related with the change of attitude of the Cypriot Communist movement towards this issue. But for these developments to become comprehensible there will have to be some initial mention of the stance of the Communist movement in Cyprus after 1931.

The ban on the functioning of the party following the failed revolt complicated, but did not halt, its activity. To be precise, in the first five-year period there was a gradual upturn in its interventions but after the return of P. Servas[2] and his assumption of the party leadership things changed. The cadres working with him played a front-line role in the unfolding social struggles of the working people and from the six recognized trade unions ("syntechnies" or "guilds" as they are called in Cyprus) which existed in 1937 with 367 members, by 1940 this number would rise to 62, with 3,389 members. Characteristic of the dynamic which had been created was the fact that during this period there was an increased number of strikes to the point where the mere inclination of the dock-workers of Varosha to come out on strike obliged the employers to accept their demands. It was in the following context that the joint action of the trade union movement emerged: In 1938, a common memorandum by four Nicosia "syntechnies" was submitted and 101 representatives of the 30 recognized unions and 27 unions under development participated in the first Pancyprian conference of the "syntechnies" which was held in Varosha in August 1939 (Katsouridis 2013: 132–133).

The outbreak of the Second World War reshaped the scene and made possible (1941) the establishment of a legal political organization[3] in which the members of the Communist Party of Cyprus participated, aiming at maximizing the overall political and ideological appeal of the communist movement's perspective.

The establishment of the new party was commenced at the initiative of the progressive lawyer G. Vasileiadis. The aim, of the communists, was to be organized a legal progressive party within which all the members of the illegal Communist Party of Cyprus could be active. The non-Communist wing thought that the time had come for the establishment of the first Pancyprian party of principle, and disclosure of the British inclination to lift the ban on conducting local elections had contributed

[2] After the banishment from Cyprus of the general secretary of the Cyprus Communist Party C. Vatyliotis (Vati) because of his participation in the 1931 revolt, the position of secretary was taken over by Kostas Kononas (1931–1933). But he was subsequently expelled from the party because after much persecution he signed the declaration renouncing Communism (Chrysanthou 2013: 71). In the period 1933–1935, Christos Savvides was the party secretary and from 1935 until the incorporation of the Party into AKEL in 1945 it was led by Ploutis Servas-Savvides brother.

[3] In 1941, by the decision of the Governor William Battershill the functioning of political parties was legalized.

to this. The collaboration would have to be based on two axes: that the anti-colonial struggle would have *Enosis* with Greece as its final goal and that small and industrially underdeveloped Cyprus could not be a terrain for "social experimentation" (Protopapas 2012: 335). The Central Committee of the Cyprus Communist Party accepted this plan and on 14th April 1941 AKEL was founded the Anorthotiko Komma Ergazomenou Laou (Progressive Party of Working People) (Servas 1985: 118–119). My view is that the Communist Party of Cyprus took this decision so that there could be legal activity in the shifting context created by the Second World War, judging that on the strength of its organizational functioning and politico-ideological composition it would be able to become the leading influence on the progressive bourgeois with whom it was allying itself. This would become evident from the fact that on the party's first Central Committee members of the Cyprus Communist Party were in the majority (Sakellaropoulos and Alecou 2019: 76).

The general conditions favoured the functioning of the new party, chiefly focussed on two parameters: The first has to do with the British need to construct major defensive works, which obliged them, under pressure from AKEL, to make important concessions to the working class. And indeed, the trade unions through intervention by the cadres of AKEL pressured for higher wages and better working conditions. They staged strikes like that on the railway in June 1941, which resulted in the network being put out of operation for ten days (Protopapas 2012: 358). All in all, AKEL put forward several progressive demands such as universal compulsory education up to the age of 14, the institution of labour legislation and social welfare, extensive measures for the protection of farmers, more just taxation and tariff policy, a broadening of women's rights, etc. Working conditions improved, the eight-hour day was instituted, wages were increased and medical care was made available for working people.

The second parameter is linked to the participation of Cypriot volunteers, members and supporters of AKEL, in the ranks of the British army. This development consolidated social peace on the island (Drousiotis 1998: 13) and made it possible for municipal elections to be held. Specifically, as early as AKEL's First Congress, the decision was taken that any member who wished to could join the British army, without an open call being issued. The non-open nature of the invitation was due to fear of a possible German invasion. Then, with the opening of the Eastern front, this possibility ceased to exist and AKEL called openly for its members to enrol in the British forces. It is estimated that more than 500 members of AKEL volunteered (Asmussen 2006: 173–175) including 11 of the 17 members of the Central Committee. At the political level, this was expressed through a call for united anti-fascist action and solidarity with the long-suffering people of Greece.

It should be mentioned that in AKEL's founding documents there was no explicit reference to the demand for *Enosis* with Greece. This must be due on the one hand to the fact that when the Governor finally consented to the founding of the party, he let it be understood that the new party would not be able to aim at *Enosis*,[4] and on the other to the fact that time was needed for the Communist Party cadres to shift from the perspective of independence to that of *Enosis*.

In any case, the first explicit reference to the demand for *Enosis* was in the declaration by the Central Committee of AKEL published on 16th November 1941 in the *Anexartitos* (Independent) newspaper: "The Progressive Party of Working People AKEL believes that as a result of the present war, which is being waged against absolutism and national subjugation, Cyprus will be given the opportunity to unite its fortunes with a free and democratic Greece" (quoted in the *Historical Encyclopedia of Cyprus* 1979–1980, Vol. 7: 91).

This was an important shift for the Cyprus Communist Party which, by virtue of its participation in AKEL, adopted the perspective of *Enosis*, even if in the remark about *Enosis* "with a free and democratic Greece" there was an implication that *Enosis* would not be acceptable with a dictatorial regime like the one which ruled Greece prior to the Italian and German occupation.[5] But even with this presumption, which was not to be voiced again by AKEL, it is a fact that conservative circles were taken by surprise by this change. A basic element that enabled them to unite against the communist adversary was being taken away from them. The initial embarrassment was succeeded by a series of attacks. On 17th March 1942, the Archimandrite of the Diocese of Kyrenia Iakovos Arnopoulos proclaimed: "The 25th March is the national festival of all Hellenes

[4] According to the testimony of Phaedon Kyriakidis, who participated in the relevant deliberations, George Vasiliadis mentioned to him that in his response to the demand for creation of the party, Governor Battershill said: "I willingly grant permission because I believe in the good sense and political tact of the delegates" (quoted in the *Historical Encyclopedia of Cyprus* 1979–1980, Vol. 7: 85).

[5] The parliamentary life of Greece had been ended on 4th August following the coup carried out by I. Metaxas.

and no party, including AKEL, of another nation and another religion, can appropriate it as its own festival." In a similar letter the Pancyprian Gymnastics Association of Nicosia, to whom a request had been made by AKEL for its stadium to be made available for a function of commemoration of the Greek Revolution of 1821, would say: "It amazes us that you become involved and that you attempt to undertake the initiative for a festival clearly Hellenic in nature, given that you represent an organization in whose ranks elements of other nationalities are included" (quoted in *Historical Encyclopedia of Cyprus* 1979–1980, Vol. 7: 136). The two extracts quoted show that the foundations for Right/Left conflict, in a way to be differentiated from that of the 1920s and 1930s, had been laid. The question would no longer be *Enosis* or not *Enosis* but rather in what way it was most likely for *Enosis* to be achieved. On the other hand, it is evident that the disparaging comments about the participation of Turkish Cypriots in AKEL were part of an attempt to show that having Turkish Cypriots in its ranks meant that AKEL was not serious about *Enosis*.[6]

Above and beyond their realization that the national question could serve as a lever not only for pursuing the anti-colonialist struggle but also for achieving broader social changes, given that in Cyprus the popular strata were doubly oppressed (both by the British colonial power and by the Cypriot bourgeoisie) there were other reasons for AKEL's turn. The first has to do with Greece's occupation by foreign powers, something provocative for Greek Cypriots also, and the second with Germany's attack on the USSR in June 1941 which, *inter alia*, had the consequence of changing the stance of the Communist International, as it now summoned the peoples to anti-fascist struggles and the defence of the USSR. For the regions not under Axis occupation that meant organizing all the anti-Nazi forces in a national front movement under the leadership of the communist parties.

3 The 1943 Local Elections

The municipal elections of 21st March 1943, which were held after an initial postponement because of the difficulties being faced by Britain in the early phase of World War II, were the first elections in Cyprus with a clearly political focus, at least in the big towns (Nicosia, Larnaca,

[6] But it seems that there was very limited Turkish Cypriot participation in AKEL. Characteristic is the expression of regret at the founding congress in Skarinou "because it was not possible the Turkish element to be represented in it" (quoted in Protopapas 2012: 355).

Limassol, Paphos, Kyrenia and Famagusta). Essentially, they were around a conflict where on one side were the candidates of the Right and on the other AKEL with its centre-Left allies.

On the level of articulation of political discourse, the candidates of the Right put forward anti-communist positions and inveighed against the Left and their fellow-travellers as enemies of the nation, the motherland, religion and the traditional values of Cypriot society. On the other hand, besides the national question, the Leftist candidates emphasized such demands as universal suffrage for men and women over 18, the provision of free meals to the unemployed, low-rent housing for workers, the securing of political freedom and condemnation of those who had collaborated with the Palmer regime[7] (Protopapas 2012: 370–371).

As far as the results are concerned, in Nicosia—a city notably linked with the power centres, the Right predominated. The same was true of Larnaca, Kyrenia and Paphos. In contrast, the towns of more working-class composition, Limassol and Famagusta, the AKEL general secretary Ploutis Servas and Adam Adamantos, member of the AKEL Central Committee, were elected majors (Katsiaounis 2000: 76). Overall, in the urban municipalities the Right obtained 54.1% and the Left 49.9%.[8] In several rural municipalities (Lefkoniko, Morfou, Kythraia and Polis) the Right came first with a 56.8% vote, as against 44.3% for the Left. So, it is observed that in towns where there was a tradition of working-class struggles the Left emerged as particularly strong. In contrast, it was considerably overshadowed by the Right in rural areas, above all, which were traditionally conservative and under the influence of the Church (Protopapas 2006: 278–279).

The rise of the Left made the Greek Cypriot elite distinctly uneasy. One characteristic example is the article by the historian Achilleas Aimilianidis on 3rd April 1943 in the *Foni tis Kyprou* (Voice of Cyprus): "Precisely because of the sacred unity of our national forces we should not permit the opportunists who seek to divide the Hellenic People, who are forever directing their hopes towards its national Jerusalem, the

[7] "The people of Nicosia flock to the polls with one idea in mind: to vote for the Popular Ticket and give the torchbearers of the Palmerist regime their marching orders" (*Anexartitos* 21st March 1943, quoted in Protopapas 2012: 371). The term "Palmerist" is derived from the name of the previous British governor Palmer.

[8] The total figure for Right and Left was more than 100% given that in accordance with the electoral system the voters had the right to give a positive vote to all the candidates.

Parthenon, with foolish, indeed loathsome slander over class differences and putative exploitation by bourgeois with references to class struggles in a place where no class sentiment or difference exists and where nine tenths of citizens are from farms" (quoted in Katsiaounis 2000: 77).

4 The Founding of the Cyprus National Party and the Formation of the Cyprus Workers' Confederation

Essentially the 1943 municipal elections were the turning point that laid the foundations for the institutional organization of the conservative party. With the establishment of AKEL, the ban was lifted on the functioning of political parties and the change in the communist position about Enosis transformed the political scene and complicated the moves of independent conservative politicians. Added to this must also be the very fact of conducting municipal elections for the first time since 1929, indicating that objectively the form of the Cypriot political system was undergoing change. And they were elections from which there emerged quite a powerful Left.

So it was that on 8th May 1943 the mayor of Nicosia Themistocles Dervis, who was elected despite his corresponding term of office under the Palmer regime, and the seven municipal councillors who won their seats on his ticket, announced their intention to find the "National Alignment", addressed to all those imbued with "love of their country" who had not been corrupted by "internationalist views".

There followed a series of political contacts and attendant deliberations and in his speech in Paphos on 4th June 1943 Dervis would emphasize: "The foundations for establishing a national—in every sense of the word—Party are going to be laid firmly and unshakably and it will be a branch of the Pan-cypriot National Alignment, including all the healthy elements, inspired by a pure and uncompromising national ideology from the urban, rural and many adherent right-thinking elements of the working world [...] We are obliged to undertake a harsh struggle against the internal enemy, AKEL and all the sundry splinter groups of miscellaneous autonomists and bureaucrats [...]" (quoted in Protopapas 2012: 380–381).

The result of the deliberations between the conservative politicians was the founding of the Cyprus National Party (KEK) on 6th June

1943 in Nicosia. The central point in the charter of the new party was Article 2 where the demand was proclaimed for *Enosis* with Greece: "The aim of the party is the unification and co-ordination of all the national forces of the Hellenic Cypriot people in the interest of providing every feasible contribution to the service of the inalienable right of Hellenes to incorporate in the free Hellenic state all Hellenic, from the ethnological viewpoint, territory [...]" (quoted in Alecou 2011: 53). We see that there was a reference not only to *Enosis* but to the need for unification of all the conservative ("national") forces in a single political body.

But there was a second point resolved at the Congress which deserves a mention and it has to do with the party's relations with the Church, given that the "teaching by the Greek people of attachment to the salutary truth of the Hellenic Orthodox Christian Religion, cultivation of the idea of the motherland and safeguarding of the cohesion of the family" are included among the objectives of the party (quoted in Alecou 2011: 53). So what was decided was that the new party should strengthen the Ecclesiastical Hierarchy (the "Ethnarchy") and collaborate with the National Council established by it, on the proviso that the Council would raise the issue of *Enosis*. It is noticeable that the KEK was very quick to forge alliances with the Church. This alacrity shows two things: one is anxiety over the prospect of the conservative alignment being outflanked by the communists and their allies. The other is apprehension that circles in the Church might turn towards support for AKEL. This is not as strange as it may appear at first sight. For a start, unlike a significant section of the Church, leading figures on the Right were key supporters of the "Palmerocracy". Then there was the example of Greece, where a section of the clergy supported EAM.[9] Finally in Cyprus, given the participation of the people in the election of bishops, the hierarchy necessarily reflected aspects of the social process.

At the same time, there were secessions from the Pan-cyprian Labour Committee (i.e. the federation of the Cypriot trade unions), which they considered to be under the control of AKEL, and new "syntechnies" began to be established, starting from Limassol, with a view to accommodating right-wing workers, enlisting the argument of Workers' Union embroilment in the 1943 elections. In October 1944, these new

[9] The National Liberation Front (EAM) was the political body which had been established by the Communist Party of Greece together with other Left and progressive forces with a view to liberating Greece from the German occupation.

"syntechnies" established the Cyprus Workers' Confederation (Synomospondia Ergaton Kyprou-SEK).

The fact is that this about-face by AKEL on the question of *Enosis* produced great consternation in the ranks of the Right, complicating the task of operating as they had in the past. As aptly remarked by the Greek Consul A. Kountouriotis "The founding of the KEK was devised by the class of Cypriot big capitalists as a weapon against the Left alignment, and indeed the communists. Its founders manipulated the alluring but at the same time deceptive title 'National' for internal party consumption [...] Many of the higher officials of the KEK, including its General Secretary T. Dervis served the detested (by every Greek Cypriot) 'Palmerocracy', making these people antipathetic and suspect (unfortunately not without reason)" [quoted by Protopapas 2012: 385).

5 The Question of *Enosis* and the Political Controversies Inside the Greek Community in the 1943–1945 Period

The basic issue was not only that AKEL had changed orientation adopting the demand for Enosis but that it had opted for a flexible alliance policy for the purpose of achieving that objective.

Accordingly, the intense confrontation between the political forces which was notable in the 1943 municipal elections would not deter AKEL two months later, in May 1943, from calling for a meeting of the National Council with participation from all the island's political forces:

> Unification of the national endeavours is required and has become imperative. Unification, however, without party-political exploitation, without any exclusion. "Unification" with exclusion of one organization or another would mean division, conflict, national bickering, serving the interests of those who are opposed to vindication of our demands, destruction of our national project. (quoted in *Historical Encyclopedia of Cyprus* 1979–1980, Vol. 7: 245)

This initiative did not go ahead at that time but in August 1944 on the occasion of the visit to the island by Sir Cosmo Parkinson, representing the Secretary of State for the Colonies, the Locum Tenens of the Archiepiscopal throne Leontios would see it as an opportunity for joint promotion of the demand for *Enosis*. He accordingly invited AKEL, the KEK and the PEK (Pan-cypriot Farmers' Union)[10] to clarify whether they wished to participate in the drafting of a joint memorandum that would raise the subject of *Enosis*. The position of AKEL and PEK was favourable but that of KEK was not. It argued that the best solution was for each party to proceed towards the implementation of its own programme (Ioannou 2005: 94).

But the immediate prospect of liberation of Greece[11] was to highlight with striking clarity the question of *Enosis* with Greece, with the result that the KEK would revise its stance and on 25th September accept Leontios' invitation. So, the four largest political formations AKEL,[12] KEK, PEK and PESP (the Pan-cyprian National Socialist Vanguard[13]) agreed on 11th October on a protocol of collaboration for the achievement of *Enosis* with Greece. But retreat soon began on the right-wing side, primarily out of opposition to AKEL's participation in the relevant discussions.[14] The result was that doubts started to emerge about the whole collaboration.

[10] PEK (Pan-cyprian Farmers Union). Founded on 31st May 1942 as part of attempt to represent the interests of the conservative farming milieu in the face of the growing influence of AKEL. There was representation at the founding congress from 272 villages and an impression was made by the presence of the British director of Agriculture. Indicative of the conservative character of PEK is its summons to every Cypriot "who believes in the religious and family traditions of the ethnos" and in the inaugural address there was harsh rhetoric against AKEL, which previously through the cultural associations it controlled had criticized the founding of PEK (Alecou 2011: 51–52).

[11] Greece would finally be freed from the German occupation in October 1944.

[12] In an announcement on 9th October, AKEL proposed that an agreement be concluded on the basis of the following principles: "(1) An organized and systematized struggle for *Enosis* of Cyprus with Greece under any regime that the Greek people wish to elect. (2) A truce between the parties covering every issue linked to the national question and (3) collaboration between Parties and Organizations on all matters whose resolution in one way or another promotes the national struggle" (quoted in *Historical Encyclopedia of Cyprus* 1979–1980, Vol. 7: 250).

[13] PESP (Pan-cyprian National Socialist Vanguard- Pagkypria Sosialistiki Protoporeia): A political formation whose reach was confined mostly to the Paphos area. Its leading figure was the Mayor of Paphos Christodoulos Galatopoulos.

[14] The PEK would call upon Locum Tenens Leontios to take a position against communism, regarding his stance towards AKEL as too friendly, and the Socialist Vanguard sought guarantees that AKEL would not undermine the Hellenic race (*Historical Encyclopedia of Cyprus* 1979–1980, Vol. 7: 251).

With this degree of suspicion already established, the *Dekemvriana*[15] events would have a catalytic effect on subsequent developments. Step by step all the political formations, and the Church too, began to demand the non-participation of AKEL in united action for *Enosis*.

The KEK made the first move on the same day as the clashes in Athens (3rd December 1944) with an announcement asserting that the developments in Greece showed that mainland Greek communists were not struggling for the advancement of national issues but for overturn of the social order. Consequently

> Given the identity of views of the Communists in Greece and in Cyprus as acknowledged explicitly and unreservedly by the AKEL delegation during the last meeting at the Archdiocese, the present gathering excludes the possibility of any collaboration with the Cypriot communists if the evolution of the situation in Greece indicates that the communists there want *Enosis* not for promotion of parts of our nation but to use it as a bridge for violent overturn of the social order [...]. (quoted in the *Historical Encyclopedia of Cyprus* 1979–1980, Vol. 7: 256)

There is a direct link between both the developments and the attitude of the KKE towards the events in Cyprus. So, it could be argued that the *Dekemvriana* was the pretext that the leadership of the Cypriot Right had been looking for throughout the preceding period so as to be able to reject collaboration with a unifying front for *Enosis* with Greece.

But above and beyond the inclinations of the KEK the reality is that the aftermath of the *Dekemvriana* had brought matters to the point where the Church, whose stance on the question of participation by the Left in the united front had been positive, was now espousing the same logic as the KEK. Accordingly, one day after the *Dekemvriana* the acting Archbishop of Kyrenia Archimandrite Anthopoulos sent an encyclical to the teachers and the ecclesiastical commissioners of the Metropolitan region of Kyrenia to be read in the churches on 17th and 24th December in

[15] These were armed clashes which took place in Greece where the alliance of the George Papandreou government and the British faced the very powerful Greek communist party and its allies. They started on 3rd December 1944 after police opened fire on an EAM demonstration which had been organized in reaction to a government ultimatum for disarmament of all the rebel groups. They resulted in the death of 33 demonstrators and the wounding of another 148. Battles ensued for 33 days within Athens city and were terminated on 5th–6th January 1945.

which it was mentioned that "denying the existence of God, Communism regards our Holy faith as a human fabrication, professing and teaching hatred, violence and subversion" (quoted in the *Historical Encyclopedia of Cyprus* 1979–1980, Vol. 7: 256).

AKEL for its part sided openly with EAM and ELAS[16] and in a related announcement by its Central Committee argued *inter alia*:

> 1. The EAM programme was to struggle for the liberation of Greece and the securing of people's democracy, ELAS played a decisive role in the achievement of the former objective. [...] That left the latter objective: the achievement of popular democracy. It is precisely for the achievement of this objective that EAM is now struggling, following the liberation. [...] 2. ELAS is today the sole guarantor for the safeguarding of the rights of the people against every attempt at reimposition of a new fascist dictatorship. EAM could accordingly not accept the disbanding of this People's Army without simultaneous disbanding of those military organizations that present the danger of imposing fascist dictatorship [...] 5. AKEL condemns before the Greek people the murderous attack of the [...] police against Greek men and women armed solely with the Allied national banners. The responsibility for that crime, whose consequence was that the streets of Athens would be drenched with the blood of its liberators, belongs entirely to the Papandreou government. 6. The political crisis in Greece in no way influences the declared views of AKEL on the necessity for national unity in Cyprus in the interest of the endeavours being pursued for the national restoration of the Island. (quoted in the *Historical Encyclopedia of Cyprus* 1979–1980, Vol. 7: 256–257)

It is clear that AKEL had a twofold reading of developments. On the one hand, it stood unequivocally shoulder to shoulder with EAM-ELAS; on the other, it made it clear that developments in Greece cannot pose an obstacle to building a common political front for the achievement of *Enosis*. Undoubtedly the position of AKEL was difficult given that it could neither omit to condemn the massacre in Athens nor leave the subject of *Enosis* to be managed by the Cypriot Right.

Nevertheless, it would soon become evident that AKEL's goal of the common front was not feasible. At the end of December 1944, the KEK issued a proclamation charging that EAM and ELAS "massacre,

[16] ELAS (Ellinikos Laikos Apeleftherotikos Stratos, Hellenic Popular Liberation Army) was the military wing of EAM.

plunder, arrest party leaders, abduct innocent and peaceful people" and then ventured the accusation that "the Cypriot Communists have similarly taken up the practice of psychological violence among us [...]" concluding with the slogan "down with the Bolshevik dictatorship, terrorism and fascism [...]" (quoted in *Historical Encyclopedia of Cyprus* 1979–1980, Vol. 7: 257). In the same vein, they expressed their gratitude to the British for their military intervention, which functioned as a "protective shield for the great majority of the Greek people who were in danger of being massacred by the hordes of armed communists" (*Pyrsos* 5th January 1945 quote in Antoniou 2014: 6).

The consequence was that the Locum Tenens Leontios would decide that members of AKEL could not participate in the Ethnarchy Council, except for G. Clerides, who collaborated with AKEL but was not a member. This action would signify the end of the attempt by the four formations to work together. From then on, the KEK, the PEK and the PESP would stage a co-ordinated effort to isolate AKEL, and the new expansion of the Ethnarchy Council in August 1945 would involve exclusively figures of the Right (Protopapas 2012: 390). Naturally, this was not an arbitrary stance of Leontios but came in consequence of the joint announcement issued on 9th August 1945 by KEK, PEK and PESP.

> The three parties also declare that they will at all costs and with all their strength reinforce every National organization that the Cypriot Ethnarchy seeks to establish, on the proviso that in it there will not be included nationally stigmatized and/or suspect elements and individuals who to this day through their antipatriotic and anti-Hellenic stance have damaged the national cause of Cyprus and Hellenism in general [...]. (quoted in Katsiaounis 2000: 131)

The rift was becoming clearer and with the passage of time ever deeper. It would no longer affect only participation in the Ethnarchy Council but would gradually embrace a variety of aspects of political and social life.

One such type of serious development was the deepening of the already existing split in the trade union movement when the Cyprus Workers' Confederation (SEK) in September 1945 organized its founding congress:

> Its organization it was imposed because of the anti-national propaganda which methodically and surreptitiously spread among workers attached to

> the old syndicalism and the sold-out agents of panslav interests [...] it was then imposed by AKEL authoritarianism, the party dictatorship [...] it was imposed by the corruption of working-class consciences and the criminal attempt to repudiate our national traditions [...] it was imposed by the socialist and democratic idealism of Cypriot workers. (cited in Protopapas 2012: 383)

The establishment of the Cyprus Workers' Confederation (SEK) would have immediate repercussions for the organizational resonance of the old workers' associations, that is to say those influenced by AKEL, whose membership fell from 11,259 in 1947 to 9,447 in 1949, with that of the SEK rising from 1,145 in 1947 to 3,599 in 1949.

The same year there was also a tightening of the repressive measures being imposed by the British forces against the Cypriot communist movement. In the autumn of 1945, the police raided all the premises of the PSE,[17] confiscated all the union's documents and arrested 18 trade unionists, who were committed for trial on the charge, *inter alia*, of "conspiracy to overthrow the legal order through revolution". The indictment linked the leftist affiliations of the accused with propagation of the *Enosis* demand (both undesirable for British colonialism).[18] Based on such accusations all those charged were found guilty and sentenced to imprisonment, and the PSE was outlawed and dissolved. This development met with the approval of the anti-AKEL political camp. As observed by the Governor in a confidential report to the Colonial Office on the non-Left political parties "they were [...] enthusiastic, hoping that the time had

[17] The PSE had been founded in 1941 in Nicosia, amalgamating 62 trade union organizations. Following its abolition in 1945 the Pan-cyprian Federation of Labour (PEO) was established. Both these groupings were (and to this day the PEO still is) under the influence of AKEL.

[18] "The accused benefit from the popular sentiment on *Enosis* with Greece to serve their purpose, i.e. to establish Socialism as they understand it. And though ostensibly they present the movement for national liberation as a genuine desire for *Enosis,* nevertheless you will perceive from their declarations that they have adopted this movement as a slogan and part of their general policy in accordance with the communist theory that the preliminary move towards establishment of Socialism must be the national liberation of all countries so that they can fight together for institution of the socialist regime [...] And knowing how tender and profound is the sentiment of the honourable people, they (AKEL and the accused) impel the workers towards violence" (quoted in Ioannou 2005: 142–143).

come for the Government to shut down the entire organizational basis of AKEL" (quoted in Alecou 2011: 29–30).

Fierce conflict between Government and AKEL was renewed in October 1945 when soldiers of the Cyprus regiment on leave in Cyprus staged a demonstration demanding their discharge given that the war was over. But the British were including this army corps in their plans for repressing national liberation movements in the Middle East. The result was that an Indian military unit undertook to force two Cypriot battalions aboard ship in Famagusta, with one Cypriot soldier killed and another five injured and finally the regiment was disbanded because all sense of discipline between the soldiers had collapsed (Antoniou 2014: 3).

6 The 1946 Local Elections

What was most influencing the situation in 1946 was perpetuation of the climate of polarization that had started after the *Dekemvriana*. The municipal elections were held in that climate. There was an increase in electoral participation, reflecting the tension of the political conflict, and the political balance had been overturned with the predominance of the Left. Specifically in the large urban centres, in addition to Limassol and Famagusta, where it had emerged as victor in the previous elections, the Left would win both Nicosia and Larnaca, limiting the Right to Paphos and Kyrenia. The overall result in these six cities was 56.3% for the Left and 48.4% for the Right. Of the rural municipalities the Left clearly won Morfou, Kythea, Lapithos and marginally Lefkoniko, and the Right was confined to Polis and Lefkara. The overall result in these six rural municipalities was 59.3% for the Left and 48.5% for the Right (Protopapas 2006: 281–282).

The factors that lay behind this development are to be sought in the strategy pursued by each party in the interval between the two electoral confrontations. The Right placed particular emphasis on the anti-communist content of its ideology but did not find it easy to free itself from the stigma of many of its top leaders having collaborated with the authoritarian regime that ruled in the period following the revolt of 1931, with Palmer as Governor. AKEL on the contrary spoke more concretely of the everyday problems of the popular strata (Protopapas 2006: 280) and projected the question of *Enosis* dynamically, emphasizing the anti-colonial content such a course necessarily entailed without from the outset positing divisions.[19] It could also be argued that the repressive policies pursued against AKEL in the preceding period by the British administration similarly played a role in strengthening the Left, inducing reaction among progressive citizens.

In any case the Left was for the first time emerging as the strongest political force on the island and that, as could be expected, caused concern and consternation in the opposing faction—the more so when AKEL persisted in a unifying policy on the national question. From that viewpoint, it is characteristic that the newly elected municipal councillors of the Left alliance not only hastened to meet with Leontios but—criticizing the ineffectiveness of the Ethnarchy Council—proposed the creation of a Pan-cyprian national organization in which every Greek Cypriot over the age of 18 would be a member. It was a stance that attracted vehement opposition from the hard-line right-wing Polykarpos Ioannidis:

> Mighty wolves have rushed to devour the Hellenic race. These poisonous and corrupted instruments of foreign propaganda and foreign interests have turned their attention now to children, your children. Agents of foreign ideologies and foreign motherlands, they lurk in every town and every village, in every street and on every corner, in associations and in remote houses to snare in their Bolshevik communist nets the innocent children of Greece, your children. (cited by Protopapas 2012: 414–415)

The issue, of course, is not the elegant content of Ioannidis' discourse but the direction in which it points, essentially laying the foundation for passage from acute conflict to the phase of an undeclared civil war. It is a development that would become particularly conspicuous in 1947 in the shadow of the Greek civil war.[20] In this context, any attempt at assembling a Pan-cyprian united front for *Enosis* came up against the entirely negative reactions of the Right. To put it somewhat differently

[19] In this connection he proposed that seats on the municipal councils should be allotted consensually. For example, in Famagusta, where he was indisputably in control, he proposed that three of the seven councillor positions and the position of deputy mayor should be held by the Right. But the Right rejected every such proposal (Alecou 2011: 64).

[20] The Greek civil war (1947–1949) was a confrontation between on the one side the forces of the Right and the Centre and on the other those of the Communist Party of Greece (KKE). Given the decisive assistance of the British initially and then the Americans, the centre-right faction emerged victorious.

both the rise in the strength of the Left and the impact of the Greek civil war injected an existential fear into the dominant Greek Cypriot forces which led not only to rejection of any joint action but also to a need to expand hostility on every level. The next stage in the conflict would be the archiepiscopal elections of 1947.

7 The Twin Elections for the Archiepiscopate

In the context on the one hand of attempting to propitiate the demand for *Enosis* and on the other the more general tendency towards liberalizing the regime that had been introduced by the authorities in the 1940s, the British proclaimed Archiepiscopal elections for May 1947. Because such a move entailed the risk that the new Archibishop would play an active role in the movement for *Enosis*, the British exerted pressure on the Greek government that the new Archbishop should be a person "at the same time capable of positive co-operation with the British authorities" (quoted in Protopapas 2012: 421). The desideratum was therefore that the candidate should neither be the Locum Tenens Leontios who had played a leading role in the creation of a Pan-cyprian front for *Enosis* nor the Kyrenian Makarios, who was also regarded as a strong proponent of *Enosis* (indeed he had been exiled for that reason in 1931).

The elections were scheduled for 5th May so the 1,004 special delegates were also appointed who would vote for the 66 general representatives (44 lay and 22 clerical) who would decide on the new Archbishop. The voters were Orthodox men who had lived for 12 months permanently in the relevant parishes and were not serving an ecclesiastical penance (prohibition from receiving holy communion).

AKEL decided to support the existing Locum Tenens of the Archiepiscopal Throne, acknowledging the moderate stance he had maintained, which distinguished him from the prevailing anti-communism of the Right. The Right supported Porphyrios, who had the disadvantage of being "extraclimatic", that is to say a priest from outside Cyprus; to be precise he served as Archbishop of Sinai.

The conflict was once again fierce. The Right Faction maintained:

> No other election of an Archibishop has been as important as the present one. Your Archbishop has never had to solve more, and more serious, issues than those that will be faced by whoever is elected in a few days. But above all it has never been attempted in any part of the world and in

any age that that an Archibishop should be chosen by the DENIERS OF RELIGION, THE ATHEISTS [...] The Communists are endeavouring through lies and slander to cloud your mind. They want an Archbishop of their own to help them spread anarchocommuism. (quoted in *Historical Encyclopedia of Cyprus* 1979–1980, Vol. 8: 44–46)

On the part of the Left, as reported in the testimony of E. Papaioannou, later general secretary of AKEL:

AKEL [...] insisted on the election of Leontios, who was indisputably the best candidate who indeed supported general patriotic unity of the people in the national liberation struggle [...] The reactionary right in Cyprus did not want Leontios as Archbishop because he supported the patriotic unity of the People in the liberation struggle while it pursued a divisive class policy that served only the interests of imperialism and colonialism. (Papaioannou 1988: 80)

Finally, the supporters of Leontios elected more than 900 special representatives[21] and in the council of electors Leontios received 58 votes and Porphyrios 17. Despite being triumphantly elected Leontios hesitated to indicate acceptance and only after intervention by the Patriarch of Constantinople was, he prepared to accept (Richter 2007: 726). Makarios of Kyrenia refused initially to enthrone Leontios because he thought that *both* of them had agreed not to be candidates and it was only after pressure that he relented and performed the enthronement.

The sudden death of Leontios on 26th July 1947 brought new opportunities for the Right to win hegemony in the ecclesiastical milieu, and not only there. The decision was therefore taken to support the Metropolitan of Kyrenia Makarios as candidate for the succession to Leontios. The Greek Ambassador Achilleas Kyrou agreed with that and wrote to the Greek Foreign Minister: "it is no longer permissible under the deceptive pretext of unity in the Cypriot struggle to create a united national front together with the communists" (quoted in Protopapas 2012: 427). Correspondingly, the Radio station of Athens took a clear position in favour of Makarios (*Historical Encyclopedia of Cyprus* 1979–1980, Vol. 8: 74).

[21] Chiefly because of the majoritarian system—given that around 48% of those voting chose special representatives who supported Porphyrios.

So, the confrontation was *both* heated *and* continuing in parallel with the Greek civil war. On the eve of the election AKEL said:

> Remember that those who yesterday insulted you, calling you a vulgar mob, the usurers who left you without a house and without a field, the collaborators with the Government, the heroes of the Palmer regime, the people with the decorations and the titles [...] the traitors and arch-traitors in practice of our national rights, the splitters of our popular forces, [...] the thieves and bloodsuckers of the people, the creatures of darkness, of hatred and destruction, come today to demand your vote [...]. (quoted in *Historical Encyclopedia of Cyprus* 1979–1980, Vol. 8: 76)

On the other hand, the *Ethnos* wrote:

> What must be rejected once and for all is the devious offensive by atheistic Communism and the national traitors against the Church and our Ethnarchy. IN THE FRONT LINES! To deal the death blow against the cunning enemies of Religion and our Motherland" (quote in *Historical Encyclopedia of Cyprus* 1979–1980, Vol. 8: 77).

Finally on the day of the elections the Pan-cyprian Front for Makarios emphasized: "[...] The votes are bullets that will lodge in the body of atheistic and countryless Communism and will transform it forever into a fleshless and motionless corpse" (quoted in the *Historical Encyclopedia of Cyprus* 1979–1980, Vol. 8: 78).

The colonial government itself would acknowledge:

> The battle is a direct trial of strength between the Communists and the anti-communists. The Right Faction, which has been very seriously shaken by the victory of the Left with the Leontios candidacy, displayed more energy than it has ever shown in the past. They utilized all the pre-election measures that were previously employed only by the Left Faction and they expended a large sum of money, the provenance of which is still unknown, and in time the initial climate of defeatism was replaced by a sense of increased self-confidence. (quoted in Protopapas 2012: 427)

The Left had as its candidate, from outside of the Cypriot hierarchy, the Metropolitan of Derkoi Ioakeim, who did not stand up to the pressures, however, and left the island. On 5th October, when the elections were held, the supporters of Makarios secured a wide lead with the special representatives (47 against 19) even though in the overall votes the difference was not particularly great. Makarios was elected by acclamation of the 61 electors in attendance, given that Derkoi had declared that he was not interested in the throne, and the general representatives of the left stayed away from the process, which they denounced as the result of fraud.[22] This victory of the Right was magnified even further when in the ensuing elections for the Metropolitans of Paphos, Kition and Kyrenia, the candidates supported by the Right won (Protopapas 2012: 428).

The reasons for this first, after 1943, defeat of the Left can be summarized as follows:

a. The acceptance of participation in the Consultative Assembly (see below) was seen as compromising *Enosis*, giving the impression of lack of stability in the politics of AKEL, leading to questioning of how much it wanted *Enosis*—the more so in the light of the stance of the Cyprus Communist Party in the pre-war period.
b. The choice for Archbishop of a person from outside the Cypriot hierarchy also pointed to lack of stability because in the previous election one of AKEL's basic arguments was that an extraclimatic like Porphyrios should not be elected Archbishop (*Historical Encyclopedia of Cyprus* 1979–1980, Vol. 8: 79).
c. It was logical that Derkoi's not having clearly accepted his candidacy would work in favour of Makarios.
d. The changes that were made to the electoral rolls also influenced the composition of the electorate and so the final result.

After the election of Makarios II, there were new amendments to the electoral rolls so that in future the Left would be able to elect its own candidate. In the relevant amendment to the statutes of the Church of Cyprus, it states that

> Those completing a religious penance cannot be included in the electoral rolls. Nor can those professing views in any way opposed to the Orthodox

[22] It seems that these allegations were not without substance. The death of Leontios helped the right-leaning mechanism of the Archiepiscopate to proceed with expulsion of leftists and supporters of Derkoi. According to assessments by the Left, the expulsions are to be numbered in tens of thousands (for example, just in Neo Chorio 20 people were expelled) (Graikos 1991: 261).

> Christian teaching, those expressing themselves in a disrespectful manner towards it or towards the Church or those serving it, behaving in such a way or collaborating with such behaviour, unless they persuade the Bishop of their sincere repentance. (quoted in Katsiaounis 2000: 486)

When the amendments to the statutes had been decided an archiepiscopal encyclical was promulgated on 19th October which also included provisions even for cancellation of the vote of a person who had been ascertained/judged, retrospectively not to have fulfilled the prerequisites for possession of the right to vote. This made it possible for any undesirable result to be overturned through mass cancellation of ballot papers:

> If the name of a parish subject to one or a number of the above obstacles is found registered on the approved list, the Bishop may order that prior to the election this parish be excluded and after the election the vote and any person characterized as commissioner be deemed invalid. [...] Any negligence or omission in this connection will be punished. (quoted in Katsiaounis 2000: 486)

After that the transformation of the right-wing forces away from a stance of indecisiveness over supporting a common Cypriot front to clear anti-communism and from there to proclamation of the struggle against AKEL as the first priority was consummated. From this viewpoint, the 17th December 1947 statement of Makarios II to the journalist Gibson Gowan is typical:

> It is declaredly in favour of the unification of Cyprus with Greece but the struggle against Communism is for the moment more urgent. It is impossible to ignore the fact that Britain today is the principal bastion against communism in the Eastern Mediterranean.
>
> We will never [...] attack Britain in order to achieve *Enosis*. Nor will we participate in an attack by any country against Britain. We hope, though, that Britain will recognize the rightness of our cause and the honesty of our inclinations. (quoted in Katsiaounis 2000: 403)

It should be underlined that this sharpening of the conflict unfolds against the backdrop of two events: The first has to do with the two consecutive electoral victories of the Left (Local elections 1946, first archiepiscopal elections of 1947) and the second with the bloody course of the civil war in Greece. The combination of these two factors generated an explosive atmosphere in Cypriot political life and great alarm on the Right, which saw its influence continually eroding.

To put it another way, Cyprus lived under the weight of the Greek civil war. The Greek Cypriot political forces could not ignore this reality. For AKEL in particular, though, the situation presented a special difficulty: it was struggling against the British for *Enosis* of Cyprus with Greece but also against the British who were fighting the fraternal Communist Party in Greece. This was objectively a point of weakness which the Right focussed on to win back its lost influence.

So, an undeclared second Greek civil war was being waged in Cyprus also, reflecting the peculiarities of the Cypriot social formation but always framed in the more general context of the Greek civil war. The longer the civil war continued the closer became the links between Cypriot political currents and their counterparts in Greece. As regards AKEL there was a relevant internal discussion of how they could be of assistance to the Democratic Army of Greece (DSE).[23]

In that connection, in the resolution of its 5th Congress (September 1947) it would refer to "admiration, sympathy and solidarity towards the heroic and invincible fraternal Greek people, towards its political vanguard as represented by the National Liberation Front and the Communist Party of Greece", deciding at the same time to proceed with tangible support for the DSE. Campaigns were organized to raise money and collect clothing. It should be noted that at the level of the Central Committee, following a meeting between F. Ioannou and G. Fotiou and the member of the Political Bureau of the KKE M. Porphyrogenis AKEL had examined the possibility of *also* sending people to assist. In fact, in the summer of 1948 various possibilities were investigated for the dispatch of a corps of 350 volunteers, but there were problems to be overcome such as the cost of transport and the non-possession of travel documents. Different approaches were investigated such as secret transport using Romanian and Polish ships going to Cyprus but finally the plan was not implemented because approval was needed from the governments in question (Protopapas 2012: 435). But this did not mean that AKEL ceased to proclaim in fiery speeches its solidarity with the KKE or organize rallies

[23] The Democratic Army of Greece- Dimokratikos Stratos tis Elladas (DSE) was the armed wing of the KKE, which was engaged in military conflict with the "official" Greek army.

in support of *Enosis* at which photographs of M. Vafeiadis, chief strategist of the DSE and Zachariadis, general secretary of the KKE, were on sale (Protopapas 2012: 447–448).

Of course, these practices of AKEL elicited sharp responses from the other side, augmenting the climate of anti-Communism. Correspondingly vehement was the reaction of the Cyprus Workers' Confederation when AKEL began to attempt to raise money for the Democratic Army of Greece:

> To hell with the plans of the sold-out national traitors working in every way to subject Greece to the Slavs and communism. Tomorrow they will be pouring out onto the streets to raise money to send to Greece to the paid subversives of EAM, to the treacherous criminals against the Nation, to the Bulgarians, to the Albanians[24] who are massacring Greeks our brothers. Do not put a single penny in the coffers of treachery. Don't give a cent for the Bulgarians to buy weapons[25] and murder Greece. (quoted in Alecou 2011: 19–140)

But it was not only the Greek civil war that fomented the continuing tension between the Greek Cypriot forces. The Organization of the Consultative Assembly by the British also played a role. The different positions put forward on participation or non-participation contributed to the even greater inflation of the internal disagreements between Greek Cypriots. There will be a further reference to the question of the Consultative Assembly and its consequences following a presentation of the stance of the Turkish Cypriot forces during this period.

8 The Stance of the Turkish Cypriots

The first Turkish Cypriot political formations were established in 1943 to participate in the municipal elections on 22nd March of the same year. The reference is to the People's Party (Halk Partisi) of Fasil Kucuk[26] and the party of the lawyer Fadil Niyazi Korkut (Richter 2007: 673). But a

[24] Meaning Slavophone and Albanian-speaking Greek citizens fighting as part of DSE.

[25] The language spoken by Slavophone Greeks had many similarities with Bulgarian.

[26] In an article of his in the *Soz* of 10/3/1943 Kucuk had anticipated the developments: "For many years there has been a Turkish Cypriot community whose member are unconnected with each other and unorganized. Who is responsible for this situation? We must confess that neither the government nor other communities are at fault. We Turks

little later, after elections had been held in which the younger generation of Kemalists headed by Kucuk had eclipsed the old guard and their leader Necati Ozkan (Moudouros 2014: 64),[27] it was perceived that in order to have better chances of success it would be necessary to shelve the differences of the past and construct a united political formation which would include the two newly formed parties but also Turkish Cypriot politicians belonging to the entourage of Evkaf (Evkafcilar). The initiative was taken by Munir Bey, who had secured the relevant encouragement from the British[28] and when two preliminary meetings had been held, finally on 18th April 1943 in the Evkaf offices the decision was taken to establish the Turkish Cypriot organization "Association for the Protection of the Turkish Minority on the island of Cyprus" (Kibris Adasi Turk Asinlik Kurumu-KATAK) (Ktoris 2013: 177–178). Note that the term "minority" was used by the founders of the party themselves rather than "community", which was to be an essential point of disagreement in the relations between the two nationalities in the following years. This was because the traditionalists continued to exert an influence which, when the issue was raised by the modernizers, had an inhibiting effect on acceptance of the term "community" (Ktoris 2013: 180–181).

From the 76 people present at meeting a nine-member committee was elected from the city and the province of Nicosia and it was decided that this body would be supplemented by another eight members to be elected from the rest of Cyprus. The pluralistic character of the whole undertaking is evident from the fact that the nine-member committee included Kemalists like Kucuk and Nejati but also representatives of the traditionally pro-British Turkish Cypriot elite with characteristic representatives Munir, Rauf Bey and the former judge Izzet Bey. The two last-mentioned, who were also members of the Advisory Board, occupied the position of President and Vice president, respectively. The founding of KATAK seemed to signify overcoming of the old rift between Kemalists and conservatives and the decision by the totality of the Turkish Cypriot

are responsible because we have not managed to take advantage of the rights which the government has ceded to us from the beginning" (quoted in Gennaris 2000: 67).

[27] Specifically, in the municipal elections in Nicosia, which were conducted by single ballot, the Kucuk side elected three municipal councillors as against just one for Nejati, namely Nejati himself (Arslan 2012: 123).

[28] The British wanted a more solid Turkish Cypriot collectivity as a bulwark against the growing pressures from the Greek Cypriots for *Enosis* (Moudouros 2014: 64).

elite to react in a unified manner to the increased activity of the Greek Cypriots in favour of *Enosis* (Katsiaounis 2000: 182).[29]

On the other hand, the fact that two members were backed by the central government and had been appointed by the British and that the founding conference had been held in the offices of Evkaf, which was a state instrumentality, was a symbol of explicit support on the part of the British. This is also clear from the fact that immediately after the founding of the party the President and Vice president visited the provincial administrator in Nicosia to assure him of the law-abiding character of the party, which aimed at preventing *Enosis* and improving the living conditions of the Turkish Cypriots (Katsiaounis 2000: 180–181).

One of the basic decisions that were taken when the new party was founded was the splitting of the mixed-nationality intercommunal trade union organizations and the establishment of purely Turkish Cypriot ones (Tenedios 1995: 389). Accordingly, under the guidance of KATAK in the field of agriculture, it has been the creation of the Union of Turkish Farmers who broke away from the Pan-cyprian Farmers' Union. The activities of the Union of Turkish Farmers focussed on fighting for the rights of Turkish Cypriots. In a memorandum of 18th May 1943, they protested that there was no Turkish Cypriot employee in the Transport Department to hear their complaints, demanding the establishment of schools for Intermediate Level Education and Technical Training for Turkish Cypriots. On 26th January 1944 in a meeting with the Colonial Secretary Hugh Foot, they condemned the injustices they believed were being perpetrated to the disadvantage of Turkish Cypriots in public works and military-related projects.

As regards labour issues in May 1943 KATAK assembled the first purely Turkish Cypriot trade union organization with 43 Turkish Cypriot workers[30] coming from a split in the woodworkers' union. Shortly afterwards, in 1944, the Federation of Turkish Trade Unions (Kibris Turk Isci Birlikleri Kurumu) was founded, bringing together 13 unions, with

[29] As we are informed by Ktoris "In his intervention Nejati Ozkan stressed that the differences that divided the community in the 1930 elections [...] but also the recent elections of 1943, deserved to be forgotten" (Ktoris 2013: 178–179).

[30] For a very interesting presentation of the joint struggles waged up to that point by the Greek Cypriot and Turkish Cypriot workers through joint trade unions see Michaelides (1993).

fewer than 1,000 members altogether (Richter 2007: 674). This Federation too made national distinctions a priority. In a letter in the Turkish Cypriot newspaper *Soz* the Turkish Cypriot workers argued that because of the stance of the Greek Cypriots they faced difficulties finding work because the Greek Cypriot public works supervisors did not hire Turkish Cypriot workers. The letter demanded that recruitment be controlled by a Greek Cypriot and a Turkish Cypriot supervisor who would be appointed by the Labour Administrator and by a committee selected by the union. The ratio in hiring workers would be required to correspond to the Pancyprian ratio between the two nationalities and if the supervisor was Greek Cypriot his assistant would be required to be Turkish Cypriot and vice versa (Katsiaounis 2000: 183–184).

But the indictments above do not seem to have corresponded to reality. In a note of 31st January 1944, R. Wayne, Administrator of the Labour Division, said that there is no data pointing to instances of ethnic discrimination. At the Province Engineer department in Nicosia Turkish Cypriot technicians comprised 46% of the total at a time when the Turkish Cypriots made up just one-third of the total population in Nicosia, 14% of the workers at the Greek mining company, and only five percent employed on public works in Limassol, were Turkish Cypriots but this was because Turkish Cypriots did not make applications for such jobs (Katsiaounis 2000: 184).

The emergence of purely Turkish Cypriot trade union organizations would not prove capable of exerting an inhibiting effect on the appearance of frictions inside KATAK. The Kemalists led by Kucuk and the newspaper *Halkin Sesi* (Voice of the People) began to emphasize the need for the Turkish Cypriot community to establish independence from the patronage of the British and the cadres of Evkaf. The dispute this time would be focussed on the apparent willingness of the British to accept self-government for the Cypriots. The traditionalist side seemed positively disposed towards such a prospect but the modernizers were dismissive because they thought that such an action would open the way for *Enosis* with Greece, and they began to raise the issue of Cyprus' return to Turkey in the event of British departure (Kalantzopoulos 2015: 146). So once again the traditionalists intimated partnership with British policy and the modernists a break with it. The result was that in April 1944 Kucuk, together with other cadres, left KATAK to establish, on the 23rd of the same month, the National Turkish Unity of Cyprus—Kibris Turk Milli Birlik Partisi—KTMBP) (Ktoris 2013: 184–185). As a choice of date, it was by no means fortuitous because it was on that day that the Turkish National Assembly was founded. Not long afterwards, the Federation of Turkish Institutions of Cyprus—Kibris Turk Kurumalri Fererasyonu was also established. This was the cultural-economic wing of Kucuk's party. But not all Kemalists were united behind this development: disagreeing with the more intransigent way the Kucuk group had chosen to clash both with the Greek Cypriots and with the British administration, Nejati Ozkan did not participate. He established the Turkish Cypriot Union Independence Party (Kibris Turk Birligistiklal Partisi) remaining in the shadow of the other two parties (Moudouros 2014: 65).

KATAK, for its part, which was traditionally dependent on the Turkish Cypriot bureaucracy's links with the affluent strata of the countryside and had the support of Evkaf and the newspaper *Hursoz* (Free Speech), succeeded in retaining control of the Turkish Farmers' Union. In contrast, Kucuk's received more support from working people in the cities. Accordingly, a new union was soon founded, the Union of Turkish Trade Associations—LSTB—which would attract the great majority of the LTIB Lefkosa Turk Isciler Birligi (Union of Turkish Workers of Nicosia) who were linked with KATAK.

On 1st May 1946 the provincial organizations of the Turkish trade unions, which were now controlled by the KTMBP,[31] submitted a memorandum to the Colonial Secretary in which they reiterated their protests against discrimination on the part of Greek Cypriots, against exploitation by Greek Cypriots of their municipal office to promote the politics of *Enosis*, demanded that there be rotation of a Greek Cypriot mayor and Turkish Cypriot deputy mayor and vice versa and protested at the absolute government control that prevailed at the Turkish high school and at Evkaf. Most interesting is the remark that: "In all the world religion is something different from nationality. *Our* nationality is Turkish, just as our religion is Muslim [...] Since that is how things are, we want our schools, which belong to the Turkish community of Cyprus,

[31] Although a little later, in 1948, the Pan-cyprian Federation of Labour was to sign an agreement with the Turkish Cypriot unions for collaboration and condemnation of racial hatred, the decisive step towards a separation of the trade unions had been taken (Pan-cyprian Trade Union Committee-Pan-cyprian Federation of Labour 1991: 250–251). It was a legitimated practice although in the first phase it was not characterized by success: the Turkish Federation in 1945 had a membership as high as 843 people. By 1946, it had fallen to 681; by 1947, 640; and by 1951, 131 (Pan-cyprian Trade Union Committee-Pan-cyprian Federation of Labour 1991: 252).

to be called, beginning from the senior high school, Turkish schools" (cited in Katsiaounis 2000: 185–186). At the end of the memorandum, it is asserted that the Turkish language should be used in parallel with the Greek in all governmental announcements and the Arabic alphabet on banknotes and the seals of the mukhtars should be replaced by the Turkish. The national festivals of the Turks should be considered public holidays for Turkish workers since this has been enacted for Greek workers to celebrate 25th March. Finally, family law for Turkish Cypriots should be adapted to existing law in the Turkish Republic (Katsiaounis 2000: 186).

The confrontation with the Greek Cypriots would reach the point where the KTMBP would consider positions on municipal councils staging posts for promotion of *Enosis* by Greek Cypriots so that there was no reason for Turkish participation in municipal elections. Accordingly in the elections of May 1946, the KTMBP and *Hallin Sesi* called upon Turkish Cypriots to abstain. This dynamic of the position exerted an influence on the *Hursoz* newspaper but also on KATAK in Nicosia, with the result that the two Turkish Cypriot parties did not run candidates in the capital of Cyprus. In the remaining municipalities, KATAK stood for election normally and the KTMBP was accordingly not represented anywhere in the new municipal councils. But this development did not affect the influence of the KTMBP inside the Turkish Cypriot community, where it remained a significant force (Katsiaounis 2000: 189–190).

Another dimension that warrants underlining has to do with a strategy of the Kemalist Turkish Cypriot elite in relation to economic development. As already mentioned, throughout the entire period from the coming of the British until the 1940s the Turkish Cypriots lagged significantly behind the Greek Cypriots. The choice made by the new Turkish Cypriot leading group to remedy this problem was one of creating strong merchant capital. But because that could not easily be done given the situation where Greek Cypriot merchant capital already occupied a very strong position in the Cypriot economy as a whole, what was opted for was the establishment of capital accumulation under separate conditions and a purely Turkish Cypriot market which would function in a geographically unified manner through stable communications and transport, i.e. a unified national territory (Arslan 2012: 121). It is obvious that in their mind they had the corresponding example of economic development of Turkey but note that the Turkish economic development was contingent on heavy state intervention. In Cyprus, in contrast, the only solution on offer was to assume control of Evkaf (Arslan 2012: 122). And indeed, that was accomplished at the end of the 1940s once Munir Bey had first resigned from the Evkaf management and the British subsequently cancelled their audit of that agency (Moudouros 2014: 70–71) (see below).

At the political level, this development made a significant contribution to KATAK and the party of Kucuk amalgamating to found, at the end of 1949, the National Turkish Unity Party of Cyprus—Kibris Milli Turk Birligi Partisi—under the leadership of Kucuk (Arslan 2012: 123–124), with a little previously to this all the Turkish Cypriot trade union organizations establishing the Federation of Turkish Cypriot Associations (Kalantzopoulos 2015: 155). Another reason for the creation of the united party was the fear stemming from the content of the proposals being made to the British in the Consultative Assembly (see below) that they draft institutional reforms upgrading the position of the Greek community (Kalantzopoulos 2015: 146).

In any case, the founding of a unified Turkish Cypriot party and adoption of the strategy of creating a purely Turkish Cypriot economy injected further momentum into the strategy for promoting partition (*taksim*), which was to be the key objective of the Turkish Cypriot elite in the 1950s (Sakellaropoulos 2017).

9 The Deliberations of the British, Organization of the 1947 Consultative Assembly and Its Aftermath

The end of World War 2 abruptly brought the Cyprus issue to the forefront. It is interesting that the establishment of the United Nations and the Charter that was accordingly signed introduced new factors into the equation, with article 73 providing that "Members of the United Nations which have or assume responsibilities for the administration of territories whose peoples have not yet attained a full measure of self-government recognize the principle that the interests of the inhabitants of these territories are paramount, and accept as a sacred trust the obligation to promote to the utmost, within the system of international peace and security established by the present Charter, the well-being of the inhabitants of these territories, and, to this end, [...] to develop self-government, to take due account of the political aspirations of the peoples, and to assist them in the progressive development of their free political institutions, according to the particular circumstances of each territory and its peoples and their varying stages of advancement".

An important role in determining the content of the article in question was played by the increase in influence of the Soviet Union but also the beginning of the crisis of colonialism. However, in relation to the Cyprus question, the end of the war found Britain wary of any development that might lead to loss of its military control of Cyprus. Thus in a relevant document compiled by the British Foreign Office experts A. F. Brooke, C. Portal and A. Cunningham, the following conclusions were drawn:

> Without knowledge of possible alternatives that may be proposed [...] the retention of Cyprus under British rule is desirable from a military point of view because:
>
> a) Although possession of Cyprus only confers limited strategic advantages on us, control of the island by a hostile power would be a very great embarrassment.
> b) In war, the island is strategically placed to assist in the defence of our interests in the Middle East.
> c) In peace, it provides us with alternative air staging bases, and naval and air facilities for the security control of the Eastern Mediterranean.
> d) It is the only territory in the Middle East where such measures as we consider necessary for the defence can be carried out unfettered by treaties. (quoted by Alexander 1979: 88)

To these arguments the Colonial Office added the following: "We remind you that in the speech delivered at the London City Hall in November 1942 the Conservative Prime Minister Churchill declared that the inclination of the British Government was to preserve the full integrity of the British Empire. Similarly on 8th November 1944 and 17th January 1945 the Labour Prime Minister Attlee in response to questions in the British Parliament stated that no part of the British Empire or of the Commonwealth is excepted from the abovementioned declaration of Churchill" (quoted in Economides 1993: XX–XXI). A little later the Colonial Secretary in a letter to the Foreign Secretary Ernest Bevin cited an additional argument: "Apart from our strategic and defence interests we should bear in mind that the cession of Cyprus to Greece would mean abandonment of our faithful friends in the Muslim Community" (quoted in Economides 1993: XX–XXI).

So, the conclusion of the relevant British officials is that British rule in Cyprus should be preserved to safeguard the strategic planning of the Empire. Nevertheless, although during the war it seems that this policy was predominant, a study of the archives reveals that after the war the British were divided over the idea of ceding Cyprus.

Very briefly, the argument for the viewpoint favouring cession, which was articulated in 1947[32] primarily by Sir Oliver Harvey, a senior official in the Foreign Office, was that because Cyprus had been rejected by the chiefs of staff as suitable for any long-term strategic goal and because the acceptance of Indian and Burmese independence had had a very positive impact on public opinion internationally, the cession of Cyprus to Greece would have only favourable effects: the resort to violence by the Greek Cypriots would be averted, as with the example of Ireland, and it would be made more difficult for EAM to intervene in the island under the pretext Britain's srefusal to accept movement towards *Enosis*.[33]

Senior Foreign Office counsellor Wallinger responded as follows to the abovementioned argumentation: "In more normal circumstances, the early cession of Cyprus to Greece might well be a wise policy, justified by considerations not only of justice, but also of expediency. But present circumstances are not normal" (cited by Mallinson 2005: 14). The abnormal circumstances are the outbreak of civil war in Greece—a development that would significantly influence the thinking of the British, compounded by the increased distrust between East and West.

And according to one official: "Cyprus is in fact the only firm bit of ground in the Middle East left to our strategic planners. From the purely strategic point of view, to sacrifice this one remaining asset at a time when it is not even certain that we shall get any strategic rights or facilities in

[32] Corresponding argumentation in favour of *Enosis* was put forward at the beginning of September 1945 by Orme Sargent, under-secretary of State conveying the views of the southern department of Britain's Foreign Ministry (Alexander 1979: 79–80). Also for the related correspondence, in September 1945, and the exchange of views, between the Secretary of State for the Colonies George Hall, who was opposed to *Enosis* and the Foreign Secretary Ernest Bevin, who was in favour, see Rizas (1998): 218–221.

[33] It should be noted that the USA too in 1947 appeared favourable to the prospect of ceding Cyprus to Greece. In a relevant 1947 document there is the comment that "we favour the cession of Cyprus to Greece if such transfer can be made to the satisfaction of the two countries involved and if due provision is made for the security of legitimate lines of communication in the Eastern Mediterranean and for the protection of the interests of the non-Greek population of the island" (cited in Kontos 2014: 187).

any part of Libya would seem inconsistent with the policy of the firm hold on the Middle East which has been endorsed by the Prime Minister and Secretary of State, as well as by the Chiefs of Staff [...] with Cyprus ceded to a Greece gone Communist, we should not only have created a vacuum in the Middle East, we should have gone halfway towards letting the Russians fill it" (cited by Mallinson 2005: 15).

Given the British decision to withdraw from Palestine and the unsuccessful Soviet attempts to secure naval facilities in the Dodecanese after its integration into Greece, but also given Soviet demands for participation in defence of the Straits, the Empire's fear of naval conflict with the USSR in the Eastern Mediterranean was palpable. And this would be the view that prevailed. As very aptly observed by Mallinson "Clearly, the perceived Communist threat was played on as an argument, and connected almost automatically to the Soviet Union. Thus, the Greek civil war played a major role in British calculations, and was used as a lever to rebuff the *Enosis* argument" (Mallinson 2005: 15).

In addition to all this, in peacetime Cyprus was a useful staging point in the aerial route to India, made possible a certain control over navigation in the Eastern Mediterranean, and Britain could implement whatever measures it wished without the stumbling blocks of international treaties (Rizas 1998: 217–218).

The key decisions would be taken in 1947, when following a proposal by Bevin, in consultation with the Greek government, that the subject not be raised for ten years, after which the Cypriots would exercise their right to self-determination, the reaction of the Prime Minister Clement Attlee was negative. He argued that on the one hand the majority of the cabinet did not agree with such a prospect and on the other there should be no mention of the possibility of self-determination and Greece should not be encouraged to broach the issue (Yiagou 2013: 26–27).

In reality, and in the maelstrom of internal conflicts, Athens had no desire to posit such a question and come into confrontation with the British. Accordingly, not even in the speech delivered by the Prime Minister of Greece G. Papandreou in Athens immediately after the end of the German occupation (October 1944) was the subject of *Enosis* mentioned. Nor was it included among the demands submitted by the Greek representative P. Dragoumis at the Paris Conference (November 1945) (Tounta-Fergadi 2010: 87). A little later, in December 1946, a similarly negative response was made by members of the Greek government to the Cypriot delegation visiting Athens. The Greek Prime Minister

K. Tsaldaris would issue a corresponding pronouncement during his visit to London in August 1947 (Katsiaounis 2001: 153, 155).

So, the prospect of *Enosis* was deflected. On the other hand, the British presence did not necessarily mean perpetuation of the regime of coercion that had been introduced after the 1931 revolt. Under these circumstances Britain would proceed, in conjunction with the dynamic generated by the participation of Greeks and Cypriots on the side of Britain in the war, but also the initiation of international efforts by the Greek Cypriots to achieve *Enosis*,[34] through the Colonial Secretary Creech-Jones, to formulate the following declaration on 23rd October 1946, in the British Parliament: "With a view to seeking opportunities to establish a more liberal and progressive regime in the internal affairs of the island [...] I propose [...] to call together a Consultative Assembly drawn from representative elements in the island, to consider the framing of proposals for constitutional reform, including the re-establishment of a Central Legislature. It is hoped that the result will be the creation of a Council which will bring representatives of the Cypriot people into full consultation with the Government in the conduct of their local affairs" (quoted in Richter 2007: 713). In addition to this, a ten-year economic development programme was announced, along with abolition of the legislation preventing election of the Archbishop.

Based on this thinking the Consultative Assembly was convened. From the outset the Ethnarchy, but also AKEL, started that they would not accept any settlement that did not provide for *Enosis* as the definitive solution to the Cyprus problem.

Specifically in the immediate aftermath of the clarification of British intentions, on 24th October 1946, AKEL presented to the Right specific proposals for both inside and outside of Cyprus.

[34] Characteristic from this viewpoint is the letter sent by Archbishop Leontios of Cyprus to the Archbishop and Regent of Greece Damaskinos in which he mentioned to him the desire of the Greek Cypriots to send a delegation to London with a view to working for implementation of *Enosis*. Apprehensive about the displeasure of the British, Damaskinos discouraged him, saying vaguely that the matter in question will be examined favourably by the British and its evolution will be monitored continuously by Greece (Katsiaounis 2000: 112–113).

1. Interparty agreement with the capacity to unite the people in a combative front for national liberation.
2. Radical revision of the programmatic framework of national representation to reflect the new conditions introduced by the British communiqué, i.e. reorientation in the direction of internationalizing the Cyprus question as a guiding strategy, and of rejection of reservations based on British altruism.
3. Establishment of a united pan-Cyprian organization for *Enosis*. Such an organization under the leadership of the Archbishop will have the responsibility for managing the national question.
4. Joint action to deal with the problems caused by the new reality in Cyprus.
5. Mass mobilization on a pan-Cyprian basis as a guarantor for reversal of colonialistic projects (Leventis 2002: 165–166).

AKEL took advantage of the platform of the Congress of communist parties of the British Empire, which was held between 26th February and 2nd March 1947, introduce—successfully—the subject of *Enosis*. Thus, in the concluding resolution, there was reference the Congress's agreement to implementation of *Enosis* (Leventis 2002: 168).

At the same time, a right-wing delegation was dispatched to London and to Athens. In February 1947, the delegation was received by the Colonial Secretary, who excluded any thought of ceding the island to Greece. The same opposition was conveyed simultaneously by the Turkish Cypriots through relevant telegrams to the British government. In contrast, the Greek parliament, the same month, unanimously passed a resolution favouring *Enosis*.

The Turkish Cypriots, for their part, stepped up their reactions against the prospect of *Enosis*. Characteristically, on 19th April 1947, KATAK, the KTMBP, the Union of Turkish Farmers and the Federation of Turkish Cypriot Associations jointly submitted a memorandum to the Governor. The memorandum began with the demand for recomposition of the office of Mufti with full attribution of its powers and with election by the totality of the island's Muslims. Then the question was posed of abolishing governmental control of Evkaf (Katsiaounis 2000: 290). Evkaf should come under the control of the community and the Seri courts should acquire independence from Evkaf and become real courts again as they were until 1927. In this framework, the family court of the community was described as medieval and incompatible with Turkish Cypriots' present-day reality, exerting a corrosive effect on the social cohesion of the community.

On the issue of the central administration, it was argued that in every department where the Greek Cypriots predominated, a Turkish Cypriot deputy should be added, and vice versa. Correspondingly there should be a review of the mode of operation of municipal authorities on the following basis: rotation of the council seat between Greek Cypriot and Turkish Cypriot should take place on the basis of demographic proportionality. When the Mayor is a Greek Cypriot the Deputy Mayor will be a Turkish Cypriot and vice versa. Decisions of the municipal council with which the Turkish municipal councillors disagree should be subject to veto by the Governor.

That said, the Turkish Cypriots judged that the institution of a regime of self-government "would be harmful for minorities and for the Turkish minority in particular." It was for this reason that the Turkish community expressed its strong opposition to any form of self-government that would leave the future and vital interests at the mercy of the majority. The signatories also ascertained that the real name for their nationality, i.e. "Turks", had to date been ignored by the government and that in its official documents they were called "Muslims", a terminology which had been overtaken by historical developments. Finally, the Turkish Cypriots wanted the Turkish community to be represented in the proposed Consultative Assembly (Katsiaounis 2000: 291).

It must be noted that this step involved two basic parameters. The first is linked to the mode of self-management of the Turkish Cypriots. It is clear that the demands that are projected are precisely those supported for many years by the pro-Kemalist wing. The fact of the erstwhile "conservative" wing's convergence with them on the one hand shows that the times had changed and on the other that the Kemalist line had secured complete hegemony. The second parameter has to do with the common rejection of the prospect of *Enosis*.

During the same period, on 9th July 1947, Lord Winster invited the Cypriot organizations to nominate their representatives for the Consultative Assembly which would elaborate the new constitution and would go down in history as the "Consultative Assembly". The proposal was accepted by the Turkish Cypriots but met with a divided response from the Greek Cypriots: The Ethnarchy refused to participate. In his statement, the Locum Tenens Metropolitan of Kyrenia Makarios said: "Until the moment that Great Britain [...] agrees to restore Hellenic Cyprus to

Mother Hellas, the Cypriot people [...] will continue steadily and unyieldingly this sacred and legitimate struggle for their national restoration [...] rejecting all enticing promises and avoiding every trap artfully constructed for them. We wish to hope that whoever may happen to be drawn into the question of Constitutional Reforms [...] will encounter as rapidly as possible disciplined and combative soldiers [...] abstaining from any participation in government for imposition of a Constitution, sabotaging or retarding the national demand of this land [...]. With this conviction we proclaim once again the demand of Cypriot People for *Enosis* and only *Enosis*" (quoted in *Historical Encyclopedia of Cyprus* 1979–1980, Vol. 8: 89–90).

Seeing that an unfavourable climate had begun to develop among a significant section of Greek Cypriots, Governor Winster tried to apply pressure, declaring that there was no chance of Cyprus being ceded to Greece, so that the only route for the Greek Cypriots to follow was to agree to participation in the Consultative Assembly[35] (*Historical Encyclopedia of Cyprus* 1979–1980, Vol. 8: 91).

In contrast to the line, it had adopted since the early 1940s, AKEL began to alter its stance. There were two reasons for this: for a start, the British position was that there was no question of *Enosis*, as it was becoming clear that Cyprus had been excluded from the framework of post-war territorial settlements and on the other it was impossible for AKEL to form a common front with the Right and the Ethnarchy. So, the conclusion was that what was needed was a parliamentary assembly within which the Leftist forces would be able to continue the struggle for *Enosis*, without that meaning that the basic prerequisite for achievement of that goal did not remain the party's capacity to mobilize the people (Leventis 2002: 168).

The attempted collaboration with the Right did not bear fruit despite the efforts of Archbishop Leontios to find common ground potentially acceptable to both sides and a uniform stance against the constitutional proposals. The conservative faction reaffirmed its policy of not collaborating with communists and their fellow travellers and staying away from the meeting summoned by the Archbishop.

The proposal put forward by AKEL in July 1947 was that of "guaranteed abstention" on the basis of which it invited the Right to provide

[35] For the full content of the declaration see *Historical Encyclopedia of Cyprus* (1979–1980, Vol. 8: 91).

guarantees that they would not participate in the Consultative Assembly or in future elections held under the proposed constitution. The PES[36] again asked the Ethnarchy to form a pan-Cyprian national organization, i.e. a body to co-ordinate the anti-colonial struggle. The resignation of all Greek Cypriots appointed by the British Administration was demanded by the PES as a prerequisite for collaboration with the Right and as a clear sign from the latter that it would persist in the policy of non-co-operation with the colonial government (Leventis 2002: 169). To ensure that the resignations of the Greek Cypriots from the Executive and Advisory councils would proceed, the PES requested the intervention of the Ethnarchy. If this were not done, the Left indicated that it would instruct its members who had been summoned to the Consultative Assembly to accept the invitation, making it clear—however—to the British that such participation did not in any way imply abandonment of the demand for *Enosis*.

The PES criticized the existing situation where "on the one hand we insist on *enosis* and *nothing but enosis* and on the other we perpetuate today's autocratic and unaccountable regime by accepting appointments to various administrative, advisory and managerial offices, whereas the holders of this posts should have been elected by the people" (cited by Leventis 2002: 170).

The Right, for its part, announced its categorical refusal either to participate in the Consultative Assembly or to accept a regime of self-government, a refusal also expressed in a resolution adopted on 21st August by the right-wing political forces, with the participation of the Locum Tenens of the archiepiscopal throne and later Archbishop Makarios II (*Historical Encyclopedia of Cyprus* 1979–1980, Vol. 8: 90).

As for the stance of the Greek state on participation in the Consultative Assembly, the situation appears quite contradictory. The Greek Deputy Foreign Minister P. Pipinelis appeared acceptant of participation so as to achieve institution of the regime of self-government, without renouncing the objective of *Enosis* (Koumas 2013: 33–34). But there were a range of other factors moving the issue in the opposite direction. Specifically, the Interior Minister G. Papandreou and the parliamentary deputy D.

[36] The Parataxi Ethnikis Synergasias (PES) (National Collaboration Grouping): Comprised of AKEL, mayors collaborating with it and other personages from the intellectual milieu.

Sfaelos, Chairman of the External Affairs Committee of the Greek Parliament, were said, according to the British archives, to be arguing that *Enosis* was imminent, so that there should not be any participation in the Consultative Assembly, the more so given the presence of Leftist Greek Cypriots in it (Katsiaounis 2000: 265ff.). This contradictory situation is interpretable from the bipolar anti-communist/pro-British stance that set its seal at that time on the politics of the Greek government. On the one hand, legitimation of the proceedings of the Consultative Assembly could not be accepted by right-wing Greek Cypriots given the probability of a regime of self-government elevating the communists to the status of most powerful political pole on the island. On the other, it was not legitimate to provoke the British resentment that would be caused by projection of the demand of *Enosis* and abstention from the Consultative Assembly. Different people were therefore found to put forward different aspects of the bipolar scenario.

As far as AKEL is concerned, at the Fifth Congress, which was held in September 1947, an idiosyncratic, if not contradictory, document was adopted on the political situation. On the one hand, the Central Committee document presented constitutional change proposed by Great Britain and the ten-year development as "a bitter impasse in the crisis of imperialism". Taking this decision "imperialism aims openly at blunting the national liberation struggle and diverting the attention of the people to reformist channels within the colonialist framework". On the other, the same document portrayed participating in constitutional negotiation as a measure of popular self-defence with the potential to thwart the attempts to dissolve the popular movement and lead to paralysis. The Central Committee judged that the party should avail itself of the advantages of the proposed political changes for the benefit of the people and the demand for national liberation. Essentially AKEL decided that from the moment that the question of *Enosis* was off the agenda for the foreseeable future, adoption of self-government could prove a favourable basis from which to intensify the campaign for *Enosis*, particularly if there were a left majority in the new parliamentary body.[37]

AKEL's basic position on participation in the Consultative Assembly was that the designing of a Constitution was no obstacle to the struggle

[37] As is mentioned in the political report of the Congress: "[...] only our movement could ensure a truly popular nationally liberating utilization of the political concessions" (cited in Ioannou 2004: 228).

for *Enosis* and it would not be understood why it was preferable for a Briton to govern Cypriots without a Constitution rather than for there to be an elected government. The assessment from AKEL was that Britain was not inclined to give Cyprus to Greece and therefore it was better for there to be a regime of self-government where the Greek Cypriot side would have control of the education system, the police and the judiciary (Richter 2007: 730–731). I think that there is a *second element* that should be added to this argumentation of AKEL: in Greece, a civil war was being waged and the official regime was one of deadly hostility towards any expression of the Communist movement. If *Enosis* were to prevail this would lead Greek Cypriot communists into much grimmer conditions of life and action than was the case with British rule.

The final resolution of the Fifth Congress makes it even clearer how convinced AKEL was that the Cyprus issue depended on developments in Britain. "The key to resolving the Cyprus problem is first and foremost to be found in radical change in the foreign policy of Great Britain, which as an ally of the United States is bound hand and foot to its decisions [...]. Only when Britain's Labour government perceives that the well-being of the British people themselves is best served by a policy of peace, honest collaboration with the democratic regimes of Europe and the Soviet Union, the development of trade relations with them, abandonment of the politics of intervention in the internal affairs of foreign countries, liberation of the colonized peoples and the institution of collaboration as equals, not to mention the decisive socialist internal restructuring of their country, only then—we say—will the most basic problems be solved, which do not concern only Cyprus but are world problems today endangering international peace and security" (cited in AKEL 1949).

What can be seen is that to a considerable extent there is a judgement that the Cyprus problem can be solved if in the government of Britain the Labour Party pursues radical policies and the basic lever is the activation of international contacts. At the same time, it is considered that the securing of a Constitution with guidance from AKEL can genuinely promote national liberation.

The first observation that might be made is that to a significant extent change for the better is linked to international developments and contacts, with corresponding downplaying of the internal struggle and popular mobilization, which are not clearly referred to at all. The second has to do with the contradictory character of its stance vis-à-vis the Constitution: if the Right agreed on abstention, AKEL would abstain; from the moment that the Right rejected it, AKEL accepted the prospect of the Constitution. But either the Constitution is a negative development, in which case a political movement does not accept it irrespective of whether it will find political allies, or it is a favourable development and it will participate in its institutions. In every other circumstance, it will be confronted by the impasses that AKEL faced at the end of the 1940s (see below).

At the same time, the Right was apprehensive of the prospect of self-government, given the left electoral victory of the previous year. They were worried that a Leftist government might proceed with social reforms contrary to the interests of the bourgeois class (chiefly as regards taxation), and the opposition to self-government on the grounds of renouncing the strategic goal of *Enosis* on the one hand sounded more appealing to a significant section of the popular strata, and on the other safeguarded bourgeois interests.

After the AKEL Congress there were no developments worth mentioning on the part of the Ethnarchy, and AKEL duly attended the Consultative Assembly in which took place the mayors of Nicosia, Limassol, Larnaca, Famagusta and Morphou (Clerides, Servas, Sandamas, Adamantos and Nikolopoulos), two representatives of the PEO (Ziartides and Fantis), the representative of the Co-operative Central Bank (Hatzimichail), two other Greek Cypriots (Arapidiotis and Evangelides) a Maronite (Houris) and seven Turkish Cypriots, one of whom was Rauf Denktaş.[38]

The proceedings got underway on 1st November 1947 in London and a few days later the seven representatives sought the institution of a regime of self-government whereby the Greek Cypriot side would assume responsibility for more Ministries. They accordingly submitted a relevant memorandum signed by all the Greek Cypriots except Arapidiotis and Evangelides.[39] But the British[40] were not inclined to accept anything of this kind. At the same time, the Ethnarchy launched attacks

[38] It is interesting that the British continued to favour KATAK over the KTMBP, with the result that in the seven-member delegation they appointed five of the members came from KATAK and only two (Denktaş and the leader of the Association of the Turkish trade unions Hasan Sasmaz) came from the KTMBP (Kalantzopoulos 2015: 151).

[39] For the full text of the memorandum see Economides (1993: 2–3).

[40] The nuances of the Britons' dismissive response are interesting to reflect on. In December 1947, the Colonial Secretary Creech Jones proposed that the Greek Cypriot

against the Left, which it accused of accepting the introduction of a "pseudo-constitution".

On 13th May 1948, the British announced that the content of the Greek memorandum could not be accepted, and they would therefore submit new proposals. It should be noted that an important role in the elaboration of their content, apart from anxiety over the possibility of communist success, was played by the emerging Arab–Israeli conflict, which made Cyprus the last secure foothold in the area (Katsiaounis 2006: 500). So, according to the proposals for the Constitution, provision was made for a Legislative Council which would be comprised of 26 members, four of whom would be elected by the Turkish Cypriots, 18 by other Cypriots and four appointed by the Governor (Colonial Secretary, Prosecutor General, General Treasurer of the island and one Provincial Administrator). An extra-parliamentary figure would be appointed President of the Parliament and it was a matter for discussion whether he/she would have the right of a vote. The Parliament would not be permitted to discuss the status of Cyprus as a Colony. Laws related to constitutional changes, foreign policy and defence policy, the economy and minorities would require ratification from the Governor. Governmental decisions on public order or administration were the exclusive prerogative of the Governor. The Governor was also granted the power to proclaim a bill or proposal and bring it into force even if it had not been voted on (!) from the moment that he believed that it would be beneficial to public order and governance. There was also a provision for the Governor to send bills back to the Legislative Council with recommendations for amendment. Executive power would be exercised by the Governor with the assistance of an Executive Council Advisory Group composed of four Britons who would participate in the Legislature together with four elected deputies

initiative be rejected but at the same time that the right to self-government be acknowledged, and revision of the Constitution be promised with the passage of five years. But Prime Minister Attlee objected that the granting of self-government would lead to *Enosis* with a Greece in which the Communist Party would have prevailed (given that the Greek Civil War had just started, and its outcome was considered uncertain). The British side therefore counterproposed that its control should be retained over Defence and Foreign Policy and self-government be conceded for other sectors. But even this more moderate variant met with a sceptical reception from the Secretaries of State for Foreign Affairs and for Defence, who thought Cyprus was too important to be allowed to govern itself, and even Winster's outline constitution was characterized as too liberal. What was decided finally was that the process of drafting a proposed constitution should be continued, and this task was completed in May 1948 (Katsiaounis 2006: 498–499).

(three Greek Cypriots and one Turkish Cypriot) who would be appointed by the Governor. The Cypriots who would be members of the Executive Council would function as advisors in different governmental sectors such as Education, Agriculture, etc.[41]

The above point was the key bone of contention of the Greek Cypriot representatives demanding that they vindicate ministries and not to have a merely advisory presence. The Ethnarchy, for its part, was totally dismissive. On 21st May 1948, the Consultative Assembly was convened again and when the Greek Cypriot representatives ascertained that their demand for ministries to be assigned to them was not accepted, they voted against the draft Constitution[42] and withdrew, thus sealing the fate of the Consultative Assembly.[43]

Evaluating the whole process, it could be argued that by comparison with the regime that existed prior to 1931, let alone what prevailed from 1931 onwards, more political rights were being conceded to the Greek Cypriot side. In the Legislative Council, it would no longer be possible as before for a majority to be assembled by the Turkish Cypriots and the British, and the Governor would no longer have the casting vote.

But that said, the problems that were emerging were neither few nor negligible in importance. Given what other colonies had achieved, the proposed Cyprus Constitution was not comparably progressive. In the constitution of Malta, for example, ministers were members of the Legislative Council and in Ceylon the leader of the parliamentary party with majority support became Prime Minister. In both cases, the Governor could not implement plans which did not have the support of the Parliament. Essentially, although the new system was more representative, what was missing was the concept of governmental responsibility (Richter 2007: 740).

[41] For full presentation of the British proposal, see Katsiaounis (2000: 535–543).

[42] In contrast to the Greek Cypriot representatives the three Greek Cypriot-nominated right-wingers (Hadjimichalis, Arapidiotis, Evangelides) would declare agreement with the proposed plan (Katsiaounis 2006: 500).

[43] It should indeed be noted that Athens too recommended against acceptance of the British proposals and Pipinellis in a letter of his to the Greek consul in Nicosia Alexandros Kountouriotis said: "The content [...] or rather the absence of any real content—from the viewpoint of participation by the people of Cyprus in the exercise of political power—in Sir Edward Jackson's Constitution, consigns to absolute irrelevance any policy of political manoeuvring and gradualistic, as it were, campaigning, obliging us to revert to a policy of total refusal" (cited in Koumas 2013: 35).

Nevertheless, the basic structural problem was what Holland pointed out: "Not only was the Labour Government not prepared to leave Cyprus, but the fact that the British strategic stakes in both Egypt and Palestine were simultaneously under pressure meant that the imperial value of the island was rising rather than falling" (Holland 1998: 115). The implication of this reality is that in the existing conditions it would be utopian to believe that the adoption of a colonial Constitution could lead, even gradually, to abolition of the colonial regime. Another problematic point is the fact that the asymmetric distribution of power so characteristic of the relation between Governor and Legislative Council would very soon bring to the surface significant disagreements which, under popular pressure, would lead parliamentary deputies to mass resignations (Katsiaounis 2000: 527ff.). This is not a simple prediction, but an assessment of structurally different interests expressed in the two opposite sides. In the most moderate variant, the Greek Cypriots demanded self-government with a view to *Enosis* and the British government sought to improve the terms of representation. Seen objectively the gap was very wide: post-war Cyprus was not the Cyprus of the interwar period. The fact indeed that there was a section of Greek Cypriots participating in the deliberations of the Consultative Assembly served to confirm the assessment that not even this presence could overturn Britain's basic plans. That said, the Consultative Assembly showed the true magnitude of the problem that existed with the Turkish Cypriots, who were not inclined to accept any solution that would give more power to the Greek Cypriot side. In essence, the Consultative Assembly was a tactical move on the part of the British to preserve the status quo through conceding certain elements of self-government which did not, however, touch the heart of the problem.

10 AKEL After the Consultative Assembly

After the failure of the Consultative Assembly, the Right found itself in a position of advantage, not only because the policy of AKEL had failed but because it was able to use the end of the Consultative Assembly as a way to connect with Greece and strengthen the prestige of political power there, given that King Paul had also come out in favour of *Enosis*, a stance which was interpreted as opposition to the Consultative Assembly.[44] So it was that after a particularly massive demonstration on 3rd October 1948, the following resolution was approved:

> The Greek Cypriot people [...] 1. Censure with some impatience the obsequious and officious statements of the British government made under the authority of His Excellency the Governor of Cyprus to the effect that no change is intended for the sovereignty of the island given that the Cyprus issue is closed. 2. Declare that for the Greek Cypriot people and the nation as a whole the Cyprus question will be resolved through *Enosis* and only through *Enosis*, with no-one entitled to close the door on freedom, justice and political morality [...] [...] 5. Express their deepest gratitude to His Majesty King of the Greeks Paul for his paternal provision in favour of Greek Cyprus [...] 7. Address themselves respectfully towards the Government of the Motherland and ask that they continue their efforts more intensively towards achievement of *Enosis*, exhausting all available means to deliver justice to a people worthy of it. (quoted in *Historical Encyclopedia of Cyprus* 1979–1980, Vol. 8: 188)

On the part of the Communist Party strong concerns began to emerge within the leadership of AKEL regarding the correctness of the participation and the demand for self-government. The Central Committee divided in two, with some believing that AKEL was doing the right thing, others believing that a mistake had been made and others not having a clear opinion (Leventis 2002: 237).

[44] Specifically, in his statement Paul asserted on 28th July 1948: "Certainly Greece desires, and will continue to desire, the *Enosis* of Cyprus with itself and it is difficult to understand why it has not yet been achieved. The argument that *Enosis* could be contrary to British security is unfounded. If Cyprus were ceded to Greece, as the vast majority of its population wish, this would in no way preclude the maintenance of British military bases on the island. Moreover, if the matter could be settled within the framework of the United Nations, Greece would be prepared to provide Great Britain and the United States with further facilities through bases in Crete and elsewhere, with the exception—of course—of the Dodecanese, which was ceded to Greece on the condition that it remain unfortified. These bases would be in every way of benefit to Greece, and to the world, and at the same time the restoration of Greek sovereignty in Cyprus would be in line with the wishes not only of Cyprus but of Greeks everywhere" (mentioned in *Historical Encyclopedia of Cyprus* 1979–1980, Vol. 8: 179). But it should be noted on the one hand that the declaration was made two months after the end of the work of the Consultative Assembly and on the other that there is no reference to it in this connection.

Total confusion reigned at the leadership level and given the delay in the new proposals from the British side it was decided that a delegation from AKEL should meet with the general secretary of the Communist Party of Greece N. Zachariadis. This happened because it was considered crucial that they also have the opinion of the leader of the Greek communists, which should be taken seriously into account.

The general secretary of AKEL F. Ioannou and the general secretary of the Pancyprian Federation of Labour A. Ziartides participated in the delegation. In the meeting which took place in November 1948, N. Zachariadis expressed disapproval of the approach adopted by the AKEL leadership and counter-proposed development of an armed movement that would fight colonialism in collaboration with the corresponding armed struggle that was being waged in metropolitan Greece. The slogan "a free Cyprus in a free Greece" would place priority on the struggle in the existing Greek state as a basic prerequisite for the liberation of Cyprus (Ioannou 2005: 336–337). In that way, the Cyprus issue was linked to the prospect of KKE victory, with concomitant downplaying of the significance of Cyprus as an autonomous anti-imperialist focus, of special importance to Cypriots wishing to cast off the colonialist yoke.

Following the Zachariadis intervention, AKEL's position changed again, and the Consultative Assembly process was condemned. Specifically, after Ioannou's return to Cyprus—Ziartides had returned earlier—several sessions of AKEL's Central Committee were held in early 1949 where the decision was taken, with only one dissenting vote, that the Central Committee would resign and leadership of the party would be assumed, until the Sixth Congress, by a seven-member provisional central leadership (*Historical Encyclopedia of Cyprus* 1979–1980, Vol. 8: 205).

After that in its announcement of 16th March 1949, the Provisional Central Committee would make a self-critical statement to the effect that the orientation to self-government "had proved a delusion [...]. From direct life experience the Party and the people had been persuaded that nothing can save Cyprus and its people but the Island's immediate liberation from the British Imperialist yoke and *Enosis* with Greece" (cited in the *Historical Encyclopedia of Cyprus* 1979–1980, Vol. 8: 209). Similar resolutions were passed in May 1949 by the Pan-cyprian Federation of Labour at its national convention. Finally, at the party's sixth Congress (27th–28th August 1949), AKEL ratified the change of line and the adoption of *Enosis*.

Notwithstanding AKEL's vigorous self-criticism, the consequences of its participation in the Consultative Assembly were conspicuous and had a dampening effect on its political influence. To put it another way, prior to the Consultative Assembly the great advantage that AKEL had was the respect that it enjoyed from the popular and petty bourgeois strata both because of its tough stance vis-à-vis everyday problems and because of its stable unifying policy when it came to the demand for *Enosis*. On the other hand, it had to deal with the Cypriot ruling class and its political representatives, the British administration, and the Greek government. All these generated intense pressures within AKEL which was no easy task to cope with. Participation in the Consultative Assembly reflected all these contradictions and difficulties. The failure of the Consultative Assembly would reinstate the demand "*Enosis* and only *Enosis*" but in a context where they were required to continue the undeclared civil war from more unfavourable positions.

The Right, by contrast, on account of the outcome of the Consultative Assembly, the favourable (for the Right) evolution of the Greek civil war but also because of its victory in the second archiepiscopal elections, was able to step up its attacks on the Left. The 1947–1949 period saw these attacks reaching a climax at every level.

11 The Sharpening of the Undeclared Civil War After the Failure of the Consultative Assembly, up to the Municipal Elections of 1949

The Strikes of 1948

In 1948, there were three very powerful strikes[45] which influenced the political climate. They were the miners' strike which lasted from 13th January to 16th May, the strike in the asbestos mines which lasted from 2nd August to 31st August, and the building industry strike which started on 26th August and continued until 18th December.

[45] Apart from what will be said about the three workers' strikes, it is worth mentioning the fact that after the war there were farmers' mobilizations which led to the establishment of four agricultural collectives by landless farmers: in Dikomo in the Kyrenia district in 1946, in Pervolia near Larnaca in 1947, in Kouklia near Paphos in 1949 and in Avgorou, south-west of Famagusta in 1951. For a detailed presentation of this form of social struggle, see Ioannou (2006) and Alexandrou (2006).

As regards the miners, the demands submitted to the management of the Cyprus Mining Corporation (CMC), both by the Pancyprian Federation of Labour and by the Federation of Turkish Trade Unions had to do with wages,[46] improving working hours and observing the holidays of Christians and Muslims (Alecou 2012: 163). Rejection of the demands triggered, initially, a five-day strike and then a continuing strike. In the meantime, the employers had stopped the provision of milk to the miners' children and ordered expulsion from the company hospital of any patients who were not gravely ill. But the workers had to face not only the employers but also the Right in all its variants. The Cyprus Workers' Confederation came out against the strike from the outset, arguing that it was happening because the Pancyprian Federation of Labour was trying to restrict the spread of the Cyprus Workers' Confederation in the mining sector. The opposition did not remain merely verbal but assumed concrete forms. The Cyprus Workers' Confederation not only did not participate in the Pan-cyprian strike in support of the strike of the miners but began to recruit strikebreakers from the surrounding villages (Alecou 2011: 123–124). At the same time, the Church too played a strikebreaking role, on 20th March issuing an encyclical in which it enjoined the strikers to return to work and not be misled by the "godless Communists". The newspaper *Efimeris* for three months came out with the header: "MINERS! Kick out the communists who are taking advantage of you and go back to work!" (Alecou 2011: 125).

In March the strikebreakers' attempt to start work led to clashes, the police opened fire with the result that eight of those who were presents were injured. This triggered a 24-hour Pan-cyprian strike. A similar incident took place a few days later, with six injured in consequence.

The tension was soon transmitted to the centre, given that the strike was continuing in tandem with the Consultative Assembly. The Right reminded Britons that a regime of self-government where the Left would be in the majority on the one hand would be contrary to the interests of the business world and on the other would create favourable conditions for assisting the Communist forces in the Greek civil war. The *Efimeris* therefore advised the British to arrest not only the trade unionists of the Greek Federation of Labour but also all the senior cadres of the Left (Katsiaounis 2000: 414–415).

[46] Between 1946 and 1948 wages increased by 20% but inflation was in the order of 36% (Antoniou 2017: 121).

Essentially what the Cypriot Right was saying was that the basic problem was not the British but the communists. Within that context insistence on the object of "*Enosis* and only *Enosis*" acquired a new dimension to it. It did not mean unyielding struggle for an abiding claim and against acceptance of the retreat symbolized by any goal of self-government but rather communicated the anxiety of the dominant Greek Cypriot strata at the prospect of formation of a Leftist Cypriot administration in a context of self-government.

> So, *Enosis* and only *Enosis* and nothing else but *Enosis*. And until that blessed hour let England govern responsible and alone. Even with Storrs and Palmer as governors. But never 'power in the hands of the people', as Fifis and Clerides demand. We proclaim this openly and without hesitation. (*Efimeris* of 10th April 1948, quoted in Katsiaounis 2000: 416)

Finally, as far as the miners' strike is concerned, after the descent on Cyprus of CMC's American director Mudd, negotiations got under way and ended with an agreement on 16th May 1948. Among the positive aspects of the agreement are that wage increases were approved, and other demands were also satisfied (overtime, worker housing and addition of a day off) (Fantis 2006: Varnava 1989: 65). Among the negative points for the workers' movement are that CMC decided not to recognize the existing trade union there the Pancyprian Federation of Labour as representative of the workers (Antoniou 2017: 118) and around ten percent of the workers were not able to work anymore in the company (Lavender 1962: 299; The Struggles on Strike 1979: 153, 160; Varnava 1989: 66).

As regards the struggles of the asbestos miners at the Anglo-Danish-Swedish Asbestos company's mines in June 1948, the workers submitted several demands for wage rises, a new way of determining overtime payments, house repairs, recognition of the worker dispute resolution committee and reinstatement of dismissed workers. Note that the overwhelming majority of workers were members of the Pan-cyprian Federation of Labour, with very few belonging to the Cyprus Workers' Confederation. Faced with the formulation of these demands, the company management tried to sabotage the functioning of the Pancyprian Federation of Labour. In August 1948 following the election of exclusively leftist workers to the medical care committee, the company fired the trade unionists who had been elected but also 15 active workers, ordered the union secretariat to leave the area and issued a warning to

150 workers (Fantis 2006: 510–511). This action triggered the calling of a strike and clashes between asbestos miners and the police. The Cyprus Workers' Confederation for its part not only did not participate in the mobilization but also supplied the company with strikebreakers (Alecou 2011: 128).

The seriousness of these events induced the unions of the Pan-cyprian Federation of Labour to call a strike throughout Cyprus on 13th August. Finally, on 28th August the strike ended because the demands of the strikers were to be accepted by the company, including that of reinstatement of all the strikers (Fantis 2006: 523).

The building industry strike, which started on 28th August, was prompted by the fact that the collective agreement with the contractors was to expire at the end of August, with the result that demands had been formulated for wage increases, increases in employer contributions, and compensation in the event of rain or bad weather. But the great standoff was over the contractors' refusal to establish a Labour Office to be managed on the basis of equality by the Pan-cyprian Federation of Labour and the Cyprus Workers' Confederation, and by means which workers would be able to find employment in construction. The strike in question was centred on Nicosia, whereas the two previous ones had taken place in farming areas, imparting a more central character to this specific mobilization, which was perceived by all the political forces.

And so it was that on 18th August the Cyprus Workers' Confederation, together with the conservative associations and organizations in a relevant announcement would declare:

> A number of indisputable facts is revealing to all that the communist leaders, devoted BODY AND SOUL TO MOSCOW is working and will continue to work on the basis of the principle of THE SLAV INTEREST, subverting religion and undermining the Motherland [...] It has by now become evident to every person of goodwill that the strikes started by the communists aim primarily at causing confusion and chaos, poisoning relations between employer and worker, to the incalculable detriment of both, and of our entire economy. (quoted in Alecou 2011: 131)

The answer given by the general secretary of the Pan-cyprian Federation of Labour Andreas Ziartides was also characterized by a tone oriented to the central political scene:

> This 'freedom' demanded by the contractors is something they will never get. The only freedom they had, have and will have is the freedom to sack every worker who in their opinion does not meet their demands technically. It is the freedom to retain every worker who is productive qualitatively and quantitatively in their work. But that is not the freedom they want. The freedom they want is the freedom to blackmail politically. [...] Either you renounce Communism, or we have no work for you. [...] Either you vote for the right-wing Mayor, or you lose your daily bread. (quoted in Alecou 2011: 131–132)

The final phrase includes overt hints that the entire campaign, for the Right, is being conducted against the time-frame for the next municipal elections. As mentioned, after the 1946 defeat, and with the civil war continuing in Greece, the Cypriot bourgeoisie had no appetite for a second consecutive electoral defeat in Pan-cyprian elections. The more so when now the strikes were against Cypriot contractors and not against two foreign companies.

Given all this, the strike was conducted in a much tenser climate than the other two strikes of 1948: the Cyprus Workers' Confederation was finding strikebreakers, the building workers tried to obstruct them and there were skirmishes (Alecou 2011 132), and there was also the factor of Cypriot Organization X members (see below) being mobilized. Intimidating trade unionists they also accompanied strikebreakers to the building sites that were on strike.

It should not, therefore, be any surprise that a number of cases were recorded where the clashes were accompanied by deployment of dynamite, there were incidents of violent assaults, serious injuries and arson (Richter 2007: 753) to the point where the Governor himself would admit in a report he compiled in September 1948: "The general view of the events during the month includes scenes of intensified division between Left and Right. These scenes amounted to a spectacle almost recalling pictures of civil war" (quoted in Alecou 2012: 176).

Finally, the strike ended in December 1948 with acceptance of the strikers' demand that contractors should not be able to appoint workers only from among those enroled in the new unions (i.e. the Right-wing unions), following previous acceptance of the demand for a wage increase (Fantis 2006: 536–539).

These three big strikes came to be intertwined on the one hand with the important economic problems known to Cypriot society and on the other with the specific conflicts which had arisen between the Greek Cypriot political forces. The intensity of the confrontation, its augmentation of the whole range of factors such as the Church, foreign capital but also the organization X, with its origins in Greece[47] contributed to further expansion of the undeclared Cypriot civil war. This became particularly obvious if the inquiry is extended to the other forms of quasi-civil war that took place in 1948.

Other Aspects of the Undeclared Civil War

One basic aspect of the undeclared civil war was the attempt at social (in the full sense of the word) isolation of the cadres of the two sides.

For example, the Cyprus Nationalist Party enjoined Cypriots to isolate the Communists socially also, not supporting them:

> Support for the atheistic communists, either through various contributions or through employing old-line trade unionists to do various tasks is a deplorable practice and we are obliged to send this warning [...] Arm yourselves with a combative stance and with fanaticism and support nationalists everywhere and always. Our grocer, our baker, our greengrocer, our clerk, our worker, must be nationalists. There is no justification for those who continue to have old-line trade unionists in their employ [...] The New Unions are in a position to find you the workers you need. (quote in Alecou 2011: 152)

The Left issued invitations to similar practices. In a relevant article F. Ioannou in September 1948 would argue:

> Turn the sacking of one of our people by the right into immediate sacking of one of their people by the left [...] Buy only from our grocer, go only to our barber, to our shop [...]. (quoted in Protopapas 2012: 438)

Another parameter which exacerbated the already disturbed climate was the arrival in the island of the far-right paramilitary grouping X, which

[47] The Organization X was a far-right paramilitary grouping operating in Greece and targeting the action and the members of the Greek Communist Party. It was led by the Cypriot colonel G. Grivas who from 1955 onwards was leader of EOKA (*Ethniki Organosi Kyprion Agoniston*: National Organization of Cypriot Fighters), which waged armed struggle (1955–1958) with a view to unification with Greece.

started to become perceptible in the run-up to the archiepiscopal elections of 1947, though it did not have the institutional status it enjoyed in Greece. The "Chites" tried to frighten their opponents, sending them threatening letters and in some cases, wearing masks, they entered the houses of leftists for the purpose of terrifying them (Alecou 2018: 146). Their activity would continue, particularly during the three big workers' strikes, to the degree that the conservative *Ethnos* newspaper of Nicosia would rejoice that:

> The peaceable and law-abiding people of the capital expresses its deep gratitude to the brave lads who protect the city and thwart the satanic, criminal plans of the communists. The "chites" are their avenging sentries and they panic at the sight of them [...]. (cited in Alecou 2011: 110)

What is most impressive is that the "chites" had reached the point of replacing the police in their duties: they proceeded to arrest individuals they considered suspect for participation in disturbances, and they then handed them over to the police (Alecou 2011: 110).

Of course, the "chites" were able only to intimidate but not suppress such a massive, by the measures of this island, communist movement. For something like that it would be necessary for the colonial administration to intervene, and some right-wing circles were demanding that they do so. The *Efimeris* newspaper of 3rd April 1948 said that all the communists should be locked in concentration camps "[...] as a democratic measure for the security of the many through restrictions on the dangerous few" (quoted in Alecou 2011: 141). Almost simultaneously, on learning that Britain was removing from public services employees who were communists, the Cypriot right asked that the same be done in Cyprus (Katsiaounis 2000: 408; 487).

So, a whole range of pressures came to be exerted primarily against educators for obedience to the summonses of right-wing ideology through adoption of resolutions in support of the Greek King and more general compliance with propagation of the Helleno-Christian civilization. One of the effects was that on 19th July 1948 three well-known Leftist teachers lost their jobs.[48] Anti-communism in education would

[48] From the spring of 1948 reports began to be compiled supporting proscription of AKEL or at least a curbing of its activities. In September of the same year Governor Winster asked the Secretary of State to increase the size of the police force and appoint

not stop there but would be extended to students. On 24th July 1948 the *Efimeris* newspaper wrote:

> We do not think that we need to prove that the authorities should unhesitatingly introduce separation everywhere, and should exclude communist students from school. (cited in Katsiaounis 2000: 484)

Even sports clubs sought to exclude leftists. Priests received orders do not perform sanctifications at clubs in which leftists participated, such as the Kinyras in Paphos, the Pezoporikos in Larnaca, the EPA in Larnaca and the Olympiakos. Olympiakos in particular not only expelled its leftist members but from a certain point on was clearly under the influence of the Cypriot Chites (Katsiaounis 2000: 407).[49] These developments were significantly affected by the intervention of the Greek SEGAS (*Syndesmos Ellinikon kai Athlitikon Somateion*—Hellenic Amateur Athletic Association), which had the Cypriot associations under its supervision. In the spring of 1948, it sought[50] a public declaration from the clubs in favour of "patriotic views" and by extension refusal to accept the participation of leftist sportspeople and supporters. There was immediate reaction from the left:

an expert to assist in government action against AKEL. In 1949 circulation of the pro-AKEL newspaper *Anexartitos* was suspended for three months, and its editor jailed, and in the summer of the same year the subject of proscription of AKEL came up again for discussion (Kalantzopoulos 2015: 213–214). The same anti-communist scenario was activated in the US. The latter drew the attention of the British to the need to prevent any spread of the influence of AKEL. At the same time, US, given the opposition of their British allies to cession of the island to Greece, they adopted the position of preserving the *status quo,* on the one hand discouraging Greece on the other maintaining the stance of disapproval towards Turkish demands (Foreign Relations of the United States 1949: 166).

[49] It is characteristic that the chairman of Olympiakos E. Zemenides was at the same time head of the Cypriot Chites (Alecou 2018: 148).

[50] Overall, in the first postwar years the stance of the official Greek state was particularly hostile towards the Cypriot left. This initially had to do with the announced contact between the Greek diplomatic representation and personages of the Cypriot right. But it subseqhently acquired a symbolic dimension also. In 1948 the Greek Consul A. Kountouriotis excluded the organizations and representatives of the Left from the customary 25th March function for the Greek Revolution of 1821. The later Consul A. Liatis was acting in the same spirit when at the beginning of 1949 he refused to meet the mayor of Nicosia I. Clerides and the municipal councillors because of their collaboration with AKEL and the Greek communists (Alecou 2012: 195).

> Dozens of athletes from all cities refuse to participate in the Pancyprian track events. In their declaration they strongly condemn the outragous party-political interference of right-wing elements in sport [...]. (*Dimokratis* 3/1/48 quoted in Alecou 2011: 153)

Corresponding developments developed within APOEL (Athlitikos Podosfairikos Omilos Ellinon Lefkosias—Athletic Football Club of Greeks of Nicosia) prompted by a telegram of 23rd May 1948 from the club's board of directors to SEGAS. In the telegram, *inter alia*, APOEL expressed the wish "that the nationally murderous revolt be brought to an end". The result was that the leftist supporters and sportspeople concluded that the club was acquiring a party-political identity, separated their position and were expelled from APOEL.

The outcome of this was that in the course of 1948, new associations would begin to be established by leftists: in March New Salamina was founded in Famagusta, in April Alki in Larnaca, in May Orfeas and in June Omonoia in Nicosia (Alecou 2011: 154).

The 1949 Municipal Elections

The battle for political hegemony was to be decided in the course of 1949 when municipal elections were held but the Greek civil war was also concluded. The evident downturn of the Cypriot left in the former on conjunction with the disappointment brought by the defeat of the Greek communist party to the ranks of the Greek Cypriot left would have an inhibiting effect on the political influence of the Left, not only in this conjuncture but for the following decades. Notwithstanding its considerable political and electoral weight, the Cypriot left was forced to follow in the wake of events, failing, in contrast to the situation in the early 1940s, in articulating a hegemonic strategy within the Cypriot social formation.

In other words, the Right had managed to emerge as hegemonic force in the population precisely because it projected the anti-colonial slogan "*Enosis* and only *Enosis*". The contradictions and hesitations of AKEL about the Consultative Assembly rendered it vulnerable to criticisms that it did not desire *Enosis* with the Motherland, that it was deeply influenced by the "Slavocommunist" ideology of the KKE and that its politics were what was responsible for the movement away from the goal of *Enosis*. At the same time, AKEL's relations with I. Clerides, who had been supported for the mayoralty of Nicosia in 1946 was plagued with tension that ultimately led to a rift.[51] The reasons are to be sought in AKEL's intense involvement in the question of the Greek civil war, AKEL's desire that EAS (National Liberation Coalition) has a more dynamic presence both on social questions and on the question of self-government, and the *Eleftheros Typos* newspaper, representing the views of Clerides, come under the jurisdiction of EAS. So, it may be seen that at a time when the Right was developing an alliance with the church and succeeding in constructing unity politically and ideologically, the communist left was losing its key underpinnings (Protopapas 2012: 445–446). Among the negative factors for AKEL, there must be included the problem of leadership faced by the party due to the purging of the Central Committee but also due to the activity of the consulates of Greece and the US (Protopapas 2012: 452).

The municipal elections were conducted in a climate of harsh confrontation, with mobiliaztion, immediate and indirect, both of local right-wing political and religious personnel and the British administration, not to mention the Greek state, flanking the conservative candidates. But this was not enough for the Right to win the elections. From as early as 1948 amendment law 34 had been adopted which increased the period one had to be resident in a municipality from 12 to 24 months to have the right to vote. This meant that several workers who moved frequently because of their working conditions were not able to vote. At the same time, it was provided that the compilation of the electoral rolls would be undertaken by regional governors appointed by the British (Alecou 2012: 222). In the midst of all this, the publication of the AKEL newspaper *Dimocratis* was suspended for three months and AKEL was constrained to respond with publication of the *Neos Dimocratis* (Alecou 2012: 222).

Above and beyond that, the climate of polarization was intense, the Greek consul himself, Alexis Liapis, issued statements in support of right-wing candidates and at the celebrations for 25th March Archbishop Makarios II would declare:

[51] Typically, because Clerides realized that he had no chance of being elected without the support of AKEL, he called upon the people to vote against T. Dervis, candidate for the Right in the Municipality of Nicosia, without generalizing that negative vote to extend to the other municipalities (Alecou 2012: 221).

> But bearing in mind [...] what our forefathers did for freedom and seeing how much evil bad Greeks, having become instruments of age-old enemies, have accumulated against the motherland, it is our duty to condemn, in the strongest terms, the genocidal revolt[52] [...]. (quoted in *Historical Encyclopedia of Cyprus* 1979–1980, Vol. 8: 190)

On 30th April 1948, a joint communiqué was issued by the nationalist associations of Larnaca:

> The [...] enemy in the struggle against our Nation has as its instruments the fifth-column communist murderers of Greece [...] Here in Cyprus too they have linked their fate to the communist traitors of Greece. (quoted in Alecou 2011: 171)

Given that context, the general climate for conducting the elections (which were held on 22nd May 1949) was stamped with features of polarization, culminating in fighting that left two dead. In the words of a report in the *Dimokratis* newspaper of AKEL:

> Last Sunday's municipal elections in the six cities of Cyprus took place in an electrified atmosphere, with repeated incidents and clashes being reported at regular intervals from everywhere [...] Every three minutes there were urgent telephone calls to various police stations in the capital announcing Homeric battles between members and supporters of the two opposing combinations. [...] Over one hundred different incidents and clashes just in Nicosia from the Saturday night, eve of the elections, to the time of completion of the voting. Hundreds of people were detained by the police and transported in custody to the police stations of Nicosia and the central prisons. Dozens of injured people were taken for treatment in hospital, many quite seriously injured. (quoted in Alecou 2011: 171–172)

But the side of the right too, via the *Ethnos* newspaper, did not present a different picture:

> Many large automobiles of the communists, full of young louts and hangers-on of AKEL from different villages, armed with clubs, stones and bottles, roamed the city [...] and launched attacks against every nationalist

[52] He means the Greek civil war.

element. (quoted in *Historical Encyclopedia of Cyprus* 1979–1980, Vol. 8: 232)

In any case, the result was that the Right won again in Nicosia and scored a triumph in Paphos and Kyrenia. The Left managed to keep Limassol, Larnaca and Famagusta. Overall, in the urban centres the Right took 55.1% and the Left was limited to 44.9%. The Right won all the big farming municipalities (Lefkoniko, Kythraia, Poli, Lapitho and Karava) with one exception (Morfou). In the total of the six big farming municipalities the Right won 56.5% and the Left 43.5%. What should be noted is that apart from the symbolic fact of winning back Nicosia, where from the 55% that the Left slate of Clerides had taken in 1946, the corresponding list of A. Ziartides dropped to 39%, the Right's wins in the provinces but also in the other urban centres were landslides, whereas those of the Left were near marginal (Protopapas 2006: 85–87).

After the downturn in its influence in the 1949 elections AKEL would offer a particularly apposite interpretation of this result, highlighting the following external factors: (a) the outbreak of the Cold War, with the consequences it had for an island with the special military significance of Cyprus and located in the sphere of influence of the second most powerful Western country, (b) the effect of the Greek civil war in the context of the increasingly evident defeat of the KKE, and (c) the role of the Church of Cyprus, "transformed into pre-electoral propagandist of the Right". As for the mistakes that AKEL itself had committed, there is mention of: (a) the mistake of "self-government" because in that way "[...] we managed to alienate ourselves from a section of the middle-class patriotic elements which previously had believed in and had followed political guidance from the party, (b) the failure of the National Liberation Coalition (EAS) as a political organization: in the two years of its life EAS did not have to show even one spirited and combative national struggle [...], (c) [...] the resignation of the party's Central Committee and the decision in favour of purging the Party and the party leadership of all the opportunistic elements" (AKEL 1949).

Truly, the conjuncture of 1949 did not have much in common with that of 1946. That was not as much for the reasons mentioned by AKEL (the growth of anti-communism internationally, the Church of Cyprus had previously played a more moderate role, the Greek left was not on the verge of military collapse) as for reasons it disregards: on the one hand was the overall pressure to which AKEL was subjected by the British, the Greek Cypriot Right, the Church, the Greek government, but on the other there was the absence of an alternative plan for the eventuality that the Consultative Assembly should end, as it did, in failure. To put it differently, the issue with the Consultative Assembly was that AKEL lost the moral advantage it had acquired. The great strengthening in the influence of the Communist Party was linked on the one hand to its trade union activity and on the other to its stance about Enosis. The complicity of personages of the Right with the authoritarian regime that prevailed after the 1931 revolt rendered them untrustworthy on the national question. In that sense AKEL was right when it asked the Right not to participate in the colonialist administrative mechanism because then there could not be a political front when one side was condemning the British and the other was operating within the colonial institutions. But the response to the right-wing's insistence that one should not resign could not be participation in the Consultative Assembly. The response to a mistaken stance should not be a stance that is even more mistaken. The result was that after AKEL opted for its chosen reaction, the Right and the ethnarchy acquired legitimation in presenting themselves as the unwavering defenders of *Enosis*, in contrast to the "traitorous" and "pro-Soviet" AKEL.

12 The *Enosis* Issue from the End of the Consultative Assembly to the 1950 Referendum

In July 1948 by the resolution of the Holy Synod of the Church of Cyprus, the Ethnarchic Council was formed to undertake direction of the struggle on the national question. AKEL and every Leftist would be excluded from the Council, which would be comprised of figures such as old politicians, representatives of (right-wing) organizations, right-wing mayors, etc. An Ethnarchy Bureau was also established consisting of the Archbishop, as President, and the metropolitans of Kition Makarios and Kyrenia Kyprianos, together with Polykaropos Ioannides and Xenofontas Koubaridis (Konstantinidis 2011: 131–132).

But the basic issue is that irrespective of the composition of the Ethnarchy Bureau the demand for self-government-*Enosis* immediately began to acquire a very considerable dynamic and arouse unease in colonialist circles. On 9th October in the Greek newspaper *Vima* reprinted an article from the *Times* which said: "At the basis of the movement in support of *Enosis* is the Greek Orthodox Church, whose influence is very great [...] *Enosis*, which is still essentially an expression of spiritual desire, could become a seriously divisive movement [...]". Even more interesting is the continuation of the article where the argument is pursued that in its tactics against the movement for *Enosis* the British government should not ignore the Turkish Cypriot minority.

The Turkish Cypriot minority began to mobilize more actively within this context against the prospect of *Enosis*. They were given encouragement by the British side with creation, immediately after the Consultative Assembly, in June 1948, of a Committee on Turkish Affairs, so that there would be a counterweight to the Greek demand for *Enosis*, with at the same time Turkey openly expressing interest in Cyprus (Katsiaounis 2001: 160). For this reason, in contrast to the composition of the Turkish Cypriot delegation in the Consultative Assembly, the eight-member committee now included leading nationalists.[53] In 1948 in the main towns of Cyprus rallies and demonstrations were accordingly held to express the opposition of Turkish Cypriots to *Enosis*. In one of the meetings in Nicosia, held on 28th November 1948, the decision was taken to send a telegram to the President and Prime Minister of Turkey with the statement that: "Fifteen thousand Turkish Cypriots resolved unanimously to reject the Greek demand for annexation of Cyprus by Greece and for autonomy. They believe that annexation and autonomy would have the consequence of disappearance of the Turkish community" (quoted in Terlexis 1971: 64).

AKEL for its part at its Sixth Congress (August 1949) would (again) decide to seek joint action with the Right. On 11th September 1949, the 2nd Pancyprian Congress of EAS invited the Ethnarchy to mobilize jointly for the purpose of submitting a common memorandum to the United Nations, sending a delegation abroad and organizing rallies throughout Cyprus. The right-wing press characterized these proposals as "unprecedently impudent" and the Ethnarchy Bureau through its secretary X. Koubaridis added that there cannot be any collaboration with

[53] A few months after the establishment of the committee in question (January 1949) the British administration revealed its intention to satisfy long-standing demands of the Turkish Cypriots such as family law, Shericourts, Evkaf, education and elections. There was also a revival of the position of Mufti as religious, but not political, leader, with Ankara given the task of appointing the individual to fill the role (Nevzat 2010: 167).

organizations and people who on the one hand have sided with the enemies of the Greek nation and on the other have betrayed the struggle of the Cypriot people for *Enosis* (Protopapas 2012: 486).

After the refusal from the conservative forces, AKEL chose 4th December as the day for launching a petition in support of *Enosis*. At this, seeing the danger of being outflanked by the AKEL initiative, the Archiepiscopate on 2nd December 1949 announced that it was calling for a referendum to promote *Enosis* on 15th January 1950.

The Archiepiscopate's announcement imposed pressure on AKEL and obliged it on 3rd December to accept the holding of a referendum by the Ethnarchy on 3rd December, and the relevant proclamation by EAS was along the same lines.

It was becoming obvious that after its self-criticism for the mistaken choice about the Consultative Assembly AKEL was moving proactively when it sought the conducting of a referendum. But the point now was not who was taking the initiative but who was able to impose a political orientation. And that, after AKEL's participation in the Consultative Assembly and after the defeat of the KKE, was the Church. Participation in the Ethnarchy's referendum signified recognition of the unfavourable balance of forces.

In any case, despite the pressures from the Greek Cypriots, the British not only refused to conduct the referendum themselves but also initiated a series of behind-the-scenes moves to induce the government in Athens to condemn the actions of the Ethnarcy. On 15th December 1949, the Prime Minister Alexandros Diomedes declared "[...] Bearing in mind the sensitivity of today's situation and the need to keep the frank collaboration between the Great Allies undisturbed [...] the Greek government is obliged to bring it to everyone's attention that under present conditions further continuation of the controversy in public opinion over Cyprus does not move the issue forward but on the contrary risks being a cause of damage to the international position of our country" (quoted in Linardatos 1977, Vol. I: 50–51).

It is clear from this declaration that the plans of the Greek Cypriots and those of the government in Athens were in a different phase altogether. Only a few months before, Greece had emerged from a civil war which had come close to ending the reign of the bourgeoisie. An important role in this development had been played by the British and this was not something that Athens could quickly forget. In Cyprus, on the contrary, the situation was entirely different. The Cypriots understood that the colonial system was on its last legs, and this was why all were united, conservatives and communists, around the demand for *Enosis*. That is why when these declarations in Cyprus became known there was displeasure in Cyprus but satisfaction in London.

As might be expected, the Turkish Cypriots came out against the referendum. The Kucuk-supporting newspaper *Halkin Sesi* asked the authorities to ban it and on 15th December a Turkish Cypriot rally was organized where the demand was raised for Cyprus to return to Turkey in the event of the British abandoning it (Katsis 2005: 114–115). At the same time, in various declarations the Turkish Foreign Minister Nehmettin Sadak argued that a possible departure of the British should lead to discussions with Turkey (Ktoris 2013: 374–376).

Nevertheless, despite the objections from Britain, Turkey, from the Turkish Cypriots and also from Greece, on 15th January 1950 the referendum was held in Cyprus in a festive atmosphere: Greek flags waved, bells rang merrily and people went to the churches to vote.[54] The British administration had forbidden its employees to take part, but many teachers and civil servants defied the ban and participated in the process. Finally, of the 224,757 Greek Cypriots who had the right to vote, 215,108 (95.7%) voted in favour of *Enosis*. It is interesting that many Armenians voted in favour of *Enosis*. It is estimated that the 4.3% of Greek Cypriots who abstained were civil servants and their relatives (Richter 2011: 39).[55]

13 Brief Presentation of the Developments After the Referendum

Following the overwhelming approval in the referendum of the demand for self-government, a committee comprised of personages of the Right

[54] To be precise, to sign the relevant registers.

[55] A whole mythology has been constructed around the participation of the Turkish Cypriots. As Richter puts it "Of course the overwhelming majority of Turkish Cypriots abstained from the referendum but from Strovolos, Doli and Potamia there are reports that around 800 Turkish Cypriots also voted in favour of *Enosis*" (Richter 2011: 39). Richter's source is Servas, who cites this specific number (Servas 1980: 151). Even Denktash in an interview with Ktoris admitted there could have been up to 200 Turkish Cypriot signatures. But Ktoris scrupulous study of the registers with the signatures found only 42 Turkish Cypriot signatures. They were either Greek Cypriots who had converted to Islam or Turkish Cypriots who did not have links with their compatriots (Ktoris 2013: 378–380).

and the Church went to Athens to submit the registers with the signatures. The Greek government was in a difficult position because if they were accepted this would be like legitimation of the referendum. Finally, after a period of two months the registers were accepted, but by the President of the Parliament and not by the King or the Prime Minister. The Greek Cypriot delegation subsequently travelled to London also but without gaining a reception from the British Government.

The beginning of the 1950s would be marked by demonstrations on the Cyprus question in Greece and Cyprus, spearheaded by pressure to have the question put up for discussion at the United Nations General Assembly. But the Greek government, anxious about the British reaction, was evidently most unwilling to support this. And Turkey simply declared "present" during the procedures, maintaining that there was no need for change in the legal status of Cyprus. Finally, after much vacillation, there was a first report on the question, not to the General Assembly but to the Trusteeship Council. What is of significance is that for the first time the question was aired, so it was seen as an existent problem, which Greece was making public under pressure from the mobilizations of the Greek Cypriots and the Greeks.

In 1952 the Greek Cypriot side continued to pressure Athens to file an appeal to the UN. But Athens remained hesitant, though Greek Cypriot pressures with the passage of time were intensifying. At the end of 1953, when the British side emphasized to the Greek Prime Minister Papagos that there was no Cyprus question, the Greek government concluded that it had to break with the routine of Greek-British dialogue. It therefore announced that if a solution was not found by 22nd August, Athens would appeal to the UN. The US, for its part, seeing that there was a possibility of Greek-British relations being disrupted, intervened and requested that Greece not appeal, promising American mediation. It was the first time that the US became directly involved in the Cyprus issue, functioning as the dominant imperialist power.

And the Greek Cypriots stepped up the pressure. They thought that the rise of Nasser in Egypt showed that violence is indispensable if one is to be rid of a repressive regime. This was a qualitative shift because for the first time there was now a hint of the possibility of going over to armed struggle. The British sought to manoeuvre, proposing a new Constitution, but this was rejected by the Greek Cypriots, who perceived it as being less democratic even than the Consultative Assembly. Faced with the impending debate at the UN, the British administration decided to harden its stance, instituting a range of prohibitions whose basic axis was the transformation into a penal offence any action aimed at changing sovereignty on the island. These practices generated even greater reactions in Cyprus, with the result that Papagos was obliged not to back down about the appeal.

Submission of the appeal secured a majority, in which however no powerful Western country participated. The US in its pronouncements evoked the danger that the Eastern countries would profit from this controversy. Throughout this period the key American concern was that two, possibly three, NATO countries, might come into conflict over it. Britain was a powerful Western country, so it was Greece that was called on to make concessions. As far as the appeal is concerned, the stance of the USA is considered particularly unpropitious for its progress. The result was that in a relevant question Archbishop Makarios III, who from 1950 succeeded Makarios II, replied that if the appeal was rejected, the Ethnarchy would not be able to restrain the Greek Cypriots from resorting to violent measures.

Finally in the debate that took place in the UN the overwhelming majority—including Greece (only the Eastern countries abstained) declared in favour of the position that there was no point, for the moment, in the question being discussed further. The Greek government regarded it as something positive that for the first time the Cyprus question was being aired in the UN. Nevertheless, in many Greek towns there were fierce clashes, and the prevailing mood was one of condemnation of the USA, but also censure of the moves at the governmental level.

On the Greek Cypriot side, it was being ascertained those discussions within the UN were futile and Makarios in his statements indicated that the Greek Cypriots could no longer rely exclusively on the UN, where the power balance was given and static, and the struggle was going to intensify. It was obvious that the conditions were being created for EOKA's armed struggle.

14 Conclusion

The outbreak of the Second World War led to an upgrading of the position of Cyprus in British calculations, given the hostilities that were unfolding in North Africa and the Middle East. This generated the need for the construction of significant infrastructures to reinforce the island's defences, and it was now obvious that the authoritarian type of government of the Palmerocracy period had to liberalize.

Within this context, the activation of the Communist Party of Cyprus, metamorphosed into AKEL, was stepped up. The needs of the British for the construction of large-scale defence infrastructures would lead, under pressure from AKEL, to the enactment of significant concessions to the working class and in a second year in the direction of more general economic and political concessions, with the result that in 1943 municipal elections were once again permitted. This development was made by the need for a consensus between Cypriots and the British. Significantly, in the municipal elections of 1943 AKEL emerged as particularly strengthened and in those of 1946 the party achieved the status of being the strongest political force on the island. An active factor in this outcome was the change in AKEL's line on the subject of *Enosis*. The reasons for the change also have to do with the occupation of Greece but also with Germany's attack on the USSR.

AKEL's rise to influence, in conjunction with adoption of the demand for *Enosis*, exerted pressure on the conservative political milieu, let alone with the segment of the latter that had been linked with the Palmerocracy. The Greek Cypriot Right accordingly attempted to force an alliance with the Church, an alliance which would be erected on terrain of the Greek Civil War's aftermath. This fact would operate refractively on the Cypriot social formation, contributing to the creation of two not just rival but indeed enemy factions. Given this situation, AKEL's endeavours to ensure that there would be a common front of the Greek Cypriot forces to demand *Enosis* would fall by the wayside. AKEL's dynamic, together with the outbreak of the Greek Civil War would generate an existential anxiety in the Greek Cypriot ruling class. Step by step the Greek Cypriot Right moved from embarrassed rejection of collaboration with AKEL for *Enosis* to anti-communism and from there to projection of AKEL and not the British as the key political opponent. AKEL for its part was in a difficult situation given that it was obliged simultaneously to wage a twofold anti-British struggle: both for dissolution of the colonialist regime and for the victory of the Democratic Army in Greece. On both of those levels, the Greek Cypriot conservative faction intervened, forging alliances with the British to neutralize AKEL.

With their decision to convene the Consultative Assembly the British confirmed the orientation of maintaining their rule in Cyprus. This did not occur without vacillations given that immediately after the war two viewpoints had emerged within the British Establishment. According to one of them, Cyprus was no longer useful for the achievement of any strategic objective, and given the favourable response there had been to the granting of independence to India and Burma, the conclusion was that the island should be ceded to Greece. The other view, which ultimately prevailed, was that on the one hand Cyprus was now the only British territory in the wider geographical region and on the other that a possible victory of the communist forces in Greece could contribute to this sensitive area passing under the influence of the USSR.

The Consultative Assembly of 1947 was represented by the British side as part of an endeavour for Cyprus to acquire a more progressive Constitution. But from the outset AKEL and the Ethnarchy declared that they could not accept any settlement that did not provide for *Enosis* as the final solution to the issue. The British side rejected any such thought and the Turkish Cypriots in a relevant resolution of their own adopted a similar orientation. This stance of the British led to the Ethnarchy abstaining from the Consultative Assembly, unlike AKEL and certain other Greek Cypriot personages. Throughout the proceedings of Consultative Assembly, the Greek Cypriot side demanded self-government with parallel assumption of further ministries.

The problem AKEL had to face was not only that the British were not inclined to accept self-government but also that the Ethnarchy denounced the Left for accepting a "pseudo-constitution" which compromised the strategic objective of *Enosis*. The Right's refusal to accept a regime of self-government did not mean only refusal to compromise with something that did not make specific provisions for *Enosis*. It meant also that in the context of self-government there was a serious probability of it being in opposition. The British for their part were finally proposing a very moderate plan which in essence reserved for the Greek Cypriots a role more consultative than invested with decision-making powers. Of course, compared with the situation prevailing prior to 1931, let alone the years following the revolt, more political rights were being ceded to the Greek Cypriots, and the possibility of forming a majority out of the support of Britons and Turkish Cypriots was being done away with. Nevertheless, there were a range of issues that were not easy to be wished away. Times had changed, colonial regimes were crumbling and the demand for self-determination was being generalized. Given their recruitment into the war on the side of the Allies, the Greek Cypriot Leftists participating in the Consultative Assembly were expecting some recompense, particularly when other colonies had been granted more progressive constitutions. The problem in Cyprus had to do with the fact that from the moment that British strategic interests were under pressure in Egypt and the Middle East it was difficult for Britain to withdraw from Cyprus, which is why there was the proposal for a democratic Constitution and not the *Enosis* with Greece. But at the same time, the Turkish Cypriots did not want either self-government or *Enosis*, or any solution that would upgrade the position of the Greek Cypriots. So, there could be no convergence between the interests of the three sides and the Consultative Assembly ended in failure.

But of all the sides the worst injured was AKEL, which was clearly incapable of pursuing a stable strategic line. Its efforts for self-government failed, it came under fire from the Church and in the end turned to the Greek Communist Party to see what should be done. Zachariadis regarded the Cypriot issue as of little importance and a diversion from the struggle of the Greek Democratic Army, whose victory would establish the conditions for *Enosis* with Greece, and finally AKEL was induced to perform self-criticism for its participation in the Consultative Assembly. The outcome of all this was creation of a deficit of trust in AKEL, which appeared not to be able to steer a stable course on the national issue. The Ethnarchy came out strengthened and was easily able to take the initiative. Excluding AKEL it established the Ethnarchy Council, which undertook leadership of the struggle. Note that the primacy of the Ethnarchy was also upheld by the fact that although in the 1946 municipal elections the Left had emerged as the strongest protagonist, in the 1949 elections it would see considerable contraction of its influence, precisely because of its chopping and changing about Enosis but also because of the impact of the Left's defeat in Greece. Of course, for things to get to this point a significant role was played by the rallying of the bourgeois forces, a phenomenon clearly visible throughout the 1948 strikes.

The changes of tack around the subject of Enosis would engender a variety of responses on the side of the Turkish Cypriots also. In the first phase, political formations were established through bridging, at least for a time, the old divisions between traditionalists and kemalists[56] and founding independent Turkish Cypriot trade unions. Through these

[56] The split in KATAK is more attributable to the remnants of old differences than to the development of separate strategies for facing the new realities. In any case, examining the orientations adopted by KATAK and the KTMBP one sees differentiations only on

initiatives, an effort was made both to wage a fight at the centre against the Greek Cypriot activities for *Enosis* and to give autonomous expression to the needs of Turkish Cypriot workers and farmers. In a second phase, these organizations were led to conduct rallies and demonstrations against *Enosis*, with diplomatic assistance being canvassed from the official Turkish state.

The Ethnarchy Council for its part decided to proceed with a referendum on the issue of self-determination. The Greek government's response was lukewarm. After all it was only a few months after the win in the civil with the help of the British, and the British indeed announced that they would not recognize the result of any such referendum. AKEL invited the Greek Cypriots to participate in the Ethnarchy's referendum. They were unable to propose any autonomous political activity, in consequence of the defeat of the Cypriot Left, irrespective of the fact that the idea of the Referendum had originated with them.

The outcome of the Referendum would lead the Cyprus question into a new historical phase. It would very soon become an issue of international politics, implicating not only the immediately interested parties (Britain, Greece and Turkey) but also the USA and the USSR, behind whom their respective allies were assembled. The confrontations between all the parties involved would also take place within the framework of the UN, reproducing the correlations and the priorities of the Cold War period. A new era began that would culminate in the creation of the independent state of Cyprus but also the new contradictions that the formation of the latter would bring to light.

References

AKEL (Progressive Party of Working People). 1949. AKEL Central Committee Action Report, September 1947–May 1949. Contemporary Social History Archives (ASKI), Greek Communist Party archive 371. File=20/21/21 (in Greek).

AKEL. 1952. *The Road Towards Freedom - For a Minimum AKEL Program for Constructing the United Liberation Front of Struggle* (in Greek).

Alecou, A. 2011. *Political Developments in Cyprus, 1945–1955*. Doctoral thesis, Panteion University (in Greek).

tactics. The dominant strategy is the same for both parties: eradicate the prospect of *Enosis*.

Alecou, A. 2012. *1948. The Greek Civil War and Cyprus.* Nicosia: Power Publishing (in Greek).

Alecou, A. 2018. Imported Nationalism: The Appearance and Evolution of X' Organization in Cyprus. In *Cypriot Nationalisms in Context. History, Identity and Politics*, ed. T. Kyritsi and N. Christofis, 135–153. London: Palgrave.

Alexander, G. 1979. British Policy on the Question of Enosis. *Kupriakai Spoudai*, mc: 79–94.

Alexandrou, I. 2006. The Revolt of the 18 of the Farmers' Union of Cyprus. In *First Scientific Symposium of Pissouri, History, Society, Politics and Communications Media*, ed. E. Antoniadis, 121–129. Nicosia: Epiphani Editions (in Greek).

Antoniou, A. 2014. December in Cyprus: Perception and Political Management of the Facts by AKEL. Intervention at the Congress "From Liberation to the December Events: A Rift in the Present-Day History of Greece", 1–8 (in Greek).

Antoniou, A. 2017. Economics and Politics: The Joint Strike of the Cyprus Mines Corporation Miners. In *The Crucial Decades of the 1940s and 1950s: Intercommunal and Intracommunal Relations in Cyprus*, 107–136. Nicosia: Prometheus Research Institute (in Greek).

Arslan, H. 2012. Turki-Cypriot Nationalist Drive Toward State-Building: Politics, Violence and Political Economy. In *Beyond a Divided Cyprus*, ed. N. Trimikliniotis and U. Bozkurt, 120–134. London Palgrave.

Asmussen, J. 2006. 'Dark-Skinned Cypriots Will Not Be Accepted!' Cypriots in the British Army. In *Britain in Cyprus: Colonialism and Post-Colonialism 1878–2006*, ed. H. Faustmann and N. Peristianis, 167–186. Mannheim: Bibliopolis.

Chrysanthou, C. 2013. The Leadership of the Left 1920–1940. In *The Cypriot Left in the First Period of British Colonial Rule: Emergence, Organization, Development, Appearance*, G. Georgis and Yiannos Katsourides, 59–74. Athens: Taxideftis (in Greek).

Drousiotis, M. 1998. *EOKA. The Dark Side.* Athens: Stachi (in Greek).

Economides, C. 1993. *Demythologized History of the Cyprus Issue in the Last 50 Years.* Nicosia: Economides Publishing House (in Greek).

Fantis, A. 2006. *The Cypriot Trade Union Movement in the Years of British Rule (1870–1960)*, vol. II. Nicosia (in Greek).

Foreign Relations of the United States. 1949. Conference at Istanbul Turkey, of American Chiefs of Mission in the Near East, November 26–29, 1949. https://history.state.gov/historicaldocuments/frus1949v06/d71. Accessed on 10 September 2020.

Gennaris, K. 2000. *From the East.* Athens: Kastaniotis (in Greek).

Graikos, K. 1991. *Cypriot History.* Nicosia (in Greek).

Historical Encyclopedia of Cyprus. 1979–1980. Ed. P. Papadimitris. Nicosia (in Greek).

History of the Cyprus Communist party-AKEL (Progressive Party of Working People), vol. I, 1926–1941. 1981. Unpublished document (in Greek).

Holland, R. 1998. *Britain and the Revolt in Cyprus*. Oxford: Oxford University Press.

Ioannou, F. 2004. The Stance of AKEL: Self-government-*Enosis*. In *Fifis Ioannou, the Left and the Cyprus Question*, ed. Nikos Peristanis, 223–234. Nicosia: Intercollege Mass Media Institute (in Greek).

Ioannou, F. 2005. *This Is the Way the Cyprus Issue Started. Following the Footsteps of a Decade (1940-1950). Relations Between AKEL and the KKE in the Civil War Years*. Athens: Filistor-Paralos (in Greek).

Ioannou, G. 2006. Agricultural Collectives in Cyprus-Focusing on a Hybrid of the Late Colonial Period. *Yearbook of the Scientific Research Centre*, XXXII: 449–476 (in Greek).

Kalantzopoulos, D. 2015. *Competing Political Spaces in Colonial Cyprus, 1931-1950*. Doctoral thesis, University of London.

Katsiaounis, R. 2000. *The "Diaskeptiki 1946–1948. A Review of the 1878–1945 Period*. Nicosia: Centre of Scientific Research (in Greek).

Katsiaounis, R. 2001. The Cyprus Question and the Discussions for Its Resolution in the 20th Century. In *Our Neighbours the Arabs*. Municipality of Nicosia Editions, 143–162. Nicosia (in Greek).

Katsiaounis, R. 2006. Politics and Constitutional Reform in Cyprus During the Late 1940s'. *Yearbook of Centre of Scientific Research*, XXXII: 487–501.

Katsis, A. 2005. *From the "Diaskeptiki" to EOKA*. Limassol: Argo (in Greek).

Katsouridis, Y. 2013. The Relation Between the Cyprus Communist Party and the Trade Unions and Syndicalist Movement. In *The Cypriot Left in the First Period of British Colonialist Rule: Emergence, Organization, Evolution*, ed. G. Georgis and Y. Katsouridis, 117–134. Athens: Taxideftis (in Greek).

Konstantinidis, S. 2011. *Review of Modern Cypriot History, Social Structures, Institutions, and Ideology. From Ottoman Rule and British Rule to Independence*. Athens: Taxideftis (in Greek).

Kontos, M. 2014. The 'Anglo-American Factor' in Greek Cypriot Politics: English, American or 'Anglo-American?'. In *Great Power Politics in Cyprus: Foreign Interventions and Domestic Perceptions*, ed. M. Kontos, S.-C. Theodoulou, N. Panayiotides, and H. Alexandrou, 181–195. Cambridge Scholars Publishing.

Koumas, M. 2013. Greek Governments and the Cypriot Referendum on *Enosis*. In *The Cyprus Question and the International System, 1945–1974: In Search of a Place in the World*, ed. P. Papapolyviou, A. Syrigos and E. Hadjivasileiou, 31–46. Athens: Patakis (in Greek).

Ktoris, S. 2013. *Turkish Cypriots, From the Margins to Association (1923–1960)*. Athens: Papazisis (in Greek).

Lavender, D. 1962. *The Story of the Cyprus Mines Corporation*. San Marino: The Huntington Library.

Leventis, Y. 2002. *Cyprus: The Struggle for Self-Determination in the 1940's. Prelude to Deeper Crisis*. Frankfort: Peter Lang.

Linardatos, S. 1977. *From the Civil War to the Junta*, vol. I. Athens: Papazisis (in Greek).

Mallinson, W. 2005. *Cyprus. A Modern History*. London: I.B. Tauris.

Michaelides, M. 1993. 'The Turkish Cypriot Working Class and the Cyprus Labour Movement, 1920–1963.' *Cyprus Review* 5 (2): 33–67.

Moudouros, N. 2014. Political Power, Violence and Economy: The Turkish Cypriot Elite's Struggle for Ethno Communal Formation. *Journal of Mediterranean Studies*, 23 (1): 61–74.

Nevzat, A. 2010. Securing the Office of Muftu: Nationalism, Religion and the Turks of Cyprus. In *Nationalism in the Troubled Triangle*, ed. A. Aktar, N. Kizilyurek, and U. Ozkirimli, 160–174. London: Palgrave Macmillan.

Pancyprian Trade Union Committee-Pancyprian Federation of Labour. 1991. *History of the Pancyprian Trade Union Committee - Pancyprian Federation of Labour*. Nicosia (in Greek).

Papaioannou, E. 1988. *Recollections from My Life*. Nicosia: Pyrsos (in Greek).

Protopapas, V. 2006. The Rise of a Bi-Polar Party System, Municipal Elections 1940–1955. In *Britain in Cyprus: Colonialism and Post-Colonialism 1878–2006*, ed. H. Faustmann and N. Peristianis, 269–294. Mannheim: Bibliopolis.

Protopapas, V. 2012. *Electoral History of Cyprus. Politicians, Parties and Elections Under British Rule 1878-1960*. Athens: Themelio (in Greek).

Richter, H. 2007. *History of Cyprus*, vol. 1 (1878–1949). Athens: Estia (in Greek).

Richter, H. 2011. *History of Cyprus*, vol. 2 (1950–1959). Athens: Estia (in Greek).

Rizas, S. 1998. The Elaboration of British Policy on the Cyprus Question. *Bulletin of the Research Centre on Modern Greek History* I: 203–223 (in Greek).

Sakellaropoulos, S. 2017. *The Cypriot Social Formation (1191–2004). From Formation to Partition*. Athens: Topos (in Greek).

Sakellaropoulos, S., and A. Alecou. 2019. The Paradoxical Co-existence of Two Communist Parties Within One: The Case of the Communist Party of Cyprus and AKEL (1941–1944). *Theseis* 147: 65–92 (in Greek).

Servas, P. 1980. *Cyprus Question: Responsibilities*, vol. I. Athens: Grammi (in Greek).

Servas, P. 1985. *Cyprus Question: Responsibilities*, vol. II, semi-vol. I. Athens: Grammi (in Greek).

Tenedios, I. 1995. Political Shifts in Turkish Cypriot Society. In *Anatomy of a Transformation. Cyprus After 1974 (Society, Economy, Politics, Culture)*, ed. N. Peristianis and G. Tsaggaras, 387–400. Nicosia: Intercollege Press (in Greek).

Terlexis, P. 1971. *Diplomacy and Politics of the Cyprus Question. Anatomy of a Mistake*. Athens: Rappa Publications (in Greek).

The Striking Copper Miners' and Asbestos Miners' 1948 Struggles. 1979. Nicosia: Publication of the Pancyprian Miners' Union. Pancyprian Federation of Labour (in Greek).

Tounta-Fergadi, A. 2010. The Exclusion of the Cyprus Issue from National Demands During the Second World War. *Filelefteri Emfasi*, 44: 80–91 (in Greek).

Tsekouras, T. 1984. Cyprus Question: From *Enosis* to Zurich. *Theseis* 7: 83–104 (in Greek).

Varnava, P. 1989. *A Miner Remembers*. Nicosia: Pancyprian Federation of Labour (in Greek).

Yiagou, A. 2013. British Diplomacy and the Cyprus Question. In *The Cyprus Question and the International System, 1945–1974: Searching for a Place in the World*, ed. P. Papapolyviou, A. Syrigos, and E. Hadjivasileiou, 23–30. Athens: Patakis (in Greek).

CHAPTER 7

Conclusion

What I have attempted to show in this book is that there are two very basic parameters that should be part of any attempt to make the political, economic and social development of Cyprus over the centuries into something comprehensible. The first has to do with the island's geographical position and the interests of the great powers in each epoch. The second relates to the existence, from 1571 onward, of two communities which throughout the period of emergent modernism would begin to transform their religious specificities into national identity, placing its seal on later intercommunal differences and making a decisive contribution to the dramatic developments of the twentieth century's final decades.

The repeated conquests of Cyprus but also the continuous interest that came to exist for the island give an insight into its wider economic and geostrategic importance. The Franks and the Venetians were to occupy the island to use it as a barrier against Ottoman expansion into the region. And in turn, the Ottomans would conquer Cyprus seeking to extirpate the Christian domination in the South-East Mediterranean. The transition to capitalism would upgrade Cyprus' status as a commercial-entrepreneurial centre and Western merchants would again become a conspicuous presence from the mid-eighteenth century onwards. The generalized crisis of the Ottoman Empire and the advance of the Russian army would impel the Sublime Porte into an agreement with the British.

S. Sakellaropoulos, *The Evolution of the Political, Social and Economic Life of Cyprus, 1191–1950*, Palgrave Studies in Economic History,
https://doi.org/10.1007/978-3-030-91839-2_7

They ceded Cyprus to Britain, and Britain in turn guaranteed the security of the "Sick Man of Europe". The British sought a presence in Cyprus because they judged that in that way, they could control the wider region of the Middle East and North Africa, inhibiting the descent of the Russians. The outbreak of the First World War and the Ottoman alliance with the Germans had the effect of rearranging the scenario and the British annexed Cyprus. After a number of vacillations over whether or not they would cede the island to Greece, they came to the conclusion that the use of aircraft as weapons of war made it urgent that the island should remain part of their Empire. The decision in favour of remaining in Cyprus would remain unchanged when the Second World War ended. Although different viewpoints would be heard, the predominant attitude was that in a changing world the geographical position of Cyprus was of such significance for British interests in the wider region as to be non-negotiable. Indeed, the fact of the creation of the Cold War framework and the stakes involved, for a time, in the question of which superpower would head the camp of which Greece would become a member functioned as an additional factor in Cyprus's staying under British occupation.

It is through this historical context that the more specific conflict between the two communities is refracted. The general conclusion which emerges is that with the passage of time relations between the two gradually worsen. In the first years of Ottoman rule, the Orthodox participated in revolts whose aim was to restore the previous order of things, something which little by little came to an end owing to the unwilling of the West to intervene. That said, with the passage of years it could be seen that the life of Orthodox and Muslims had numerous points in common but also that there were important differences. The points in common involved exploitation of the existing means of taxation by the state authorities and the tax farmers, contributing to joint participation in *certain* revolts. The differences, for their part, had as much to do with the Ottoman feeling that the state power was *also* "their" power as it did with the existence of several institutional distinctions (from the additional taxes to be paid by the Orthodox up to the prohibition on bearing arms and being appointed to the civil service). The whole arrangement became more complicated from the moment that the Orthodox hierarchy was upgraded to become part of the state tax-collecting function. This was how it came about that the Muslims saw the Orthodox Church as a hostile oppressive mechanism.

All the above would begin to intensify from the moment that elements of the capitalist system started to penetrate the Cypriot social formation. Orthodox Christians' involvement in trade enabled them to achieve significant financial prosperity and introduce the first forms of capitalist organization of labour in Cyprus. This fact was conducive to the acquisition of Hellenic national identity by Orthodox Cypriots. It was a development linked to the process of Hellenic ethnogenesis outside of Cyprus. The advent of the age of modernity, the appearance of Nations and Nation States, would create the context for emergence of the concept of Hellenic national identity. The use of the Greek language and the common Orthodox Christian faith, in conjunction with the tightening of relations between Greek-speaking merchants in different regions, would create the preconditions for appearance of the current of Greek Enlightenment. Initially, the view became accepted that Greek speakers belong to the Hellenic *ethnos*, which soon afterwards evolved into the thesis that they belong to the Hellenic nation, which must acquire specific state territory. In the first phase, this affected Greek-speaking entrepreneurs and intellectuals but subsequently it influenced increasing numbers of Greek-speaking Orthodox rural people. Above and beyond the common language and religion it is a development which should be linked to the reality of discrimination suffered by non-Muslims on Ottoman territory. These specific factors would accumulate to find expression in the demand for liberation from Ottoman oppression and so in the outbreak of the Greek revolution of 1821. In the case of Cyprus all the elements of *ethnogenesis* would be activated, with the specific addition of the massacre of the notables and its aftermath. The degree of acquisition of Hellenic national identity for a great section of Orthodox Cypriots would be evident from their very massive participation in the Greek Revolution.

It should not be forgotten that an important part in the process of adopting the Hellenic identity by Orthodox Cypriots was played by the very different education their parents received from that of Muslim Cypriots. Greek Cypriots pursued a course of studies which oriented them primarily towards commerce and economic activity, whereas the Turkish Cypriots were exposed to a more religious syllabus aimed primarily at staffing the machinery of administration. The result of all this was that from the end of the eighteenth century and throughout the nineteenth the socio-economic differences between the two communities widened. To this must be added the fact of the cession of Cyprus to the British, in consequence of which Cypriot Muslims were transformed from being a demographic minority within a realm where they comprised the political majority to being both a demographic and a political minority. And not only that, but they had to begin a struggle against the demands of the Greek Cypriots for *Enosis* with Greece, a development which led to them developing a Turkish national consciousness.

Of course, this was not unrelated to the more general tendency for Turkish-speaking Muslims in the Ottoman Empire to embrace Turkish nationalist assumptions. A significant role in that was played by the emergence of nation states in what had until then been the Ottoman Balkans. A connective factor in Turkish *ethnogenesis* had been the reality that the Turkish-speaking Muslim population had enjoyed several privileges compared to other *millet* and almost exclusive occupation of the top posts in the Ottoman administration. It is interesting that in the case of the Balkans what distinguishes and shapes the various nationalities is on the one hand religion and language and on the other the pre-existing social discriminations, which however derive from membership of one or other of the various *millets*.

Bear in mind that in the specific case of Cyprus the acquisition of Turkish consciousness was to come at the end of a protracted process *and* because of the fact that from 1878 there was a British administration which at certain points in time privileged the Britification of all Cypriots, but *also* because precisely on account of the British administration a significant section of the Turkish Cypriot elite collaborated very closely with the machinery of government, a practice which could be legitimated only through perpetuation of the Muslim identity.

The growth of capitalism in Cyprus in the first half of the twentieth century contributed to a section of the Turkish Cypriot working class being assimilated by a corresponding section of the Greek Cypriot working class, and thanks to the efforts of the Cyprus Communist Party participating actively in joint trade union organization. But this development (which in any case had certain social limits because many Turkish Cypriots were farmers and did not become unionized) was not capable of inhibiting the desire of Greek Cypriots for *Enosis*, which was grounded in adoption of a common national identity with the Greeks of metropolitan Greece and further fomented by the factor of very heavy, for long periods, taxation of Cypriots. It would not be able, either, to change the fact that establishment of the state of the Young Turks and the consequent spread of Kemalism to the island would further intensify the national differences. Of course, there were certain moments of collaboration between the two communities, including at the level of the Legislative Council, with their high point the rejection of imposition of new tariffs in 1931. But these instances were either isolated or else momentary conjunctures of two trajectories with different starting points and different destinations, merely happening to intersect at a certain point in their course. This would become particularly evident during the 1931 revolt but also in the immediately following years. Undoubtedly within the two communities, there were different tendencies and viewpoints: kemalists and "traditionalists" in the Turkish Cypriots, moderate nationalists, radical nationalists and communists among the Greek Cypriots. But it is worth noting that whatever internal conflicts there were significant, they could not affect the primacy of the polarization between the demand for *Enosis* among the Greek Cypriots and its avoidance in every way by the Turkish Cypriots.

The end of the Second World War and the breakup of colonialist relations would have as side effects the return, with even greater force, of the demand for *Enosis* from the Greek Cypriots, along with organized Turkish Cypriot opposition to it through the creation of political parties but also Turkish Cypriot trade unions. This metamorphosis was linked to the attempt to develop a more co-ordinated and upgraded contingency plan against the possibility of *Enosis,* but this is not the only relevant factor. The passage of time, general proliferation internationally of the institution of the mass political party, modernization of the structures of the Turkish political system, but also liberalization of the British administration, all played their own specific role. It is also worthy of note that the Turkish Cypriot elite, above and beyond protests, rallies and memoranda, opted for something that was to place its seal on developments for the next decades: the construction of a closed Turkish Cypriot economy through top-down limitation of transactions with Greek Cypriots. There were two axes underpinning this option: the first involved the low competitiveness of Turkish Cypriot enterprises compared to their Greek Cypriot counterparts, due to their chronic backwardness in that respect, a backwardness dating back to the time of the Ottoman Empire and associated with the different education prescribed for Muslims and the priority assigned to staffing the state sector. The second is linked to the prospect of partition (*taksim*), of dividing the island into Greek Cypriot and Turkish Cypriot sectors, a political orientation which was to be a permanent feature of Turkish and Turkish Cypriot strategy in the following years leading up to the 1974 and self-proclamation of the so-called "Turkish Republic of Northern Cyprus" in 1983 (Sakellaropoulos 2017).

The Greek Cypriots, for their part, besides the demand for *Enosis*, had to face internal polarization. The Right-Left clash, a product not only of the dramatic strengthening of AKEL in the early 1940s but also of reflection from the Greek Civil War and the international conflicts of the first post-war years, was to place a decisive stamp on internal developments within it. The Right was apprehensive at the prospect of losing political supremacy, which is why they chose to make the Left their prime opponent, without abandoning the demand for *Enosis*. In its relations with the Right the Left would attempt to negotiate a knife-edge, advancing from collaboration on the question of *Enosis* to harsh confrontation over social issues. Finally, the ineffectual choice to participate in the Consultative Assembly and on the other hand the impact of the defeat of the Greek Communist Party in the Greek civil war would reset the power balance in the internal Greek arena, giving a clear lead to the forces of the Right and the Church hierarchy.

The refusal the British to accept the demand for *Enosis* led the Greek Cypriot side to carry out the 1950 referendum that would confirm the Greek Cypriot desire for *Enosis*. Above and beyond the flat refusal of both Britain and Turkey to accept such a prospect, the fact of the referendum would mark a turning point in the history of the island because henceforth the subject would acquire an international dimension, involving apart from Greece, Turkey and Great Britain both the USA and the USSR and their allies, complicating the situation even further and in the following years at times transforming the question into a factor in the Cold War. But these developments are the subject for another study.

Reference

Sakellaropoulos, S. 2017. *The Cypriot Social Formation (1191–2004). From Formation to Partition*. Athens: Topos (in Greek).

Bibliography

AKEL (Progressive Party of Working People). 1949. AKEL Central Committee Action Report, September 1947–May 1949. Contemporary Social History Archives (ASKI), Greek Communist Party archive 371. File=20/21/21 (in Greek).

AKEL. 1952. *The Road Towards Freedom - For a Minimum AKEL Program for Constructing the United Liberation Front of Struggle* (in Greek).

Alastos, D. 1976. *Cyprus in History. A Survey of 5000 Years*. London: Zeno.

Alecou, A. 2011. *Political Developments in Cyprus, 1945-1955*. Doctoral thesis, Panteion University (in Greek).

Alecou, A. 2012. *1948. The Greek Civil War and Cyprus.* Nicosia: Power Publishing (in Greek).

Alecou, A. 2018. Imported Nationalism: The Appearance and Evolution of X' Organization in Cyprus. In *Cypriot Nationalisms in Context. History, Identity and Politics*, ed. T. Kyritsi and N. Christofis, 135–153. London: Palgrave.

Alexander, G. 1979. British Policy on the Question of Enosis. *Kupriakai Spoudai* mc: 79–94.

Alexandrou, I. 2006. The Revolt of the 18 of the Farmers' Union of Cyprus. In First Scientific Symposium of Pissouri, *History, Society, Politics and Communications Media*, ed. E. Antoniadis, 121–129. Nicosia: Epiphani Editions (in Greek).

Anagnostopoulou, S. 1999. The Church of Cyprus and Its Role as Ethnarch: 1878–1960. The 'religiofication' of 'Cypriot' Political Activity: *Enosis. Synchrona Themata,* 68–69–70: 198–227.

S. Sakellaropoulos, *The Evolution of the Political, Social and Economic Life of Cyprus, 1191–1950*, Palgrave Studies in Economic History, https://doi.org/10.1007/978-3-030-91839-2

Anagnostopoulou, S. 2002. Les rapports de l' Eglise Orthodoxe avec le Kapudan Pacha (fin du XVIIIeme debut XIXeme siècle). In *The Kapudhna Pasha, His Office and His Domain*, ed. E. Zachariadou, 265–289. Rethymnon: Crete University Press.

Antoniou, A. 2014. December in Cyprus: Perception and Political Management of the Facts by AKEL. Intervention at the Congress "From Liberation to the December Events: A Rift in the Present-Day History of Greece", 1–8 (in Greek).

Antoniou, A. 2017. Economics and Politics: The Joint Strike of the Cyprus Mines Corporation Miners. In *The Crucial Decades of the 1940s and 1950s: Intercommunal and Intracommunal Relations in Cyprus*, 107–136. Nicosia: Prometheus Research Institute (in Greek).

Antonopoulou, M.-E. 2013. *The Social Position of Farmers (Parici and Frangomata) in Venetian-Occupied Cyprus (15th and 16th Centuries).* Athens: Poreia (in Greek).

Antreou, M. 2007. *How Turkish Cypriots Are Represented in the "Eleftheria" Newspaper in the 1930–1958 Period.* Postgraduate dissertation in the Department of Political Science and History. Athens: Panteio University (in Greek).

Apeyitou, E. 2003. Turkish-Cypriot Nationalism: Its History and Development (1571–1960). *The Cyprus Review* 15 (1): 67–98.

Apostolopoulos, C. 2001. An Attempted Approach to the Ottoman Empire by the *parici* of Venetian-Occupied Cyprus (1551). In *Proceedings of the Third Cyprological Congress*, vol. II Medieval Section Nicosia, 669–689 (in Greek).

Arbel, B. 1986. Urban Assemblies and Town Councils in Frankish and Venetian Cyprus. In *Proceedings of the Second International Cypriological Congress*, ed. T. Papadopoulos and V. Egglezakis, vol. II, 203–213. Nicosia: Association of Cypriot Studies.

Arbel, B. 1995. Cyprus Under Venetian Rule. In *History of Cyprus*, ed. T. Papadopoulos, vol. IV, Medieval Kingdom Venetian occupation, Part I, 455–536. Nicosia: Makarios III Institute (in Greek).

Argyriou, S. 2014. *The National Movement of the Greek Cypriots in the Final Period of British Rule: 1945–1960.* Doctoral thesis, Panteion University (in Greek).

Aristeidou, A. 1980. *Unpublished Documents on Cypriot History from the Archives of Ragusa (16th century).* Nicosia: Cyprus Centre of Scientific Research (in Greek).

Aristeidou, A. 1984. Production and Commerce in Cyprus in the 18th-19th Centuries. In *Life in Cyprus in the 18th and 19th Centuries*, 33–62. Nicosia: Municipality of Nicosia (in Greek).

Aristeidou, A. 1990. *Unpublished Documents on Cypriot History from the Archives of Venice. Vol. I (1474–1508)*. Nicosia: Centre of Scientific Research (in Greek).

Aristeidou, A. 1998. Rich and Poor in Venetian-Occupied Cyprus. In *Rich and Poor in the Community of the Greco-Latin Orient*, ed. C. Maltezou, 373–385. Venice: Hellenic Institute of Venice (in Greek).

Aristeidou, A. 2001. Unknown Attempts to Organize Revolts or Insurrections During Venetian Rule. In *Proceedings of the Third Cyprological Congress*, vol. II, Medieval Section, 570–598. Nicosia (in Greek).

Arslan, H. 2012. Turki-Cypriot Nationalist Drive Toward State-Building: Politics, Violence and Political Economy. In *Beyond a Divided Cyprus*, ed. N. Trimikliniotis and U. Bozkurt, 120–134. London Palgrave.

Asdrahas, S. 2003. The Political Terms of the Economic. The Conquests and Their Economic Logic. In *Greek Economic History 15th-16th*, vol. 1, ed. S. Asdrahas, et al., 249–288. Athens: Piraeus Bank Group Cultural Foundation (in Greek).

Asmussen, J. 2004. Early Conflicts Between the Greek and Turkish Cypriot Communities in Cyprus. *Cyprus Review* 16 (1): 87–106.

Asmussen, J. 2006. 'Dark-Skinned Cypriots Will Not Be Accepted!' Cypriots in the British Army. In *Britain in Cyprus: Colonialism and Post-Colonialism 1878–2006*, ed. H. Faustmann and N. Peristianis, 167–186. Mannheim: Bibliopolis.

Attalides, M. 1979. *Cyprus. Nationalism and International Politics*. Edinburg: Q Press.

Aymes, M. 2004. 'Position Delicate' ou ile sans Histoiries? L' integration de Chypre a l' Etat Ottoman des Premieres Tanzimat. In *Insularites Ottomanes*, ed. N. Vatin and G. Veinstein, 241–275. Paris: Maisonneuve & Larose.

Barkan, O.L. 1975. The Price Revolution of the Sixteenth Century: A Turning Point in the Exconomic History of the Near East. *International Journal of Middle East Studies* 6 (1): 3–28.

Berberoglu, B. 1982. *Turkey in Crisis*. London: Zed Press.

Bouleti, E. 2008. *British Policy Against the Turkish Cypriot Community 1878–1950. The Course Towards Nationalization of the Muslim-Cypriot Community.* Doctoral thesis. Athens: Panteion University (in Greek).

Bouleti, E. 2011. The Muslin Community on Cyprus and British Colonial Policy 1878–1915. *Cyprus Review* 23 (2): 39–56.

Branch, D. 2010. Identity, Violence and Co-operation in Cyprus During the State of Emergency. In *Unorthodox Wars: Macedonia, Civil War, Cyprus*, ed. V. Gounaris, S. Kalyvas, and Ioannis Stefanidis, 396–419. Athens: Patakis (in Greek).

Braudel, F. 1996. *The Mediterranean and the Mediterranean World in the Age of Philip II*, vol. II. Oakland: University California Press.

Bryant, R. 2004. *Imagining the Modern*. London: Tauris.

Choisi, J. 1995. The Greek Cypriot Elite- Its Social Function and Legitimization. *The Cyprus Review* 7 (1): 32–68.

Choisi, J. 2010. The Turkish Cypriot Elite-its Social Function and Legitimisation. In *Colonial Cyprus 1878–1960. Selected Readings From the Cyprus Review*, ed. E. Solomou and H. Faustmann, 277–300. Nicosia: University of Nicosia.

Christodoulou, D. 1959. *The Evolution of the Rural Land Use Pattern in Cyprus*. London: A. P. Tayler & Co.

Christodoulou, D. 1992. *Inside the Cyprus Miracle. The Labours of an Embattled Economy*, vol. 2. Minneapolis: University of Minnesota.

Christodoulou, D. 1995. Life Chances in Cyprus: Occupational and Social Structures and Mobility Viewed in Perspective. *Cyprus Review* 7 (1): 7–33.

Christodoulou, M. 1999. *Relations Between Athens and Nicosia. Rise and Fall, Emergence and Regeneration*. Nicosia: Proodos (in Greek).

Chrysanthis, K. 1983. Historical Data on the Movement of the Year 1931. In *Hellenic Cyprus: The Cypriot revolt of 1931*, 84–89. Nicosia: Hellenic Cultural Association of Cyprus (in Greek).

Chrysanthou, C. 2013. The Leadership of the Left 1920–1940. In *The Cypriot Left in the First Period of British Colonial Rule: Emergence, Organization, Development, Appearance*, G. Georgis and Yiannos Katsourides, 59–74. Athens: Taxideftis (in Greek).

Collenberg de Rudt, W.H. 1982. Le declin de la societe franque de Chypre entre 1350 et 1450. *Kypriakai Spoudai* 46: 71–83.

Collenberg de Rudt, W.H. 1995. Structure and Origin of the Class of the Nobility. In *History of Cyprus*, ed. T. Papadopoulos, vol. IV, Medieval Kingdom Venetian rule, Part I, 785–841. Nicosia: Makarios III Institute (in Greek).

Conomos, N. 1972–1973. Moves Towards Contracting of a Cypriot Loan During the Greek Uprising. *Yearbook of the Scientific Research Centre*, VI: 237–268 (in Greek).

Coureas. N. 2009. Stunted Growth: The Latin Clergy of Cyprus During the Ottoman Period. In *The Minorities of Cyprus: Development and the Identity of the Internal-Exclusion*, ed. A. Varnava, N. Coureas, and M. Elia, 92–110. Newcastle: Cambridge Scholars Publishing.

Crouzet, F. 1973. *Le Conflit en Chypre 1946-1959*. Tome Premier-Tome Deuxième, Bruxelles: Etablissements Emile Bruylant.

Cvetkova, B. 1978. *Les Institutions Ottomanes en Europe*. Wiesbaden: Franz Steiner Verlag GMB.

Cvetkova, B. 1979. The Evolution of the Turkish Feudal Regime from the End of the 16th to the Mid-18th Century. In *The Economic Structure of the Balkan Countries in the Years of Ottoman rule*, ed. S. Asdrahas, 89–112. Athens: Melissa (in Greek).

Dertilis, G. 2018. *History of Modern and Contemporary Greece*. Heraklion: University Editions of Crete (in Greek).

Dimaras, K.T. 2002. *Modern Greek Enlightenment*. Athens: Ermis (in Greek).

Dionysiou, G. 1988. *Church and Terminology in Cyprus in the Last Century of Turkish Rule (1779–1856)*. Doctoral thesis, University of Athens (in Greek).

Dionyssiou, G. 2009. *The Implementation of the Tanzimat Reforms in Cyprus (1839–1878)*. Nicosia: MAM.

Divtcioglou, S. 1979. Economic Model of Ottoman Society (14th and 15th Century). In *The Economic Structure of the Balkan Countries*, ed. S. Asdrahas, 115–131. Athens: Melissa (in Greek).

Drousiotis, M. 1998. *EOKA. The Dark Side*. Athens: Stachi (in Greek).

Economides, C. 1993. *Demythologized History of the Cyprus Issue in the Last 50 Years*. Nicosia: Economides Publishing House (in Greek).

Edbury, P. 1991. *The Kingdom of Cyprus and the Crusades, 1191–1374*. Cambridge: Cambridge University Press.

Erdentug, N. 1973. The Cultural Unity of the Turkish Traditional Societies of Cyprus and Turkey. In *Proceedings of the First International Cypriological Congress*, ed. T. Papadopoulos and M. Christodoulou, vol. III, second part, 125–130. Nicosia: Association of Cypriot Studies.

Fantis, A. 2006. *The Cypriot Trade Union Movement in the Years of British Rule (1870–1960)*, vol. II. Nicosia (in Greek).

Faustmann, H. 1998. Clientelism in the Greek Cypriot Community of Cyprus Under British Rule. *The Cyprus Review* 10 (2): 41–77.

Faustmann, H. 2006. Clientelistic Relations in Greek Cypriot Society Under British Colonial Rule. In *The Cyprus Question in Foreign Eyes*, ed. A. Stergiou and H. Richter, 177–229. Athens: Roes (in Greek).

Foreign Relations of the United States. 1949. Conference at Istanbul Turkey, of American Chiefs of Mission in the Near East, November 26–29, 1949. https://history.state.gov/historicaldocuments/frus1949v06/d71. Accessed on 10 September 2020.

Fotakis, Z. 2008. The Naval Policy of Great Britain and the Prospect of Ceding Cyprus to Greece, 1912-1914. In *Eleftherios Venizelos and Cyprus*, ed. G. Kazakias and P. Papapolyviou, 88–97. Athens: Kastaniotis (in Greek).

Gasparis, C. 2001. Race for Predominance: Venice and Genoa in the Medieval Kingdom of Cyprus. In *Cyprus Crossroads of the Mediterranean*, 61–82. Athens: National Research Foundation (in Greek).

Gazioglou, A. 1990. *The Turks in Cyprus. A Province of the Ottoman Empire (1571-1878)*. London: K. Rustem & Brother.

Gennaris, K. 2000. *From the East*. Athens: Kastaniotis (in Greek).

Georgalis, K. 2016. *The British in Cyprus. Taxation and Politics in the First Period of British Rule and the Question of Tribute*. Athens: Kastanioris (in Greek).

Georghallides, G.S. 1969–1970. Churchill's 1907 Visit to Cyprus: A Political Analysis. *Yearbook of Cyprus Research Centre*, III: 167–220.

Georghallides, G.S. 1971–1972. Memorandum by Mr. Headlam-Morley and Mr. Childs Respectinf Cyprus. *Yearbook of Cyprus Research Centre* V: 189–240.

Georghallides, G.S. 1979. *A Political and Administrative History of Cyprus 1918-1926*. Nicosia: Cyprus Research Centre.

Georghallides, G.S. 1985. *Cyprus and the Governorship of Sir Ronald Storrs: The Causes of the 1931 Crisis*. Nicosia: Cyprus Research Centre.

Georgis, G. 2010. The Contribution of Cyprus to the Revolution of 1821. *Pergamini* 5: 31–43 (in Greek).

Giannopoulos, G. 1975. The Decline of the Ottoman State. The Adaptation of Institutions to the New Reality. In *History of the Greek Nation*, vol. XI, 98–110. Athens: Ekdotiki Athinon (in Greek).

Graikos, K. 1991. *Cypriot History*. Nicosia (in Greek).

Graikos, K. 1994. *The Movement of October and the Communist Party of Cyprus*. Nicosia (in Greek).

Gramsci, A. 1978. Some Aspects of the Southern Question. In *Selections from Political Writings 1921-1926*, 441–462. London: Lawrence and Wishart.

Grivaud, G. 1983. L' ile de Chypre en 1697 d' après un memoire du consul Francois Luce. *Yearbook of Cyprus Research Centre*, XII: 171–183.

Hadjianastasis, M. 2004. *Bishops, Agas and Dragomans: A Social and Economic History of Ottoman Cyprus 1640–1704*. Ph.D. thesis, University of Birmingham.

Hadjianastasis, M. 2011. Crossing the Line in the Sand: National Officials, Monopolization of State Power and 'Rebellion". The Case of Mehmed Aga Boyacioglu in Cyprus, 1685–1690. *Turkish Historical Review* 2: 155–176.

Hadjianastasis, M. 2015. Between the Porte and the Lion: Identity, Politics and Opportunism in Seventeenth Century Cyprus. In *Frontiers of the Ottoman Imagination*, ed. M. Hadjianastasis, 139–167. Leiden/Boston: Brill.

Hadjidemetriou, K. 2002. *A History of Cyprus*. Nicosia.

Hadjiioannou, K. 1976. The Origins of Turkish Cypriots and the Cyprus Question. http://www.lykionellinidon.org.cy/likeio/userfiles/documents/kiriakos_Xatziioannou_i_katagogi_ton_tourkokiprion.pdf. Accessed on 5 May 2017 (in Greek).

Hadjikyriakou, A. 2011. *Society and Economy on an Ottoman Island: Cyprus in the Eighteenth Century*. Doctoral thesis, University of London.

Hadjikyriakou, A. 2014. Local Intermediaries and Insular Space in late-18th Century Ottoman Cyprus. *The Journal of Ottoman Studies*, XLIV: 427–456.

Hadjikyriakou, A. 2016. The Ottomanisation of Cyprus: Towards a Spatial Imagination Beyond the Centre-Province Binary. *Journal of Mediterranean Studies* 25 (2): 81–96.

Hadjikyriakou, A. 2019. Beyond the *Millet* Dabate: Communal Representation in Pre-Tanzimat-Era Cyprus. In *Poltical Thought and Practice in the Ottoman Empire*, ed. M. Sariyannis, 71–96. Rethymno: Crete University Press.

Hadjivasileiou, E. 1998. *The Cyprus Question, 1878–1960: The Constitutional Aspect*. Athens: Ellinika Grammata (in Greek).

Hadjivasileiou, E. 2009. Britain, Mediterranean Geopolitics and Cyprus (1878–1960). In *Cyprus, Geopolitical Developments in the 21st Century*, ed. V. Horafas and L. Rizas, 229–233. Athens: Monthly Review (in Greek).

Hadjivasileiou, E. 2010. Unorthodox War as Political Lever in Greek History 1904–1959. In *Unorthodox Wars. Macedonia, Civil War. Cyprus*, ed. V. Gounaris, S. Kalyvas and I. Stefanidis, 23–38. Athens: Patakis (in Greek).

Hasiotis, I., ed. 1972. *Spanish Documents on Cypriot History (XVIth and XVIIth century)*. Nicosia Scientific Research Centre: Sources and Studies on Cypriot History (in Greek).

Heraclidou, A. 2017. *Imperial Control in Cyprus*. London: I.B. Tauris.

Hidiroglou, P. 1975. Some Administrative Institutions of Turkish Rule in Cyprus. *Kypriakai Spoudai*, XXXVIII–XXXIX: 91–110 (in Greek).

Hill, G. Sir. 1951. *A History of Cyprus, vol. 3, The Frankish Period 1432-1571*. Cambridge: Cambridge University Press.

Hill, G. Sir. 1952. *A History of Cyprus, vol. 4, The Ottoman Province, The British Colony 1571-1948*. Cambridge: Cambridge University Press.

Historical Encyclopedia of Cyprus. 1979–1980. Ed. P. Papadimitris. Nicosia (in Greek).

Historical Essay on the Communist Party of Cyprus and AKEL. 1968. Unpublished document (in Greek).

History of Cyprus. 2010. Vol. II. Nicosia: Odysseia (in Greek).

History of the Cyprus Communist party-AKEL (Progressive Party of Working People), vol. I, 1926–1941. 1981. Unpublished document (in Greek).

Holland, R. 1998. *Britain and the Revolt in Cyprus*. Oxford: Oxford University Press.

Holland, R., and D. Markides. 2007. *The British and the Greeks*. Athens: Patakis (in Greek).

Inalcik, H. 1973a. Application of the Tanzimat and Its Social Effects. *Archivum Ottomaticum* 5: 97–127.

Inalcik, H. 1973b. Ottoman Policy and Administration in Cyprus After the Conquest. In *Proceedings of the First International Cypriological Congress*, ed. ed. T. Papadopoulos and M. Christodoulou, vol. III, first part, 119–136. Nicosia: Association of Cypriot Studies.

Inalcik, H. 1985. The Emergence of Big Farms, ciftlicks: State, Landlords and Tenants. In *Studies in Ottoman Social and Economic History*, ed. H. Inalcik, 105–126. London: Valorium Reprints.

Inalcik, H. 1997. Introduction: Empire and Population. In *An Economic and Social History of the Ottoman Empire*, ed. H. Inalick and D. Quataert, vol. I: 1300–1660, 11–43. Cambridge: Cambridge University Press.

Indianos, A. 1938. The Dragoman regime and Dragomans in Cyprus. *Kypriakai Spoudai* 2: 141–195 (in Greek).

Ioannou, F. 2004. The Stance of AKEL: Self-government-*Enosis*. In *Fifis Ioannou, the Left and the Cyprus Question*, ed. Nikos Peristanis, 223–234. Nicosia: Intercollege Mass Media Institute (in Greek).

Ioannou, F. 2005. *This Is the Way the Cyprus Issue Started. Following the Footsteps of a Decade (1940-1950). Relations Between AKEL and the KKE in the Civil War Years*. Athens: Filistor-Paralos (in Greek).

Ioannou, G. 2006. Agricultural Collectives in Cyprus-Focusing on a Hybrid of the Late Colonial Period. *Yearbook of the Scientific Research Centre*, XXXII: 449–476 (in Greek).

Ioannou, T. 1996. *Commercial Relations Between Cyprus and France in the 18th Century*. Doctoral thesis, National and Capodistrian University of Athens (in Greek).

Irakleidis, A. 2006. *The Cyprus Problem 1947-2004. From Enosi to Partition*. Athens: Sideris (in Greek).

Islamoglou, H., and C. Keyder. 1977. Agenda for Ottoman History. *Review (fernard Braudel Center)* 1 (1): 31–55.

Itzkowitz, N. 2008. *Ottoman Empire and Islamic Tradition*. Athens: Papazisis (in Greek).

Jennings, R. 1993. *Christians and Muslim in Ottoman Cyprus and the Mediterranean World 1571-1640*. New York: New York University Press.

Kalantzopoulos, D. 2015. *Competing Political Spaces in Colonial Cyprus, 1931-1950*. Doctoral thesis, University of London.

Kafkarides, C. 2010. *Turkey and Cyprus 1923–1960*. Athens: Amorgos (in Greek).

Kalogirou, A. 1994. The Clash Between the Latin and Orthodox Church in Cyprus. In the collective volume, *Some Crucial Hours in Cypriot History*, 19–61. Nicosia: Municipality of Nicosia (in Greek).

Karouzis, G. 1977. *Land Ownership in Cyprus-Past and Present* (with special reference to Greek and Turkish ownerships). Nicosia: "Strabo".

Karpat, K. 1972. The Transformation of the Ottoman State, 1789–1908. *International Journal of Middle East Studies* 3 (3): 243–281.

Katsiaounis, R. 1994. Electing and Being Elected in the First Parliamentary Elections Under British Rule in 1883. *Yearbook of the Centre of Scientific Research*, XX: 309–345 (in Greek).

Katsiaounis, R. 1996. *Labour, Society and Politics in Cyprus During the Second Half of the Nineteenth Century*. Nicosia: Cyprus Research Centre.

Katsiaounis, R. 2000. *The "Diaskeptiki 1946–1948. A Review of the 1878–1945 Period*. Nicosia: Centre of Scientific Research (in Greek).

Katsiaounis, R. 2001. The Cyprus Question and the Discussions for Its Resolution in the 20th Century. In *Our Neighbours the Arabs*. Municipality of Nicosia Editions, 143–162. Nicosia (in Greek).

Katsiaounis, R. 2004. Social, Ethnic and Political Conflicts in Cyprus During the Period of British Rule 1878–1950. In Lectures at the People's University, *British Rule Themes in Cyprus*, pp. 19–43. Nicosia (in Greek).

Katsiaounis, R. 2006. Politics and Constitutional Reform in Cyprus During the Late 1940s'. *Yearbook of Centre of Scientific Research*, XXXII: 487–501.

Katsis, A. 2005. *From the "Diaskeptiki" to EOKA*. Limassol: Argo (in Greek).

Katsouridis, Y. 2009. *The Party System in Cyprus 1878–1931: Construction and Peculiarities*. Doctoral thesis, Nicosia: University of Cyprus (in Greek).

Katsouridis, Y. 2010. The Church as a Vehicle for Ideological and Political Processes. *Elliniki Epitherisi Politikis Epistimis* 36: 37–71.

Katsouridis, Y. 2013. The Relation Between the Cyprus Communist Party and the Trade Unions and Syndicalist Movement. In *The Cypriot Left in the First Period of British Colonialist Rule: Emergence, Organization, Evolution*, ed. G. Georgis and Y. Katsouridis, 117–134. Athens: Taxideftis (in Greek).

Katsourides, Y. 2014. *The History of the Communist Party of Cyprus*. London: I.B. Tauris.

Katsourides, Y. 2017. *The Greek Cypriot Nationalist Right in the Era of British Colonialism*. London: Springer.

Kazamias, G., and M. Panayiotou. 2016. Cyprus' Trade with the Levant, 1881–1946/47. In *The Greeks and the British in the Levant, 1800–1960s*, ed. A. Yangou, G. Kazamias, and R. Holland, 111–122. London: Routledge.

Kitromilides, Paschalis. 1977. "Cyprus" Entry. *History of the Greek Nation*, XIV: 387–395 (in Greek).

Kizilyurek, N. 2007. Relations Between Greek Cypriots and Turkish Cypriots. From the Traditional Ottoman Period to Modernity. In *Cyprus in the 20th Century*, 111–136. Nicosia: Municipality of Nicosia (in Greek).

Kizilyurek, N. 2009. *Turkish Cypriots, Turkey and the Cyprus Question*. Athens: Papazisis (in Greek).

Kizilyurek, N. 2015. Modenrity, Nationalism and Secularization: The Tyrkish Cypriot case. In *Religious Communities and Modern Statehood*, ed. M. Michael, T. Anastassiadis, and C. Verdeil, 173–181. Berlin: Klaus Schwarz Verlag.

Kizilyurek, N. 2019. *A Story of Violence and Resentment, The Origins and Evolution of the Ethnic Dispute in Cyprus*. Nicosia: Heterotopia (in Greek).

Klapsis, A. 2013. The Strategic Importance of Cyprus and the Prospect of Union with Greece 1919–1931. The Greek Perspective. *The Journal of Imperial and Commonwealth History* 41 (5): 765–782.

Kondylis, T. 2009. *Eleftherios Venizelos and Greece (1928–1932). Diplomatic Policy and Economy*. Athens: Iamvos (in Greek).

Konstantinidis, S. 1995. *The Cyprus Problem, Structures of Cypriot Society and the National Question*. Montreal-Nicosia: Metoikos (in Greek).

Konstantinidis, S. 2011. *Review of Modern Cypriot History, Social Structures, Institutions, and Ideology. From Ottoman Rule and British Rule to Independence*. Athens: Taxideftis (in Greek).

Kontos, M. 2014. The 'Anglo-American Factor' in Greek Cypriot Politics: English, American or 'Anglo-American?'. In *Great Power Politics in Cyprus: Foreign Interventions and Domestic Perceptions*, ed. M. Kontos, S.-C. Theodoulou, N. Panayiotides, and H. Alexandrou, 181–195. Cambridge Scholars Publishing.

Kostis, K. 1991. Communities, Church and Millet in "Greek" Areas of the Ottoman Empire in the Period of Reforms. *Mnimon* 13: 57–76 (in Greek).

Koumas, M. 2013. Greek Governments and the Cypriot Referendum on *Enosis*. In *The Cyprus Question and the International System, 1945–1974: In Search of a Place in the World*, ed. P. Papapolyviou, A. Syrigos and E. Hadjivasileiou, 31–46. Athens: Patakis (in Greek).

Koumoulides, J. 1971. *Cyprus and the War of Greek Independence 1821–1829*. Athens: National Centre of Social Research.

Koumoulides, J. 1973. An Attempt for the Liberation of Cyprus During the Struggle for Greek Independence. In *Proceedings of the First International Cypriological Congress*, ed. T. Papadopoulos and M. Christodoulou, vol. III, first part, 149–154. Nicosia: Association of Cypriot Studies.

Koumoulides, J. 1987. Sir John Stavridi and British Offer of 1915. *Journal of Modern Hellenism* 4: 93–119.

Koupanou, A. 2017. *The Shaping of Relations Between Christians and Muslims in Cyprus During the First Period of Colonial Government (1878–1914)*. Doctoral thesis, University of Cyprus (in Greek).

Koureas, N. 2001. Social Aspects of Latin Rule in Cyprus, A Politics of Separation. *Yearbook of Cypriot Society for Historical Studies* V: 254–284 (in Greek).

Ktoris, S. 2013. *Turkish Cypriots, From the Margins to Association (1923–1960)*. Athens: Papazisis (in Greek).

Kyriakidis, H. 2016. *The Legislative Council of Cyprus (1878–1931)*. Nicosia: House of Representatives.

Kyrris, K. 1964. *The Dispute Between Dragomans Markoullis and Georgis (1669–1674) and the Relations Between Greek and Turkish Cypriots at That Time*. Nicosia (in Greek).

Kyrris, K. 1970–1971. Unpublished Accounts of Hatzigeorgakis Kornessios. *Yearbook of the Scientific Research Centre*, IV: 283–328 (in Greek).

Kyrris, K. 1973. The Role of the Greeks in the Ottoman Administration of Cyprus. In *Proceedings of the First International Cypriological Congress*, ed. T. Papadopoulos and M. Christodoulou, vol. III, first part, 155–179. Nicosia: Association of Cypriot Studies.

Kyrris, K. 1984. Anatomy of the Ottoman Regime in Cyprus 1570–1878. In the collective *Life in Cyprus in the 18th and 19th Centuries*, 65–82. Nicosia: Municipality of Nicosia (in Greek).

Kyrris, K. 1985. *History of Cyprus*. Nicosia: Nicocles Publishing House.

Kyrris, K. n.d. Diplomatic Background to the Revolution of 1821 in Relation to Cyprus. *Morphosis*, part IV, 6–8 (in Greek).

Lanitis N.-C. 1944 [1992]. *Rural Indebtedness and Agricultural Co-operation in Cyprus*. Limassol: Proodos.

Lavender, D. 1962. *The Story of the Cyprus Mines Corporation*. San Marino: The Huntington Library.

Dwight, Lee. 1931. A Memorandum Concerning Cyprus, 1878. *The Journal of Modern History* 3 (2): 235–241.

Lee, D. 1934. *Great Britain and the Cyprus Convention Policy of 1878*. Cambridge: Harvard University Press.

Lefkis, G. 1984. *The Roots. Historical Study*. Limassol (in Greek).

Leventis, Y. 2002. *Cyprus: The Struggle for Self-Determination in the 1940's. Prelude to Deeper Crisis*. Frankfort: Peter Lang.

Linardatos, S. 1977. *From the Civil War to the Junta*, vol. I. Athens: Papazisis (in Greek).

Loizidis, S. 1983. National Radical Union and 1931 Revolt. In *The Cypriot Revolt of 1931*, 30–38. Nicosia: Hellenic Cultural Society of Cyprus (in Greek).

Loizos, P. 1977. Politics and Patronage in a Cypriot Village, 1920–1970. In *Patrons and Clients in Mediterranean Societies*, ed. E. Gellner and J. Waterbury, 115–126. Duckworth: Center for Mediterranean Studies of the American Universities.

Louis, K. 2006. *Forms of Economic relations in Cyprus (1817–1839)*, vol. 1. Nicosia (in Greek).

Louis, K. 2013. Makarios I, The Tanzimat and the Role of the Archbishop-Ethnarch. In *The Archbishops of Cyprus in the Modern Age*, ed. A. Varnava and M. Michael, 88–105. Newcastle: Cambridge Scholars Publishing.

Loukaidis, L. 1986. The History of Local Self-Government. In *Kypriaka 1878-1955*, 63–76. Nicosia: Publication of the Municipality of Nicosia (in Greek).

Luke, H., Sir. 1969. *Cyprus Under the Turks, 1571–1878*. London: C. Hurst and Co.

Lympouridis, A. 1985. *British Rule in Cyprus. From the Occupation to the End of the First World War*. Nicosia (in Greek).

Lympouridis, A. 1997. *Cyprus' Contentious Archiepiscopal Question and the l Ten Years Adventured Course of 1900 -1910*. Nicosia: Fakos (in Greek).

Marios, Lyssiotis. 1990. An Analysis of the Cyprus Legislative Council. *Cyprus Review* 2 (2): 55–69.

McHenry, J.-A. 1981. *The Uneasy Partnership on Cyprus, 1919-1939: The Political and Diplomatic Interaction Between Great Britain, Turkey and the Turkish Cypriot Community*. Doctoral thesis, University of Kansas.

Mallinson, W. 2005. *Cyprus. A Modern History*. London: I.B. Tauris.

Mandel, E. 1996. The Asiatic Mode of Production and the Historical Prerequisites for Capital Growth. *Theseis*, 57. http://www.theseis.com/1-75/theseis/t57/t57f/mandel.htm. Accessed on 13 September 2012 (in Greek).

Mantran, R. 1989. L' Etat ottoman au XVIIIe siècle: la pression européenne. In *Histoire de l' Empire Ottoman*, ed. R. Mantran, 265–286. Paris: Fayard.

Maratheftis, F. 1982. The Growth of Cities in Cyprus in the 18th and 19th Centuries. In *Life in Cyprus in the 18th and 19th Century*, 135–152. Nicosia: Municipality of Nicosia (in Greek).

Mariti, T. 1994. On an Uprising Which Took Place a Short Time Ago on the Island of Cyprus. In *Cyprus Through the Centuries in Texts of Visitors from Abroad. From the 1st Century to the 20th*, ed. Andros Pavlides, vol. II, 874–881. Nicosia: Filokypros (in Greek).

Markides, D., and G.S. Georghallides. 1995. British Attitudes to Constitution-Making in Post-1931 Cyprus. *Journal of Modern Greek Studies* 13 (1): 63–80.

Melamid, A. 1956. The Geographical Distribution of Communities in Cyprus. *Geographical Review* 46 (3): 355–374.

Michael, M. 2003. *The Kykkos Monastery in the Ottoman Economic Context on the Basis of Code 56 (1844 1890)*. Nicosia: Kykkos Monastery Research Centre (in Greek).

Michael, M. 2005. *The Church of Cyprus in the Ottoman Period (1571–1878). Its Step-by-Step Formation as an Institution of Political Power.* Nicosia: Cyprus Scientific Research Centre (in Greek).

Michael, M. 2006. Mouchasilis, the Dragoman, the Archbishop and Claims on Political Power in the Cyprus of the Ottoman Regions, 1789–1810. *Yearbook of the Scientific Research Centre*, XXXII: 209–240 (in Greek).

Michael, M. 2008. Ottoman Rights of the Senior Clergy of the Church of Cyprus and the British Administration. *Yearbook of the Scientific Research Centre*, XXXIV: 333–367 (in Greek).

Michael, M., 2009. An Orthodox Institution of Ottoman Polititical Authority: The Church of Cyprus. In *Ottoman Cyprus. A Collection of Studies on History and Culture*, ed. M. Michael, M. Kappler and E. Gavriel, 209–230. Wiesbaden: Harrassowitz Verlg.

Michael, M. 2010. History, Myth and Nationalism: The Retrospective Force of National Roles within a Myth-Constructed Past. In *Nationalism in the*

Troubled Triangle, ed. A. Aktar, N. Kizilyurek, and U. Ozkirimli, 149–159. London: Palgrave Macmillan.

Michael, M. 2015a. From the Ottoman Meclis-I Idare to the British Legislative Council. In *Religious Communities and Modern Statehood*, ed. M. Michael, T. Anastassiadis, and C. Verdeil, 105–130. Berlin: Klaus Schwarz Verlag.

Michael, M. 2015b. Revolts and Power Negotiating in Ottoman Cyprus During the First Half of the Nineteenth Century. In *Archivium Ottomanum*, ed. G. Xazia, vol. 32, 117–138. Gottingen: Hubert & Co.

Michael, M. 2016. *Insurrections as Terrain for Negotiation with Power. Ottoman Cyprus, 1804–1841*. Athens: Alexandria (in Greek).

Michael, M., and K. Kokkinoftas. n.d. The Church of Cyprus. In the collective *Cyprus*, 646–705. Athens: Domi A.E. (in Greek).

Michaelides, M. 1993. The Turkish Cypriot Working Class and the Cyprus Labour Movement, 1920–1963. *Cyprus Review* 5 (2): 33–67.

Milios, G. 1996. The Asiatic Mode of Production. *Theseis*, 57. http://www.theseis.com/1-75/theseis/t57/t57f/asiati.htm. Accessed 4 September 2020 (in Greek).

Milios, G. 2000. *The Greek Social Formation. From Expansionism to Capitalist Growth*. Athens: Kritiki (in Greek).

Moudouros, N. 2014. Political Power, Violence and Economy: The Turkish Cypriot Elite's Struggle for Ethno Communal Formation. *Journal of Mediterranean Studies* 23 (1): 61–74.

Moustaka, S. 2010. *The Workers' Movement in Cyprus During the Period of British Rule 1878–1955*. Doctoral thesis, Athens: Panteion University (in Greek).

Moutsis, I. 2014. *The Turkish Cypriots (1918–1931): From a Religious Community to an Ethnic Minority*. Doctoral thesis, University of London (in Greek).

Myrianthopoulos Konstantinos. 1973. Cyprus Under Turkish Rule (1570–1878). *Kypriakai Spoudai*, XXXVII: 85–102 (in Greek).

Nevzat, A. 2005. *Nationalism Amongst the Turks of Cyprus: The first Wave*. University of ULU. herkules.oulu.fi/isbn9514277511/isbn9514277511.pdf. Accessed on 3 June 2012.

Nevzat, A. 2010. Securing the Office of Muftu: Nationalism, Religion and the Turks of Cyprus. In *Nationalism in the Troubled Triangle*, ed. A. Aktar, N. Kizilyurek, and U. Ozkirimli, 160–174. London: Palgrave Macmillan.

Nevzat, A., and M. Hatay. 2009. Politics, Society and the Decline of Islam in Cyprus: From the Ottoman Era to the Twenty-First Century. *Middle Eastern Studies* 45 (6): 911–933.

Onurkan-Samani, M. 2018. The Legislative Council and Its Historical/Political Implications in Cyprus (1882–1931). In *Cypriot Nationalisms in Context. History, Identity and Politics*, ed. T. Kyritsi and N. Christofis, 75–92. London: Palgrave.

Orhonlu, C. 1973. The Ottoman Turks Settle in Cyprus (1570-1580). In *Proceedings of the First International Cypriological Congress*, ed. T. Papadopoulos and M. Christodoulou, vol. III, first part, 257–261. Nicosia: Association of Cypriot Studies.

Orr, C.W.J. 1972. *Cyprus Under British Rule*. London: Zeno Publishers.

Pampalos, C., and I. Theoharides. 2008. *The Turkish Press on Cyprus (1928–1945)*. Nicosia: Holly Monastery Research Centre of Cyprus (in Greek).

Panayiotou, A. 1999. *Island Radicals: The Emergence and Consolidation of the Cypriot Left, 1920-1960*. Doctoral thesis, University of California.

Panagiotou, M. 2016. Harbours, *Harbour Works and Foreign Trade in Cyprus, 1878–1927*. Doctoral thesis, University of Cyprus (in Greek).

Pancyprian Trade Union Committee-Pancyprian Federation of Labour. 1991. *History of the Pancyprian Trade Union Committee - Pancyprian Federation of Labour*. Nicosia (in Greek).

Pantelis, S. 1986. *The Modern History of Cyprus*. Athens: I. Floros Publications (in Greek).

Papadopoullos, T. 1965a. *Social and Historical Data on Population (1570–1881)*. Nicosia: Cyprus Research Centre.

Papadopoulos, T. 1995b. Structure and Functioning of the Feudal Polity. In *History of Cyprus*, ed. T. Papadopoulos, vol. IV Medieval Kingdom Venetian Rule, Part I, 759–784. Nicosia: Makarios III Institute (in Greek).

Papadopoulos, T. 2011. Hellenic Education in Cyprus Under the Ottomans. In *History of Cyprus*, ed. T. Papadopoulos, vol. VI, 379–468. Nicosia: Makarios III Institute (in Greek).

Papageorgiou, S. 1990. *Kapodistrias and the Roots of the Cyprus Question*. Nicosia: K. Epiphaniou Publications (in Greek).

Papageorgiou, S. 1996. *The First Period of British Rule in Cyprus [1878–1914]. Political Modernization and Social Inertia*. Athens: Papazisis (in Greek).

Papaioannou, E. 1988. *Recollections from My Life*. Nicosia: Pyrsos (in Greek).

Papapolyviou, P. 1997. *Cyprus and the Balkan Wars. Contribution to the History of Cypriot Voluntary Service*. Nicosia: Scientific Research Centre, Sources and Studies of Cypriot History XXVI (in Greek).

Papapolyviou, P. 2004. Cyprus 1922–1940. The 1931 Revolt and the Colonialist Counter-Revolution. In *History of Modern Hellenism*, vol. 7, 325–336. Athens: Ellinika Grammata (in Greek).

Papapolyviou, P. 2010. Cypriot Voluntary Service in Greek Wars, 1866–1945. In the volume of the National and Capodistrian University of Athens. Committee for Cyprus, ed. Andreas I. Voskos, 204–229. Cyprus: Freedom Struggles in Greek History. Athens (in Greek).

Papapolyviou, P. 2019. An Unknown Text on the Cypriot Revolts of 1833. *Yearbook of the Kykkos Monastery Research Centre* 12: 365–374 (in Greek).

Papapolyviou, P. 2020. Cypriot Fighters of 1821. https://papapolyviou.com/2020/03/25/kiprioi-agonistes-tou-1821/. Accessed on 12 September 2020 (in Greek).

Pardos, A. 2001. The Ideological and Cultural Platform of Cypriot Resistance (12th-16th Century). In National Research Institute, *Cyprus Crossroads of the Mediterranean*, 109–152. Athens (in Greek).

Pavlidis, A. 1992. *History of the Island of Cyprus*, vol. 3: From 1192 to 1571. Nicosia: Filokypros (in Greek).

Pavlidis, A. 1993. *History of the Island of Cyprus*, vol. 4: From 1571 to 1964. Nicosia: Filokypros (in Greek).

Perikleous, C. 2007. *The 2004 Referendum. The Regional and International Environment. The Conception of a Solution and the Conjuncture*. Athens: Papazisis (in Greek).

Philippou, L. 1975. *The Church of Cyprus Under Turkish Rule*. Nicosia: Cyprological Library (in Greek).

Pikros, G. 1980. *Venizelos and the Cyprus Question*. Athens: Philippotis (in Greek).

Pizanias, P. 2015. *The History of the Modern Greeks. From 1400 to 1800*. Athens: Estia (in Greek).

Polis, A. 1979. Colonialism and Neo-colonialism: Determinants of Ethnic Conflict in Cyprus. In *Small States in the Modern World. The Conditions of Survival*, ed. P. Worsley and P. Kitromilides, 45–80. Nicosia.

Poulantzas, N. 1978. *Classes in Contemporary Capitalism*. London: New left Books.

Protopapas, V. 2006. The Rise of a Bi-Polar Party System, Municipal Elections 1940–1955. In *Britain in Cyprus: Colonialism and Post-Colonialism 1878–2006*, ed. H. Faustmann and N. Peristianis, 269–294. Mannheim: Bibliopolis.

Protopapas, V. 2012. *Electoral History of Cyprus. Politicians, Parties and Elections Under British Rule 1878-1960*. Athens: Themelio (in Greek).

Protopsaltis, E. 1954. Plans for an Expedition from Lebanon and the Liberation of Cyprus, in 1827. *Elliniki Kypros*, January: 16 (in Greek).

Protopsaltis, E. 1971. *Cyprus in the Struggle of 1821*. Athens: Publication of the Cypriot Union of Greece (in Greek).

Psyroukis, N. 1983. *History of Contemporary Greece (1940–1967)*, vol. II. Athens: Epikairotita (in Greek).

Psyroukis, N. 1987. *The Cypriot Drama (1958–1986)*. Athens: Epikairotita (in Greek).

Rappas, A. 2014. *Cyprus in the 1930's*. London: I.B. Tauris.

Reddaway, J. 1987. *Burdened with Cyprus. The British Connection*. London: Weidenfeld & Nicolson.

Report on the Census of Cyprus 1891.

Report on the Census of Cyprus 1901.

Report and general Abstracts on the Census of Cyprus 1911.
Report and general Abstracts on the Census of Cyprus 1921.
Report of the Census of 1931.
Rey P.-P. 1973. *Les alliances de classes*. Paris: Maspero.
Richard J. 1977. Une Economie Coloniale? Chypre et ses Ressources agricoles au Moyen-Age. In *Byzantinische Forschungen. Internationale Zeitschrift fur Byzantinistik, herausgegeben*, ed. von Adolf M. Hakkert and Peter Wirth, Band V, 331–352. Amsterdam: Verlag Adolf M. Hakkert.
Richard, J. 1995a. The Political and Social Institutions of the Medieval Kingdom. In *History of Cyprus*, ed. T. Papadopoulos, vol. IV, Mediterranean Kingdom Venetian Rule, Part I, 333–374. Nicosia, Makarios III Institute (in Greek).
Richard, J. 1995b. The Formation and the Foundations of the Medieval Kingdom (1192-1205). In *History of Cyprus*, ed. T. Papadopoulos, vol. IV Mediterranean Kingdom Venetian Rule, Part I, 1–20. Nicosia: Makarios III Institute (in Greek).
Richter, H. 2006. Benevolent Aristocracy. In *Britain in Cyprus. Colonialism and Post-colonialism 1878-2006*, ed. H. Faustmann and N. Peristianis, 133–150. Wiesbaden: Harrassowitz.
Richter, H. 2007. *History of Cyprus*, vol. 1 (1878–1949). Athens: Estia (in Greek).
Richter, H. 2011. *History of Cyprus*, vol. 2 (1950–1959). Athens: Estia (in Greek).
Rizas, S. 1998. The Elaboration of British Policy on the Cyprus Question. *Bulletin of the Research Centre on Modern Greek History* I: 203–223 (in Greek).
Rizopoulou-Egoumenidou, E. 1996. The Economy of Cyprus Under Ottoman Rule with Special Emphasis on the Late 18th and Early 19th Centuries. In *The Development of the Cypriot Economy. From the Prehistoric Period to the Present Day*, ed. V. Karageorghis and D. Michaelides, 193–208. Nicosia: University of Cyprus-Bank of Cyprus.
Sakellarios, A.A. 1890. *The Cypriot Question, i.e. Geography, History and Language of the Island of Cyprus from Antiquity Until Today*, vol. 1. Athens (in Greek).
Sakellaropoulos, S. 2017. *The Cypriot Social Formation (1191–2004). From Formation to Partition*. Athens: Topos (in Greek).
Sakellaropoulos, S. 2019. The Debate on *Enosis* Between Greeks and Turks of Cyprus in the Legislative Council. *Deltos* 4: 67–86 (in Greek).
Sakellaropoulos, S., and A. Alecou. 2019. The Paradoxical Co-existence of Two Communist Parties Within One: The Case of the Communist Party of Cyprus and AKEL (1941–1944). *Theseis* 147: 65–92 (in Greek).
Samaras, P. 1987. *The Greek Origin of the Turkish Cypriots*. Athens (in Greek).

Sarris, N. 1990. *Ottoman Reality. Systemic Juxtaposition of Structures and Functions. Vol. 2, Administration Dose by Dose*. Athens: Arsenidis (in Greek).
Servas, P. 1980. *Cyprus Question: Responsibilities*, vol. I. Athens: Grammi (in Greek).
Servas, P. 1985. *Cyprus Question: Responsibilities*, vol. II, semi-vol. I. Athens: Grammi (in Greek).
Shaw, J.S., and E.K. Shaw. 1977. *History of the Ottoman Empire and Modern Turkey*, vol. II. Cambridge: Cambridge University Press.
Sophokleous, A. 1993. Geographical Determinism in the Future Development of Cyprus. In *The New International Order, Greece and Turkey and the Cyprus Problem*, ed. C. Giallouridis and P. Tsakonas, 515–546. Athens: I. Sideris (in Greek).
Sophokleous, K. 2003. *Struggle for Freedom. Internal Conflicts*, vol. I. Nicosia (in Greek).
Stavrianos, L.S. 1958. *The Balkans Since 1953*. New York: Rinehart & Company Inc.
Stavridis, T. 2003. The Defection of Mehmed Boyacioglou (1683–1690). *Yearbook of the Scientific Research Centre*, XXIX: 115–143 (in Greek).
Stefanidis, I. 1991. The Cyprus Question, 1949–1952: British Attitude, American Reactions and Greek Dilemmas. *Byzantine and Modern Greek Studies* 15: 212–267.
Stojanovitc, T. 1980. Balkan Farmers and Landowners and the Ottoman State: Family Economy, Market Economy and Modernization. In collective volume *Modernization and Industrial Revolution in Balkans During the 19th Century*, 157–198. Athens: Themelio (in Greek).
Storrs, R. 1937. *The Memoirs of Sir Ronald Storrs*. New York: Putnam.
Stubbs, J., and B. Taseli. 2014. New Press, Nationalism and Empire. The Turkish Cypriot Press in the British Colonial Period and Its Aftermath. *Media History* 20 (3): 284–301.
Stylianou, P. 1975. The Cypriot Revolution of 1606 Under Petros Aventanios. *Kypriakos Logos* 41–42: 337–341 (in Greek).
Stylianou, P. 1976. "The 1609 Cypriot Appeal to the Spanish King Philip III for Liberation of Cyprus, Examined Historically. *Kypriakos Logos* 43: 3–13 (in Greek).
Stylianou, P. 1984. *The Movement of October 1931 in Cyprus*. Doctoral thesis, Nicosia (in Greek).
Stylianou, P. 2013. The Revolt of October 1931 (Oktovriana). In the collective *The Struggles Prior to the Struggle of 1955. Aspects of the Preparation for Organization of the Struggle*, 11–108. Nicosia: Academy of Historical Studies (in Greek).
Sugar, P. 1996. *Southeastern Europe Under Ottoman Rule, 1354–1804*. Seattle: University of Washington Press.

Surridge, B.J. 1930. *A Survey of Rural Life in Cyprus*. Nicosia: Government Printing Office.

Svolopoulos, K. 1978. The Stance of the Greek Government during the Cypriot Crisis of 1931. *Epistimoniki Epetirida tis Panteiou Anotatis scholis Politikon Epistimon*, 485–511. Athens (in Greek).

Svolopoulos, C. 1985. The Lausanne Peace Treaty and the Cyprus Problem. In Proceedings of the International Symposium, *Greece and Great Britain During World War I*, 233–245. Thessaloniki: Institute for Balkan Studies.

Tenedios, I. 1995. Political Shifts in Turkish Cypriot Society. In *Anatomy of a Transformation. Cyprus After 1974 (Society, Economy, Politics, Culture)*, ed. N. Peristianis and G. Tsaggaras, 387–400. Nicosia: Intercollege Press (in Greek).

Terlexis, P. 1971. *Diplomacy and Politics of the Cyprus Question. Anatomy of a Mistake*. Athens: Rappa Publications (in Greek).

Theoharidis, I. 1987. On the Institution of the Dragoman in Cyprus Under Turkish Rule. In *Proceedings of the Second International Cyprological Congress*, vol. III (modern section), 65–75 (in Greek).

Theoharidis, I. 1995. The Cypriot Forerunners of 1821 According to an Unknown Ottoman Source. *Dodoni* 24: 67–109 (in Greek).

Theoharidis, I. 1999. *Ottoman Documents 1840–1912*, vol. I 1840–1872. Nicosia: Kykkos Monastery Research Centre (in Greek).

Theoharidis, I. 2010. The Turkish Cypriots in the Turkish Press (1928–1945). *Yearbook of the Kykkos Monastery Research Centre* 9: 311–336 (in Greek).

Theoharidis, I., and S. Andreev. 1996. *Sequel to the 1821 Tragedy. Ottoman Source on Cyprus 1822–1832*. Nicosia: Kykkos Monastery Research Centre (in Greek).

The Striking Copper Miners' and Asbestos Miners' 1948 Struggles. 1979. Nicosia: Publication of the Pancyprian Miners' Union. Pancyprian Federation of Labour (in Greek).

Tounta-Fergadi, A. 2010. The Exclusion of the Cyprus Issue from National Demands During the Second World War. *Filelefteri Emfasi*, 44: 80–91 (in Greek).

Tsalakos, G. 1981. Brief Review of Certain Aspects of British Rule in Cyprus. In *Cyprus, History, Problems and Struggles of Its People*, ed. G. Tenekidis and G. Kranidiotis, 137–166. Athens: Estia (in Greek).

Tsekouras, T. 1984. Cyprus Question: From *Enosis* to Zurich. *Theseis* 7: 83–104 (in Greek).

Tsiknakis, K. 2001. Cyprus in the Maelstrom of Competition Between the European Powers (15th-16th Century). In *Cyprus Crossroads of the Mediterranean*, 83–108. Athens: National Research Foundation (in Greek).

Varnava, A. 2009. *British Imperialism in Cyprus, 1878–1915. The Inconsequential Possession*. Manchester: Manchester University Press.

Varnava, A. 2013. Sophronios III, 1865–1900: The Last of the 'Old' and the First of the 'New' Archbishop-Ethnarchs? In *The Archbishops of Cyprus in the Modern Age*, ed. A. Varnava and M. Michael, 106–147. Newcastle: Cambridge Scholars Publishing.

Varnava, A. 2019. *British Cyprus and the Long Great War, 1914–1925*. London: Routledge.

Varnava, P. 1989. *A Miner Remembers*. Nicosia: Pancyprian Federation of Labour (in Greek).

Vergopoulos, K. 1975. *The Agrarian Question in Greece*. Athens: Exantas (in Greek).

Weir, W.W. 1952. *Education in Cyprus. Some Theories and Practices in Education in the Island of Cyprus Since 1878*. Cyprus.

Woodhouse, C.M. 1985. The Offer of Cyprus: October 1915. In Proceedings of the International Symposium, *Greece and Great Britain During World War I*, 77–97. Thessaloniki: Institute for Balkan Studies.

Xypolia, I. 2011. Cypriot Muslims Among Ottomans, Turks and Two World Wars. *Bogazici Journal* 25 (2): 109–120.

Yiagou, A. 2013a. English Policy 1931–1950. In *The Struggles Prior to the Struggle of 1955. Aspects of the Preparation for Organization of the Struggle*, 109–127. Nicosia: Academy of Historical Studies (in Greek).

Yiagou, A. 2013b. British Diplomacy and the Cyprus Question. In *The Cyprus Question and the International System, 1945–1974: Searching for a Place in the World*, ed. P. Papapolyviou, A. Syrigos, and E. Hadjivasileiou, 23–30. Athens: Patakis (in Greek).

Zachariadou, E. 1997. *Cyprus in the First Century of Ottoman Occupation (1570–1670)*. Nicosia: Leventis Foundation (in Greek).

Zanettos, F. 1910. *History of the Island of Cyprus*, vol. I. Larnaca (in Greek).

Zanettos, F. 1911. *History of the Island of Cyprus*, vol. II. Larnaca (in Greek).

Index

S. Sakellaropoulos, *The Evolution of the Political, Social and Economic Life of Cyprus, 1191–1950*, Palgrave Studies in Economic History,
https://doi.org/10.1007/978-3-030-91839-2

G

H

I

J

K

The manufacturer's authorised representative in the EU is Springer Nature Customer Service Centre GmbH, Europaplatz 3, 69115 Heidelberg, Germany. If you have any concerns regarding our products, please contact ProductSafety@springernature.com

Printed and bound by CPI Group (UK) Ltd, Croydon, CR0 4YY
30/09/2026
02225689-0003